"L'être situé", Effectiveness and Purposes of International Law

Professor Ryuichi Ida

"L'être situé", Effectiveness and Purposes of International Law

Essays in Honour of Professor Ryuichi Ida

Edited by

Shotaro Hamamoto
Hironobu Sakai
Akiho Shibata

BRILL
NIJHOFF

LEIDEN | BOSTON

Library of Congress Cataloging-in-Publication Data

"L'être situé," effectiveness and purposes of international law : essays in honour of Professor Ryuichi Ida / edited by Shotaro Hamamoto, Hironobu Sakai, Akiho Shibata.
  pages cm
 Includes bibliographical references and index.
 ISBN 978-90-04-26888-3 (hardback : alk. paper) -- ISBN 978-90-04-29428-8 (e-book) 1. International law. 2. Foreign trade regulation. I. Hamamoto, Shotaro, 1970- editor. II. Sakai, Hironobu, 1963- editor. III. Shibata, Akiho, 1965- editor. IV. Ida, Ryuichi, honouree.

 KZ3410.E87 2015
 341--dc23

                       2015010265

This publication has been typeset in the multilingual "Brill" typeface. With over 5,100 characters covering Latin, IPA, Greek, and Cyrillic, this typeface is especially suitable for use in the humanities. For more information, please see www.brill.com/brill-typeface.

ISBN 978-90-04-26888-3 (hardback)
ISBN 978-90-04-29428-8 (e-book)

Copyright 2015 by Koninklijke Brill NV, Leiden, The Netherlands.
Koninklijke Brill NV incorporates the imprints Brill, Brill Hes & De Graaf, Brill Nijhoff, Brill Rodopi and Hotei Publishing.
All rights reserved. No part of this publication may be reproduced, translated, stored in a retrieval system, or transmitted in any form or by any means, electronic, mechanical, photocopying, recording or otherwise, without prior written permission from the publisher.
Authorization to photocopy items for internal or personal use is granted by Koninklijke Brill NV provided that the appropriate fees are paid directly to The Copyright Clearance Center, 222 Rosewood Drive, Suite 910, Danvers, MA 01923, USA.
Fees are subject to change.

This book is printed on acid-free paper.

Contents

Préface   VII
Acknowledgements   X
List of Figures and Tables   XII
List of Contributors   XIII

PART 1
"L'être situé": Deconstruction of Universality

1 L'État situé dans le droit international de l'investissement   3
   Shotaro Hamamoto

2 "L'État situé" in the Context of the Accession of Developing Countries to the WTO   23
   Tomonori Mizushima

3 The Functional Approach in *le droit international de développement*: A Theoretical Appraisal   37
   Zhian Wang

4 Emerging Economies and International Economic Law: A Case Study on Thailand   63
   Sakda Thanitcul

5 Universal Jurisdiction in a Context: From Dialectic to Dialogue   89
   Mari Takeuchi

PART 2
Effectiveness: Formality of Law and Amorphous Reality

6 Running Many FTAs is Like Balancing between Many Bicycles: A Multidimensional Comparison of Institutional Provisions in Japan's FTAs   115
   Tomohiko Kobayashi

7   Provisional Measures in Investor-State Dispute Settlement:
    Reappearance of *Community of Investment Interests?*   144
    Dai Tamada

8   New Relationship between the United Nations and Regional
    Organizations in Peace and Security: A Case of the African
    Union   165
    Hironobu Sakai

PART 3
Law-Making: International Law Catching Up with the Globalizing Community

9   International and Domestic Laws in Collaboration: An Effective
    Means of Environmental Liability Regime-Making   193
    Akiho Shibata

10 New Perspectives on Soft Law: Towards More Effective Regime
    Governance   214
    Tatsuya Abe

11 The Defence of Necessity as Customary International Law:
    The Fisheries Jurisdiction Case (Spain v. Canada) Re-examined   238
    Takuhei Yamada

12 Catching Up with Society – What, How, and Why: The Regulation
    of the UN Security Council's Targeted Sanctions   255
    Machiko Kanetake

    Bibliography of Professor Ryuichi Ida
    (with abbreviations used in this book)   285
    Index   296

Préface

Au milieu des années quatre-vingt, alors que je donnais mon enseignement dans le cadre des enseignements de doctorat en droit international, je connus une surprise que je ne suis pas près d'oublier. Alors que je consultais la notice d'information que devait remplir chacun des participants nouvellement inscrits à mon séminaire de doctorat, je dus constater que, parmi une trentaine d'étudiants, tous invités par moi à donner des indications sur leur cursus universitaire antérieur, figurait un japonais, un peu plus âgé que la moyenne, certes, mais pas tant que cela ! A la rubrique consacrée aux activités professionnelles, il indiquait simplement qu'il était professeur de droit international à la prestigieuse université impériale de Kyoto !

Ainsi, se trouvait, parmi mes élèves, un collègue confirmé ! J'en fus non seulement très surpris mais aussi vaguement inquiet ! Devant un public entièrement composé d'étudiants, un professeur peut parfois se permettre quelques synthèses un peu rapides, certaines simplifications dont il espère qu'elles seront au moins pédagogiquement efficaces, des raccourcis faisant image mais qu'il conviendra ensuite de compléter...Devant un auditoire au sein duquel se trouve un collègue, en revanche, le recours à de tels procédés s'avère beaucoup plus risqué. Une fois sorti de la salle de cours, ce dernier ne va-t-il pas souligner les faiblesses, les approximations voire les incohérences de l'enseignement entendu ? Diable, me disais-je, il va falloir être particulièrement vigilant et faire encore plus attention que d'habitude à ce que je vais dire; vérifier mes sources plutôt deux fois qu'une; formuler ma pensée avec le plus de précision possible; ne pas oublier de faire état d'autres courants doctrinaux que de celui dont je me réclame. Autant d'exigences auxquelles, certes, je me soumettais et me soumets encore dans les cours et conférences que je suis appelé à donner mais qui trouvaient en cette année où l'un de mes étudiants était aussi un collègue une occasion toute particulière d'être respectées. Bref, la présence au sein des participants à mon séminaire de droit international économique du professeur Ida fut d'emblée très bénéfique pour mon enseignement.

Elle fut aussi particulièrement agréable et stimulante. Car, loin d'affirmer une quelconque prétention, le professeur Ida considérait visiblement qu'il était à Paris pour travailler, sérieusement quoique bien sûr sans difficulté, pour obtenir son diplôme d'études approfondies (DEA) de droit international ! Nous fumes rapidement amis. Je me rendais très vite compte, en effet, non seulement de la modestie mais de l'esprit de mesure et de l'intelligence pénétrante de Ryuichi. Nous pouvions bien entendu parler d'égal à égal des aspects les plus divers du droit international mais aussi de sujets portant notamment sur les aspects les plus variés de la comparaison entre l'histoire, la civilisation et les mentalités comme les points de vue souvent différents existant entre les Européens et les Asiatiques, mais, plus précisément encore, entre la France et le Japon, deux pays également marqués par l'ancienneté de leurs racines historiques et la richesse de leur culture.

Comme beaucoup de mes condisciples anciennement étudiants parisiens, j'étais très cinéphile et admirateur en particulier du cinéma japonais; je connaissais un certain nombre des films de Akira Kurosawa, Masaki Kobayashi et Kenji Mizoguchi, mais cela me renvoyait plutôt au Japon des Samouraï qu'à celui de la fin du XX° siècle, en dépit des compléments plus contemporains apportés par certaines des créations de Yasujiro Ozu. Ryuichi me fit connaître le Japon d'aujourd'hui et pas seulement celui d'hier. Il le fit au cours de nos conversations parisiennes mais plus encore lorsqu'à son invitation, je vins plus tard moi-même donner une série de conférences à Kyoto. J'y retrouvais, avec un plaisir renouvelé, la science, l'amicale simplicité et la finesse de la pensée de mon ami japonais. A mon égard, mais aussi pour beaucoup d'autres de mes collègues français et européens, Ryuichi Ida a été et reste un irremplaçable intermédiaire entre les cultures, européennes et asiatiques, et ceci pas seulement dans le domaine juridique.

Le professeur Ida est cependant d'abord un juriste, et l'un de ceux qui ont su étudier des domaines variés du droit international. La question de la formation des normes de ce droit l'intéresse particulièrement, de longue date, mais aussi, parmi bien d'autres, celle de la pratique et des formes de coopération interétatique régionale, particulièrement en Asie. En relation avec ce cadre mais aussi à l'échelle universelle, il a abordé à plusieurs reprises divers aspects du droit international de la mer, mais aussi du droit international économique, notamment en relation avec l'impératif du développement économique dans le respect de la protection de l'environnement. Tous ces domaines de la coopération internationale, hors ou dans le cadre des organisations internationales, ont fait l'objet de son étude attentive et perspicace, pour ne parler ici que de sa production en français et en anglais, l'accès à la lecture de la langue japonaise m'étant malheureusement impossible.

Toutefois, sans quitter le domaine normatif et plus particulièrement la question qui l'a toujours fasciné de la « soft law » ou de ce que mon père, René-Jean Dupuy, appelait « le droit programmatoire », Ryuichi Ida a su attacher son nom au domaine de la bioéthique et des normes, souples dans leur forme instrumentale mais fermes dans leur contenu, qui doivent permettre de concilier le développement de la recherche biologique et le respect de la dignité de la personne humaine. Son rôle au sein du Comité international de bioéthique de l'UNESCO dont il a aussi assuré la présidence demeure fondamental. Il a ainsi notamment contribué à mettre au service de l'éthique internationale des sciences sa connaissance approfondie du phénomène normatif international tel qu'il a pu l'observer dans le cadre du droit de la communauté des Etats mais aussi des peuples, dans le respect de la diversité des cultures. Lui qui notait comment la négociation internationale, multidimentionnelle, évolue entre la recherche du consensus et le recours au « package deal », il a su œuvrer concrètement pour faire aboutir en particulier les difficiles discussions en vue de l'adoption de la Déclaration universelle sur le génome humain et les droits de l'homme, finalement adoptée en 1997. Il s'agit d'une œuvre d'une richesse toute particulière, dont certains des développements comportent des prolongements philosophiques très spécifiques.[1]

J'aurais tendance à dire, et c'est pour moi le meilleur hommage que l'on puisse rendre à un professeur de droit international authentiquement internationaliste que mon ami Ryuichi Ida incarne par excellence l'idéal de l'intellectuel cosmopolitique au sens où l'entendait Immanuel Kant à la fin du XVIII° siècle : celui qui sait rester fidèle à ses racines tout en s'ouvrant sur la pluralité des cultures du monde dont il faut constamment œuvrer pour assurer l'entente universelle, toujours menacée par les fanatismes, d'où qu'ils viennent. Les Mélanges qui lui sont ici offerts sont non seulement bien mérités. Ils sont aussi un encouragement pour la poursuite de sa contribution à une culture de la paix entre les nations fondée sur le respect des droits de l'homme.

Pierre-Marie Dupuy
Professeur émérite à l'Université de Paris (Panthéon-Assas) et à L'Institut de Hautes Etudes Internationales et du Développement de Genève. Membre associé de l'Institut de Droit International.

---

1 Voir notre étude Bioéthique et droit international. Elaboration progressive d'un cadre juridique pour la définition d'une morale universelle, *in Etudes à la mémoire du professeur Xavier Linant de Bellefonds, Droit et Technique,* Paris, Litec, 2007, pp. 167–181.

Acknowledgements

Although we knew that, as Socrates said (in Plato, *Phaedo* 114d), we "should feel confident concerning (our) soul...who have pursued the pleasures that go with learning and made the soul fine with...their own proper refinements, moderation and justice and courage and freedom and truth", we did not expect this "journey to the world below" would take so long....

It was around June 2005 when three of his former students exchanged e-mails regarding a possible Festschrift congratulating Professor Ryuichi Ida for his expected retirement from Kyoto University (Kyodai) in 2012. The three, who ultimately became the editors of this book, proposed that this Festschrift would be a token of appreciation from those who had studied directly under Professor Ida at Kyodai and later pursued academic careers, and that it would be written in English and French, as Professor Ida always encouraged us to "compete with the world". Following a suggestion from Professor Ida, we then organised a study group, open to interested scholars and graduate students at Kyodai and Kobe University (Shindai), in order to establish a coherent concept that would reflect Professor Ida's approach to the study of international law. This study group ran from April 2007 to May 2009 culminating in a final proposal on the overall structure of the book consisting of three parts: être situé, effectiveness, and law-making. Our first gratitude, therefore, goes to those who participated in this study group and provided advice during this early but extremely important phase of our long journey, some of whom could not contribute to the final product.

The study group and, later, the review group, which considered in-depth the drafts submitted by the contributors from September 2009 to February 2011, were financially supported by KAKENHI: Grant-in-Aid for Scientific Research (B) of Japan Society for the Promotion of Science (JSPS). Without this fund, we could not have organised, for example, a long interview session with Professor Ida in December 2007, or an intensive two-day review session amongst the contributors in September 2009 at Arima Onsen. Since the fund was attached to Kobe University, the administrative staff of its Graduate School of International Cooperation Studies (GSICS) assisted us in managing and executing the fund. Our gratitude, therefore, goes to JSPS and GSICS for their kind support.

Our thanks also go to many of the graduate students at Shindai who helped us in organising meetings of the study/review groups and supporting our research, including the production of Professor Ida's bibliography. These able students at Shindai either at GSICS or Graduate School of Law include: Mai Fujii, Tomoko Yamashita, Mai Okumura, Sayaka Adachi, and Kosuke Ichinomiya.

The editors would also like to express their gratitude to two graduate students at Kyodai, Haruka Ito and Hinako Takata, who, during the final phase of the book production in 2014, have undertaken the most cumbersome work of checking and formatting the final drafts of all chapters, finalising Professor Ida's bibliography, and producing the index for the book. Without their tireless and speedy work, the publication of this book would have again been delayed for several months.

Finally, the editors must express their appreciation to the contributors of this book for their patience in producing this book. This unexpectedly long journey, spanning almost 10 years, would not have come to its finale unless all the contributors shared a strong commitment to express their gratitude to Professor Ryuichi Ida in the form most appropriate for such a purpose.

This book, *L'Être situé, Effectiveness and Purposes of International Law: Essays in Honour of Professor Ryuichi Ida*, is dedicated to Professor Ryuichi Ida, Professor emeritus of Kyoto University and the Distinguished Visiting Professor, Graduate School of Global Studies, Doshisha University.

S.H.H.S.A.S.
December 15, 2014
Kyoto and Kobe, Japan

List of Figures and Tables

Figures

6.1 Target Country RTAs   120
6.2 Partner RTAs   120
6.3 Parallel Agreements   121
6.4 Three-dimensional comparison   121
10.1 Relation between Soft Law X and Hard Law   220
10.2 Relation between Soft Law A to D and Hard Law X   220

Tables

4.1 Litigation costs   76
6.1 Provisions relating to the institutional structure of Japan's FTAs   123
6.2 Provisions relating to the relationships with other agreements   129
6.3 Provisions relating to subsequent modifications   137

List of Contributors

Tatsuya Abe
is Associate Professor of International Law at School of International Politics, Economics and Communication, Aoyama Gakuin University. He earned his LL.M. in 1999 and LL.D. in 2008 from Kyoto University. His recent articles include 'Non-proliferation of Chemical Weapons: Strengthening the Obligation on National Implementation through Collaborative Institutional Frameworks,' *Aoyama Journal of International Politics, Economics and Communication*, No.82 (September 2010), pp. 85–119 and 'Effectiveness of the Institutional Approach to an Alleged Violation of International Law: The Case of Syrian Chemical Weapons,' *Japanese Yearbook of International Law*, Vol.57 (2014), pp.333–370.

Pierre-Marie Dupuy
is Emeritus Professor of Public International Law at the University of Paris (Panthéon-Assas) and at the Graduate Institute of International and Development Studies in Geneva. He is an Associate Member of the *Institut de droit international* and he has been awarded the 2015 Manley Hudson Medal by the American Society for International Law. He appeared in many contentious cases before the International Court of Justice as Counsel for Governments. He is an international arbitrator (in foreign investor/State arbitrations, ICSID, UNCITRAL, PCA). He delivered the General Course of Public International Law at the Hague Academy of International Law in 2000 (Vol. 297, 2002). His latest article, co-autored with his son Florian DUPUY is entitled 'What to Expect from Legitimate Expectations ? A Critical Appraisal and look into the Future of the 'Legitimate Expectations' Doctrine in International Investment Law,' to be published in 2015 in the Essays in Honor of Dr. Ahmed El Kosheri.

Shotaro Hamamoto
is Professor of the Law of International Organizations at Graduate School of Law, Kyoto University. He holds LL.M. from Kyoto University (1995) and *docteur en droit* from the Université de Paris II (Panthéon-Assas) (2007). He was advocate and counsel for Japan in *Hoshinmaru* (Japan v. Russia, ITLOS, 2007), *Tomimaru* (Japan v. Russia, ITLOS, 2007) and *Whaling in the Antarctic* (Australia v. Japan: New Zealand intervening, 2014). His recent publications include: 'Méthodologie extraordinaire pour trouver le sens ordinaire ? : Le sens ordinaire pour les tribunaux compétents en matière d'investissement,' in *Unité et diversité du droit international : Ecrits en l'honneur du Professeur Pierre-Marie Dupuy* (Martinus Nijhoff Publishers, 2014), pp. 689–707; 'Requiem for Indirect

Expropriation: On the Theoretical and Practical Uselessness of a Contested Concept,' PILAGG e-series/IA/1 (École de Droit, Sciences Po de Paris, 2013), pp. 1–28.

Machiko Kanetake

is a Lecturer in Public International Law at Utrecht University. She received Ph.D. from Kyoto University, LLM at the London School of Economics (LSE), and MA in Law from the University of Sheffield. She was also appointed as a Hauser Visiting Doctoral Researcher of the Global Fellows Program at New York University (NYU) School of Law (2010–11), a Visiting Researcher of the University of Sydney (2012), and a Visiting Fellow at the Human Rights Program, Harvard Law School (2014–2015). Her recent publications include: *The Rule of Law at the National and International Levels: Contestations and Deference* (Hart Publishing, 2015) (co-edited with André Nollkaemper); 'The Application of Informal International Instruments Before Domestic Courts,' *George Washington International Law Review*, Vol.46 (4) (2014) (co-authored with André Nollkaemper).

Tomohiko Kobayashi

is Associate Professor at the Department of Law, Otaru University of Commerce. He earned his B.A. in 1999 and LL.M. in 2001 from Kyoto University. He is an LL.M. candidate 2015 at the University of California, Berkeley. His recent publications include 'Revisiting the Role of Anti-Circumvention Provisions Under the WTO Agreement: Lessons for East Asia,' *Korean Journal of International and Comparative Law*, Vol. 2 (2) (2014), pp. 139–163; 'Redefining US-Japan Economic Relations: A Japanese Perspective,' in Madhuchanda Ghosh, Raj Kumar Kothari, Takehiko Yamamoto (eds.), *US Policy Towards China, India and Japan: New Challenges and Prospects* (Atlantic, 2013), pp. 48–62; 'Pinning Down the Circling Concept of Circumvention: a Comprehensive Approach to Anti-Circumvention Disciplines under the WTO Agreement on Agriculture,' *Japanese Yearbook of International Law*, Vol. 54 (2011), pp. 365–385; and 'Dynamic Process of Transnational Dispute Settlement as Autopoietic System?' in Junji Nakagawa (ed.), *Multilateralism and Regionalism in Global Economic Governance : Trade, Investment and Finance* (Routledge, 2011), pp. 91–107.

Tomonori Mizushima

is Professor of International Law at the Graduate School of Law, Nagoya University: LL.B. (Tokyo, 1993); LL.M. (Kyoto, 1995); LL.M. (London, 1999); LL.D. (Kyoto, 2008). His recent publications include *Public International Law Aspects of Foreign State Immunity* (The University of Nagoya Press, 2012) (*in Japanese*),

'The Significance of the Recent Enactment of Japan's Sovereign Immunity Act in the New Age of Globalization,' in Andrew Byrnes, Mika Hayashi and Christopher Michaelsen eds., *International Law in the New Age of Globalization* (Martinus Nijhoff Publishers, 2013), pp. 367–387 and 'Case Report: Korean Film Export & Import Corp. v. Fuji Television Network, Inc., Supreme Court of Japan, December 8, 2011,' *American Journal of International Law*, Vol.107 (2013), pp. 627–631.

Hironobu Sakai
is Professor of International Law at Graduate School of Law, Kyoto University. He earned his B.A. in 1987 and LL.M. in 1989 from Kyoto University. His recent publications include '"As if" *Acting* under Chapter VII of the UN Charter? : Rigidity of the Threshold between Chapter VII and non Chapter VII,' *Asian Yearbook of International Law*, Vol.13 (2007), pp. 103–125, 'Legitimization of Measures to Secure Effectiveness in UN Peacekeeping: The Role of Chapter VII of the UN Charter,' in Teruo Komori & Karel Wellens (eds.), *Public Interest Rules of International Law. Towards Effective Implementation* (Ashgate, 2009), pp. 119–139, and '*La bonne administration de la justice* in the Incidental Proceedings of the International Court of Justice,' *Japanese Yearbook of International Law*, Vol.55 (2012), pp. 110–133.

Akiho Shibata
is Professor of International Law at Graduate School of International Cooperation Studies (GSICS), Kobe University, Japan. He holds LL.M. from Kyoto University (1992) and New York University School of Law (1993). His recent publications in English include: *International Liability Regime for Biodiversity Damage: The Nagoya-Kuala Lumpur Supplementary Protocol* (editor, Routledge, 2014); 'The Court's Decision *in silentium* on the Sources of International Law: Its Enduring Significance,' in Karine Bannelier, Theodore Christakis & Sarah Heathcote (eds.), *The ICJ and the Evolution of International Law: The Enduring Impact of the Corfu Channel Case* (Routledge, 2012), pp. 201–210; and 'International Environmental Lawmaking in the First Decade of the Twenty-First Century: The Form and Process,' *Japanese Yearbook of International Law*, Vol. 54 (2011), pp. 28–61.

Mari Takeuchi
is Professor of International Law at Graduate School of Humanities and Social Sciences, Okayama University. She earned her B.A. and LL.M. from Kyoto University and Ph.D. from Glasgow University. Her recent publications include 'Passive Personality Principle in the Japanese Penal Code,' *Japanese*

Yearbook of International Law, Vol. 54 (2011), pp. 418–433, and 'Beyond Dichotomy between Deduction and Induction—Critical Appraisal on the Approaches to Universal Jurisdiction—,' *Okayama Law Review*, Vol.64 No.2, pp. 1–40.

Dai Tamada
is Professor of Public International Law at Graduate School of Law in Kobe University. He earned B.A., Kyoto University (1998), LL.M., Kyoto University (2000), and Ph.D., Kyoto University (2014). He started his academic career as Assistant Professor (Kyoto University, 2003–2005), Associate Professor (Okayama University, 2005–2009), Associate Professor (Kobe University 2009–2013) and now is Professor (Kobe University 2014-). Professor Tamada specialises in procedural law of international courts and arbitration, international investment law and law of State responsibility. His recent publication includes *Legal Effects of the International Courts' Judgments* (Yuhikaku, 2012) (*in Japanese*). He advises METI (Ministry of Economy, Trade and Industry) and RIETI (Research Institute of Economy, Trade and Industry) on the economic policy of the Japanese government.

Sakda Thanitcul
is Professor of Law at Faculty of Law, Chulalongkorn University. He earned his LL.B. from Chulalongkorn University, LL.M. and Ph.D. (Law) from University of Washington School of Law and also LL.M. and LL.D. from Kyoto University. He was a member of the advisory team to the chief negotiators in US-Thailand FTA negotiation and Japan-Thailand Economic Partnership Agreement negotiation. His recent publications include 'Thailand,' (co-author with R. Ian McEwin) in R. Ian McEwin (ed.), *Intellectual Property, Competition Law and Economics in ASIA* (Hart Publishing, 2011), pp. 279–291, 'Thailand,' (co-author with R. Ian McEwin) in Mark Williams (ed.), *The Political Economy of Competition Law in ASIA* (Edward Elgar, 2013), pp. 251–282, 'Compulsory licensing of chronic disease pharmaceuticals in Thailand,' (co-author with Matthew L. Braslow) *The Thai Journal of Pharmaceutical Sciences*, Vol.37 No.2 (2013), pp. 61–83, and 'Balancing accountability for adverse drug reactions under American product liability law: lessons for Thailand?' (co-author with Matthew L. Braslow) *The Thai Journal of Pharmaceutical Sciences*, Vol.38 No.3 (2014), pp. 106–120.

Wang Zhi-an
is Professor of International Law at Faculty of Law, Komazawa University. He earned his B.A. in 1985 from East China School of Law and Doctor Degree of

Law in 1996 from Kyoto University. His recent publications include 'The Function of International Adjudication in International Order: Is There a Possibility of Dialogue between E.H. Carr and H. Lauterpacht,' Part 1, *SJTU Law Review*, Vol.1 (2012), pp. 148–162, Part 2, Vol.2 (2012), pp. 155–166 (*in Chinese*), 'Non-recognition as a Legal Sanction in International Law: A Theoretical Analysis of the Evolution Process from a Doctrine to a Rule,' *Komazawa Law Review*, Vol.12, No.1 (2012), pp. 1–54 (*in Japanese*), and 'Territorial Sovereignty in International Law: Rethinking the Significance of its Historical Origin in Europe,' *Komazawa Law Review*, Vol.14, No.1 (2014), pp. 23–82 (*in Japanese*).

Takuhei Yamada
is Professor of International Law at Ryukoku University. He earned his B.A. in 1996 and LL.M. in 1998 from Kyoto University. He has written many articles mainly on the law of international responsibility of States. His latest work is *Necessity in International Law* (Yuhikaku, 2014) (*in Japanese*). He has been an editorial committee member of *Journal of International Law and Diplomacy* [Kokusaiho-Gaiko-Zassi] published by the Japanese Society of International Law. He was a Visiting Fellow at Lauterpacht Centre for International Law, University of Cambridge, in 2003–2005 and 2014–2015.

PART 1

"L' être situé" : Deconstruction of Universality

∴

CHAPTER 1

L'État situé dans le droit international de l'investissement

Shotaro Hamamoto

Introduction

« [Dans le monde de l'après-Seconde Guerre mondiale,] les écarts entre les États en voie de développement et les États développés deviennent si importants qu'est perdue l'homogénéité de la communauté internationale. Dans ce monde hétérogène, l'égalité formelle, qui finit par élargir les inégalités de fait, n'a plus sa raison d'être. Paradoxalement, l'égalité fait progresser les inégalités…

On cherche [aujourd'hui] la possibilité de rectifier, par le moyen du droit, les inégalités nées depuis la fin de la Seconde Guerre mondiale. Il est espéré que le droit fonctionne de manière proactive pour garantir substantiellement l'égalité souveraine, qui en constitue un des principes fondamentaux. Son objectif n'est plus d'assurer l'égalité au niveau de l'application du droit mais celle des fruits, c'est-à-dire l'égalité réelle…

L'« État » dans ce monde n'est plus un « État souverain » abstrait et homogène. Il s'agit de l'« État situé », placé sous de diverses circonstances concrètes. »[1]

Le fondement philosophico-politique du « droit international du développement » repose, selon ses promoteurs, sur une dualité des normes : les normes qui s'appliquent entre États hétérogènes (celles qui s'appliquent entre États développés et États en voie de développement) sont différentes de celle qui s'applique entre États homogènes (États développés)[2].

Aujourd'hui, les experts s'accordent, pourtant, à dire que le droit international du développement n'est pas parvenu à l'instauration de cette dualité[3] et qu'« il n'est plus guère question de nouvel ordre économique international »[4]

---

1 Ryuichi Ida, "Statut juridique des pays en voie de développement" (1985), pp. 614–615.
2 Ryuichi Ida, "La doctrine du droit international de developpement" (1989), pp. 58–59.
3 Pierre-Marie Dupuy & Yann Kerbrat, *Droit international public* (11e éd., Pedone, 2012), p. 784.
4 Patrick Daillier, Mathias Forteau & Alain Pellet, *Droit international public* (8e éd., LGDJ, 2009), p. 1176.

puisque les principes néo-libéraux sont fortement réaffirmés au cours des deux dernières décennies[5]. Et c'est le droit international de l'investissement qui est fréquemment accusé d'être l'incarnation de ces principes néo-libéraux[6]. Le « nouvel ordre économique international » se trouve remplacé par le droit international de l'investissement basé sur un réseau de traités bilatéraux et multilatéraux de promotion et de protection des investissements[7], qui incarnent les principes néo-libéraux universellement applicables aux États parties sans égard à leur niveau du développement économique. Les États en voie de développement n'ont aucun choix. Ils ne peuvent que les accepter pour survivre dans un monde totalement marchéisé[8].

On s'étonnera dès lors de rencontrer la phrase suivante dans une sentence arbitrale en matière d'investissements :

> « [T] he Tribunal considers it imperative to recall the particular context in which the dispute arose, namely, that of a renascent independent state, coming rapidly to grips with the reality of modern financial, commercial and banking practices and the emergence of state institutions responsible for overseeing and regulating areas of activity perhaps previously unknown. This is the context in which Claimants knowingly chose to invest »[9].

Et le tribunal dans cette affaire de rejeter la demande des investisseurs pour cette raison, tout en considérant que certains comportements des autorités de l'État d'accueil étaient « contrary to generally accepted banking and regulatory practice »[10]. Peut-on en conclure que le droit international de l'investissement reconnaît aujourd'hui une dualité des normes contrairement à ce que l'on tend à croire?

Pour répondre à cette question, nous allons d'abord faire un bref bilan de la dualité des normes dans le droit international économique (1). Nous

---

5   Emmanuelle Jouannet, *Qu'est-ce qu'une société internationale juste?* (Pedone, 2011), pp. 42–52.
6   *Voir* M. Sornarajah, "The Clash of Globalisations and the International Law on Foreign Investment," The Norman Paterson School of International Affairs, 12 September 2002, Ottawa, Centre for Trade Policy and Law, Ottawa, pp. 4–5. <http://archive.ctpl.ca/> [dernière visite: le 1er mai 2014].
7   Rudolf Dolzer & Christoph Schreuer, *Principle of International Investment Law* (2nd ed., Oxford University Press, 2012), p. 5; Jeswald Salacuse, *The Law of Investment Treaties* (Oxford University Press, 2010), p. 75.
8   Samuel K.B. Asante, "Droit international et investissements," in Mohammed Bedjaoui, sous la direction de, *Droit international : Bilan et perspectives*, t. 2 (Pedone, 1991), p. 711, pp. 720–721.
9   Genin v. Estonia, Award (25 June 2001), ICSID Case No. ARB/99/2, para. 348.
10 *Ibid.*, para. 364.

examinerons ensuite si les normes sont appliquées de manière différente selon le niveau économique ou les circonstances économiques et/ou politiques de l'État (II).

I La place des Etats situés vue par les Etats : formation des règles juridiques

1 *Les Etats en voie de développement en tant que catégorie(s) : du nouvel ordre économique international à l'OMC*

Le professeur Ida a attiré notre attention sur les efforts de la communauté internationale de créer un « droit international du développement » qui octroierait aux États en voie de développement un statut particulier. L'Accord général sur les tarifs douaniers et le commerce (GATT) a été amendé en 1955 pour inclure un nouvel article XVIII portant sur l'aide de l'État en faveur du développement économique. Cette nouvelle disposition introduit une dualité des normes puisqu'elle prévoit que les règles qui ne s'appliquent qu'aux « parties contractantes dont l'économie ne peut assurer à la population qu'un faible niveau de vie et en est aux premiers stades de son développement » (para. 1). A la suite de la première réunion de la Conférence des Nations Unies sur le commerce et le développement (CNUCED) en 1964, un nouveau chapitre a été ajouté au GATT en tant que Partie IV « Commerce et développement ». Cette nouvelle Partie spécifie les droits et les obligations des parties contractantes développées et de celles « peu développées ». Ensuite, en 1971, le Système généralisé de préférences s'est fait introduire par le jeu d'une dérogation conformément à l'article XXV du GATT. Cette dérogation a été ensuite consolidée par l'adoption de la « Clause d'habilitation » en 1979. Comme l'indique son titre (« Traitement différencié et plus favorable, réciprocité et participation plus complète des pays en voie de développement »), la Clause permet aux parties contractantes de la GATT d'introduire une dualité des normes.

Les accords de l'Organisation mondiale du commerce (OMC), adoptés en 1994, confirment la dualité normative. Comme le fait remarquer le professeur Ida, presque tous les accords de l'OMC se réfèrent au statut particulier des États en voie de développement[11]. De plus, une troisième catégorie des « pays les moins avancés » a été introduite dans de nombreux accords de l'OMC[12].

---

11   Ryuichi Ida, "Le système international du commerce et les pays en voie de développement" (1998), p. 54.
12   *Ibid.*, pp. 54–55.

Le dédicataire de ces lignes trouve insatisfaisant de l'état actuel du statut des États en voie de développement au sein de l'OMC. En effet, s'il est vrai que de nombreuses dispositions des accords de l'OMC octroient « un traitement différencié et plus favorable » aux États en voie de développement, elles n'imposent pas d'obligation concrète aux États développés et ne précisent pas les droits accordés aux États en voie de développement[13].

2 *L'absence de statut particulier des Etats en voie de développement dans les traités d'investissements*

Il est bien connu que le premier traité de protection et d'encouragement d'investissements a été conclu en 1959 entre le Pakistan et la République fédérale d'Allemagne. Ayant perdu tous ses investissements à l'étranger à la suite de sa défaite dans la Seconde Guerre mondiale, cet Etat était particulièrement attentive à la protection des investissements. Pour cette raison, elle a conclu plusieurs traités d'investissement avec de nombreux États en Afrique et en Asie dans les années 1960–1970[14]. Plusieurs pays exportateurs de capitaux ont suivi. C'est le cas de la Suisse (depuis 1962), de la Belgique (depuis 1966), de la France (depuis 1972), du Royaume-Uni (depuis 1975), du Japon (depuis 1978) et des États-Unis (depuis 1982)[15].

Contrairement au GATT, ces traités ne contiennent pas de clause relative à « un traitement différencié et plus favorable » applicable aux États en voie de développement. Ils créent simplement des droits et des obligations réciproques. Il va sans dire que ces droits et obligations concernent la protection et l'encouragement d'investissements. Les États en voie de développement ont-ils besoin de règles qui assureraient une meilleure protection de leurs investissements aux États développés que celle accordée aux investissements de ceux-ci dans leurs territoires? Dans la mesure où les États en voie de développement demeurent importateurs de capitaux, le plus important pour eux reste d'attirer dans leurs territoires autant d'investissements étrangers que possible en octroyant à ceux-ci un certain niveau de traitement garanti sur le plan du droit international. Ils ne s'intéresseraient ainsi guère au niveau de la protection d'éventuels investissements de leurs ressortissants dans les États développés, dans la mesure où la protection est accordée de manière réciproque.

---

13 *Ibid.*, p. 59.
14 Jeswald W. Salacuse & Nicholas P. Sullivan, "Do BITs Really Work?" *Harvard International Law Journal*, Vol. 46 (2005), p. 67, p. 73.
15 Jean-Pierre Laviec, *Protection et promotion des investissements* (PUF, 1985), pp. 8–9.

On sait aujourd'hui que la propagation de traités d'investissement a eu pour effet d'ébranler le fondement même du projet du Nouvel ordre économique international[16]. Il faut dire en effet que ce n'est rien d'autre que ce dernier qui a incité les États développés à négocier et conclure ces traités[17]. Selon l'article 2(2) de la Charte des droits et devoirs économiques des États (1974)[18]: « Chaque État a le droit... c) de nationaliser, d'exproprier, ou de transférer la propriété des biens étrangers, auquel cas il devrait verser une indemnité adéquate, compte tenu de ses lois et règlements et de toutes les circonstances qu'il juge pertinentes », sans faire la moindre référence au droit international[19]. Ainsi, la conclusion des traités d'investissements, qui assure la protection des investissements étrangers par le droit international, va précisément à contre-courant du Nouvel ordre économique international[20]. Les États en voie de développement, pour leur part, avait besoin d'accepter ces traités pour attirer des capitaux qui leur faisaient cruellement défaut[21]. Comme nous l'a fait remarquer le professeur Ida, alors qu'ils soutenaient le NOEI sur le plan multilatéral, les États en voie de développement ont mis l'accent en réalité sur les rapports bilatéraux[22]. On comprend alors qu'une partie importante de la doctrine considère que les traités de protection et d'encouragement d'investissement sont des instruments d'une nouvelle forme d'impérialisme[23]. Cependant, avant d'arriver à une quelconque conclusion sur le rôle des traités d'investissement, il faut savoir comment ils sont mis en œuvre en pratique.

---

[16] Thomas W. Wälde, "A Requiem for the 'New International Economic Order'," in *Liber Amicorum Professor Seidl-Hohenveldern* (Kluwer, 1998), pp. 771–804; Maurice Kamto, "Requiem pour le droit international du développement," in *Mélanges en l'honneur de Madjid Benchikh* (Pedone, 2011), p. 493.

[17] C'est ce que Guzman qualifie d'un dilemma du prisonnier. Andrew T. Guzman, "Why LDCs Sign Treaties That Hurt Them," *Virginia Journal of International Law*, Vol. 38 (1998), p. 639, p. 666, pp. 669–671.

[18] ONU Doc. A/RES/3281 (XXIX) (1974).

[19] Guy Feuer & Hervé Cassan, *Droit international du développement* (2e éd., Dalloz, 1991), p. 215.

[20] Kenneth J. Vandevelde, "A Brief History of International Investment Agreements," U.C. Davis Journal of International Law and Policy, Vol. 12 (2005), p. 157, p. 170.

[21] Nida Mahmood, "Democratizing Investment Laws," *Journal of World Investment and Trade*, Vol. 14 (2013), p. 79, p. 83.

[22] Ryuichi Ida, "La doctrine du droit international de developpement" (1989), pp. 52–53.

[23] Kate Miles, "International Investment Law: Origins Imperialism and Conceptualizing the Environment," *Colorado Journal of International Environmental Law and Policy*, Vol. 21 (2010), p. 1, pp. 37–40.

II La place des Etats situés vue par les arbitres

Comme la sentence *Genin c. Estonie* à laquelle nous nous sommes référés dans l'introduction de la présente étude, il existe des décisions arbitrales qui tiennent compte des circonstances économiques et/ou politiques de l'État d'accueil pour interpréter des dispositions prévues par les traités d'investissements (1). En revanche, il existe aussi une autre série de sentences arbitrales qui ne le font pas alors même qu'il s'agit d'affaires similaires (2).

1 Considération par les tribunaux de la situation dans laquelle l'État est situé

On sait qu'il existe des décisions arbitrales d'après lesquelles les circonstances politiques et économiques dans lesquels se situe l'État d'accueil jouent un certain rôle dans l'application des traités d'investissements. Des études qui ont examiné de telles décisions se réfèrent aux affaires suivantes: *AMT c. Zaïre* (1997), *Genin c. Estonie* (2001), *Olguin c. Paraguay* (2001), *Nagel c. République tchèque* (2003), *Generation Ukraine c. Ukraine* (2003), *LG&E c. Argentine* (2006), *Parkerings c. Lithuanie* (2007), *Duke Energy c. Equateur* (2008), *National Grid c. Argentine* (2008), *Bayindir c. Pakistan* (2009), *Toto c. Liban* (compétence, 2009) et *Pantechniki c. Albanie* (2009)[24].

Maria Gritsenko, affirme, cependant, que cela ne signifie pas nécessairement que les tribunaux considèrent que les États en voie de développement appartiennent à une catégorie distincte à laquelle s'appliquent les provisions des traités d'investissements de manière différente[25]. Et pourtant, quand on regarde des décisions arbitrales plus récentes, on s'aperçoit d'une tendance qui consiste à mettre en exergue le fait que l'État d'accueil-défendeur est un État en voie de développement pour examiner si l'obligation d'offrir un traitement juste et équitable est méconnue (1). De surcroît, lorsqu'ils appliquent la clause du traitement juste et équitable, les tribunaux tiennent compte des situations particulières et spécifiques où se situe l'État d'accueil-défendeur (2).

---

24 Ursula Kriebaum, "The Relevance of Economic and Political Conditions for Protection under Investment Treaties," *Law and Practice of International Courts and Tribunals*, Vol. 10 (2011), p. 383; Ursula Kriebaum, "Are Investment Treaty Standards Flexible Enough to Meet the Needs of Developing Countries?" in Freya Baetens, *Investment Law within International Law* (Cambridge University Press, 2013), p. 330; Maria Gritsenko, "Relevance of the Host State's Development Status in Investment Treaty Arbitration," in Freya Baetens, *Investment Law within International Law* (Cambridge University Press, 2013), p. 341.

25 Gritsenko, *supra* note 24, p. 346.

(1) Le niveau du développement de l'État en question

Dans l'affaire *Sergei Paushok c. Mongolie* (2011), des investisseurs russes ont contesté la taxe exceptionnelle sur l'or promulguée par le Gouvernement mongol après l'établissement des investissements. Ils ont considéré que cette taxe exceptionnelle frustrait leurs attentes légitimes et transgressait ainsi la clause relative au traitement juste et équitable contenu dans le TBI entre la Mongolie et la Russie[26]. Le tribunal, tout en reconnaissant que la taxe en question était généralement considérée comme excessive par des membres du parlement et du gouvernement mongol, a décidé que l'imposition de cette taxe ne portait pas atteinte aux attentes légitimes des investisseurs pour les raisons suivantes :

> « foreign investors are acutely aware that significant modification of taxation levels represents a serious risk, especially when investing in a country at an early stage of economic and institutional development. In many instances, they will obtain the appropriate guarantees in that regard in the form of, for example, stability agreements which limit or prohibit the possibility of tax increases.... In the absence of such a stability agreement..., Claimants have not succeeded in establishing that they had legitimate expectations that they would not be exposed to significant tax increases in the future. »[27]

Il est donc possible que la même imposition violait la clause du traitement juste et équitable si elle est promulguée dans un État développé. Cependant, dans cette affaire, puisque la Mongolie est un État en « early stage of economic and institutional development », le tribunal a considéré que l'imposition en question n'était ni injuste, ni inéquitable. Dans le même sens, le tribunal dans l'affaire *El Paso c. Argentine* (2011) a soutenu, s'agissant de la même obligation relative au traitement juste et équitable, que les attentes légitimes des investisseurs pourraient être différentes selon le niveau du développement de l'État d'accueil[28].

L'affaire *White Industries c. Inde* (2011) porte sur le défaut d'exécution par les autorités judiciaires indiennes d'une sentence arbitrale rendue par la Chambre de commerce international favorable à l'investisseur. Ce dernier a estimé que « the Indian courts' delay in delaing with teh enforcement of the Award (i.e., a failure to provide justice to White by allowing the enforcement process—and the dispute and setting aside proceedings—to continue for more than nine years without any realistic end in sight) » constituait une frustration des attentes

---

26   Sergei Paushok v. Mongolia, Award on Jurisdiction and Liability (28 April 2011), para. 258.
27   *Ibid.*, para. 302.
28   El Paso v. Argentina, Award (31 October 2011), ICSID Case No. ARB/03/15, para. 360.

légitimes et un déni de justice, d'où une violation de la clause du traitement juste et équitable contenue dans l'article 3 du TBI entre l'Australie et l'Inde[29].

Le tribunal arbitral affirme que la durée de la procédure indienne est « certainly unsatisfactory » et « regrettable ». Se référant à une sentence arbitrale rendue durant les des années 1930!—considérant qu'un retard comparable montre le caractère défectueux du système judiciaire de l'État en question[30], le tribunal arbitral a rejeté néanmoins la réclamation de l'investisseur et refuse de reconnaître une violation de la clause du traitement juste et équitable. Pourquoi un tel retard ne constitue-t-il pas une frustration des attentes légitimes de l'investisseur ? Selon le tribunal,

> « White...either knew or ought to have known at the time it entered into the Contract that the domestic court structure in India was overburdened.... [O]n these facts, and absent an express assurance from India that any award would be enforced in a particular manner or timeframe, it is simply not possible for White, legitimately, to have had the expectation as to the timely enforcement of the Award that it now asserts. »[31]

Puisque la procédure judiciaire indienne est réputée pour sa lenteur extrême, les investisseurs ne peuvent pas espérer qu'elle se déroulera comme dans d'autres États. Mais un retard de neuf ans ne constitue-t-il pas, tout de même, un déni de justice ? Le tribunal répond à la négative comme suit:

> « it [is] relevant, when examining the behaviour of the courts, to bear in mind that India is a developing country with a population of over 1.2 billion people with a seriously overstretched judiciary.... [T]here being no suggestion of bad faith, [the delay] does not amount in the Tribunal's mind to "a particularly serious shortcoming" or "egregious conduct that shocks or at least surprises, a sense of judicial propriety". »[32]

Il s'ensuit qu'un retard dans une procédure judiciaire qui constituerait normalement une violation de la clause du traitement juste et équitable si ce retard a lieu dans un État en voie de développement[33].

---

29 White Industries v. India, Final Award (30 November 2011), paras. 10.1.1, 10.3.1, 10.4.1.
30 *Ibid.*, paras. 10.4.22–10.4.23.
31 *Ibid.*, paras. 10.3.14–10.3.15.
32 *Ibid.*, paras. 10.4.18, 10.4.23.
33 Le tribunal estime pourtant que ce même retard dans la procédure judiciaire n'est pas compatible avec une autre obligation d'offrir des moyens effectifs pour revendiquer et mettre en œuvre des droits, importée d'un autre traité en application de la clause de la nation la plus favorisée du traité applicable en l'espèce. *Ibid.*, paras. 11.4.8–11.4.10.

(2) La situation économique ou politique dans l'État en question pendant une période donnée

Ursula Kriebaum nous fait remarquer que « some arbitral tribunals have been prepared to consider the social, economic and political situation prevailing in the country when applying the standards in particular cases »[34]. Par exemple, dans l'affaire *Genin c. Estonie*, la privatisation d'une succursale d'une banque estonienne et la révocation d'une licence octroyée à un investisseur américain ont fait surgir un différend entre celui-ci et le Gouvernement estonien. Le tribunal établit sur la base d'un traité bilatéral d'investissements (TBI) entre les Etats-Unis et l'Estonie apporte une remarque générale suivante avant d'examiner de près la compatibilité de la révocation de la licence en question avec le TBI:

> « the Tribunal considers it imperative to recall the particular context in which the dispute arose, namely, that of a renascent independent state, coming rapidly to grips with the reality of modern financial, commercial and banking practices and the emergence of state institutions responsible for overseeing and regulating areas of activity perhaps previously unknown. This is the context in which Claimants knowingly chose to invest in an Estonian financial institution, EIB [, qui a acheté la succursale privatisée]. »[35]

Le tribunal met ensuite en cause la procédure qui a abouti à la révocation de la licence. La procédure était, d'après le tribunal, « contrary to generally accepted banking and regulatory practice », parce que:

> « (1) No formal notice was given to EIB that its license would be revoked unless it complied with the Bank of Estonia's demands within a reasonable time;
> (2) no representative of EIB was invited to the session of the Bank of Estonia's Council that dealt with the revocation to respond to the charges brought by the Governor;
> (3) the revocation of the license was made immediately effective, giving EIB no opportunity to challenge it in court before it was publicly announced. »[36]

Et pourtant, cette procedure « contrary to generally accepted banking and regulatory practice » ne constitue pas, dit le tribunal, une violation de la clause

---

34 Kriebaum, *supra* note 24, p. 403 ["The Relevance of"].
35 Genin v. Estonia, Award (25 June 2001), ICSID Case No. ARB/99/2, para. 348.
36 Genin v. Estonia, *supra* note 9, para. 364.

du traitement juste et équitable dans le TBI applicable parce qu'il ne s'agit pas d' « acts showing a wilful neglect of duty, an insufficiency of action falling far below international standards, or even subjective bad faith »[37]. Elle n'enfreint pas la clause de non-discrimination non plus, parce que « the circumstances of political and economic transition prevailing in Estonia at the time justified heightened scrutiny of the banking sector »[38].

Le tribunal affirme ainsi que, si les comportements « contrary to generally accepted banking and regulatory practice » ne constituent pas une méconnaissance d'un traité et en particulier d'une clause de non-discrimination, c'est parce que l'État d'accueil se trouve dans une période de transition. Il s'ensuit que les mêmes comportements pourront constituer une violation de la même clause, lorsque l'Estonie sorte de la période de transition. Si la norme—celle de non-discrimination—demeure identique, elle s'applique de manière différente selon les situations dans lesquelles l'Etat d'accueil est placé.

Sans avoir besoin d'entrer plus dans les détails des affaires qui ont été analysées dans les études précitées[39], il convient d'examiner, dans les lignes suivantes, des décisions arbitrales récentes qui vont dans le même sens.

La crise économique et financière qu'a traversée l'Argentine dans la période 2000–2002 est trop bien connue pour que l'on s'y attarde ici[40]. L'Argentine a adopté une loi d'urgence qui a mis fin à la dollarisation de l'économie argentine et aux mécanismes d'indexation des tarifs des services publics sur des indices des États-Unis. Une question importante soulevée par ces mesures argentines est celle de savoir si elles sont justifiées par la norme coutumière de la nécessité ou par l'exception prévue dans le TBI applicable, s'il y en a[41]. Une

---

37   Genin v. Estonia, *supra* note 9, para. 367. Le tribunal considère que la clause du traitement juste et équitable dans le TBI américano-estonien prévoit l'application d'un "international minimum standard."

38   Genin v. Estonia, *supra* note 9, para. 370.

39   *Voir* les études cite dans la note 24.

40   *Voir* par ex. Esther Kentin, "Economic Crisis and Investment Arbitration: The Argentine Cases," in Philipe Kahn and Thomas W. Wälde, sous la direction de, *Les aspects nouveaux du droit des investissements internationaux* (Nijhoff, 2007), p. 629.

41   *Voir* Charles Leben, "L'état de nécessité dans le droit international de l'investissement," *Gazette du Palais*, 14–15 décembre 2005, p. 4003; Mathieu Raux, "La reconnaissance de l'état de nécessité dans la dernière sentence relative au contentieux argentin : LG&E c/ Argentine," *Gazette du Palais*, 13–14 décembre 2006, p. 3799; Patrick Jakob & Franck Latty, "Arbitrage transnational et droit international général," *Annuaire français de droit international*, t. 57 (2011), p. 533, pp. 553–556.

autre question, celle qui nous intéresse ici, est de savoir si ces mesures argentines contreviennent l'obligation d'offrir le traitement juste et équitable, vu les circonstances extrême où se trouvait l'Argentine.

Le tribunal dans l'affaire *Metalpar c. Argentine* (2008) a rejeté la réclamation avancée par l'investisseur qui alléguait que les mesures argentines constituaient une violation de la clause du traitement juste et équitable. Selon le tribunal,

> « It cannot be denied that there are countries in the world that enjoy greater stability than others. Claimants' representatives, businesspersons with international experience who are knowledgeable of Argentina's situation, were aware…of the problems Argentina had suffered on several prior occasions…. When Claimants invested in Argentina, they knew that the Convertibility Law No. 23,298, published on March 28, 1991, was in effect, and that, in the event of certain external events impacting on Argentina, the factual situation upholding what was provided in that law could become unreal and a new crisis would lash such nation. In spite of this, Claimants' representatives decided to invest large sums of money in Argentina. »[42]

Dans l'affaire *Total c. Argentine* (2010), le tribunal a considéré qu'une partie des mesures argentines n'enfreignaient pas la clause du traitement juste et équitable pour des raisons suivantes :

> « In the case of a "normal" devaluation of the peso, the de-dollarisation of the gas tariffs would not have been economically justified nor socially necessary, and might thus be objectionable under the fair and equitable treatment clause of the BIT (Article 3). In contrast, the "bankruptcy" of Argentina in 2001–2002, the forced abrupt abandonment of the US dollar parity and the devaluation of the peso by more than 300%, support the conclusion that the pesification of the tariffs and their de-linkage from the US PPI [United States Producer Price Index] were not unfair or inequitable. »[43]

En revanche, le tribunal a estimé que l'État d'accueil violait l'obligation du traitement juste et équitable lorsqu'il a refusé une augmentation des tarifs de gaz

---

42 Metalpar v. Argentine, Award on the Merits (6 June 2008), ICSID Case No. ARB/03/5, paras. 204, 207.
43 Total v. Argentine, Decision on Liability (27 December 2010), ICSID Case No. ARB/04/1, para. 161.

demandée par l'investisseur pour rendre ses activités rentables et durables conformément aux termes du droit argentin. Le tribunal précise que ce refus est décidé et annoncé après que l'Argentine est sortie de la crise[44].

Dans l'affaire *Toto Costruzioni c. Liban* (2012), la partie demanderesse, une société italienne de travaux publics engagée dans la construction d'une autoroute au Liban, a soutenu que la hausse des droits de douane sur certains produits nécessaires à la construction transgressait la clause du traitement juste et équitable contenue dans le TBI entre l'Italie et le Liban[45]. Le tribunal a rejeté la réclamation de l'investisseur pour des raisons suivantes:

> « The Tribunal considers that fair and equitable treatment does not, in the circumstances prevailing in Lebanon at the time, entail a guarantee to the investor that tax laws and customs duties would not be changed.... [T]he post-civil war situation in Lebanon, with substantial economic challenges and colossal reconstruction efforts, did not justify legal expectations that custom duties would remain unchanged. »[46]

2 *L'absence de considération par les tribunaux de la situation dans laquelle l'État est situé*

Il existe certes des tribunaux qui ne prennent pas en considération le niveau du développement ou les circonstances politiques et économiques de l'État d'accueil lorsque la question du respect des obligations imposées par le traité d'investissements applicable s'est posée. Maria Gritsenko nous fait remarquer que les tribunaux arbitraux refusent de tenir compte de ces éléments dans cinq affaires[47]. Cependant, dans quatre de ces cinq affaires, les tribunaux rejettent les demandes des investisseurs et ne trouvent aucune violation des TBIs applicables par les États d'accueil, sans avoir besoin de se référer aux circonstances économique et politiques dans lesquelles les États répondeurs se situent[48]. La seule parmi ces cinq affaires, *Lemire c. Ukraine*, dans laquelle le tribunal arbitrale se prononce en faveur de l'investisseur, signale que le niveau

---

44 *Ibid.*, paras. 171–172.
45 Toto Costruzioni v. Lebanon, Award (7 June 2012), ICSID Case No. ARB/07/12, para. 239.
46 Toto Costruzioni v. Lebanon, *supra* note 45, para. 245.
47 Gritsenko, *supra* note 24, pp. 346–347.
48 GAMI v. Mexico, Final Award (15 November 2004), para. 137; World Duty Free v. Kenya, Award (4 October 2006), ICSID Case No. ARB/00/7, para. 192; Tokios Tokeles v. Ukraine, Award (26 July 2007), ICSID Case No. ARB/02/18, para. 147; Pantechniki v. Albania, Award (30 July 2009), ICSID Case No. ARB/07/21, para. 105.

du développement ou les circonstances politiques et économique de l'État d'accueil ne joue aucun rôle lorsque celui-ci fait intentionnellement subir des pertes à un investisseur étranger particulier en prenant des mesures bien ciblées qui ne sont pas justifiées par des intérêts publics[49].

Dans la section précédente, nous avons vu les affaires dans lesquelles les tribunaux arbitraux ont pris en considération le niveau du développement économique de l'État d'accueil ou les circonstances économiques et politiques dans lesquelles celui-ci se situait pour arriver à la conclusion qu'il n'a pas transgressé la clause du traitement juste et équitable. Dans les lignes qui suivent, nous allons examiner les décisions arbitrales par lesquelles les tribunaux affirment que la clause du traitement juste et équitable est violée dans des situations similaires. Notre analyse montrera que les décisions arbitrales dans ces affaires s'alignent généralement sur celle prise dans l'affaire *Lemire c. Ukraine*. Cette concordance donne à penser qu'il existe un certain standard minimum auquel aucun État ne peut échapper, indépendamment de son niveau du développement économique ou des circonstances économiques et politiques dans lesquelles il est situé.

(1) L'absence de considération du niveau du développement de l'État en question

(a) *Retard dans la procédure judiciaire*

Dans l'affaire *White Industries c. Inde*, le tribunal tient compte des difficultés éprouvées par le système judiciaire indien pour affirmer qu'un retard considérable dans la procédure judiciaire n'est pas constitutif d'une transgression de la

---

49 Dans cette affaire, le demandeur, un investisseur américain, soutient que l'État d'accueil a détruit ses investissements dans une chaîne de radio, Gala, très populaire, en allouant les fréquences additionnelles systématiquement à ses concurrents. Le tribunal considère que cette pratique est constitutive d'une violation de la clause du traitement juste et équitable pour des raisons suivantes : "In six years Gala Radio, although it tried insistently, and presented more than 200 applications for all types of frequencies, was only able to secure a single licence (in a small village in rural Ukraine). Gala's main competitors were much more successful and each received between 38 and 56 frequencies. Although this macro-statistical analysis does not provide conclusive evidence that Respondent, when awarding radio licences, has been violating the FET standard, there are factors (the strikingly different success rates of Gala and of its competitors, the inexistence of any information regarding the real owners of the competing stations, the impossibility of verifying the reasons why Gala was rejected) which can be construed as indications that at least some of the decisions of the National Council when it awarded frequencies were arbitrary and/or discriminatory." Lemire v. Ukraine, Decision on Jurisdiction and Liability (14 January 2010), ICSID Case No. ARB/06/18, para. 420.

clause du traitement juste et équitable. En revanche, le tribunal dans l'affaire *Pey Casado c. Chili* ne se réfère pas au niveau du développement économique ou institutionnel de l'État d'accueil lorsqu'il affirme qu'un retard dans la procédure judiciaire chilienne enfreint la clause du traitement juste et équitable du TBI entre le Chili et l'Espagne.

Dans l'affaire *Pey Casado c. Chili* (2008), l'investisseur espagnol-chilien[50] est revenu au Chili après la chute du gouvernement Pinochet afin d'obtenir réparation pour les préjudices qu'il avait subis pendent la dictature. N'étant pas en mesure d'obtenir de réparation par des négociations amiables ou devant les juridictions chiliennes, celui-là a déposé une requête d'arbitrage sur le fondement du TBI entre le Chili et l'Espagne. Il invoque notamment un déni de justice de la part des tribunaux de l'État d'accueil incompatible avec l'obligation de garantir un traitement juste et équitable.

Le tribunal dans cette affaire affirme que :

> « l'absence de toute décision par les tribunaux civils chiliens sur les prétentions de M. Pey Casado s'analys[e] en un déni de justice. En effet, l'absence de décision en première instance sur le fond des demandes des parties demanderesses pendant sept années…doit être qualifiée comme un déni de justice de la part des tribunaux chiliens. »[51]

Ce qui est particulièrement intéressant dans le contexte de notre étude est le fait que le tribunal, à l'appui de sa conclusion, fait appel à une décision de la Cour européenne des droits de l'homme, d'après laquelle les sept ans que les juridictions étatiques ont mis pour examiner une demande en compensation à la suite d'une expropriation étaient bien supérieurs à un délai raisonnable, ce qui constitue une violation du droit d'être entendu dans un délai raisonnable garanti par la Convention européenne des droits de l'homme[52]. Le tribunal tient ainsi compte de la pratique développée dans le contexte d'un traité

---

50 "De l'avis du Tribunal arbitral, il n'existe pas de condition de nationalité 'effective et dominante' pour les double-nationaux dans [le TBI]. Un double-national n'est pas exclu du champ d'application [du TBI], même si sa nationalité 'effective et dominante' est celle de l'Etat de l'investissement…. En toute hypothèse, [à] partir de 1974, la nationalité « primaire » de M. Pey Casado est la nationalité espagnole, cette nationalité étant également sa nationalité d'origine." Pey Casado c. Chili, sentence arbitrale (le 8 mai 2008), CIRDI Aff. N° ARB/98/2, paras. 415, 417.

51 *Ibid.*, para. 659.

52 *Ibid.*, para. 662, qui cite CEDH, Ruiz-Mateos c. Espagne, Arrêt de la Cour plénière du 26 juin 1993, Requête n° 12952/87, série A n° 262.

multilatéral dont la plupart des membres sont des États développés pour examiner le comportement d'un tribunal d'un État en voie de développement. Pourtant, mis à part le fait que l'État défendeur n'a pas développé sa position sur les demandes relatives au déni de justice[53], il est à noter qu'il s'agit d'un cas de discrimination manifeste[54]. La sentence dans l'affaire *Pey Casado c. Chili* peut ainsi se placer dans la même logique que *Lemire c. Ukraine* : le niveau du développement ou les circonstances politiques et économique de l'État d'accueil ne joue aucun rôle lorsque celui-ci fait intentionnellement subir des pertes à un investisseur étranger particulier en prenant des mesures bien ciblées qui ne sont pas justifiées par des intérêts publics.

(b)   *Mesures fiscales*

Dans l'affaire *Paushok c. Mongolie*, le tribunal justifie les mesures fiscales prises par l'État d'accueil en se référant au niveau du développement économique et institutionnel. Au contraire, le tribunal dans l'affaire *Yukos c. Russie* (2014) affirme que les mesures fiscales de l'État défendeur enfreignent le traité sur la Charte d'énergie, sans aucune référence à son niveau du développement économique.

Ceci est dit, il s'agit ici aussi d'un bel exemple de la situation *Lemire* où l'État d'accueil fait intentionnellement subir des pertes à un investisseur étranger particulier en prenant des mesures bien ciblées qui ne sont pas justifiées par des intérêts publics. Selon le tribunal statuant dans le contentieux *Yukos c. Russie*, une série de mesures fiscales prises par les autorités russes, dont le recouvrement de la taxe sur la valeur ajoutée infligés à Yukos qui s'élève à 13,5 milliard USD mais ne se fonde pas sur le droit interne russe révèlent que « the primary objective of the Rusian Federation was not to collect taxes but rather to bankrupt Yukos and appropriate its valuable assets. »[55] Le tribunal affirme ainsi que ces mesures constituent des mesures « ayant des effets équivalents à une nationalisation ou à une expropriation » (l'Article 13(1), Traité sur la

---

53   Pey Casado c. Chili, *supra* note 50, paras. 646–649.
54   "[E]n accordant des compensations—pour des raisons qui lui sont propres et sont restées inexpliquées—à des personnages qui, de l'avis du Tribunal arbitral, n'étaient pas propriétaires des biens confisqués, en même temps qu'elle paralysait ou rejetait les revendications de M. Pey Casado concernant les biens confisqués, la République du Chili a manifestement commis un déni de justice et refusé de traiter les demanderesses de façon juste et équitable." Pey Casado c. Chili, *supra* note 50, para. 674.
55   Yukos v. Russia, Final Award (18 July 2014), PCA Case No. AA 227, para. 756. *Voir aussi* paras. 757–760; Hulley Enterprises v. Russia, Final Award (18 July 2014), PCA Case No. AA 226, paras. 756–760; Veteran Petroleum v. Russia, Final Award (18 July 2014), PCA Case N. AA 228, paras. 756–760.

Charte de l'énergie) qui ne remplissent pas les conditions précisées dans le traité. Bien que le tribunal n'aborde pas la question de savoir si la clause du traitement juste et équitable a été transgressée[56], il aurait facilement conclu à la violation de la clause, étant donné qu'il considère que les mesures russes en question ne sont pas « effectuée avec les garanties prévues par la loi » (l'Article 13(1)(c))[57].

(2) La situation économique ou politique dans l'État en question pendant une période donnée

(a) *Mesures prises pour faire face à des crises économiques et/ou politiques*

Dans les affaires *Metalpar c. Argentine, Total c. Argentine* et *Toto Costruzini c. Liban*, les tribunaux prennent en considérations les difficultés économiques et politiques lorsqu'ils examinent la question de savoir si l'obligation d'offrir un traitement juste et équitable est méconnue par les mesures qu'ont prises les États d'accueil pour faire face à des crises politiques et/ou économiques. Nous avons également vu que le tribunal dans l'affaire *Total c. Argentine* précisait que les mesures argentines qu'il considérait comme constitutives d'une violation de l'obligation du traitement juste et équitable avaient été prises après que l'État défendeur était sorti de la crise économique.

Il est vrai que trois des premières sentences arbitrales traitant de la crise économique argentine considèrent que les mesures adoptées par l'Argentine pendant la crise sont également constitutives de violations de l'obligation du traitement juste et équitable sans analyse approfondie de la pertinence des circonstances extrêmes dans laquelle l'État d'accueil était alors situé[58]. Cependant, indépendamment du fait que toutes ces sentences sont annulées ou sévèrement critiquées par les comités *ad hoc* à la suite de recours en

---

56 Yukos v. Russia, *supra* note 55, para. 1585; Hulley Enterprises v. Russia, *supra* note 55, para. 1585; Veteran Petroleum v. Russia, *supra* note 55, para. 1585.

57 Yukos v. Russia, *supra* note 55, para. 1583; Hulley Enterprises v. Russia, *supra* note 55, para. 1583; Veteran Petroleum v. Russia, *supra* note 55, para. 1583. Il est inutile, aux points de vue à la fois théorique et pratique, de distinguer une expropriation indirecte d'une violation de l'obligation du traitement juste et équitable. *Voir* Shotaro Hamamoto, "Requiem for Indirect Expropriation: On the Theoretical and Practical Uselessness of a Contested Concept," PILAGG e-series/IA/1, École de Droit, Sciences Po de Paris (2013), pp. 1–28.

58 CMS v. Argentina, Award (12 May 2005), Case No. ARB/01/8, paras. 275, 281; Enron v. Argentina, Award (22 May 2007), ICSID Case No. ARB/01/3, paras. 266–268; Sempra v. Argentina, Award (28 September 2007), ICSID Case No. ARB/02/16, paras. 303–304.

annulation[59], il est à noter que la plupart des autres sentences examinent minutieusement les effets de la crise économique qu'affrontait l'Argentine sur l'interprétation et l'application de la clause du traitement juste et équitable, en parvenant généralement à la même solution que retient la sentence *Total*[60].

(b) *Mesures prises pendant la privatisation par un État d'accueil en transition*

Dans l'affaire *Genin c. Estonie*, le tribunal tient compte de la situation de l'Estonie en tant qu'un État en transition pour conclure que les mesures prises dans le processus de la privatisation d'une banque ne sont pas constitutive d'une violation de la clause du traitement juste et équitable.

En revanche, la sentence *Eureko c. Pologne* (2005) affirme que les mesures qu'a prises la Pologne dans le processus de la privatisation d'une institution financière enfreignent la clause du traitement juste et équitable. Dans cette affaire, il était convenu entre l'investisseur néerlandais et l'État d'accueil que celui-là deviendrait actionnaire majoritaire d'une institution d'assurances, jusqu'à lors une société à capital détenu 100% par l'État. Cependant, le défaut des autorisations nécessaires a empêché la réalisation de l'opération. Le tribunal déclare que l'État d'accueil transgresse l'obligation du traitement juste et equitable « by the conduct of organs of the State, acted not for cause but for purely arbitrary reasons linked to the interplay of Polish politics and nationalistic reasons of a discriminatory character. »[61]

Dans l'affaire *Saluka c. République tchèque* (2006), le demandeur, une entreprise néerlandaise, a pris le contrôle d'une banque tchèque, dont le capital

---

59 Sur ces décisions controversées des comités *ad hoc*, voir Shotaro Hamamoto, "New Challenges for the ICSID Annulment System: Another Private-Public Problem in the International Investment Dispute settlement," in Rüdiger Wolfrum and Ina Gätzschmann eds., *International Dispute Settlement: Room for Innovations?* (Springer, 2013), pp. 393–416.

60 Continental Casualty v. Argentina, Award (5 September 2008), ICSID Case No. ARB/03/9, paras. 220, 22, 264; Suez v. Argentina, ICSID Case No. ARB/03/19 and AWG v. Argentina, Decision on Liability (30 July 2010), para. 235; Impregilo v. Argentina, Award (21 June 2011), ICSID Case No. ARB/07/17, paras. 325-331; SAUR c. Argentine, Décision sur la compétence et sur la responsabilité (le 6 juin 2012), CIRDI Aff. N° ARB/04/4, paras. 505–506; EDFI v. Argentina, Award (11 June 2012), ICSID Case No. ARB/03/23, paras. 1009–1012. La seule exception est l'affaire El Paso c. Argentine, dans laquelle le tribunal estime que l'Argentine a commis "creeping violations of the FET standard" par des mesures qu'elle a prises pendant la période de la crise, tout en reconnaissant que chacune de ces mesures était raisonnable pour faire face à la crise. El Paso v. Argentina, *supra* note 28, paras. 515, 518.

61 Eureko v. Poland, Partial Award (19 August 2005), para. 233.

avait été détenu 100% par l'État. Lorsque la banque traversait des difficultés financières et demandait à l'État une aide financière, celui-ci l'a refusé alors qu'il a fourni des aides à d'autres banques dans une situation similaire. Ensuite, la Banque centrale tchèque a placée sous administration forcée la banque en question qui était au bord d'une faillite et qui a finalement été rachetée par une banque tchèque. Le gouvernement de l'État d'accueil a alors décidé de lui fournir une aide financière importante. Le tribunal conclut à la violation de la clause du traitement juste et équitable à raison de la discrimination exercée par l'État défendeur, qui ne pouvait apporter aucune justification raisonnable pour ce traitement différencié[62].

Les sentences *Eureko* et *Saluka* s'alignent ainsi à la solution adoptée dans l'affaire *Lemire c. Ukraine* : le niveau du développement ou les circonstances politiques et économiques de l'État d'accueil ne joue aucun rôle lorsque celui-ci fait intentionnellement subir des pertes à un investisseur étranger particulier en prenant des mesures bien ciblées qui ne sont pas justifiées par des intérêts publics. Les autres affaires dans lesquels les tribunaux condamnent les États en voie de développement nous amène à la même conclusion[63].

Conclusion: De la dualité des normes à la pluralité infinie de l'application

Les sentences arbitrales que nous venons d'examiner nous font remarquer deux points. En premier lieu, il est tout à fait possible de tenir compte des circonstances dans lesquelles l'État est situé lorsque l'on apprécie la licéité des mesures prises par celui-ci. En seconde lieu, c'est toujours dans le contexte de l'obligation de traitement juste et équitable que les tribunaux arbitraux considèrent les circonstances pertinentes.

L'obligation du traitement juste et équitable est notoirement mal définie[64] et le « sens ordinaire » des termes « traitement juste et équitable » est difficile

---

62   Saluka v. Czech Republic, Partial Award (17 March 2006), paras. 337, 344, 347.
63   Par ex. Tecmed v. Mexico, Award (May 29 2003), ICSID Case No. ARB(AF)/00/2, paras. 163–164; CAA & Vivendi v. Argentina, Award (20 August 2007), ICSID Case No. ARB/97/3,para. 7.4.19; Siag v. Egypt, Award (1 June 2009), ICSID Case No. ARB/05/15, para. 454; Occidental v. Ecuador, Award (5 October 2012), ICSID Case no. ARB/06/11, paras. 450–452; Deutsche Bank v. Sri Lanka, Award (31 October 2012), ICSID Case No. ARB/09/02, para. 479; Stati v. Kazakhstan, Award (19 December 2013), SCC Arbitration V (116/2010), paras. 1086, 1095.
64   "[I]t is a vague and ambiguous expression on its face.... [I]t is a flexible term that applies to all kinds of investments in all industries and economic endeavors." Suez v. Argentina, ICSID Case No. ARB/03/19, AWG v. Argentina, Decision on Liability (30 July 2010), para. 187.

à identifier⁶⁵. Puisqu'il s'agit d'une norme d'une abstraction extrême, son application exige de tenir compte de tous les éléments factuels et circonstanciels d'un différend auquel la norme est censée s'appliquer⁶⁶. Il n'y a ainsi rien d'étonnant à ce que le niveau du développement ou les circonstances politiques et économiques de l'État d'accueil soient pris en compte par des tribunaux arbitraux lorsque ceux-ci examinent si l'obligation du traitement juste et équitable est violée. La malléabilité de cette obligation est souvent considérée comme problématique au point de vue des États en voie de développement⁶⁷. Au contraire, précisément grâce à sa malléabilité, les tribunaux arbitraux peuvent tenir compte de la situation dans laquelle chaque État est situé.

Le droit du développement, au sein duquel ses promoteurs souhaitaient établir une dualité des normes ou un double standard de droits en faveur des États en voie de développement, se passe aujourd'hui dans l'oubli général, à tel point qu'un manuel réputé de droit international économique explique que les résolutions de l'Assemblée générale portant sur le NOEI « relèvent de la protohistoire du droit international de l'investissement »⁶⁸. Il est vrai que les traités d'investissement ne semblent rien à voir avec l'idée même de dualité des normes. Les parties à ces traités bénéficient des mêmes droits et assument les mêmes obligations. On comprend donc que certains auteurs écrivent des requiem pour le droit international du développement sur la base de la prolifération de traités d'investissement⁶⁹.

Cependant, vu la tendance de la jurisprudence arbitrale que nous avons examinée dans cette brève étude, il paraît trop hâtif de déclarer le décès du droit du développement. Certes, on ne peut pas trouver une dualité des normes

---

65 "An inquiry into the ordinary meaning of the expression 'fair and equitable treatment' does not clarify the meaning of the concept. 'Fair and equitable treatment' is a term of art, and any effort to decipher the ordinary meaning of the words used only leads to analogous terms of almost equal vagueness." Lemire v. Ukraine, Decision on Jurisdiction and Liability (14 January 2010), ICSID Case No. ARB/06/18, para. 258. Voir aussi Micula v. Romania, Award (11 December 2013), ICSID Case No. ARB/05/20, para. 504.

66 "[T]wo aspects stand out: the idea of even-handedness and the need to consider all the facts and circumstances of an individual case." National Grid v. Argentina, Award (3 November 2008), para. 168. Voir aussi Duke Energy v. Ecuador, Award (18 August 2008), ICSID Case No. ARB/04/19, para. 340; Oostergetel v. Slovakia, Final Award (23 April 2012), para. 224; Swisslion v. Macedonia, Award (6 July 2012), ICSID Case No. ARB/09/16, para. 273.

67 Jason Haynes, "The Evolving Nature of the Fair and Equitable Treatment (FET) Standard," Journal of World Investment and Trade, Vol. 14 (2013), p. 114, p. 115.

68 Dominique Carreau & Patrick Juillard, Droit international économique (5ᵉ éd., Dalloz, 2013), p. 443.

69 Wälde, supra note 16; Kamto, supra note 16.

dans les traités d'investissement. Mais, les décisions arbitrales analysées plus haut nous fait remarquer que l'application n'en est pas toujours complètement réciproque. La clause du traitement juste et équitable, inscrite dans de très nombreux traités d'investissement et la provision la plus fréquemment invoquée dans les procédures arbitrales instituées sur la base des traités d'investissement, s'applique de manière différente selon le niveau du développement économique et les circonstances économiques et politiques de l'État d'accueil.

Pas de dualité des normes, mais une pluralité dans l'application de ces normes. En plus, cette pluralité est pratiquement infinie, car le tribunal arbitral peut tenir compte de toutes les circonstances qui entourent l'État d'accueil. La clause du traitement juste et équitable instaure ainsi un droit véritablement « situationnel », une idée chère au professeur Ida[70].

---

70   Ryuichi Ida, "Statut juridique des pays en voie de développement"(1985), p. 615, p. 619, n. 16. *Voir aussi* René-Jean Dupuy, *L'Océan partagé* (Pedone, 1979), pp. 28–38.

CHAPTER 2

"L'État situé" in the Context of the Accession of Developing Countries to the WTO

Tomonori Mizushima

I   Introduction

Professor Ryuichi Ida, in an article of 1974, examined problems concerning the accession of developing countries to the General Agreement on Tariffs and Trade (GATT), and pointed out that "[i]n acceding to the GATT, a developing country immediately and unconditionally enjoys existing concessions [granted by other contracting parties], but the acceding State must, in order to accede to the GATT, offer considerable tariff concessions to all the contracting parties, as 'an accession fee'."[1]

We may make a similar observation about accession to the World Trade Organization (WTO), which was established by the WTO Agreement of 1994 and succeeded the GATT. Indeed, the WTO Appellate Body confirmed in 1996 as follows:

> The *WTO Agreement* is a treaty—the international equivalent of a contract. It is self-evident that in an exercise of their sovereignty, and in pursuit of their own respective national interests, the Members of the WTO have made a bargain. In exchange for the benefits they expect to derive as Members of the WTO, they have agreed to exercise their sovereignty according to the commitments they have made in the *WTO Agreement*.[2]

As will be seen, however, the accession to the WTO of some developing countries, especially those in transition to a market economy (e.g., China in 2001, Viet Nam in 2007 and Tajikistan in 2013), has caused problems that apparently did not exist in the GATT era. Professor Ida has not addressed these new problems directly, but his past writings, especially those concerning "l'État situé", provide us with various suggestions that are valuable in considering them. The purpose of this paper is to analyse the accession to the WTO of developing

---

1   Ryuichi Ida, "La revendication d'une réelle égalité (1)" (1974), p. 41 (my translation).
2   *Japan—Taxes on Alcoholic Beverages*, WT/DS8/AB/R, WT/DS10/AB/R, WT/DS11/AB/R, October 4, 1996, *Dispute Settlement Reports 1996:1*, p. 108.

countries in the light of the concept of "l'État situé" as presented by Professor Ida. Section I examines the role of "l'État situé" in the international law of development and in the weighted voting system. Section II examines problems concerning the accession of developing countries to the GATT and the WTO from the viewpoint of "l'État situé".

II "L'État situé" as Presented by Professor Ida

Professor Ida has referred to and analysed the role of the concept of "l'État situé" not only in the context of the international law of development but also in the weighted voting system. An examination of "l'État situé" in each of these areas (Sections 1 and 2) will demonstrate that the concept has two distinct aspects (Section 3).

1 "L'État situé" in the International Law of Development

The international law of development, which first began to be discussed in the middle of the 1960s, aims at settling the problem of differences in levels of economic development among States, i.e., the North–South problem.[3] Professor Ida points to three basic principles that underlie the international law of development: economic sovereignty, solidarity (the idea of the international community) and substantive equality.[4]

Under traditional international law, the principle of the equality of States was based on the concept of the State as understood in the abstract, i.e., the *formal* equality of States. However, the application of such a principle in the international society where there are considerable differences in development among States, may result in increases in actual inequality among States.

> Thus, the international law of development endeavors to achieve the equality of results by giving reasonable differential treatment in the light of actual differences between developed and developing countries (differences in levels of economic development). This is called "substantive equality". This law takes States in concrete situations, "Etat situé", such as the size of population, the degree of economic development, and the social structure.[5]

---

3 See e.g., Michel Virally, "Vers un droit international du développement," *Annuaire français de droit international*, Vol. 11 (1965), p. 3. *See also* Ryuichi Ida, "La doctrine du droit international de développement" (1989), pp. 47–50.

4 See Ryuichi Ida, "La doctrine du droit international de développement" (1989), pp. 54–59.

5 *Ibid.*, p. 58 (my translation).

This principle of substantive equality thus calls for compensatory inequality. Under the international law of development, States are classified into two groups: those States at a similar stage of economic development and those States at different stages. Each group has different rights and obligations. In other words, different rules apply to each group of States. Such co-existence of equality (substantive equality) and inequality (compensatory inequality) is an important element of the international law of development.[6]

Professor Ida also states that the international law of development, which applies to the specific field of development against the background of the existence of developed and developing countries, may be considered to be "special law" in the contemporary international legal system.[7] He suggests that the international law of development may then be taken to be "temporary law".[8]

Lastly, mention should be made of the principle of solidarity. As pointed out above, the international law of development protects developing countries through compensatory inequality. This is not simply a matter of imposing an obligation to protect developing countries on developed countries. The international law of development is based on the idea that underdevelopment is a problem of the international society as a whole and that the development of developing countries leads to that of the international society as a whole. There must thus exist a sense of solidarity among the members of the international society, or rather "the international community".[9]

2 "L'État situé" in the Weighted Voting System

As stated above, Professor Ida finds that the concept of "l'État situé" has a positive aspect in the context of the international law of development. However, he seems to take a different view of its role in the context of the weighted voting system such as that which is used in the International Monetary Fund (IMF) and the International Bank for Reconstruction and Development (IBRD).

Under traditional international law, most international organizations adopted the one-country-one-vote system, which reflects the principle of absolute sovereign equality (the abstract concept of the State). However, and this is well-known, since World War II some international organizations, in particular those in the field of economics, have adopted a weighted voting

---

6 Ibid., pp. 58–59.
7 See Ryuichi Ida, "Statut juridique des pays en voie de développement" (1985), p. 645.
8 Ibid.
9 Ibid.

system instead of the traditional one-country-one-vote system.[10] A weighted voting system allocates voting rights to each member of an international organization in accordance with the weight of the member's function in the organization. We can thus consider this system to be based on the principle of "functional equality".[11]

The State as conceived under the principle of functional equality is, according to Professor Ida, no longer the State in the abstract. "The weighted voting system takes into account various powers of the State including the economic power and it deals with States in concrete situations, 'Etat situé', rather than sovereign States in general."[12] Taken at face value, this explanation suggests that there is similarity between "l'État situé" in the context of the international law of development and "l'État situé" in the weighted voting system.[13]

It is clear, however, that the weighted voting system does not work in favour of developing countries, though "l'État situé" in the international law of development implies their protection. Indeed, Professor Ida points out that the principle of functional equality in the weighted voting system may be taken to be a legal expression of a policy that favours great powers, i.e., developed countries.[14] The following comment of Professor Ida is very instructive, in that it suggests a negative aspect of "l'État situé" that may be found in the context of the weighted voting system.

> Although sovereign equality was established on the basis of the State in the abstract, [the weighted voting system in the IMF and the IBRD] takes into account actual and concrete inequality [among States]. This is to deviate from formal equality. In theory, however, this [voting system] has been explained in the framework of the principle of equality through the concept of functional or relative equality. Moreover, this grants privileges

---

10   See e.g., IMF's Articles of Agreement, Article XII, Section 5; IBRD's Articles of Agreement, Article V, Section 3.
11   See Ryuichi Ida, "Le développement du système du vote" (1989), p. 129.
12   Ibid., p. 130 (my translation).
13   It may be interesting to compare Professor Ida's explanation about the accession of developing countries to the GATT (see the text to note 1) with the following observation by a commentator about developing countries' accession to the IMF and the IBRD: "A weighted voting system is part of the price of [sic] developing countries pay for access to resources [of these institutions]." See Bartram S. Brown, "Multiculturalism and the Bretton Woods Institutions," in Sienho Yee and Jacques-Yvan Morin eds., *Multiculturalism and International Law: Essays in Honour of Edward McWhinney* (Martinus Nijhoff Publishers, 2009), p. 354.
14   See Ryuichi Ida, "The Evolution of Voting Systems" (1989), p. 129.

to particular States in accordance with certain facts and results in approving and maintaining actual inequality. Certainly, this does not overturn the principle of equality based on the State in the abstract. In other words, traditional international law admitted a system that reflects the difference in power insofar as the system provides the minimum protection of the weak. From a different viewpoint, this may be taken to mean that law can do nothing in the face of the actual inequality of power. Then, by no means does the [weighted voting] system that takes into account the inequality of power deviate from the assumption of the State in the abstract.[15]

It is true that an amendment to the IMF's Articles of Agreement, which leads to the 2008 Quota and Voice Reforms, has entered into force.[16] According to the then IMF Managing Director, "[t]his will represent the most fundamental governance overhaul in the IMF's 65-year history and the biggest-ever shift of influence in favor of emerging market and developing countries."[17] Needless to say, however, the Reforms do not purport to abolish the weighted voting system as such and, in terms of voting shares, the impact of the Reforms appears to be modest. For instance, the voting shares of the United States of America, Japan and the members of the European Union, taken together, still constitute a majority.[18] We should thus regard the negative aspect of "l'État situé", though slightly attenuated, as persisting in the context of the weighted voting system.

3   Two Distinct Types of "l'État situé"

Professor Ida's analysis of the weighted voting system, as outlined above, may appear to be self-contradictory. On the one hand, he argues that functional equality, as it is reflected in this system, does not take into account the State in

---

15   Ryuichi Ida, "Statut juridique des pays en voie de développement" (1985), pp. 613–614 (my translation).
16   See "The IMF's 2008 Quota and Voice Reforms Take Effect," IMF, Press Release No. 11/64, March 3, 2011, at http://www.imf.org/external/np/sec/pr/2011/pr1164.htm (as of October 31, 2014).
17   Ibid.
18   "Quota and Voting Shares Before and After Implementation of Reforms Agreed in 2008 and 2010", available at http://www.imf.org/external/np/sec/pr/2011/pdfs/quota_tbl.pdf (as of October 31, 2014). In accordance with the IMF's Articles of Agreement, Article XII, Section 5(c), "Except as otherwise specifically provided, all decisions of the Fund shall be made by a majority of the votes cast."

the abstract any longer, but "l'État situé".[19] On the other hand, we find an apparently contradictory claim that the system does not deviate from the assumption of the State in the abstract.[20]

We could perhaps dispel the apparent contradiction by distinguishing two types of "l'État situé", though Professor Ida does not himself draw such a distinction explicitly. The first type is "l'État situé" in the international law of development, or "l'État situé" as originally conceived, which aims at achieving substantive equality through compensatory inequality in favour of developing countries. This type thus represents the positive aspect of "l'État situé", at least from the viewpoint of developing countries. The second type is "l'État situé" as it is used in the weighted voting system. This type also has the character of "l'État situé" as it was originally conceived, in that it takes into account States in concrete situations rather than States in the abstract. However, it also serves to preserve actual inequality between developed and developing countries. It thus reflects the negative aspect of "l'État situé" and may be called "le *faux* État situé". We may consider that the first type is dynamic in character, but the second is static.[21]

Such an understanding of "l'État situé", inspired by Professor Ida's writings, calls for an understanding of the concept of "l'État situé", not in the abstract, but in concrete situations. When "l'État situé" is understood in this way, it could shed light upon various problems of international law, including those concerning the accession of developing countries to the WTO.

III Accession of Developing Countries to the GATT and the WTO

I now offer a brief account of developing countries in the GATT and the WTO (Section 1), and then examine problems of their accession to the GATT and the WTO (Sections 2 and 3). I focus particularly on developing countries that are in transition to a market economy, because an analysis of their situation provides us with an appropriate model of "l'État situé" in the context of accession to the GATT and the WTO. As will be seen, the two-aspect understanding of "l'État situé" that I proposed in the preceding section aids the analysis.

---

19 *See* the text to note 12.
20 *See* the text to note 15.
21 *See also* Ryuichi Ida, "Statut juridique des pays en voie de développement" (1985), p. 644 (arguing that the international law of development is dynamic, whereas traditional international law is static).

1   Developing Countries in the GATT and the WTO

The GATT aimed at establishing a free trade system by reducing tariffs on the basis of reciprocity and granting such benefits multilaterally through the general most-favoured-nation treatment.[22] Such principles of the GATT may be appropriate in a society that is based on the formal equality of States, but will lead to substantive inequality in an international society where considerable differences exist between developed and developing countries.[23] As the proportion of developing countries in the GATT increased,[24] those developing countries criticised those principles and demanded "differential and more favourable treatment".

The developing countries' demand was answered by a series of changes in the GATT system.[25] First, Part IV of the GATT, "Trade and Development", was added in 1965 and provided, among other things, that "[t]he developed contracting parties do not expect reciprocity for commitments made by them in trade negotiations to reduce or remove tariffs and other barriers to the trade of less-developed contracting parties" (Article XXXVI:8). Second, the CONTRACTING PARTIES of the GATT decided in 1971 that "the provisions of Article I [general most-favoured-nation treatment] shall be waived for a period of ten years to the extent necessary to permit developed contracting parties...to accord preferential tariff treatment to products originating in developing countries...without according such treatment to like products of other contracting parties".[26] This Generalized System of Preferences was made permanent by the CONTRACTING PARTIES' decision in 1979.[27]

---

22   See GATT, preamble and Article I.
23   See e.g., Ryuichi Ida, "Le système international du commerce et les pays en voie de développement" (1998), p. 50.
24   See e.g., Mitsuo Matsushita, Thomas J. Schoenbaum & Petros C. Mavroidis, *The World Trade Organization: Law, Practice, and Policy* (2nd ed., Oxford University Press, 2006), p. 765 ("Only ten of the original 23 GATT contracting parties were in this category [of developing countries], and developing countries continued to be in the minority until the late 1960s. By May 1970, 52 of the 77 GATT contracting parties could be classified as developing countries.").
25   See generally Ryuichi Ida, "The System of International Trade and Developing States" (1998), pp. 50–51.
26   Generalized System of Preferences, June 25, 1971, L/3545, *Basic Instruments and Selected Documents*, 18th Supplement (1970–1971), p. 24.
27   Differential and More Favourable Treatment, November 28, 1979, L/4903, *Basic Instruments and Selected Documents*, 26th Supplement (1978–1979), p. 203.

The GATT 1994 preserves these reforms,[28] and other WTO agreements also provide for so-called "special and differential treatment" for developing country Members.[29] For instance, under the Agreement on Subsidies and Countervailing Measures, export subsidies are prohibited (Article 3.1(a)), but this prohibition "shall not apply to: (a) developing country Members referred to in Annex VII [and] (b) other developing country Members for a period of eight years from the date of entry into force of the WTO Agreement" (Article 27.2). Similar consideration is given to Members that are in transition to a market economy.[30]

Developing countries may not fully be satisfied with the treatment they receive under the GATT and the WTO. Indeed, as Professor Ida correctly points out, many of the special and differential treatment provisions in WTO agreements fall short of granting developing county Members "rights" to enjoy such treatment.[31] However, the provisions are better than nothing. One cannot deny that the current treatment of developing countries in the GATT and the WTO reflects the positive aspect of "l'État situé". This is a step, small though it may be, towards the realization of the aim of the international law of development. It is against such a background that we should examine problems about the accession of developing countries to the GATT and the WTO.

2   Accession of Developing Countries to the GATT

Under international law, "[a]ll States enjoy sovereign equality. They have equal rights and duties and are equal members of the international community, notwithstanding differences of an economic, social, political or other nature. In particular, [e]ach State has the right freely to choose and develop its political, social, economic and cultural systems".[32] In principle, therefore, the political,

---

28   GATT 1994, Section 1.

29   See M. Matsushita et al., supra note 24, p. 777 ("[T]he WTO Secretariat has identified 145 separate provisions for [special and differential] treatment contained in the WTO agreements.").

30   In accordance with the Agreement on Subsidies and Countervailing Measures, "Members in the process of transformation from a centrally-planned into a market, free-enterprise economy may apply programmes and measures necessary for such a transformation" (Article 29.1) and "[f]or such Members, subsidy programmes falling within the scope of Article 3...shall be phased out or brought into conformity with Article 3 within a period of seven years from the date of entry into force of the WTO Agreement" (Article 29.2).

31   See Ryuichi Ida, "The System of International Trade and Developing States" (1998), p. 59.

32   "The principle of sovereign equality of States" in the Declaration on Principles of International Law concerning Friendly Relations and Co-operation among States in Accordance with the Charter of the United Nations, A/RES/2625 (XXV) (1970).

social, economic or cultural system of a State is of no consequence for the membership of most international organizations. However, in the case of the GATT (and the WTO), the economic system is of consequence, because a number of rules of the GATT, which "was designed by market economies and for market economies",[33] assume the existence of a market economy and the economic system of a socialist country is incompatible with the GATT system insofar as such rules are concerned.[34]

Some socialist countries nevertheless managed to accede to the GATT, under Article XXXIII of the GATT, which provides: "A government not party to this Agreement...may accede to this Agreement...*on terms to be agreed between such government and the CONTRACTING PARTIES*" (emphasis added).

This accession clause does not specify conditions for accession but leaves them to subsequent agreement. In the GATT era, such agreement was not so difficult to obtain. "Since the GATT related only to trade in goods, the main concerns of the negotiators were border measures. Such concerns could be accommodated without placing the demands on the acceding countries to reform their domestic economies."[35] Likewise, "[t]he GATT accession negotiations evolved around tariff levels and import quotas and thus did not need to penetrate inside the borders of the acceding countries."[36]

Furthermore, it should be noted that, because of the so-called grandfather clause, the original member States of the GATT undertook to apply Part II of the GATT, including Article III concerning national treatment and Article XVI concerning subsidies, "to the fullest extent not inconsistent with existing legislation".[37] Under Article XXXIII, if an acceding State and the CONTRACTING PARTIES can reach agreement on similar terms, which are to be provided for in its Protocol of Accession, the State may be able to accede to the GATT, even though "existing legislation" is inconsistent with GATT Part II obligations in that its economic system is designed to support a non-market economy.[38]

---

[33] Alexander Polouektov, "Non-Market Economy Issues in the WTO Anti-Dumping Law and Accession Negotiations: Revival of a Two-tier Membership?" *Journal of World Trade*, Vol. 36 (2002), p. 5.

[34] See e.g., Anna Lanoszka, "The World Trade Organization Accession Process: Negotiating Participation in a Globalizing Economy," *Journal of World Trade*, Vol. 35 (2001), p. 581.

[35] *Ibid.*, p. 580.

[36] *Ibid.*, p. 582.

[37] Protocol of Provisional Application of the General Agreement on Tariffs and Trade.

[38] See also A. Lanoszka, *supra* note 34, pp. 580–581.

3 Accession of Developing Countries to the WTO

The WTO accession clause is couched in terms similar to those of the GATT: "Any State...may accede to this Agreement, *on terms to be agreed between it and the WTO*" (WTO Agreement, Article XII:1, emphasis added). Like its predecessor, this clause gives no guidance on what sort of "terms" are to be agreed, leaving the matter to negotiation between an acceding State and the WTO.[39] However, in practice, despite the surface similarity between the GATT and WTO accession clauses, there are strong difference between accession to the GATT and accession to the WTO.[40]

Under the WTO system, the grandfather clause no longer applies[41] and the scope and coverage of the WTO is significantly expanded over that of the GATT. As a result, negotiation about terms of accession has become much more complex than was the case with accession to the GATT.[42] Developing countries are finding it increasingly difficult to live up to conditions and qualifications that are now emphasised in accession to the WTO.[43] As Lanoszka points out:

> To accede to the WTO means that the candidate State has to meet the requirements specified by the present WTO Members. These requirements no longer relate only to border measures. The WTO expanded the scope of international trade rules by including under its mandate trade in services, intellectual property and issues of investment. Hence the WTO obligations are quite demanding. The accession negotiations place tremendous pressure on the candidate country to make numerous concessions and also to undergo massive domestic regulatory reforms meant to create a credible and equitable system of commercial and administrative law.[44]

As pointed out at the outset, Professor Ida refers to "an accession fee", which a State must pay when acceding to the GATT.[45] An acceding State must also pay a fee when acceding to the WTO. However, the WTO fee not only differs from one acceding State to another;[46] it is also much higher than the GATT fee. In

---

39 *See also ibid.*, p. 589; A. Polouektov, *supra* note 33, p. 3; Technical Note on the Accession Process, Note by the Secretariat, WT/ACC/10/Rev.3 (2005), p. 3.
40 *See e.g.*, A. Lanoszka, *supra* note 34, p. 579.
41 GATT 1994, Section 1.
42 *See e.g.*, WT/ACC/10/Rev.3, *supra* note 39, p. 1.
43 *See e.g.*, WT/GC/M/32 (1998), p. 37 (the representative of Pakistan); A. Polouektov, *supra* note 33, p. 4.
44 A. Lanoszka, *supra* note 34, p. 602.
45 *See* the text to note 1.
46 *See e.g.*, Accession to the World Trade Organization, Procedures for Negotiations under Article XII, Note by the Secretariat, WT/ACC/1 (1995), para. 14; A. Lanoszka, *supra* note 34, p. 582.

a similar vein, it should be noted that "all countries that have acceded to the WTO since 1995 had to accept obligations, which in several cases exceeded those of many WTO Members themselves."[47] These so-called "WTO-plus" obligations tend to arouse dissatisfaction on the part of the acceding State despite the fact that the State agreed to such terms when negotiating its accession and acceded successfully to the WTO.[48]

China's accession is a typical example. In 2001, the WTO Ministerial Conference decided that "[t]he People's Republic of China may accede to the [WTO Agreement] on the terms and conditions set out in the Protocol annexed to this decision."[49] For instance, paragraph 5.1 of China's Accession Protocol provides that "China shall progressively liberalize the availability and scope of the right to trade, so that, within three years after accession, all enterprises in China shall have the right to trade in all goods throughout the customs territory of China". This obligation to grant the right to trade is an example of WTO-plus commitments, *special* law, because it does not exist under general WTO law.

Such WTO-plus commitments "are enforceable through the Dispute Settlement Mechanism of the WTO."[50] In *China—Audiovisual Services*,[51] several provisions of China's Accession Protocol, including paragraph 5.1, were at issue and the Panel stated as follows:

> [T]he Accession Protocol sets forth the terms of China's accession to the WTO. The preamble to the Accession Protocol refers to the fact that these terms are the result of negotiations between the WTO and China. This being so, we must be mindful of the possibility that the Accession Protocol may impose obligations on China that are not imposed on other Members under the WTO Agreement, or are stricter than those that are applicable to other Members. However, this element does not logically lead to the conclusion that the obligation to grant trading rights stipulated in paragraph 5.1 was intended to prejudice China's ability to

---

47 A. Polouektov, *supra* note 33, p. 34.
48 See e.g., Julia Ya Qin, "'WTO-Plus' Obligations and Their Implications for the World Trade Organization Legal System: An Appraisal of the China Accession Protocol," *Journal of World Trade*, Vol. 37 (2003), pp. 519–520.
49 Accession of the People's Republic of China, WT/L/432 (2001).
50 WT/ACC/10/Rev.3, *supra* note 39, p. 13.
51 *China—Measures Affecting Trading Rights and Distribution Services for Certain Publications and Audiovisual Entertainment Products*, WT/DS363/R, August 12, 2009, *Dispute Settlement Reports 2010:II*, p. 261, WT/DS363/AB/R, December 21, 2009, *Dispute Settlement Reports 2010:I*, p. 3.

regulate imports and exports and, incidentally, importers or exporters of the regulated goods. [O]ther elements and considerations lead us to a different conclusion. We therefore do not consider that our interpretation of the phrase "right to regulate trade" is in any way at variance with the object and purpose of allowing the WTO and China to establish, by mutual agreement, the terms under which China could accede to the WTO.[52]

The Panel, after thus stating, found that China acted inconsistently with its Accession Protocol.[53] The Appellate Body upheld the Panel's conclusions about this issue.[54]

As the Panel mentions, the terms of accession are the result of negotiations between each acceding State and the WTO. In accession negotiations, "the situation of each Applicant [is] considered on a case by case basis, while taking into account individual development, financial and trade needs."[55] The outcome of such negotiations may thus be considered to reflect "l'État situé". We should not forget, however, that negotiations in such a "one-against-all" situation tend to lead to the rule of (economic) power.[56] Equally, the WTO attitude towards the accession of developing countries may be compared to a policy of divide and rule, *divide et impera*, though the former WTO Director-General stated that "[i]n accession negotiations, the objective shared by WTO Members and acceding governments is to reach a 'win-win' agreement that benefits everyone".[57]

The process by which decisions are made at the WTO may also matter. The WTO Agreement, Article XII:2, provides: "Decisions on accession shall be taken by the Ministerial Conference. The Ministerial Conference shall approve the

---

52 *Ibid.*, WT/DS363/R, p. 520, para. 7.281.
53 *See ibid.*, pp. 891–896, para. 8.1 (China's commitments on trading rights in its Accession Protocol).
54 *See ibid.*, WT/DS363/AB/R, p. 216, para. 414.
55 WT/ACC/10/Rev.3, *supra* note 39, p. 13. *See also* "Lamy: WTO accession is an 'investment' in future competitiveness", a speech by Pascal Lamy, the then WTO Director-General, May 11, 2012, available at http://www.wto.org/english/news_e/sppl_e/sppl227_e.htm (as of October 31, 2014) ("Each accession responds to the specific needs of each acceding government. There is no 'one-size-fits-all'.").
56 *See also* WT/GC/M/32, *supra* note 43, p. 40 (the representative of Cuba); WT/ACC/10/Rev.3, *supra* note 39, p. 37; Julia Ya Qin, "WTO Regulation of Subsidies to State-Owned Enterprises (SOEs)—A Critical Appraisal of the China Accession Protocol," *Journal of International Economic Law*, Vol. 7 (2004), pp. 910–911.
57 "Lamy: WTO accession is an 'investment' in future competitiveness," *supra* note 55.

agreement on the terms of accession by a two-thirds majority of the Members of the WTO." Although at present "[a]bout two thirds of the WTO's around 150 members are developing countries",[58] "it is a well-established practice for all decisions to be taken by consensus."[59] Then, we should remember that "[w]hile the WTO's consensus-based policy-making has certain advantages, it gives particular weight to the strongest countries."[60] In this respect, we should not forget either that "in practice, only some WTO Members have the resources necessary to participate actively in the details of all the individual accession processes."[61]

IV   Concluding Remarks

The concept of "l'État situé" provides us with a useful analytical tool with which to examine the accession of developing countries to the WTO. In this process of accession, what is taken into account is not the State in the abstract but the State in concrete situations. As a result, different rules apply to each acceding State. Moreover, insofar as "WTO-plus" rules are concerned, they are examples of the "temporary law" that Professor Ida suggests is a characteristic of "l'État situé" in the international law of development.[62]

However, we cannot consider these characteristics of "l'État situé" to reflect the positive aspect of "l'État situé" that, above, we argued could be found in the context of the international law of development. It is clear that these characteristics do not constitute the type of "l'État situé" that aims at achieving substantive equality through compensatory inequality in favour of developing countries. Rather, the situation with respect to accession to the WTO reflects the actual inequality of power between an acceding developing country and the existing WTO members, especially developed countries. This is intended to maintain such inequality, even if not permanently. Thus viewed, the situation with respect to the role that "l'État situé" plays in the context of accession to

---

58   World Trade Organization, *Understanding the WTO* (5th ed., 2011), p. 93, available at http://www.wto.org/english/thewto_e/whatis_e/tif_e/understanding_e.pdf (as of October 31, 2014).

59   World Trade Organization, *A Handbook on Accession to the WTO* (Cambridge University Press, 2008), p. 4.

60   Daniel C. Esty, "Good Governance at the World Trade Organization: Building a Foundation of Administrative Law," in William J. Davey and John Jackson eds., *The Future of International Economic Law* (Oxford University Press, 2008), p. 85.

61   World Trade Organization, *Handbook, supra* note 59, p. 7.

62   *See* the text to note 8.

the WTO appears to come close to that which it plays in the context of the weighted voting system, or "le *faux* État situé".

As the above analysis suggests, what distinguishes the two types of "l'État situé" is the existence or otherwise of a sense of solidarity among the members of the international community.[63] However, it seems difficult to consider that the process of accession to the WTO of developing countries, especially those in transition to a market economy, is based on the idea that underdevelopment is a problem that the international community must address. Neither can we find in this process the belief that the development of developing countries, or the smooth transition to a market economy, will lead to the development of the international community as a whole. It is important for us to take due account of Professor Ida's suggestions concerning "l'État situé" and develop a sense of solidarity.[64]

---

63 *See* the text to note 9.
64 When the United Nations General Assembly adopted the Declaration on the Establishment of a New International Economic Order, A/RES/3201 (S-VI) (1974), this new international economic order was supposed be "based on equity, sovereign equality, interdependence, common interest and co-operation among all States". We should note that the General Assembly has recently reaffirmed "the need to continue working towards a new international economic order based on the principles of equity, sovereign equality, interdependence, common interest, cooperation and *solidarity* among all States" (Towards a New International Economic Order, A/RES/63/224 (2008), A/RES/64/209 (2009), A/RES/65/167 (2010) and A/RES/67/217 (2012) (emphasis added)).

CHAPTER 3

The Functional Approach in *le droit international de développement*: A Theoretical Appraisal

Zhian Wang

I   Introduction

"Developing country" is a political as well as a legal concept in international plane. It is much less politically charged than the other terms used to describe our divided world, such as the Third World versus the First or Second World,[1] South versus North. In many legal documents, especially in treaties concerning international trade, finance, and environment, the term developing country is used as a legal framework through which preferential treatments or reduced obligations are provided for those countries. Embedded in this legal term is a functional and pragmatic approach to international law: using legal norms and institutions as useful tools to tackle the issue of actual disparities among countries and to pursue fairness and justice as the final value or end of the international law.

While the theme of developing countries pursued actively by functionalist scholars of international law has not been reflected in the mainstream international legal thinking prevalent in Western Europe,[2] it did give birth to an important branch of international law: *le droit international de développement*. In Professor Ryuichi Ida's words:

> *Le droit international développement* is a branch of international law the central concern of which has been the disparities of economic development between developed and developing countries. However, this does not mean that international legal norms in the economic field should become its only concern. Actually, the South–north confrontation,

---

1   In Vijay Prashad's opinion, the Third World is a political project and a vehicle through which the peoples of Africa, Asia, and Latin America dreamed of a new world. Vijay Prashad, *The Darker Nations: A People's History of the Third World* (The New Press, 2007), p. xv.

2   As for the articulation of mainstream methods of international law, *see* Steven R. Ratner & Anne-Marie Slaughter eds., "Symposium on Method in International Law: Appraising the Methods of International Law—A Prospectus for Readers," *American Journal of International Law*, Vol. 93 (1999), p. 291.

viewed broadly as an active engagement after the beginning of the process of de-colonization in the early 1960s, has become inevitably an important element challenging the legitimacy of the contemporary international order and, therefore, requiring reconsideration and reconstruction of traditional international law. In this sense, *le droit international de développement*, while setting its central issue in the area of economic development, affects almost all areas of international law, such as sources of law, legal personality, and human rights.[3]

This chapter is a theoretical appraisal of the functional approach to international law constructed for tackling issues of developing countries in international law, especially in *le droit international de développement*. Such a functional approach of international law could, in my opinion, be inductively drawn from Professor Ida's research on the issues of developing countries. Professor Ida is a distinguished Japanese international law scholar who received his professional legal training in Japan and France, the latter being the birthplace of the idea of *le droit international de développement*. Professor Ida has devoted almost his entire academic life to the problems of developing countries in international law, developed a well-balanced functional approach, and consistently applied his argument for favorable treatment of developing countries.

Accordingly, Section II of this paper explores the characteristics of the functional approach in *le droit international développement* by analyzing Professor Ida's arguments for using international law to pursue substantive equality for developing countries. Section III then examines this functional approach as an intuitive sociological method of international law, and endeavors to situate the method in a broader theoretical framework by comparing it with other kinds of functional approaches. Section IV examines the real-world significance and inherent limitations of the functional approach to international law in resolving the problems of developing countries. For this purpose, the text compares the functional approach with other approaches to the same issue, especially that of the so-called Third World Approach to international law. The chapter concludes by recognizing the continuing relevance and importance of the functional approach of *le droit international développement* in addressing problems today's international society faces, but also by pointing out that this approach has not yet eliminated the aggrieved situation it addresses in the first place.

---

3   Ryuichi Ida, "Statut juridique des pays en voie de développement" (1985), p. 610.

II Pursuing Substantive Equality through an Intuitive Functional Approach

The functional approach to the problems of developing countries originates in a proper and sympathetic understanding of the huge developmental disparities between developed and developing countries. Along with such an understanding, a sense for pursuing fairness and justice through legal measures is also vital. It was well argued by former ICJ Judge Weeramantry that, when addressing the issues faced by developing countries, international law scholars should use international law with a sense of justice, fairness, and historical perspective.[4]

International law has always been and still is mainly used for maintaining the *status quo* established mainly in the process of adjustment and coordination of power politics. To make the rectification of huge existing developmental disparities a proper theme of international law, a realistic worldview and a strong sense of justice as basic mindsets are determinative. The functional approach starts with its understanding of reality: reality is only an extension of historical facts. Great efforts to understand the reality of huge economic disparities and their historical background and to transfer this understanding into effective rectifying legal measures were made by those scholars putting strong trust in the function of law in establishing fairness and justice.

As pointed out by Professor Ida, "one of the most serious problems our contemporary world faces is the developmental disparities between developed and developing countries. GNP for one person in developing countries is only one fifteenth of that for one person in developed countries."[5] Such huge developmental disparities, in the view of *le droit international de développement* scholars, crippled the foundation of international law, especially the principle of equality of States, and provided a proper basis for arguing the emergent need to grasp their repercussions for the legal system. "With the existence of so many States at quite different levels of development, any economic legal measure based on the strict equality of States could hardly function well in the real world. And for this reason, developing countries expressed their dissatisfaction with the principles and structures of GATT and some other

---

4 *See* Antony Anghie & Garry Sturgess eds., *Legal Visions of the 21st Century: Essays in Honour of Judge Christopher Weeramantry* (Martinus Nijhoff Publishers, 1998), pp. ix–x.
5 Ryuichi Ida, "Statut juridique des pays en voie de développement" (1985), pp. 609–610. Quite regrettably, the fact that the poorest 20 percent of the world's population receive only 1.0 percent of the global income and the richest 5 percent enjoy 40 percent of all income, is still a reality in the 21st century.

international economic institutions and argued for a new system of international economic cooperation."[6]

With this understanding in mind and a sense of a civilizing mission, some Western scholars turned to legal mechanisms and institutions for help. For them, international law should not be described only as a passive reflection of the power structure in the international society. Following the realist theory of international relation, international law only is a reflection of the struggle among political powers and is supposed to be a tool for maintaining a power-balanced world; any change in law can only be realized through a change in power relations. The functional approach in *le droit international de développement*, arguing for justice to rectify and adjust disparities of real economic power instead of burying such disparities in law, would have to first find ways to overcome this traditional view of international relations or at least to change the interpretation of the legal system as a passive reflection of current power structures.

As it has been convincingly pointed out, the most important question faced by contemporary international lawyers is not "is international law, law?" but "is international law fair?" Following this train of thought, it is argued that the very debatable questions of the desirability, content, existence, and effect of an international legal right of poor peoples to development deserve pre-eminent scholarly attention in the socio-economic context of today's unfair world.[7]

The functional approach to international law in focus did not go through a direct confrontation with the broadly recognized mainstream theories of international law, not even with the realist understanding of international relations and the positivist perspective of international law, to reach its conclusion.[8] Instead of rejecting the realist and positivist ways of thinking, *le droit international développement* scholars argued persuasively for the necessity of a pragmatic and functional approach to the problems of development. Their argument focused on the changing structural elements of the contemporary international society. In their opinion, the traditional international society had been a community composed of States with basic homogeneity, in which State

---

6   Ryuichi Ida, "La revendication d'une réelle égalité(1)" (1974), pp. 75–76.
7   Obiora Chinedu Okafor, "The Right to Development in Contemporary International Law," *African Journal of International and Comparative Law*, Vol. 7, No. 4 (1995), p. 865.
8   In theory, it might be said that any kind of functional or pragmatic approach in international studies has a strong inherent connection with the realist view on the world. It is argued that the doctrine of pragmatism is recognized by classical realists. Here, pragmatism means that only theories that make a difference in practice are worth the effort and the effect or "practical pay-off" is the relevant measure of value in theoretical matters. *See* Brian Leiter, "Classical Realism," *Nous*, Vol. 35, Supplement: Philosophical Issues, 11, *Social, Political, and Legal Philosophy* (2001), p. 245.

equality had been considered to be a firm and legitimate basis. In the contemporary world in which huge disparities of economic competitiveness and developmental power exist as an obvious fact among States, pursuing equality of States without taking into consideration their actual competitive power would result in and extend substantive unequal situations among States.[9]

In the opinion of *le droit international développement* scholars, new legal measures for rectifying unbearable and unequal situations were needed urgently in order to restore the foundation of law in a troubled real world. For this noble purpose, there is no need to reject the power-based structure of the international legal system. Instead, challenging it by requiring a look at the reality and outlining a more functional and more stable picture of this structure in a future world permeated only with bearable differences is enough for them. As a result, the substantive equality among States became the reason as well as the goal for using a pragmatic or functional approach to tackle the issues of developing countries. It is needed only because the legal system itself could only function well in a society maintaining some extent of physical, particularly economic, equality among States. These scholars predict that such equality can be realized through a systematic institutional design or set of measures with immediate, large scale, and effective impacts.

As for this normative and institutional design, they argued in particular that the dismissal of reciprocity between developed and developing countries as well as the general preferential treatment of developing countries are essential. In Professor Ida's view, this argument, based on the need for adjustment and adaptation of the traditional principle of State equality established in a traditional society, with basic homogeneity to the contemporary world with huge disparities, should be considered a useful guideline for moving toward establishing substantive equality. In a traditional international society, economic and trade policies had been fully under the control of State sovereignty and were hardly subject to international adjustment or control. However, what is needed in the contemporary world is a new idea of international economic cooperation: the principle of substantive equality instead of equality in formality. Here, the principle of substantive equality means that, for realizing the goal of boosting the level of development of developing countries to a bearable level or a level close to the one of developed States, reasonable differential measures should be adopted.[10] In this sense, the most important means of this functional approach should be defined through the lawmaking process.[11]

---

9   Ryuichi Ida, "La revendication d'une réelle égalité(1)" (1974), p. 35.
10 *Ibid.*, pp. 75–76.
11 *Ibid.*, p. 67.

With the great efforts in such a functional perspective, nowadays the idea of a more favorable stance of international law toward developing countries, especially in economy-related areas, has been broadly accepted. Developing countries, with their limited ability in terms of economy, technology, and law, are generally considered less capable of complying with the requirements of international agreements. Reflecting this fact, many international agreements, including treaties on trade, the environment, human rights, intellectual property, and other areas, begin to recognize that developing countries will have more difficulty complying with the standard international obligations and adopt favorable standards.[12] More importantly, such pragmatic efforts also have been accepted by many developing countries in practice and even had certain impacts on the self-identification of some of these States. For example, in the process of participating in multilateral international legal regimes, China gradually turned to using the label developing country for self-identification in the international society, instead of sticking to the more politically charged term Third World.[13]

Based upon the above analysis, we consider that the functional approach to the issues of developing countries can be described mainly in three aspects.

Firstly, this approach uses international law as a pragmatic tool and tries to actively adjust the interests among States, especially between developed and developing countries so as to be able to establish some balanced common ground for a new world. Such an active functional aspect of developing countries research has been persistently pursued. To realize the evolutionary and challenging desires of developing countries, it has been strongly argued that, many favorable measures to establish the principle of substantive equality, to secure equal participation of developing countries in the international law-making process, and to provide special and differential treatment to developing countries are necessary.

Such a functional perspective comes from a realist view on the international order. Here, international law is expected to play the role of a regulator of the different interests and to respond to different cultures and ways of thinking

---

12 As for special and differential treatment for developing countries, see Frank J. Garcia, "Beyond Special and Differential Treatment," *British Columbia International and Comparative Law Review*, Vol. 27 (2004), pp. 291–292; Peter Lichtenbaum, "'Special Treatment' vs. 'Equal Participation': Striking a Balance in the Doha Negotiations," *American University of International Law Review*, Vol. 17 (2002), p. 1010.

13 For the change of the usage of these terms in China, see Dong Minyuan, "Strategic Implications of the Division of Developing Countries," *China International Studies*, Fall (2008), pp. 4–8.

among States. International law is a system treating the particularities and diversities among States as its premise, but when the disparities among States become so large that the normal foundation of the law is crippled, this law should be used as an effective tool for narrowing such gaps. Such a balanced realistic sense of international life has been constantly maintained in *le droit international développement* research. The formation and application of international law should not be carried out for maintaining the *status quo* but rather to reformat the reality. Such a law inherently includes equality in development as one of its distinct ends. This nature of *le droit international développement* is what distinctly separates it from traditional international law.[14]

Secondly, the functional perspective used for developing countries studies encompasses a thoroughgoing pragmatic trend in its refusing a formalistic use of the concept of developing country. The concept of developing country has been used meaning a group of certain States on the one hand and more importantly, has been used intentionally identifying particular States on the other hand. It is argued that in legal arrangements for developing countries the State should not be understood as an abstract and homogenous State, but rather as an individual State exiting in a unique and concrete situation (*l'Etat situé*). In this way, the different levels of development can be more appropriately taken into account in the lawmaking process and States can be understood in their concrete situations. As a result, it is argued that, in order to ensure equality in development, particular mindsets and policies for reproducing substantial equality in accordance with concrete situations and, therefore, a new legal concept that could create harmonized effects between equality in development and legal equality is much needed.[15]

The concept of *l'Etat situé* reflects a distinct characteristic of the functional approach developed in Professor Ida's research: while arguing for the principle of equality of States, formal or substantive, it pays special attention to those States exiting in a concrete, unbearable situation that impairs the basic function and foundation of the law and hurts the sense of legal fairness and justice. Here, unequal treatment in law is designed to realize the goal of resolving unequal development in favor of weak States as a compensatory unequal treatment. In addition, equality is considered an active functional equality to ensure the continuity of equal development earned from such a process. Traditional international law had shown no interest in unequal development. By concentrating on liberalist development policies and maintaining neutrality toward facts, equality in law was only a passive reflection of reality. Contrary

---

14   Ryuichi Ida, "Statut juridique des pays en voie de développement" (1985), p. 615.
15   *Ibid.*

to this, from the functional approach perspective, the function of law is not to maintain the disparities in development, but rather to try to mitigate them to restore the function of law to its normal course. In another words, law should be used as an active tool to create equality in development and should not be neutral but rather interventional in *de facto* unbearable societal situations. This intervention means creating and applying different legal norms according to the differing development levels of States in specific situations, and can be realized by introducing double- or multi-standard legal norms, some of which are applicable to the relations among developed States, some of which are applicable to the relations between developed and developing countries, and some of which are applicable only to the relations among developing countries.[16]

Thirdly, another important characteristic of this functional perspective is its endorsement of the basic value of the Western-born international law, the unspoken premise of trying to negotiate interests among States at different levels of development while keeping the core value of the current legal system. This way of thinking is based on the basic trust put by *le droit international développement* scholars in the adaptability and great tolerance of traditional international law. For Western scholars arguing for developing countries, the creation and development of international law had always included tolerating different interests of States. Not only *le droit international de développement*, even the New International Economic Order (NIEO), despite showing clearly confrontation toward traditional law, should be understood as ideas of a particular period for adjusting conflicting interests among States and not as rejecting the modern international legal order as such. Acceptance of the legal concept of developing country does not mean to reject traditional law, but rather brings new elements or new life into it. Put another way, the West had to confront the challenge of preventing the disruption of the international order that would follow the developing world's campaign to articulate its history of exploitation and to change the rules of international law that had both justified and furthered the system of exploitation.[17] As will be explored later, this attitude has also been shared by many scholars of developing countries.

Disparities in economic development cannot be overcome by equal treatment established in liberalist legal thinking. But the concept of equality has been accepted as a basic value of the international society. Whatever the current situation might be, the common view of the international society is that eventually, equality among States must be achieved. The huge gap between the

---

16   *Ibid.*, pp. 615–616.
17   Antony Anghie, *Imperialism, Sovereignty and the Making of International Law* (Cambridge University Press, 2005), p. 235.

reality and the ultimate goal created the space for the new *le droit international de développement*. Law functions as evolutionary change pursuing equality as its final destination. In this sense, the preferential or differential treatments should not be interpreted as contradiction of the principle of equality, but rather as useful tools for realizing this principle in a more effective way.[18]

III   The Functional Approach Viewed from a Methodological Perspective

Although it is difficult to define a specific location of the functional approach to the issue of developing countries in the methodologies of international law, judging from the characteristics mentioned above, it might be described as an intuitive sociological method or an approach with some sense of justice and fairness regarding developing countries defined in a more concrete social context. By locating this functional approach in the framework of sociological methods, one cannot only reconfirm its methodological characteristics, but also can argue more persuasively for its soundness and significance as a general perspective of international law.

The functional approach or functionalism has different meanings in the field of international studies. According to Douglas M. Johnston's research, the functionalist mindset pivots on constructs such as system, context, situation, role, function, and relationship and became a dominant method in the field of social anthropology after the First World War. Immediately after the Second World War, functionalism entered the mainstream of sociology and quickly influenced the leading theorists in that discipline, especially those in the United States. By the 1960s, functionalism in one form or another had become central, if not dominant, in political science as well as in sociology throughout most of the world. The label has been found so convenient that it is no longer possible to offer a definition that is generally acceptable in all the social sciences.[19] Even considering the many interpretations, functionalism still can be seen as an approach that treats society as if it were composed of mutually dependent and determinant parts, working together to maintain and preserve the social whole.[20]

---

18   Ryuichi Ida, "Statut juridique des pays en voie de développement" (1985), p. 617.
19   Douglas M. Johnston, "Functionalism in the Theory of International Law," *Canada Yearbook of International Law*, Vol. 26 (1988), pp. 18–19.
20   *Ibid.*, p. 20.

The root of the functional approach designed for tackling the issue of developing countries is not clearly identified by *le droit international développement* scholars. In order to give a more proper theoretical appraisal, it should be useful to compare it with several other functional approaches designed for tackling general problems of the international society.

First, the functional approach to the issue of developing countries is able to revert to the traditional, specialized meaning the term has in international organizations. Functionalism in this traditional version posits that, as economic and technological interdependence grows, diplomacy and the elaboration of international legal rules will be shaped increasingly by functional concerns and less and less by ideology and "high politics."[21] One common ground between traditional functionalism and the functionalist approach to the issue of developing countries becomes apparent: using international law, particularly through institutions or norms, to reach a defined end of the international society.

Starting in the late nineteenth century, a number of scholars took the proliferation of international organizations as an indication of a growing sense of world community and as a guarantee for future international stability. David Mitrany was considered the leading scholar who best formulated the doctrine and the theory of functionalism in international organizations.[22] His essay *A Working Peace System* (1943) summarized the main arguments of the functionalists in international studies and made a challenging claim: functionalism is the road to a lasting peace. Proponents of functionalism have assumed that the growing tide of functional links and relationships eventually will dominate international relations and render political and ideological conflicts less significant.[23]

This functionalism maintains that social and economic maladjustments are the basic causes of war and that social and economic welfare is the precondition of peace. The existing State system contributes to international tensions and conflicts because it is institutionally inadequate. It cannot deal with basic

---

21 For readings on the case for functionalism, see David Mitrany, *A Working Peace System* (Royal Institute of International Affairs, 1966); Ernst B. Haas, *The Uniting of Europe: Political, Social and Economic Forces, 1950–1957* (2nd ed., Stanford University Press, 1968).

22 For an analysis of the conceptual development of functionalism in international organization study, see David Long, "International Functionalism and the Politics of Forgetting," *International Journal*, Vol. 48 (1992–1993). As for the role played by Mitrany, *ibid.*, see pp. 368–369.

23 David Mitrany, *A Working Peace System* (National Peace Council, 1943); Particularly his 1946 version, *A Working Peace System: An Argument for the Functional Development of International Organization* (National Peace Council, 1946).

global problems because it arbitrarily divides the global society into national units based on territory, and not based on the problems to be solved.[24] International institutions based on function rather than on territory are appropriate for the solution of such problems. Establishing such institutions is possible because social activities can be separated into political and non-political or technical ones. Positive experiences in certain fields of international institutions will spread and accumulate, forming part of the foundation for an international society.[25]

From this point of view, the most basic premise of functionalism is that human beings are fundamentally rational, that they see the advantages of harmony over conflict in social relations, and that they can control their destiny through the evolutionary steps that will lead to a peaceful world. Functionalists advocate building on existing foundations by extending the network of international agencies and increasing their powers. The practical and pragmatic aspect is one of the chief attractions of functionalism.[26] This kind of functionalism has also had a definite impact on the study of international law since 1945. A further reflection of this influence is the growth of international legal studies devoted to functional concerns, e.g., trade, conservation of resources, and human rights that established a firm base for the development of the neo-functional approach.

While the classical functional approach emphasizes the final aims of reduction of interstate conflicts and promotion of peace, the neo-functional approach embraces a general utilitarian perspective that may promote a wider range of additional goals. In the neo-functional view, the process of increasing interdependence generates complex problems that individual States cannot deal with effectively. This approach suggests that, in the first stage, States' policymakers identify a cooperative framework that is plausible to further the interests of involved parties. It is desirable to begin with international cooperation in relatively "low-key" and apolitical sectors (such as technical or environmental sectors) that should be of importance to the parties involved. Once the cooperative efforts in such "low political" spheres generate benefits for both parties, interest groups are expected to exert pressure on national leaders to expand integration to additional sectors, not necessarily apolitical ones.[27]

---

24   Mitrany (1943), *ibid.*, p. 42.
25   *Ibid.*, pp. 29–30.
26   As for the critics of functionalism, *see* Inis L. Claude, *Swords into Plowshares: The Problems and Progress of International Organization* (3rd ed., Random House, 1956), Chapter 16.
27   Moshe Hirsch, "The Sociology of International Economic Law: Sociological Analysis of the Regulation of Regional Agreements in the World Trading System," *European Journal of International Law*, Vol. 19, No. 2 (2008), pp. 286–287.

Second, the functional approach in *le droit international de développement* can be considered an important constructing element for the general functionalism in international law, such as the one explored by Johnston. While it was recognized that it is not easy to develop a general theory or framework on functionalism in international law, it is possible to describe the nature and future of functionalism. For Johnston, functionalism is envisaged as a "frame of reference" available to both participants (policymakers and practitioners) and observers (scholars, students, and the general public). Functionalism adopts the dynamic "policy science" perception of "international law as a process of claim and response."[28]

In conformity with the heritage of classic functionalism in political science, legal functionalism bases its ethic on the need for efficiency (effectiveness) as well as equity (justice) in international law. While it is recognized that in certain contexts effectiveness and justice may be served more directly through legitimate forms of autonomous and competitive behavior, functionalists encourage the development of international law on the basis of a co-operative ethic with a view to facilitate the confrontation of fundamental issues and the application of collective intelligence to the treatment of complex problems. Although reluctant to abandon the concept of common core values, functionalists accept the trend to diversification in the world community. They advocate a higher degree of sensitivity to the cultures and traditions of the more recently independent States, as well as to the special needs and vulnerabilities of their developing economies. In general, the ethical position adopted by functionalists in a particular context or problem situation is influenced by their awareness of the multiple functions assigned to international law by history.[29]

In particular, international law has now been assigned corrective and developmental functions: that is, the correction of distributive injustices among a concert of nation-states with the goal of a world community order based on the ethic of co-operative behavior. Nations and peoples benefit from a restructuring of the international legal system designed to bring preferential benefits to the developing and the disadvantaged States. In this process, the transformation of the international society from a concert of nation-states to a world community order based on the ethic of co-operative behavior carries signs of functionalism.[30] It is specifically argued that functionalists are sympathetic to the efforts of developing nations to raise their economy to a higher level

---

28 D. Johnston, *supra* note 19, p. 55.
29 *Ibid.*, pp. 56–57.
30 *Ibid.*, pp. 28–29.

through the removal of unfair advantages vested in the technologically advanced States. In a world community characterized by gross and widening disparities, the problem of injustice among nations must continue to be treated as a matter of priority. The corrective function of international law is, however, closely associated with the developmental gap and to some degree dependent on it. Proposals for a restructuring of the international legal system under the aegis of the New International Order must be seen as contributing, more or less directly, to the enhancement of social welfare in developing countries as well as to the overall statist goal of economic development. The problems of *le droit international de développement* are immensely complex and require sympathetic treatment at the highest level of sophistication. From the functionalist perspective, progress will depend on a precise and reasonable balance of efficiency and equity. The whole enterprise is critically dependent on good faith and ingenuity in co-operative arrangements.[31]

Third, the strong tendency of the functional approach to the issues of developing countries to emphasize the intimate relationship between the social reality and the institutional or normative design evokes another kind of functional approach to international law posited by some international law scholars, especially by Hans Morgenthau, that emphasizes the functional relationships between political, social, and economic forces and the legal rules for correcting the weakness of positivism.[32] Although the realist trend in it might be too strong to properly compare it to the functional approach used for the issue of developing countries, from a critical perspective on positivism, however, the sensibility of the latter toward reality, particularly toward the economic developmental reality of the world, is quite strong, the understanding of which, as mentioned above, has played a vital role in their great effort to use legal institutions and norms to pursue substantive equality for developing countries.

For Morgenthau, the fundamental weakness of formalism or the positivist doctrine of international law lies in its falling short of international law as it really is. A truly scientific theory of international law must avoid these mistakes in order to come closer to the reality. Although it seems a logical choice to call such a theory "realist", on second thought, Morgenthau argued that it should be called a functional approach to international law. Because this approach does not regard the legal rules as definitely determined by their legislative or judicial formulation, but searches for the psychological, social,

---

31 *Ibid.*, pp. 49–50.
32 According to Johnston, with the expansion of functionalism in the field of sociology, some of the language of functionalism was adopted by anti-formalist international lawyers in the United States. Morgenthau was one of them. D. Johnston, *ibid.*, p. 22.

political, and economic forces that determine the actual content and working of legal rules and that, in turn, are determined by them. In other words, their scientific goal is to formulate uniform functional relationships between those forces and the legal rules. Hence, realist jurisprudence is, in reality, functional jurisprudence.[33]

Morgenthau argues that international law should be comprehended as standing in a reciprocal functional relationship with the social forces of its time. Firstly, international law is the function of the civilization in which it originates, that is, of the regulative ideas laid down in the ethics and mores of a civilization, of the political, economic, and general social forces prevailing in it, and, finally, of the specific psychological factors manifesting themselves in the individuals determining it. Secondly, international law is a social mechanism working towards certain ends within the same civilization that, in turn, becomes a function of this same international law.[34]

Some important consequences[35] for a functional theory of international law described by Morgenthau also have valuable meaning for our appraisal of the functional approach in *le droit international de développement*, particularly its non-confronting stance on the basic value of international law. For Morgenthau, a functional theory of international law has to start with the recognition of the particularly intimate nature of the relationship between social forces and legal rules. It is because of this intimate relationship that in the international field, fundamental changes of the social forces and hence of the legal rules follow each other at frequent intervals and in an abrupt, often violent, manner. It follows from this analysis that two obviously different types of international law exist: one founded on the permanent and stable interests, the other one based on the temporary and fluctuating interests of States. This differentiation is not only of fundamental importance for the understanding of the validity of international law; it leads to yet more far-reaching consequences regarding the subject matter, the methods, and the scientific character of the science of international law. As a conclusion, this kind of functional theory of international law will not only fulfill the task of any scientific doctrine, that is, to know what is and why it is; it will also prepare the ground for satisfying the greater ethical and political desire to improve international relations by means of the law.[36]

---

33   Hans J. Morgenthau, "Positivism, Functionalism, and International Law," *American Journal of International Law*, Vol. 34 (1940), pp. 273–274.
34   *Ibid.*
35   Morgenthau presented six important consequences, *ibid.*, pp. 274–275.
36   *Ibid.*, p. 284.

Finally, the functional approach to the issue of developing countries also can be appraised comparatively from the point of view of the structural-functional approach as described by Moshe Hirsch for studying international law. For him, international law is a social phenomenon that reflects and aims to guide a variety of interactions in the international arena. Sociological analysis casts new light on an important dimension of international law and enriches our understanding of the social factors involved in the creation and implementation of international rules.[37] As mentioned above, the functional approach to the issues of developing countries is based on the idea that international law and other societal processes are profoundly interlinked and try to identify proper and new legal regimes to rectify the huge gaps between developed and developing countries for realizing the integrated function of law.

As pointed out by Hirsch, a sociological exploration of international law cannot limit itself to the analysis of official legal texts and their interrelationships. Although these sources of "lawyers' law" remain significant, unofficial sources of "living international law" should also be carefully studied. Socio-legal studies should take into account the variety of international interactions that reflect the social norms prevailing in the international community.[38] This trend has, as mentioned above, been shown clearly in Professor Ida's functional approach to the issue of developing countries. In addition, soft law research has actually been an important theme of Professor Ida's academic projects relating to the issues of developing countries.[39]

There are several different sociological theories on international law and, according to Hirsch, the more influential one is the structural-functional approach to international law that calls for the construction of inclusive legal regimes that have uniform provisions, binding all members, with few variations or exceptions.[40]

While it is clear that the functional approach to the issue of developing countries has not been developed by strictly following the methodology of the structural-functional approach, there are some similarities between these two perspectives. More importantly, the basic characteristics and theoretical orientations of these two perspectives are almost the same. The similarity may originate in their shared deep-rooted understanding that the relationships between the aims and functions of law and society are intimately linked, and that the legal rules constitute social control. As argued by Hirsch, the international

---

37   M. Hirsch, *supra* note 27, p. 892.
38   *Ibid.*, pp. 894–895.
39   See Ryuichi Ida, "Qu'est-ce que le 'Soft Law'? (1) (2)" (1985), pp. 1–26 and pp. 1–21.
40   M. Hirsch, *supra* note 27, p. 893.

legal literature commonly assumes, either explicitly or implicitly, that one of the functions underpinning international law is that of achieving order and integration. Thus, not surprisingly, numerous international lawyers and policymakers almost intuitively consider international cooperation, integration, and order vital goals to be pursued by international law.[41] In this sense, the functional approach in *le droit international développement* is an intuitive sociological method applied to tackle the issue of developing countries.

Two comparable characteristics of these two functional approaches can be identified. The first one is the emphasizing on the linkage between the orientation of law and the societal situation. This aspect of the functional approach has been explained clearly by reading Professor Ida's research on the issue of developing countries. The structural-functional conception of international law, on the other hand, invites scholars to ascertain the social functions of particular legal rules or institutions within the general international system. This finding may encourage scholars to suggest new rules to restore the desired balance within the system. Even without the enactment of new formal rules, in light of the inherent tendency of social systems toward an equilibrium, a move from the desired equilibrium may well impel actors to remedy the systemic malfunction informally. Under this approach, legal changes are often perceived as deriving from the tendency of international law to adapt itself to changing circumstances in the international system. "Soft law" instruments often attract a wider participation of States and introduce new international norms through broad approval. This wide endorsement frequently exerts social pressure on policymakers to comply with the norms contained by these instruments.[42]

The second comparable characteristic is the basic trust in the core values of the existing law shown by these two approaches. As mentioned above, the functional perspective of *le droit international développement* follows an unspoken premise of keeping the core value of the current legal system and trusting the nature of adaptability and tolerance of traditional international law. Evolution, not revolution, is its basic mindset. On the other hand, it is argued that the structural-functional perspective is also located at the "consensual" end of the consensus-conflict spectrum. It emphasizes the interdependence of the various components of society and the resulting tendency of societies to enhance cooperation and integration. Consequently, this perspective attributes particular significance to social stability and equilibrium. Equilibrium exists when a society attains the social patterns that are best

---

41   Ibid., p. 914.
42   Ibid., pp. 914–915.

adapted to its needs and this balance is expected to persist until external conditions change.[43]

In the study of social relations at the macro level, the structural-functional perspective is contrasted with the social conflict perspective in this aspect. For social conflict theorists, society is characterized by regular patterns of inequality in the allocation of essential resources, such as wealth and political power, among its members. The uneven distribution of resources engenders social stratification and struggle among rival groups; each is interested in advancing its own interests at the direct expense of the other groups. The existing social structures are the outcome of the competition among rival groups. Thus, while the structural-functional perspective highlights the importance of social interdependence, cooperation, and order, the social conflict perspective emphasizes social disorder and argues that the social structure is temporary and fragile. Unlike the structural-functional perspective, the proponents of the conflict perspective view social change as inevitable and desirable.[44]

This kind of contradiction between the structural-functional perspective and the conflict perspective is similar to the one existing between the functional perspective in this analysis and the Third World approach to the issues of developing countries. A comparative analysis will follow in Part 2 of Section IV.

IV The Significance and Limitations of the Functional Approach

The functional approach in *le droit international développement* has basically been put forward by Western scholars in response to the strong claims from developing countries to resolve the huge gaps in development. It is also a story told from inside of the exiting legal system to argue for the survival of this system in response to the necessity of adapting it to the changed situations. While the principles of State sovereignty and equality of States, core values of the system, have been strongly guarded, its pragmatism has been highlighted in the process of designing and applying favorable treatments to developing countries. Along with its strong sense of fairness and justice, pragmatism can be considered a credo of the functional approach in *le droit international développement*.[45]

---

43   *Ibid.*, pp. 901–902.
44   *Ibid.*, pp. 906–907.
45   See Balakrishnan Rajagopal, "From Resistance to Renewal: The Third World, Social Movements, and the Expansion of International Institutions," *Harvard International Law Journal*, Vol. 41 (2000), p. 529.

As explained above, a functional explanation of the development of international institutions, especially international economic institutions, has long been used to explain their emergence as a result of the pragmatic necessity to serve concrete functions related, for example, to trade, postal services, or the regulation of rivers. It was said that GATT was presented as an international mechanism for the multilateral reduction of tariff barriers to trade in goods and, in this respect, shared with the IMF and the IBRD some aspects of the functionalist approach to international organizations. Because they all share, firstly, the underlying rationale that specialized organizations can best serve the world community by performing specific functions and, secondly, the assumption that economic and technical matters can be effectively separated from politics. Following these assumptions, the Bretton Woods Institutions were separated from the UN and secured the appearance of economic neutrality in carrying out their activities.[46] The central proposition of this theory is that institutions are born and expanded because of top-down policy decisions that correlate with the functional needs of the international society.[47] The functional approach to the issues of developing countries followed the same way of functional thinking of international institutions.

But as criticized by Rajagopal, functionalism displays serious deficiencies when explaining the evolution of many important politically charged international institutions. To the extent that international legal scholarship continues to reiterate the apolitical and technical image of the Bretton Woods Institutions, it remains trapped in functionalism.[48] In other words, the functionalist separation between the economic and political realms of international law served to conceal the deeply political nature of the supposedly neutral economic rules and institutions put in place to promote development.[49]

In addition, the functional approach to development issues generally has been narrated as an evolution of legal mechanisms to enable the adaption of traditional international law to a changed world. The involvement of developing countries in the process of creating preferential treatment had only been accounted for as an economic or *de facto* element, but not as political power factor. As developing countries were decolonized and entered the

---

46 Antony Anghie, "Time Present and Time Past: Globalization, International Financial Institutions, and the Third World," *New York University Journal of International Law & Politics*, Vol. 32 (2000), pp. 264–265. L. Claude, *supra* note 26, p. 384.
47 B. Rajagopal, *supra* note 45, p. 530.
48 *Ibid.*, p. 531.
49 Donatella Alessandrini, *Developing Countries and the Multilateral Trade Regime: The Failure and Promise of the WTO's Development Mission* (Hart Publishing, 2010), p. 226.

international society in the middle of the previous century, international institutions were truly becoming consolidated in a wave of pragmatism. Despite this temporal coincidence, the influence that developing countries as a newly emerged block of political powers had on the creation and evolution of preferential treatment or vice versa shall be properly reflected. The institutional evolution cannot be considered simply a pragmatic and functional pursuit of substantive equality for the survival of the old legal system, but has to be explained by relating it to the grand politics of decolonization that created the stage for a long-lasting battle between the exploiting States and the exploited States.[50]

In this sense, the functional approach in development issues can only be described as a liberal or open-minded method of legal thinking. With regard to the huge disparities in development, this approach admits the beneficent character of development and the role of preferential treatment in resolving these gaps that are defined as the collective effort to eradicate poverty and raise standards of living for all. The writers adopting this position may concede that sometimes these mechanisms do not achieve their objectives, but that is all the more reason to reform and improve them.

When the functional approach is compared to the approaches of developing world scholars on international law and particularly on *le droit international de développement*, its significances and limitations become much clearer. In Gathii's view, the work of developing world scholars on international law in the past 50 years can be characterized as falling into one of two ends of a spectrum: an integrationist strand that sees promise in developing country participation in international law through legal reform; and a nationalist strand that sees no hope for developing countries within the present structure of international law without fundamental restructuring of the discipline and of international economic and political relations.[51] These earlier efforts and convictions are an enduring and important legacy of international legal

---

50   It should be realized that there are many skeptical views about whether the functional approach to international law has been able to achieve the results desired by developing countries. For one of these explorations, see Sundhya Puhuja, *Decolonising International Law: Development, Economic Growth and the Politics of Universality* (Cambridge, 2011). In her view, international law in its aspirational dimension bears an enduring relation to an idea of justice. The relation holds out a promise of universality that has inspired many attempts by the Third World to use international law as a site of political struggle, but many such attempts have had the unintended consequence of legitimizing an expanding domain of international intervention into the Third World, p. 254.

51   James Gathii, "International Law and Eurocentricity," *European Journal of International Law*, Vol. 9 (1998), p. 184.

scholarship as it relates to developing countries. The functional approach can be easily cognized as intimately relating to the integrationist strand, although it was not a direct result of legal thinking from the stance of developing countries. This makes it possible and useful to compare the functional approach with approaches adopted by developing countries scholars.

With the above-mentioned differences and possibilities in mind, it can be said that the common ground of international law scholarship shared by developed and developing countries scholars is maintaining the core values of international law and making the favorable measures toward the issues of developing countries effective. Actually, substantive equality, set as its goal by the functional approach in *le droit international de développement*, has also been shared and even vigorously pursued by many developing countries scholars.[52]

1   The Functional Approach and the NIEO

Even today, when the movement of the New International Economic Order has been criticized and somewhat muted, the pursuit of fairness and justice in the way of ensuring substantive equality nevertheless remains fundamentally vital. That is to say that developing countries must develop economically, that the gap in standards of living between developed and developing countries must narrow, and that there should be a transfer of resources from developed countries to developing countries to accomplish those ends.[53] Actually, the NIEO as well as the idea of substantive equality are firmly based on the notion of differential treatment for developing countries.

The NIEO regime began in 1970s, with the adoption of the UN resolutions at its Sixth Special session: firstly, the Declaration on the Establishment of a NIEO[54] and secondly, the Program of Action on the Establishment of a NIEO.[55]

---

[52]   Despite their increased number and activity in the WTO, developing countries still find themselves in a relatively marginalized position and experience difficulties in linking their development agenda to multilateral trade negotiations. The recent emergence of a multitude of developing country coalitions reflects fundamental changes in the landscape of developing country positions in the General Agreement on Tariffs and Trade ("GATT") and the WTO, and shows that such coalitions are beginning to change the organization's dynamics. Sonia E. Rolland, "Developing Country Coalitions at the WTO: In Search of Legal Support," *Harvard International Law Journal*, Vol. 48 (2007), p. 483.

[53]   Daniel Barstow Magraw, "Legal Treatment of Developing Countries: Differential, Contextual, and Absolute Norms," *Colorado Journal of International Environmental Law and Policy*, Vol. 1 (1990), pp. 78–79.

[54]   UNGA Res. 3201 (S-VI), GAOR, Supp. 1 (1974), pp. 3–5.

[55]   UNGA Res. 3202 (S-VI), GAOR, Supp. 1 (1974), p. 5.

The third and the legally binding document pertaining to the NIEO is the UN Charter of Economic Rights and Duties of States.[56]

The principle of substantive equality has been argued to trump the principle of State equality in its rigid formality with regard to equitable results or equity. This should also be considered the basic spirit of the NIEO claimed by developing countries. It is well known that the NIEO contains elements of contextual treatment. Each of the three basic NIEO resolutions repeatedly refers to "equity" and "equitable." Pursuing equitable results, just as argued by scholars of the functional approach in *le droit international de développement*, requires consideration of the facts and circumstances of the particular situation under examination. The concepts of "equity" and "equitable" mandate that the characteristics of developing countries are taken into account.[57]

Putting trust in the fundamental values of international law and its adaptable and changeable character and, more importantly, making efforts to design agreeable and applicable legal mechanisms of preferential treatment, become the basis upon which scholars endorsing the functional approach from both sides of a divided world can build a common ground for cooperation. When facing the question whether the international community can sufficiently reform international law to have redeeming relevance for the Third World countries, a host of Third World scholars has seen the potential in international law through which the system can be reformed from the inside in favor of Third World States.[58]

Third World scholars take the position that if they can influence the content of international law, they will purge the system of its bias, blind spots, and all that causes injustice in the system. If only they could ascertain the exact norms of international law, and if such norms were favorable, all would be well. This seems to be the overarching theme of most of the Third World struggles: struggles to influence the content of international law.[59]

---

56   UNGA Res. 3281 (XXIX) (1974).
57   Ryuichi Ida, "Statut juridique des pays en voie de développement" (1985), pp. 615–616.
58   Mohamed Bedjaoui, "Challenge and Reply: An Evaluation of the Balance of Power with a View to Changing the Present Order", in Mohamed Bedjaoui, ed., *Towards A New International Economic Order* (Holmes & Meier, 1979), p. 65; T.O. Elias, *Africa and the Development of International Law* (1988); Makau wa Mutua, "Why Redraw the Map of Africa: A Moral and Legal Inquiry," *Michigan Journal of International Law*, Vol. 16 (1995), p. 1113.
59   Joel Ngugi, "Making New Wine for Old Wineskins: Can the Reform of International Law Emancipate the Third World in the Age of Globalization?" *U.C. Davis Journal of International Law and Policy*, Vol. 8 (2002), p. 81.

The proposals for a NIEO must thus be seen as representing the culmination of a decade-long process of attempting to articulate an alternative to the mainstream approach to the international economic system. It is undisputed that the NIEO proposals represented a high point in Third World optimism about their power within the economic system. What is sometimes overlooked, however, is another source of optimism, perhaps equally as important: a faith that the Third World spokespersons had both in the adaptability of the system and the receptiveness of their First World counterparts to consider a fundamental change in orientation.[60]

2   The Functional Approach and TWAIL

The functional approach in *le droit international de développement* has long been appraised and accepted by some scholars from developing countries. Even in the so-called Third World Approaches to international law (TWAIL), we can find many common points shared with the functional approach in this analysis. Certainly, historical experiences of exploitation have been much more emphasized in TWAIL.[61] Contrary to the functional approach's character of almost apolitically and technically acknowledging the huge gaps in development, TWAIL have dug deeply into history to explain the causes of the current situation and even openly indicted Europeans for holding historical responsibility for such gaps.[62] It is argued that what these scholars share is the political, ethical, and academic commitment to look at the history, structure, and processes of international law and institutions from a particular standpoint: that of the peoples of the Third World.[63] For this reason, TWAIL have much broader perspectives on issues of developing countries and stronger ethical arguments for reform and change in international law.

TWAIL scholarship shares the common purpose of seeking the reformation or, where necessary, the retrenchment of international rules and structures that are unjust for the Third World. TWAIL perspectives seek *inter alia* to unpack the colonial history of most of the Third World, foreground

---

60   Karin Mickelson, "Rhetoric and Rage: Third World Voices in International Legal Discourse," *Wisconsin International Law Journal*, Vol. 16 (1998), pp. 365–366.

61   Andrew F. Sunter, "TWAIL as Naturalized Epistemological Inquiry," *Canadian Journal of Law and Jurisprudence*, Vol. 20 (2007), p. 479.

62   For the central features of earlier TWAIL, see B.S. Chimni, "Towards a Radical Third World Approach to Contemporary International Law," *International Center for Comparative Law and Politics Review*, Vol. 5 (2002), p. 15.

63   Special Issue, "Situating Third World Approaches to International Law (TWAIL): Inspirations, Challenges and Possibilities," *International Community Law Review*, Vol. 10 (2008), 351–353, p. 351.

colonialism's continuing influence on the international system and on Third World peoples, draw on and problematize the shared experiences of Third World peoples, and focus on achieving some form of justice for peoples of the Third World.⁶⁴ Mutua provides three objectives of the TWAIL discourse: to examine and expose the usage of international law for perpetuation and for the subordination of non-Europeans to Europeans; to provide an alternative legal structure to the present system; and finally, to eliminate underdevelopment in the Third World.⁶⁵

Even with such distinct characteristics, the functional perspective in TWAIL has still upheld its importance. For TWAIL scholars, international law can fulfill a far more noble purpose. It can serve to respond to serious problems at a global level. Some scholars of this discourse even shift the focus towards culture and policy, exploring the fairness in international law and concentrating on the requirement that international law must flow from the reality of international life. By moving beyond its present purpose, international law can be extremely useful in tackling issues of inequality.⁶⁶ Here, it is clear that the functional perspective has been inherently included in TWAIL.

Actually, one of the earlier streams of developing country scholarship recognized and analyzed the historical origins of international law in Europe; its engagement with international law was often premised on how best to reform international law and how to address the concerns of developing countries.⁶⁷ For this purpose, TWAIL is described as a collection of scholarly perspectives as well as a political movement.⁶⁸ It was argued that TWAIL are not "methods" in a traditional sense, but are distinct ways of thinking about what international law is and should be; they involve the formulation of a particular set of concerns and the analytic tools with which to explore them. For some TWAIL scholars, international law makes sense only in the context of the lived history

---

64   Ibironke T. Odumosu, "Challenges for the (Present/) Future of Third World Approaches to International Law," *International Community Law Review*, Vol. 10 (2008), 467–477, p. 468.
65   Makau wa Mutua, "What is TWAIL?" *American Society of International Law Proceedings*, Vol. 94 (2000), p. 24.
66   Madhav Khosla, "The TWAIL Discourse: The Emergence of a New Phase," *International Community Law Review*, Vol. 9 (2007), p. 295.
67   But it was pointed out that, due to this scholarship's commitment to making international law relevant outside its European origins, it understated how rules and institutions of international law reflect a process of engagement between European and non-European cultures and races. James Thuo Gathii, "Alternative and Critical: The Contribution of Research and Scholarship on Developing Countries to International Legal Theory," *Harvard International Law Journal*, Vol. 41 (2000), p. 265.
68   I. Odumosu, *supra* note 64, p. 467.

of the peoples of the Third World. Two important characteristics of TWAIL emerge from this thinking. First, the experience of colonialism and neo-colonialism has made Third World peoples acutely sensitive to power relations among States and to the ways in which any proposed international rule or institution will actually affect the distribution of power between States and peoples. Second, it is the actualized experience of these peoples, and not merely that of States that represent them in international forums, that is the interpretive prism through which rules of international law are to be evaluated. By evaluating positivist rules through the lens of the lived experience of Third World peoples, TWAIL scholars seek to transform international law from being a language of oppression to a language of emancipation—a body of rules and practices that reflect and embody the struggles and aspirations of Third World peoples and that, thereby, promote true global justice.[69]

More importantly, TWAIL adopted a non-rejectionist stance towards modern international law. TWAIL put great importance on the principles of sovereign equality of States and non-intervention, fundamentally important issues to societies that had just regained their independence. TWAIL believed that the contents of international law could be transformed to take into account the needs and aspirations of the peoples of the newly independent States. This was to be achieved principally through the United Nations system. TWAIL scholarship was closely aligned with the diplomatic initiatives undertaken by newly-independent Third World States, and TWAIL placed immense faith in the UN to bring about the changes necessary to usher in a just world order. In attempting to achieve these ends, the Third World States tried, in effect, to formulate a new approach to sources doctrine by arguing that General Assembly resolutions passed by vast majorities had some binding legal effect.

TWAIL scholarship does not seek to completely overthrow and discard international law. Although it seeks a reformation or retrenchment of international legal rules and structures that foster injustice and domination, it must continue to engage for the potential of adopting a redefined or reformed international law as a strategic means to reconstruct the Third World's place in an international system with a hegemonic character. Put differently, TWAIL must continue to develop means of seeking justice for the Third World within the international system through alternative conceptions of international legal order or governance.[70]

---

[69] Antony Anghie and B.S. Chimni, "Third World Approaches to International Law and Individual Responsibility in Internal Conflicts," *Chinese Journal of International Law*, Vol. 2 (2003).

[70] I. Odumosu, *supra* note 64, pp. 468–469.

On the other hand, quite contrary to the attitudes of the functional approach in the present analysis toward the very concrete situations of each specific State, TWAIL perceived the newly independent, post-colonial State as a unitary entity that transcended and stood above conflicts and tensions generated by class, race, and gender within Third World societies. But much like the functional approach, the earlier stream of TWAIL adopted a relatively unproblematic view of international law and saw its task in using the established techniques of international law to address Third World concerns.

IV   Conclusion

It is said that the norms, claimed by the developing world on the basis of justice, were successful. Though attacked, they remain powerful forces within the international system to this day.[71]

On the other hand, it is now broadly recognized that many attempts of developing countries to change the world order became weaker with the end of the Cold War and the dissolution of the Soviet Union. With the collective strength of the developing countries lessening, those ways of legal thinking supported by this collective strength also might become weaker. The functional approach in this analysis can also not escape this fate entirely. But contrary to the clear trends of decline and deadlock of other approaches in the field of development, such as the NIEO or TWAIL, the functional approach maintains its long lasting activity. As a conclusion of this research, I would like to argue that the functional approach in *le droit international développement* has a better chance to identify proper ways to respond to the concerns of developing countries.

Firstly, the pursuit of fairness and justice through realizing substantive equality, as strongly argued for by the functional approach in *le droit international de développement*, still has a powerful basis in reality. The concerns still exist, and to respond to them with more effective and more complicated multi-standards are still needed to rectify current gaps in development between States.

Secondly, with the weakening of the collective approach to the issues of developing countries, the functional approach in *le droit international développement* becomes a better and more appropriate choice in the sense that it takes into account the concrete situations of each developing State.

---

71   Muthucumaraswamy Sornarajah, "Power and Justice: Third World Resistance in International Law," *Singapore Year Book of International Law*, Vol. 10 (2006), p. 21.

Even with the collective strength of developing countries dispersed and weakened, the emphasis of the analyzed functional approach on the unbearable disparities in economic development among very real States is still a strong motivation to maintain current and to create new legal measures to keep international law functioning well with a reasonable sense of fairness and justice.

CHAPTER 4

Emerging Economies and International Economic Law: A Case Study on Thailand

Sakda Thanitcul

I   Introduction

The author, as a Thai foreign student of Professor Ryuichi Ida, is largely inspired by "Ida's International Law", particularly Professor Ida's academic interest in the impact of legal standards and international rules in assisting developing States such as Thailand to achieve their developmental aims. This paper, which relates to Thailand's experience with the WTO dispute settlement mechanism, is written as a tribute to Professor Ida and his work in the area of international law of development.

After the Second World War, numerous countries in Africa and Asia gained independence from colonialism and sought policy advice from the World Bank on how to accelerate their national development.[1] The years 1949 and 1950 witnessed a flurry of government activity that linked Thailand to the international development system. In May 1949, Thailand gained membership of the World Bank and the International Monetary Fund (IMF).[2] Further, although Thailand was not an original contracting party to the General Agreement on Tariffs and Trade (GATT), it joined GATT in 1982. After becoming a contracting party, Thailand has actively participated in multilateral trade negotiations, particularly during the Uruguay Round. During the 1980s, Thailand participated in bilateral trade negotiations with the United States with regard to Section 301 of the United States Trade Act of 1974 and was the respondent in the well-known Thailand cigarette case,[3] decided by a GATT panel in 1990. Recognizing that it is difficult for a less powerful country to bilaterally negotiate trade issues with a more powerful one, Thailand strongly supported the Uruguay Round multilateral trade negotiations. Moreover, together with a number of developed and developing countries, Thailand collectively negotiated on many significant

---

1   Robert J. Muscat, *The Fifth Tiger: A Study of Thai Development Policy* (M.E. Sharpe, 1994), p. 50.
2   *Ibid.*
3   *Thailand-Restrictions on Importation of and Internal Taxes on Cigarettes*, 7 November 1990, BISD 37S/200.

issues during the Uruguay Round from its inception in 1986 until its completion in late 1993.

At the outset, it should be noted that this paper is not an empirical study of trade data, and hence, the author does not argue that the accession of Thailand to the World Trade Organization (WTO) is praiseworthy in the economic context in the sense that the increase in Thailand's export volume has exceeded (even modestly) the increase in its import volume (even after taking into consideration a normal growth had Thailand not been in the WTO regime). Such an argument must be substantiated by an empirical study of adequate export–import data over a sufficiently long period of time, which is beyond the scope of this paper.[4] The purpose of this paper is to argue that the dispute settlement mechanism embedded within the WTO rule-based system provides Thailand, as a developing country, with more export opportunities and greater protection of its domestic market. This paper will first discuss the merits of the dispute settlement system with respect to Thailand, and then it will briefly examine Thailand's experience in the WTO dispute settlement mechanism for the purpose of evaluating its practical effects both in the general sense and more particularly on the Thai private sector.

II   Developing Countries in the GATT and WTO Multilateral Trading System

1   *Developing Countries in the GATT (1947–1994)*

The United Nations was established in the aftermath of the Second World War in 1945, with the ultimate aim of maintaining global peace and security through international cooperation. In this period of reconstruction and economic development to recover from the devastation of the war, the United Nations established the Bretton Woods System (GATT-IMF-World Bank) to promote economic wealth and assure liberalized free international trade by obligating countries to peg their national currencies to the US dollar and empowered the IMF to resolve temporary imbalances in countries' balance of payments.

---

4 Certain empirical studies found that WTO/GATT accessions are associated with significant increases in growth and investment for those acceding countries which have to undertake substantial reforms; *see* for example, Man-Keung Tang and Shang-Jin Wei, "Does WTO Accession Raise Income? When External Commitments Create Value," IMF Research Department. Available at <http://www.nber.org/~wei/data/tang&wei2006/wto-Accession_journal_version_060706.pdf> (13 November 2014).

With the establishment of the new economic regime, developing countries, including Thailand, realized that industrialization would be the only way to undo the structural disadvantage that they faced in the domain of international trade as predominantly primary producers confronting low price elasticity of demand, low income elasticity, fluctuation in export revenue, and deteriorating terms of trade. Referring to Jamaica's industrialization in his report in 1946, W. Arthur Lewis stated that it is as "clear as daylight" that industrialization was the key to development.[5] Therefore, by requiring deliberate efforts of States and calling for a type of planning that ensured the right allocation of scarce resources, corrected market prices, maximized savings, foreign investment oriented to the right direction, industrialization could be considered a key development during the 1940s[6] and constituted the core of most development models of the 1950s.[7]

With industrialization being given paramount importance in the process of economic development, the struggle for obtaining concessions in the name of "economic development" from GATT rules has persisted since the earliest International Trade Organization (ITO) negotiations.[8] During the final Havana Conference, developing countries spent a substantial amount of time on this issue and eventually obtained several concessions, which larger developed countries found rather distressing.[9] Despite the reactions from developed countries, developing countries continued to push the matter forward, until a decision was taken in 1964 to establish a permanent United Nations Conference on Trade and Development (UNCTAD). This marked a more vigorous phase of the economic development campaign of developing countries.

At the first session of UNCTAD in 1964, a report presented by Raul Prebisch, the first Secretary-General of UNCTAD, brought international focus on the idea that preferential tariff rates in the markets of developed countries could provide impetus for industrial development in the Third World.[10] Prebisch propounded that promoting developing countries' exports of manufactured

---

5   Gerald M. Meier, *Leading Issues in Economic Development* (Oxford University Press, 1989), p. 82.
6   Arturo Escobar, *Encountering Development: The Making and Unmaking of The Third World* (Princeton University Press, 1995), p. 74.
7   *Ibid.*
8   Robert E. Hudec, *The GATT Legal System and World Trade Diplomacy* (Butterworth Legal Publishers, 1990), p. 228.
9   *Ibid.*
10 Report by the Secretary-General of the OECD, "The Generalized System of Preferences: Review of the First Decade," in John H. Jackson, William J. Davey and Alan O. Sykes,

products could help free those countries from heavy dependence on trade in primary products, whose slow long-term growth and marked price instability contributed to chronic trade deficits.[11] By adopting a deliberate policy of export-oriented industrialization, developing countries could benefit not only from employment and production creation but also from greater export earning potential based on products for which demand in industrialized countries was strong.[12] In keeping with the proposed solution, a system of generalized non-reciprocal preferences was created under which developed countries would lower customs duties on goods imported from developing countries.[13] The legal basis for the system was founded in June 1971 when the Contracting Parties to the GATT approved a waiver to Article I of the GATT, which requires that trade policy measures be applied without discrimination to all contracting parties.[14]

Following the approval of this waiver, the Generalized Scheme of Preferences (GSP) fell quickly into place, with the first GSP being implemented by the European Economic Community in July 1971.[15] Over the following months, most other developed countries put their own schemes into effect.[16] The GSP itself became complete on January 1976, when the scheme of the United States became operational.[17]

2 Thailand's Experience with the Generalized System of Preferences (1981–1986)

After the Second World War, members of the Association of Southeast Asian Nations (ASEAN), with the exception of Singapore, included basically agrarian, primary commodity-exporting economies that were heavily dependent on advanced industrial nations to provide markets for their resource-based exports and as suppliers of imported capital goods and consumer durables.[18]

---

11 Jr. eds., *Legal Problems of International Economic Relations: Cases, Materials and Text on the National and International Economic Relations* (Thomson/West, 1995), pp. 1126–1127.
11 Ibid., p. 1127.
12 Ibid.
13 Ibid.
14 Ibid.
15 Ibid., p. 1128.
16 Ibid.
17 Ibid.
18 Soon-Beng Chew, Rosalind Chew & Francis K. Chan, "Technology Transfer from Japan to ASEAN: Trends and Prospects," in Shojiro Tokunaga ed., *The Japan's Foreign Investment and ASEAN Economic Interdependence: Production, Trade, and Financial Systems* (University of Tokyo Press, 1992), p. 122.

The aspiration of ASEAN countries was to move away from being mere suppliers of primary commodities and become markets for foreign manufactured goods, thereby paving the way to becoming industrial economies.[19] Thailand spent three decades (the 1950s, 1960s, and 1970s) shifting focus from agriculture to manufacturing and other non-agricultural sectors;[20] in 1985, the export value of textile products exceeded that of rice, which was greatly applauded by Thai economists.[21]

It was as early as May 1979 in Manila, that the then World Bank President Robert McNamara called for developing countries to "upgrade their export structure to take advantage of the export market being vacated by more advanced developing countries (e.g. Taiwan, South Korea, Hong Kong, and Singapore)".[22] The World Bank report recommended that in order to achieve rapid growth, developing countries should adopt good economic fundamentals and export promotion.[23] In Thailand, General Prem, who headed the government from 1980 to 1988, led the shift of focus from an import-substitution industrialization strategy to an export-oriented industrialization in 1981 in accordance with the World Bank, which was playing a leadership role in the process of industrialization in Thailand since the late 1950s.[24]

Following the adoption of this export-oriented industrialization strategy, Thailand utilized the GSP, particularly those related to the United States and the European Economic Community, to promote the export of its manufactured goods to those markets. However, the early 1980s witnessed the rise of the protectionist sentiment in the United States, coupled with the rise in Thai exports to the United States, which was Thailand's largest export destination. In the mid-1980s, three petitions were filed to the United States Trade Representative (USTR) under Section 301 of the Trade Act of the United States

---

19   *Ibid.*, p. 123.
20   Somsak Tambunlertchai, "Manufacturing Exports from Thailand: Performance and Prospects," in Shu-Chin Yang ed., *Manufactured Exports of East ASIAN Industrializing Economics: Possible Regional Cooperation* (M.E. Sharpe, 1994), p. 190.
21   Akira Suehiro, "Capitalist Development in Postwar Thailand: Commercial Bankers, Industrial Elite, and Agriculture Groups," in Ruth McVey ed., *Southeast ASIAN Capitalists* (SEAP, Cornell University, 1993), p. 35.
22   Robin Broad and John Cavanagh, "No More Nics," in Charles W. Kegley, Jr. and Eugene R. Wittkopt eds., *The Global Agenda: Issues and Perspectives* (McGraw-Hill, 1992), p. 273.
23   World Bank, *The East Asian Miracle: Economic Growth and Public Policy* (Oxford University Press, 1993), p. 33.
24   Sakda Thanitcul, *Industrial Ladder and Technology Import Regulation: Experiences of Japan, South Korea, Mexico and Lessons for Thailand* (Nititham Pub. House, 1999), pp. 52–53.

against Thailand.²⁵ One was by the International Intellectual Property Alliance (IIPA), alleging a lack of adequate protection of the US copyrights by Thailand. The second one was by the Pharmaceutical Manufacturers Association (PMA), which alleged a lack of pharmaceutical patent protection by Thailand. The third one was by the American Federation of Labour and Congress of Industrial Organizations (AFL–CIO) on grounds of a lack of internationally recognized workers' rights in Thailand.²⁶ These three petitions asked the US Administration to withdraw Thailand's rights under GSP.²⁷ In the overall assessment of the benefit of GSP for Thailand, below is an influential view.

> More importantly, developing countries should reconsider GSP benefits when they have to exchange them for IP protection, First GSP is a unilateral extension of benefits which imposes no legal obligation on the countries extending it. Secondly, a granting country can attach any conditions to the GSP benefits. For example, a recipient country must remain a developing country, the criterion of which is, in many cases, arbitrary. Furthermore, a granting country, such as the US, can also set forth minimum competitive need limits, i.e., an item will be deleted from the GSP list if the total exports of the product to the US in the previous year have exceeded 50% of the total US import of the product. Worse yet, if this minimum competitive need requirement is reduced to 25% (which is most likely) many GSP items will be excluded from the list. Thirdly, in the case of Thailand the data shows that approximately 80% of exports from Thailand to the US do not utilize the GSP scheme. It had been reported that Thai exporters have faced difficulties in reporting cases of raw materials and labor used in production. Often Thai exporters perceive that US import duties are low, and thus are willing to pay the duties rather than go through complicated procedures to receive GSP benefits which incur very high transaction costs. Furthermore US importers often agree to pay import duties for those products from Thailand that are eligible to receive GSP in order that both parties can avoid the time consuming process of presenting documents showing the origin of the product.²⁸

---

25   Surakiart Sathirathai, *Thailand and International Trade Law* (Graduate Institute of Business Administration, Chulalongkorn University, 1987), p. 43.
26   *Ibid.*
27   *Ibid.*
28   *Ibid.*, p. 29.

3 Developing Countries in the WTO (1994–present)

In *Developing Countries in the GATT Legal System*, Robert Hudec argued against the preferential and non-reciprocal treatment for developing countries, on the basis that the nuanced combination of economic, political, and legal analysis circumventing this treatment would not benefit developing countries. Particularly, despite the preferential market access that was designed to provide enhanced access of developed countries' markets for developing countries' products, Hudec argued that this did not provide sufficient advantage. In fact, he held that such preferences were mostly granted with strings attached or with the subsequent development of additional conditions. In other words, he did not expect the developed world to give something for nothing; the preferences are granted in ways that incur trade diversion to hurt other developing countries rather than trade creation to put the adjustment burden on developed countries.[29]

Prior to the Uruguay Round, the main purpose of developing countries' trade negotiations was to secure unreciprocated access to the Organization of Economic Cooperation and Development (OECD) countries' markets.[30] Dubbed as a "watershed" in the evolution of the GATT System, the Uruguay Round was the eighth round of multilateral trade negotiations conducted within the GATT framework and centred on issues relating to agriculture. The introductory statement in the Uruguay Round in September 1986 contained an explicit understanding that developing countries would be accorded "Special and Different Treatment" (S&D) in the negotiation.[31] However, the adoption of the "Single Undertaking (Take It or Leave It)" as the guiding principle for the round radically changed the form and content of most of the key elements of S&D provisions. In other words, the intent of the Uruguay Round agreement was that developing countries should eventually meet virtually the same set of standards as industrial countries on a broad range of market access issues.[32] Over the course of the negotiations, the hard line coalition of developing countries was replaced by coalitions of developing countries that

---

29 Robert E. Hudec, *Developing Countries in the GATT Legal System* (Gower Publishing Company Limited, 1987), p. 228.

30 Sylvia Ostry, "The Uruguay Round North–South Grand Bargain: Implication for Future Negotiation," in Daniel L.M. Kennedy and James D. Southwick eds., *The Political Economy of International Trade Law* (Cambridge University Press, 2002), p. 285.

31 Ademola Oyejide, "Special and Different Treatment," in Bernard Hoekman, Aaditya Mattoo and Philip English eds., *Development, Trade and the WTO* (The International Bank for Reconstruction and Development/The World Bank, 2002), p. 506.

32 Ibid.

concentrated firmly on liberalization of agriculture, textiles, and garments.[33] Consequently, the Grand Bargain was completed, in quite a different manner from the old GATT reciprocity, thereby resulting in the emergence of an implicit deal: the opening of OECD markets to agriculture and labour-intensive manufactured goods; in particular, textiles and garments were to be included into the trading system of trade in goods. Another landmark creation following the Uruguay Round was the creation of the World Trade Organization (WTO), equipped with what is highly acclaimed to be one of the strongest dispute settlement mechanisms in the history of international law.[34]

Therefore, with regard to the GSP, it can be concluded that the benefits derived by developing countries from the GSP have been rather small in relation to the total volume of exports of developing countries; moreover, the benefits have been heavily concentrated in a few countries.[35] Up to the mid-1980s, Hong Kong, South Korea, and Taiwan accounted for approximately 45% of the total gains from the GSP. This concentration of GSP benefits remained unchanged through the early 1990s, as 6–12 of the largest beneficiaries claimed 71–81% of the total benefit.[36]

III The WTO Dispute Settlement Mechanism and Developing Countries

The non-economic benefit, which is also rather important for lower-middle income countries such as Thailand, is the merit of the rule-based multilateral trading system that the WTO embodies. It enables Thailand to stand on equal footing with all its trading partners, large or small.

Without a means of settling disputes, the rule-based system would be less effective because the rules would not be enforceable.[37] Dispute settlement is considered as one of the main pillars of the WTO. In 1994, all members of the WTO agreed on the Understanding on Rules and Procedures Governing the Settlement of Disputes or Dispute Settlement Understanding (DSU). The aim is to resolve trade disputes through consultations among member States—that is, multilaterally—and not unilaterally. All member States are required to

---

33   Ibid.; S. Ostry, *supra* note 30, pp. 286–287.
34   Ibid., p. 287.
35   Ibid.; A. Oyejide *supra* note 31, p. 506.
36   Ibid.
37   Understanding the WTO: Settling Disputes. Available at <http://www.wto.org/english/thewto_e/whatis_e/tif_e/disp1_e.htm> (13 November 2014).

abide by the decision of the Dispute Settlement Body (DSB), which adjudicates all disputes. The merits of the WTO dispute settlement mechanism and constraints faced by developing countries in this regard are discussed below.

1 Protection against Unilateral Actions

Section 301 of the 1974 Trade Act of the United States is the principal law authorizing the US government to impose trade sanctions against foreign countries upon actions that are deemed by the US government to have violated the rights or benefits of the United States.[38] While the WTO's Dispute Settlement Understanding (DSU) does not explicitly state whether a member State could employ a unilateral action, it can be implied from the language of the DSU that a unilateral action that has not been authorized by the WTO would violate the WTO rules.[39] Such implication can be derived from, for example, Articles III and XXII of the DSU (multilateral settlement), Article I of the GATT (Most Favoured Nation), and Article II of the GATT (excessive tariffs), all of which collectively indicate that a unilateral sanction is not permitted.[40] Notwithstanding the above, Section 301 has survived a number of challenges,[41] which implies that the US government can always exercise its power pursuant to Section 301 to unilaterally impose trade sanctions against its trading partners at its own free will. Thus, Thailand is also liable to action from the United States under Section 301 as Thailand is listed on the Priority Watch List of the 2010 Special 301 Report by the Office of the United States Trade Representative.[42] The United States may choose to impose unilateral sanction against Thailand if the latter fails to satisfactorily cooperate with the former in relation to the protection of intellectual property rights (IPRs).

---

[38] Jean Heilman Grier, "Section 301 of the 1974 Trade Act," Available at <http://www.osec.doc.gov/ogc/occic/301.html> (13 November 2014).

[39] Dispute Resolution Mechanism, the International Economics Study Center. Available at <http://internationalecon.com/wto/ch2.php> (13 November 2014).

[40] Tracy M. Abels, "The World Trade Organization's First Test: The United States-Japan Auto Dispute," UCLA Law Review, Vol. 44 (1996), p. 467, p. 484.

[41] Dispute Settlement: Dispute DS152. Available at <http://www.wto.org/english/tratop_e/dispu_e/cases_e/ds152_e.htm> (13 November 2014). Chakravarthi Raghavan, "WTO Panel Upholds US Sanctions Law! Third World Network." Available at <http://www.twnside.org.sg/title/uphold-cn.htm> (13 November 2014).

[42] The placement of a trading partner on the Priority Watch List indicates that particular problems exist in that country with respect to intellectual property rights protection, enforcement, or market access for persons relying on intellectual property. Countries placed on the Priority Watch List are the focus of increased bilateral attention related to problem areas. Available at <http://www.ustr.gov/about-us/webfm_send/1906> (13 November 2014).

However, to a certain extent, it can be argued that the wide ambit of Section 301 has been curtailed by the introduction of the WTO dispute settlement mechanism. One of the reasons is that the trading partner against which the United States may impose a trade sanction, pursuant to Section 301, may retaliate against the United States by claiming that the United States has acted in violation of the DSU. Hence, the United States must be more mindful in exercising its power under Section 301. Therefore, the effectiveness of the WTO DSU is another explanation for why the United States may refrain from using Section 301. As the dispute settlement mechanism was established within the WTO regime, it is widely accepted at an international level as an effective tool for resolution of trade disputes. In fact, the United States has itself, on a number of occasions, resorted to the WTO dispute settlement to make a claim against other countries. Thus, the dispute settlement mechanism of the WTO provides the United States with a more legitimate option to protect its trade interests as compared to Section 301, as the arbitrary nature of the latter may backfire on the United States (for example, by retaliation from the affected trading partner). In addition, the United States may be reluctant to impose trade sanctions under Section 301 as such action would run counter to the movement towards a global free trade regime, which it has been promoting for decades.[43]

2 Equitable Treatment of Developing Countries

The result of trade negotiations is generally perceived as a reflection of negotiating powers. The outcomes often depend on the comparative bargaining power of the negotiating parties. Hence, bilateral agreements do not appear to be a solution to resolve the problem of power imbalance.[44] With collective bargaining power in the WTO,[45] Thailand is more likely to benefit from multilateral trade negotiations as compared to bilateral trade negotiations.

The WTO system is a law-based regime. The system has become increasingly subject to legal control derived from multilateral negotiations. The bargaining power of member countries, particularly powerful ones, decreased as such countries continue expanding their commitments to liberalize their domestic markets. One of the most notable tools to ensure that rules are respected is the DSU. The DSU effectively restricts the use of unilateral power by dominant players and compels them to implement what they agreed upon during negotiation

---

43 Dispute Resolution Mechanism, *supra* note 39.
44 Pascal Lamy, "Multilateral and Bilateral Trade Agreements: Friends of Foes?" WTO News: Speeches. Available at <http://www.wto.org/english/news_e/sppl_e/sppl46_e.htm> (13 November 2014).
45 The Role of Thailand within the WTO (in Thai), Eduzones Elibrary. Available at <http://blog.eduzones.com/offy/4475> (13 November 2014).

rounds.[46] The Dispute Settlement Body (DSB) of the WTO is responsible for adjudicating disputes among member countries; had it not been for the DSB, it would be impossible for weaker countries to force more powerful countries to behave according to their commitments towards market liberalization as evidenced in the DSU prior to the founding of the WTO.[47] As the paradigm of international economic law has shifted, international trade order aims to become increasingly freer and fairer. Less powerful countries now have a platform to challenge more powerful countries in order to bring about freer and fairer trade.[48]

Even though it is stated that the new DSU is not a meaningful source of power for developing countries, given that such countries are still unable to secure an advantageous position under the DSU as compared to the previous GATT dispute resolution mechanism which GATT panel decision must be adopted by consensus while the WTO panel decision is going to be adopted except it is rejected by consensus (negative consensus). But it cannot be denied that this dispute settlement mechanism has reduced the bargaining power gap between rich industrialized and poor developing countries. The DSU places developing countries in a better position compared to that if they were to stay outside the WTO system or to stay within the system but without the presence of the DSB. Once a developed country's action is found to be inconsistent with its commitments, the DSU provides an immediate and promising solution corresponding to the rules that have been laid down by several rounds of multilateral negotiations. The tide of the disputes has turned, even minimally, since the power-based regime of the GATT has shifted to a rule-based organization.

The Tuna Exports case of the European Community (EC) case, Tuna products from Thailand was imposed with higher tariff rate than those coming from the Africa, Caribbean and Pacific States (ACP States), is a good illustration of how Thailand can utilize the WTO regime to secure more equitable treatment from a stronger trading partner.[49] As discussed in Section II.1.(3) later, this case was

---

46   Peter M. Gerhart and Archana Seema Kella, "Power and Preferences: Developing Countries and the Role of the WTO Appellate Body," *North Carolina Journal of International Law and Commercial Regulation*, Vol. 30 (2005), p. 515, pp. 523–524.
47   In the past, members in dispute could block or delay the process of dispute resolution at almost every stage, which rendered the entire process ineffective. However, currently, it is stated that the dispute settlement system in the WTO has been a remarkable success. Chapter 4: The WTO Dispute Settlement System, Available at <http://www.wto.org/english/thewto_e/10anniv_e/future_wto_chap6_e.pdf> (13 November 2014).
48   The Victory of Thailand in the WTO (in Thai), Available at <http://www.nidambe11.net/ekonomiz/2005q4/article2005oct03p14.htm> (13 November 2014).
49   Nilaratna Xuto, "Thailand: Conciliating a Dispute on Tuna Exports to the EC," in Peter Gallagher, Patrick Low and Andrew L. Stoler eds., *Managing the Challenges of WTO Participation: 45 Case Studies* (Cambridge University Press, 2005), pp. 555–565.

settled through mediation and did not go through a formal litigation procedure. Settlement through mediation seemed to be a sensible approach as the prospect of Thailand winning the case was not contentious and that the parties were well aware that if the case were to go to the DSB, the outcome would have been binding. It was preferable for the parties to agree on a settlement during the mediation process, both in terms of time and litigation costs. In addition, this case also illustrates how developing countries can benefit from the flexibility of the WTO dispute settlement regime, such as the use of mediation and negotiation to arrive at a satisfactory outcome at less cost.

3   Constraints Faced by Developing Countries in the WTO Dispute Settlement Mechanism[50]

Developing countries are believed to face difficulties of initiating a case against other members, namely "capacity constraints" and "power constraints". [51]

(1) Capacity Constraints

"Capacity Constraints" includes both a shortage of skilled human resources and a lack of financial resources without legal assistance.[52]

The first major problem Thailand faces is the language barrier. Since the official language of the WTO is English, litigators in the DSB must be extremely fluent in English. In addition, owing to the complexity of the WTO legal structure, legal expertise in WTO law is essential. If Thailand can overcome these capacity constraints, it can benefit more from WTO legal framework, as then Thailand can more effectively utilize the dispute settlement mechanism to defend its trade interests.[53]

The short-term solution to this problem for Thailand is to employ the expertise of foreign lawyers who are native English speakers or fluent in English and who have appropriate expertise in WTO law to represent Thailand in the DSB. It is essential that such foreign lawyers must work closely together with Thai

---

50 For more details on what may hold back greater participation from developing member countries, *see* Roderick Abbott, "Are Developing Countries Deterred from Using the WTO Dispute Settlement System?" ECIPE Working Paper No. 01/2007. Available at <http://www.ecipe.org> (13 November 2014).

51 Andrew T. Guzman and Beth A. Simmons, "Power Plays and Capacity Constraints: The Selection of Defendants in World Trade Organization Disputes," *Journal of Legal Studies*, Vol. 34 (2005), p. 557.

52 *Ibid.*

53 Christina L. Davis and Sarah Blodgett Bermeo, "Who Flies? Developing Country Participation in GATT/WTO Adjudication," *The Journal of Politics*, Vol. 71 (2009), p. 1033.

officials who can then learn from such foreign lawyers and acquire appropriate knowledge, skills, and useful techniques to litigate within the legal WTO framework. In contrast, the long-term solution for Thailand is that the Thai government must invest in its own human capital and have more capable lawyers with excellent command of English and appropriate expertise in WTO law.

Recognizing that most developing countries face similar problem of capacity constraint, the WTO established the Advisory Centre on WTO Law (ACWL) in 2001 to provide general legal advice, support, and training on all matters related to WTO law and dispute settlement proceedings at reasonable fees.[54]

The 2009 ACWL reports revealed that since the date of its establishment, the ACWL has provided support to 17 members and 2 least-developed countries directly through its staff in 34 disputes and through external legal counsel in 4 disputes.[55] Among these disputes, Thailand was assisted and supported by the ACWL in at least nine proceedings:[56]

- Thailand as a respondent in the case of Customs and Fiscal Measures on Cigarettes initiated by the Philippines (DS371).
- Thailand as a complainant against the United States in the case of Anti-Dumping Measures on Polyethylene Retail Carrier Bags (DS383).
- Thailand as a third party against the United States in the case of Continued Existence and Application of Zeroing Methodology (DS350).
- Thailand as a complainant against the United States in the case of Measures Relating to Shrimps from Thailand (DS343).
- Thailand as a third party against the United States in the case of Final Dumping Determination on Softwood Lumber (DS264).
- Thailand as a complainant against the United States in the case of Provisional Anti-dumping Measures on Shrimps from Thailand (DS324).

---

54 Advisory Centre on WTO Law. Available at <http://www.acwl.ch/e/index.html> (13 November 2014). Certain articles also support the idea that developed countries must assist developing countries in improving their trade regime by supporting an independent legal aid center; see for example, Thaddeus McBride, "Rejuvenating the WTO: Why the US Must Assist Developing Countries in Trade Disputes," *International Legal Perspectives*, Vol. 11 (1999), p. 65.

55 ACWL Report on Operations (2009). Available at <http://www.acwl.ch/e/documents/reports/FINAL%20FOR%20WEBSITE%20Report_On_Operation_2009_PP_INT.pdf> (13 November 2014).

56 The support came in the form of initial assessment and preparation of the case, drafting consultation requests, drafting requests for establishment of a panel, drafting written submissions and responses, etc. Available at <http://www.acwl.ch/e/disputes/dispute.html> (13 November 2014).

- Thailand as a third party against the United States in the case of Measures relating to Zeroing and Sunset Reviews (DS322).
- Thailand as a complainant against the European Communities in the case of Customs Classification of Frozen Boneless Chicken (DS286).
- Thailand as a complainant against the European Communities in the case of Export Subsidies on Sugar (DS283).
- With regard to financial constraints, the litigation expense depends on the degree of complexity of the relevant case. The table below illustrates the correlation between the degree of complexity and estimated litigation costs.

TABLE 4.1 *Litigation costs*

Time budget (hours)	Degree of complexity		
	Low	Medium	High
Total	257	444	706
Consultations	43	80	127
Panel	143	256	411
Appeal	71	108	168
Estimated costs at the rate of US $500 per hour			
Total	1,28,500	2,22,000	3,53,000
Consultations	21,500	40,000	63,500
Panel	71,500	1,28,000	2,05,500
Appeal	35,500	54,000	84,000
Estimated costs at the rate of US $1000 per hour			
Total	2,57,000	4,44,000	7,06,000
Consultations	43,000	80,000	1,27,000
Panel	1,43,000	2,56,000	4,11,000
Appeal	71,000	1,08,000	1,68,000

SOURCE: HAKAN NORDSTROM, THE COST OF WTO LITIGATION, LEGAL AID, AND SMALL CLAIM PROCEDURES.[57]

---

57 In fact, the fee charged by first-rate law firms in Brussels and Washington, DC are in the range of $500 to $1,000 per hour plus expenses. The table reflects the conservative time budget used by the ACWL. It should be noted that there is no upper limit in highly complex cases. Available at <http://www.ppl.nl/bibliographies/wto/files/3753a.pdf> (13 November 2014).

It is believed that smaller economies tend to have smaller trade stakes; hence, these countries tend to be more sensitive to high litigation costs, because the costs may outweigh the potential gains for such countries from pursuing litigation. Consequently, fewer cases will actually be initiated by smaller economies to the DSB since some of them may not pass the simple cost-benefit analysis.[58]

However, the above assertion may not hold true for Thailand. Thus far, Thailand has been involved in precisely 55 cases: 13 cases as a complainant, 3 cases as a respondent, and 39 cases as a third party. The Thai government has paid approximately 3–5 million Baht per case to the ACWL (approximately US $1,00,000 to US $1,50,000).[59] A conclusion that can be drawn from Thailand's active participation in the WTO dispute settlement mechanism as illustrated above is that the advent of the AWCL has somewhat successfully eliminated the capacity constraints faced by Thailand, both in terms of human and financial resources.

Further, it must be noted that the amount of WTO member contribution paid by Thailand is fairly small compared to the benefits Thailand obtains from the membership. The amount of member contribution is calculated according to each member's share of international trade (in percentage), based on trade in goods, services, and IPRs for the last five years for which data is available.[60] In 2009, Thailand contributed to the WTO budget and the budget of the Appellate Body at CHF 1,984,912 (approximately US $1,786,580).[61] Such payment by Thailand is considered to be cost-effective.[62]

(2)   Power Constraints

Power constraints involve the impact of possible retaliatory action by major players if their policies or measures are challenged in the WTO by other member countries.

Initiating a case against another WTO member may be considered a hostile act against which the respondent may have a lawful right to retaliate. For example, a country that initiates a legal proceeding may face a cancellation of the GSP. Developing member countries that are dependent on trade

---

58   Ibid.
59   Based on a brief interview with a trade officer of the Ministry of Commerce of Thailand.
60   Members' contributions to the WTO budget and the budget of the Appellate Body for the year 2010. Available at <http://www.wto.org/english/thewto_e/secre_e/contrib10_e.htm> (13 November 2014). There is a minimum contribution of 0.015 per cent for Members whose share in the total trade of all members is less than 0.015 per cent.
61   Ibid.
62   Constantine Michalopoulos, "The Participation of the Developing Countries in the WTO." Available at <http://cdi.mecon.gov.ar/biblio/docelec/bm/1906.pdf> (13 November 2014).

preferences, foreign aid, and other forms of assistance may be deterred from initiating a case even if the imposed measure is illegitimate.

The GSP scheme, with the aim to achieve economic development of developing countries, offers Thailand an increase in its export earnings. However, such a scheme is unilateral and voluntary.

IV   Thailand's Experience with the Dispute Settlement Mechanism[63]

The trade jurisprudence implemented through the Dispute Settlement Mechanism (DSM) is the basis of the rule-oriented trading order and provides stability and predictability to trade relationship among WTO members.[64] Such jurisprudence may contribute positively to Thailand's trade interests in two ways. Firstly, it paves a way for more credible export opportunities to major foreign markets. This benefits Thailand since Thailand, as an emerging economy, is highly export-dependent. In the first three quarters of 2009, the exports of goods and services contributed to over 60 per cent of the country's GDP.[65] Secondly, it provides Thailand with a legal instrument to protect its domestic market from potential unfair trade practices such as dumping and export subsidies. A summary of important cases involving Thailand that may contribute to (1) the improvement of Thailand's export opportunities and (2) the protection of Thailand's domestic market are summarized below.

1   *Improving Export Opportunities*

(1)   United States—Import Prohibition of Certain Shrimps and Shrimp Products (1998)[66]

Complainants: India, Malaysia, Pakistan, and Thailand

Respondent: The United States

The four complainants requested consultations with the United States regarding a ban on the import of shrimps and shrimp products imposed by the

---

63   Most of the cases mentioned here can be found on the official WTO website. Available at <www.wto.org> (13 November 2014).

64   Mitsuo Matsushita, "The WTO's Coming of Age—Its Tenth Anniversary: A Review of Major WTO Jurisprudence." Available at <http://www.sipa.columbia.edu/wto/pdfs/MatsushitaWorkingPaper.pdf> (13 November 2014).

65   Background Note: Thailand. Available at <http://www.state.gov/r/pa/ei/bgn/2814.htm> (13 November 2014).

66   Dispute Settlement: Dispute DS58. Available at <http://www.wto.org/english/tratop_e/dispu_e/cases_e/ds58_e.htm> (13 November 2014).

United States pursuant to Section 609 of US Public Law 101–162. It was alleged that the United States nullified and impaired the benefits and violated various articles of GATT 1994.

The GATT panel found that the import ban on shrimps and shrimp products as applied by the United States was inconsistent with the provisions of GATT 1994 and was to be justified under Article XX of GATT 1994.

However, the Appellate Body reversed the panel's finding that the US measure of interest was not within the scope of measures permitted under the chapeau of Article XX of GATT 1994, but concluded that the measure—while qualifying for provisional justification under Article XX (g)—failed to meet the requirements of the chapeau of Article XX.

(2)   Egypt—Import Prohibition on Canned Tuna with
       Soybean Oil (2000)[67]

Complainant: Thailand

Respondent: Egypt

Thailand requested unofficial consultations with Egypt regarding the prohibition imposed by Egypt on the import of canned tuna with soybean oil from Thailand. Thailand considered that Egypt failed to implement its obligations under the Marrakesh Agreement that established the WTO, GATT, and SPS Agreement. The outcome of the consultations was in Thailand's favour and Egypt agreed to lift the import ban.

(3)   The European Community (the EC)—Tuna Exports (2002)[68]

Complainants: Thailand and the Philippines

Respondent: The EC

Although this case did not go to the panel and the Appellate Body, it illustrates that the DSU provided good conciliation and mediation where parties in dispute could avoid potential panel proceedings, which would be more costly and time consuming.[69] This was the first case in WTO history to be settled through mediation. The case sets a precedent that not all cases may need to be concluded in a formal litigation in order to achieve binding results.

Inequity existed primarily in the form of a preferential tariff granted by the EC to canned tuna producers from the African, Caribbean, and Pacific States (ACP countries). Subsequently, the EC and ACP countries entered into the

---

67   Dispute Settlement: Dispute DS205. Available at <http://www.wto.org/english/tratop_e/dispu_e/cases_e/ds205_e.htm> (13 November 2014).
68   N. Xuto, *supra* note 49, pp. 555–565.
69   *Ibid.*

Cotonou Agreement (ACP Agreement) to officially maintain this preferential treatment in 2000. Specifically, while ACP countries enjoyed zero tariffs on tuna imports, other countries—including Thailand—continued to face an inhibiting tariff of as high as 24 per cent, which proved to be detrimental to the legitimate economic interests of Thailand.

The appointed mediator indicated that the merits of the complainants had been accepted, and advised that the EC open up a new quota at a given tariff rate. This opinion was officially adopted in EC Council Regulation No. 975/2003.

(4)   The United States—Continued Dumping and Subsidy Offset Act of 2000 (2003)[70]

Complainants: Australia, Brazil, Chile, the EC, India, Indonesia, Japan, Korea, and Thailand.

Respondent: The United States

Under the Continued Dumping and Subsidy Offset Act (the Byrd Amendment), the US government allocated the money obtained from anti-dumping and anti-subsidies duties to domestic firms who alleged harm. These firms then spent the offset payments to cover investment activities for production of the products, subject to anti-dumping and anti-subsidy measures. The main concern was that the Act offered dual protection for US domestic producers in dumping and subsidization from abroad.[71]

The complainants, including Thailand, alleged that the Act was inconsistent with the obligations of the United States under several provisions of the GATT, Anti-Dumping Agreement, SCM Agreement, and WTO Agreement.

The Appellate Body upheld the finding of the panel that the Act was inconsistent with certain provisions of the Anti-Dumping and SCM Agreements. Consequently, the Act nullified or impaired benefits accruing to the complainants.

(5)   The United States—Measures Relating to Zeroing and Sunset Reviews (2007)[72]

Complainant: Japan

Respondent: The United States

---

70   Dispute Settlement: Dispute DS217. Available at <http://www.wto.org/english/tratop_e/dispu_e/cases_e/ds217_e.htm> (13 November 2014).

71   Yang-Ming Chang and Philip G. Gayle, "The Continued Dumping and Subsidy Offset Act: An Economic Analysis," *Southern Economic Journal* (2006). Available at <http://www.accessmylibrary.com/coms2/summary_0286-26363161_ITM> (13 November 2014).

72   Dispute Settlement: Dispute DS322. Available at <http://www.wto.org/english/tratop_e/dispu_e/cases_e/ds322_e.htm> (13 November 2014).

Third Parties: Argentina, China, the EC, Hong Kong, China, India, Korea, Mexico, New Zealand, Norway, and Thailand

The Appellate Body reversed the panel's finding and found that the United States acted inconsistently with the Anti-Dumping Agreement by maintaining zeroing, instances of shipment where a product is sold at a higher price in the international market than in the domestic one are ignored, procedures when calculating dumping margins on the basis of transaction-to-transaction comparisons in original investigations. The Appellate Body also found that by maintaining zeroing procedures in periodic and new shipper reviews, the United States acted inconsistently with the Anti-Dumping Agreement.

It should be noted that Thailand has substantial export interest in the "zeroing" issue, because the United States imposed anti-dumping duty on a number of Thailand's export products.

(6) The United States—Measure Relating to Shrimps from Thailand (2008)[73]

Complainant: Thailand
Respondent: The United States

Thailand considered that through the use of the "zeroing" negative dumping margins on imports of certain frozen warm-water shrimps from Thailand, the United States failed to make a fair comparison between the export price and normal price, because the effect of the zeroing practice was to artificially create dumping margins. Therefore, it was alleged that this calculation methodology violated the Anti-Dumping Agreement as well as the GATT 1994.

The panel found that the application of the Enhanced Bond Requirement (EBR) to shrimps from Thailand was inconsistent with the Anti-Dumping Agreement. It also upheld Thailand's claim that the United States acted inconsistently with the Anti-Dumping Agreement by using zeroing to calculate dumping margins with respect to the anti-dumping measure. Subsequently, the Appellate Body upheld the panel's finding.

(7) The United States—Customs Bond Directive for Merchandise Subject to Anti-Dumping/Countervailing Duties (2008)[74]

Complainant: India
Respondent: The United States
Third Parties: Brazil, China, the EC, Japan, and Thailand

---

73 Dispute Settlement: Dispute DS343. Available at <http://www.wto.org/english/tratop_e/dispu_e/cases_e/ds343_e.htm> (13 November 2014).

74 Dispute Settlement: Dispute DS345. Available at <http://www.wto.org/english/tratop_e/dispu_e/cases_e/ds345_e.htm> (13 November 2014).

Under the 2004 US Customs and Border Protection Act (the Enhanced Bond Requirement, or EBR), exporters are required to post a minimum bond equivalent to the anti-dumping duty margin, multiplied by the value of import of shrimps in the preceding year and to pay a cash deposit equal to the amount of anti-dumping duty per entry.[75]

The Appellate Body upheld the panel's finding that the EBR was not necessary to secure compliance with certain US laws and regulations governing the final collection of anti-dumping duties since the United States had not demonstrated that the dumping margins were likely to increase, thereby resulting in significant additional unsecured liability. Consequently, the Appellate Body upheld the panel's conclusion that the application of the EBR to shrimps was inconsistent with Article 18.1 of the Anti-Dumping Agreement, because it was inconsistent with the Ad Note to Article VI: 2 and 3 of the GATT 1994.

2   Protection of the Domestic Market from Unfair Trade Practices

The following is an account of cases that clearly illustrate that the dispute settlement mechanism of the WTO offers Thailand a legal instrument to protect its domestic market from potential unfair trade practices such as dumping and export subsidies.

(1)   Hungary—Export Subsidies for Agricultural Products (1996)[76]
Complainants: Argentina, Australia, Canada, New Zealand, Thailand, and the United States
Respondent: Hungary

In 1995, Hungary spent approximately US $280 million on export subsidies for over 300 agricultural products. Complainants claimed that Hungary violated the Agreement on Agriculture by providing export subsidies for agricultural products not specified in its Schedule (which limits export subsidies to only 16 agricultural products) as well as by providing agricultural export subsidies in excess of its commitment levels.

Although a panel was established in February 1997, it did not have to convene to hear the dispute since the parties reached a mutually agreed solution that required Hungary to seek a waiver of certain WTO obligations.

---

75   Simi T.B., India, "Thailand and US on Anti-dumping Measures Relating to Shrimps: Another Case Calling for Clarity in the WTO Rules," *Trade Law Brief*, Vol. 2 (2008). Available at <http://www.cuts-citee.org/pdf/TLB08-02.pdf> (13 November 2014).

76   Dispute Settlement: Dispute DS35. Available at <http://www.wto.org/english/tratop_e/dispu_e/cases_e/ds35_e.htm> (13 November 2014).

(2)   Thailand—Anti-Dumping Duties on Angles, Shapes, and Sections of Iron or Non-Alloy Steel and H Beams from Poland (2001)[77]

Complainant: Poland
Respondent: Thailand

In this case, Poland contended that Thailand's imposition of the provisional anti-dumping duties and the final anti-dumping duty of 27.78 per cent of CIF value on products produced or exported by Poland as well as Thailand's refusal of Poland's two requests of disclosure of findings violated Articles 2, 3, 5, and 6 of the Anti-Dumping Agreement.

The panel found (whose findings were subsequently upheld by the Appellate Body) that Thailand's imposition of the definitive anti-dumping measure on imports of H-beams from Poland was inconsistent with the requirement of Article 3 of the Anti-Dumping Agreement. Thailand's action was considered *prima facie* to constitute a case of nullification or impairment of benefits. Accordingly, it was found that Thailand had acted in violation of the provision of the Anti-Dumping Agreement and that it nullified or impaired benefits accruing to Poland under that Agreement. Finally, the Appellate Body reversed the panel's reasoning, but left undisturbed the panel's main finding of violation.

(3)   European Communities—Export Subsidies on Sugar (2005)

Complainant: Thailand
Respondent: The EC

In this case, Thailand alleged that the EC sugar regime accorded imported sugar a less favourable treatment than that accorded to domestic sugar and provided subsidies contingent upon the use of domestic goods over imported products. Further, Thailand alleged that the EC sugar regime also accorded export subsidies above its reduction commitment levels specified in Section II of Part IV of the EC's Schedule to the sugar produced in excess of its production quotas (so-called C sugar); Thailand also contended that the EC provided export subsidies (known as "export refunds") that covered the difference between the world market price and the high prices in the EC for the products in question, thereby enabling those products to be exported. Thus, Thailand considered that the above subsidies were inconsistent with the EC's obligations under Article III: 4 of GATT 1994, the SCM Agreement, and the Agreement on Agriculture.

---

77   Dispute Settlement: Dispute DS122. Available at <http://www.wto.org/english/tratop_e/dispu_e/cases_e/ds122_e.htm> (13 November 2014).

The Appellate Body found that the payments in dispute "were on the export" within the ambit of Article 9.1(c) of the Agreement on Agriculture, and that the EC had acted inconsistently with the Agreement on Agriculture by providing export subsidies in excess of its commitment levels as specified in its Schedule.

3   Analysis: Effects of Thailand's Recourse to the WTO Dispute Settlement Mechanism

It is evident from the above account that Thailand has proactively participated in the DSM of the WTO, regardless of capacity and power constraints. In fact, as evident from the cases presented above, Thailand does not appear to be discouraged by the power disparity to bring a claim against more powerful countries when it comes to protecting its own legitimate trade interests. In summary, Thailand would not hesitate to resort to WTO to (i) protect its export interest where an importing country adopts illegitimate trade barriers, and/or (ii) protect its domestic market if another country adopts unfair trade practices causing damage to Thailand's trade interests.

Although the rulings or recommendations in favour of Thailand may prompt economically strong developed countries to bring their policies into line with such rulings or recommendations, the author does not go so far as to say that Thailand's recourse to WTO dispute settlement procedures and its readiness to utilize such an option have posed a threat to stronger countries or directly induced changes in the trading behaviours of rich industrialized countries. Thailand would be willing to make a claim against another country only if an analysis of pros and cons reveals that the benefits (such as increased export volume as a result of a favourable decision) would clearly outweigh the costs involved (such as legal fees incurred in dispute settlement proceedings). The author does not assert that Thailand would deliberately make a claim against a more powerful country as a ploy to influence its trading behaviours. The viewpoint of the author is that Thailand is willing and ready to make such a claim if it is necessary and/or desirable to protect its own legitimate trade interests, and that it would only be an incidental effect, welcomed by Thailand of course, if a WTO's decision in favour of Thailand would induce such strong economies to change their unfair trade policies.

V   The Implications of a Multilateral Trading System for Developing Countries

While it is fair to say that the rule-based multilateral trading system has promoted a freer market and a more competitive, transparent, and predictable trading environment, developing countries must carefully consider the implications of such a trading system, particularly in relation to their export and import competitiveness.

The multilateral trading system has been beneficial to developing countries in terms of their export competitiveness, particularly in relation to those industries in which developing countries have a comparative advantage, such as agricultural and labour-intensive industries. In addition, trade liberalization has opened up foreign markets for these developing countries and enabled the promotion of their economic growth. Since developing countries export their products at a cheaper price to developed markets, there is a temptation for such import markets to ward off the challenge of competitive imports and call for protectionist measures, for example through the use of tariffs, import bans and quotas. Owing to trading power imbalances, developing countries would stand to lose from the imposition of trade barriers by rich industrialized countries. However, the position of developing countries would have been worse off in the absence of the multilateral trading system. Under such a system, stronger economies are required to eliminate trade barriers in accordance with their commitments, and the system also provides a platform for developing countries to challenge any illegitimate trade practices of more powerful countries. The tuna exports case by Thailand and the Philippines to the EC is a good example of cases where developing countries can successfully challenge an unfair trade practice of a powerful trading partner in relation to a product in which they clearly have a comparative advantage. There was evidence that Thailand and the Philippines managed to maintain a notable EC market presence despite the imposition of 24 per cent tariffs, while ACP countries enjoyed free access. This is a direct manifestation of the fact that tuna industries in both countries have much higher competitiveness and productivity.[78]

With regard to Thailand, the most obvious benefit would accrue to the agricultural sector. Since it is a major agricultural exporting country, Thailand is highly competitive in this sector. The country has been among the top five exporters in the world with respect to rice, sugar, tapioca, shrimp and chicken.[79] However, Thailand could not take advantage of most of its competitiveness owing to both tariff and non-tariff barriers in major foreign markets.[80] With regard to the shrimp market, after the DSB found the act of the United States to

---

78   N. Xuto, *supra* note 49, pp. 555–556.
79   *See* Top 5 Exporters in Rice, Sugar and Chicken, FAO Statistical Database, 26 September 2006. Available at <http://faostat.fao.org> (13 November 2014).
80   Zamroni Salim, "Thailand's Agricultural Sector and Free Trade Agreements," *Asia Pacific Trade Investment Review*, Vol. 2 (2006), p. 51.

be inconsistent with the Anti-Dumping Agreement, Thai shrimp exporters enjoyed increased competitiveness in the US market owing to considerably lower costs.[81]

It is also indicated that Thai readymade garments enjoy greater competitiveness over their counterparts in many other countries. Additionally, Thailand is the world's top producer of natural rubber, because of the low price and stable supply of raw material.[82] Thailand's competitiveness stands to improve further as a result of the elimination of trade barriers by developed countries in the multilateral trading system.

However, the possible adverse effect of the open trading system on developing countries is the other side of the coin. Obviously, the opening up of the markets by developing countries increases competition and poses a threat to domestic producers. For example, Thailand's gem and jewellery, textile, ceramic, and electrical and electronic industries have relatively low competitiveness and will suffer on account of trade liberalization if Thailand does not prepare itself well for the increasingly liberal trade regime.[83] While developing countries are also obligated to comply with their market access commitments, their special economic conditions require them to do so carefully with appropriate protection being put in place in the interest of their domestic producers. Developing countries require flexibility in terms of the time they take to implement trade liberalization programs and prepare themselves to take on most of the obligations that trade liberalization entails. For example, developing countries should be allowed to gradually reduce their import tariffs over time in order to mitigate any adverse effects that trade liberalization may have on their domestic market.

As in the case of export competitiveness, the rule-based system is beneficial for developing countries in the sense that it protects these weaker economies from unfair trade policies (such as dumping) employed by stronger economies. If faced with such unfair trade practices, developing countries can resort to the DSM to protect their trade interests.

Therefore, owing to their special economic conditions, developing countries must act thoughtfully to realize the full benefits of trade liberalization under the evolving multilateral trading system.

---

81   The Future of Thai Shrimps and the International Trade Measure (in Thai). Available at <www.pandinthong.com/ViewContent.php?ContentID=639> (no longer active, 13 November 2014).

82   Trade Liberalization within the Framework of WTO: Repercussions on Thailand. Available at <www.bangkokbank.com/download/Trade%20liberalization.pdf> (13 November 2014).

83   *Ibid.*

VI Conclusion

As mentioned in Section I, the aftermath of the Second World War urged developing countries to reconstruct their respective economies, shifting from an agricultural economy towards industrialization, as the latter was regarded as the only approach during the 1940s and 1950s to assist governments to elevate the living standard of a majority of the population from below the poverty line in the most immediate and efficient manner. Recognizing the necessity of having a system to support the developing countries' ability to trade, developing countries gathered to form a group to negotiate with the ultimate goal of obtaining "preference" under the GATT. This effort became successful when Part IV of the GATT received additional provisions in 1964 to include the system of S&D Treatment, comprising the principles of non-reciprocity, preferential market access, and permissive protection. The concrete outcome of having preferential market access was evident in the introduction of the GSP, under which industrialized countries accord exemptions on import tax on certain industrial products originating from developing countries. Thailand also substantially benefitted from the GSP after having acceded to GATT in 1982, as this enabled the country to export labour-intensive industrial products, such as gems and jewellery, and textiles and garments into OECD countries, particularly the United States.

Since 1981, the United States has exercised the so-called "stick and carrot" policy towards developing countries, including Thailand. The policy required Thailand to accord sufficient protection to IPRs, open its market to US products, and accord protection to labour in compliance with international standards. Failure to implement this as such, particularly by virtue of Section 301 of the United States Trade Act of 1974, would lead the United States to prohibit the granting of privileges under the US GSP on customs for certain important products originating from Thailand. The requirement of being governed by Section 301, coupled with the fact that Thailand's industrial development was in its infancy as it produced mainly labour-intensive products, made it vital for Thailand to closely cooperate with other developing countries to negotiate in the Uruguay Round. The final outcome of the Uruguay Round affected Thailand in that since it required all WTO members to adhere to all outcomes of the negotiation (Single Undertaking), Thailand, like other member countries, was compelled to accept all obligations arising from the rounds, even it did not wish to ratify TRIPS, GATS, and TRIMS.

Prior to the ratification of The Final Act Embodying the Results of The Uruguay Round at the Multilateral Trade Negotiation, the Government of Thailand established a committee to analyse the legal implications arising from the obligations under this act. The committee established 10 sub-committees to conduct analytical studies in this regard, but none of them was mandated to focus on the implication of the dispute settlement mechanisms of the Final Act, something which Thailand coincidentally benefitted from subsequently.

The DSM embedded within the WTO rule-based system provides developing countries, particularly Thailand, a platform to initiate any legal proceedings against more powerful countries. This mechanism has substantially eliminated unjustified unilateral actions taken by larger and more powerful countries in the past and ensured that more equitable treatment is provided to smaller and less powerful countries in spite of the trading power disparity. Further, it also offers Thailand important jurisprudence in the process of establishing a stable and predictable international trade order. Thus, by improving the credibility of Thailand's export opportunities and protecting its domestic market from unfair trade practices, the WTO's DSM will enable Thailand's balance of trade to provide a more accurate reflection of the competitiveness of the Thai private sector.

The author believes that the WTO dispute settlement is rather helpful for Thailand exports. In the future, if Thailand can improve productivity, the ability to produce more output with the same input of labour or capital, of its export products, it can reap larger benefit from the WTO multilateral trading system without depending on the fading away GSP benefit that it has been relying on for many decades.

CHAPTER 5

Universal Jurisdiction in a Context: From Dialectic to Dialogue

Mari Takeuchi

Introduction

Professor Ryuichi Ida has held a unique position among Japanese scholars, not only because of his focus on topics that had rarely been approached before he pioneered them (law of development, international organizations, human genome, soft laws, voting systems), but also because of his method of analyzing these topics.

As most of his topics are related to the emerging trends underpinned by social needs, it seems quite natural that he has often contrasted the trend-oriented approach, which tries to promote the change in legal rules in order to meet those needs, with a strict positivist approach, which tends to be reluctant in admitting the change in legal rules. However, this very emphasis on the confrontation between the two approaches distinguishes him from other scholars. Generally, doctrines tend to sympathize with one or the other approach, whether being aware of it or not, and focus on *whether* the establishment of certain norms can be confirmed. As a consequence, where international practices do not appear mature enough, the trend-oriented approach would have recourse to the importance or value aspect of the norms, which may allegedly compensate for the lack of practice.[1] In contrast, the strict positivist approach would deny the establishment of such norms as a rule of customary international law, insisting that such "relative normativity" threatens to "destabilize the whole international normative system and turn it into an instrument that can no longer serve its purpose".[2] The difference between these approaches is difficult to reconcile, as they are divided both in the

---

[1] This is typical in the argument for the "relative normativity". See John Tasioulas, "In Defence of Relative Normativity: Communitarian Values and the Nicaragua Case," *Oxford Journal of Legal Studies*, Vol. 16 (1996), pp. 94–104. For an overview on this argument, Dinah L. Shelton, "International Law and 'Relative Normativity,'" in Malcolm Evans ed., *International Law* (3rd ed., OUP, 2010), pp. 146–157.

[2] See e.g., Prosper Weil, "Towards Relative Normativity?" *American Journal of International Law*, Vol. 77 (1983), p. 423.

content of the norms they endorse and the ways in which they address international practices.

Professor Ida detaches himself from both approaches and focuses on *how* they are confronted with each other; it is in doing so that he sees the very essence of international law. His excellent article "L'O.N.U. et la souveraineté"[3] proves the advantage of this method of analysis. In this article, he observes first the process in which the United Nations has gradually developed and enlarged its scope of activity in order to secure its effectiveness to meet the needs of international society. This enlargement had been brought about through theoretical devices, such as the theory of implied powers, the importance of the practice of the organization itself in interpreting relevant instruments, and the assumption of validity of the activities of the organization.[4] The member States found them to be an interference into their sovereignty, due mainly to the fact that these developments did not necessarily take place within the scope of the explicit consent of the member States given by the foundational instruments of the organization. Thus, they attempted to exercise their direct and indirect control over the organization through either legal or illegal means (illegal means involved control over the secretariat and financial pressure; legal means involved nonparticipation in the activities of the organization and exerting influence from outside the organization), which Professor Ida termed a phenomenon of "resistance from sovereignty."[5] Bringing the confrontation of these two camps into dynamism in this way, Professor Ida succeeded in pointing out *at what stage* the institutionalization of international society has reached and *to what extent* the organization has gained autonomy, rather than *which side* won the day.

Nevertheless, this advantage has its own drawbacks. While his dynamic method of analysis may indeed bring out an accurate depiction of the current situation, it also confines his assessment within a sphere of empirical description that does not lead to a normative account of it. It may be suggested that this disadvantage derives in part from his taking the concepts of sovereignty and international community merely as opposing assertions and not exploring their individual normative implications. This was succinctly shown by his description of international society as "a vessel floating between these two poles [the sovereignty and the international community]."[6]

---

3   Ryuichi Ida, "L'O.N.U. et la souveraineté" (1991), p. 1ff.
4   *Ibid.*, pp. 5–18.
5   *Ibid.*, pp. 22–40.
6   *Ibid.*, p. 46.

Based on the above assumption, this study seeks a normative ground in the dialectic between opposing concepts, aiming to explore the waters half-charted by Professor Ida. The focus is on the issue of universal jurisdiction, for which Professor Ida's dialectic method of analysis seems particularly workable: there has been a stark confrontation between the assertion of universal jurisdiction grounded on the concept of community interest and that of sovereign equality. Yet there seems to be a certain embryo of dialogue between these concepts that deserves further exploration to determine upon what normative ground this dialogue is built. Against this background, Chapter 1 tries to illustrate the situation surrounding assertions of universal jurisdiction. Based on the pictures thus obtained, Chapter 2 further explores the normative content of opposing concepts and assesses how they are interrelated.

I Dialectic between Community Interest and Sovereignty

1 *Promotion of Universal Criminal Jurisdiction*

Universal criminal jurisdiction is the assertion of jurisdiction over an act that has no link to a State exercising it in terms of the locus of the crime or the nationality of the offenders or victims.[7] Having traditionally been asserted only with piracy,[8] this basis of jurisdiction was revitalized with regard to grave violations of human rights in the 1990s.

There was a sort of "zeitgeist" behind this trend: the spirit of cooperation generated among great powers at the end of the Cold War, the phenomenon of globalization in various fields, and the reemerged interventionism.[9] This climate also led the international society to activate the project of international criminal justice in face of the mass atrocities in Yugoslavia and Rwanda, which evolved into the global campaign of "fight against impunity," led mainly by NGOs.[10] Universal jurisdiction can be seen as one of the central apparatuses to promote this project, along with international criminal tribunals.

---

7   Roger O'Keefe, "Universal Jurisdiction," *Journal of International Criminal Law*, Vol. 2 (2004), pp. 745–746; The AU-EU Expert Report on the Principle of Universal Jurisdiction (2009), 8672/1/09 REV1, p. 7, para. 8.
8   *Mandat d'arrêt du 11 avril 2000 (République démocratique du Congo c. Belgique)*, arrêt du 14 fevrier 2002, *C.I.J. recueil 2002*, Joint Separate Opinion of Judges Higgins, Burgenthal and Kooijmans, p. 81, para. 61.
9   *See* Luc Reydams, "The Rise and Fall of Universal Jurisdiction," in William A. Schabas and Nadia Bernaz eds., *Routledge Handbook of International Criminal Law* (Routledge, 2011), p. 338.
10 Amnesty International and Human Rights Watch are of particular importance in this regard. *See* Amnesty International, *Universal Jurisdiction: The Duty of States to Enact and*

At the same time, the promotion of universal jurisdiction required a theoretical innovation, especially in the period of its genesis, because this basis of jurisdiction apparently lacks the jurisdictional links (territoriality, nationality, or States' own interests) that traditional jurisdictional principles have. Regarding this, its proponents tend to rely on the *jus cogens* nature of the crimes and the community interest embodied therein, from which every State's entitlement to exercise universal jurisdiction is deduced.[11] This is reflected in the oft-cited statements of the *Furundžija* case at the International Criminal Tribunal for the former Yugoslavia, in which the Trial Chamber, after observing that the prohibition of torture is a norm of *jus cogens* that enjoys "a higher rank in the international hierarchy,"[12] provides:

> Furthermore, at the individual level, that is, that of criminal liability it would seem that one of the consequences of the *jus cogens* character bestowed by the international community upon the prohibition of torture is that every State is entitled to investigate, prosecute and punish or extradite individuals accused of torture who are present in a territory under its jurisdiction. Indeed, it would be inconsistent on the one hand to prohibit torture to such an extent as to restrict the normally unfettered treaty-making power of sovereign States and on the other hand bar States from prosecuting and punishing those torturers who have engaged in this odious practice abroad.[13]

However, it is not very clear from this statement how the function of *jus cogens* to restrict "the treaty-making power of sovereign States," in which an addressee of the norm is a State, may also serve to authorize the other States' exercise of criminal jurisdiction over a crime committed by an individual in which the individual is regarded as having acted in violation of the norm. To put it another

---

Implement Legislation (2001); *Ending Impunity: Developing and Implementing a Global Action Plan using Universal Jurisdiction* (2009); *Universal Jurisdiction: Strengthening This Essential Tool of International Justice* (2012). Human Rights Watch, *Universal Jurisdiction in Europe: The State of the Art* (2006).

11 M. Cherif Bassiouni, "Universal Jurisdiction for International Crimes: Historical Perspective and Contemporary Practice," *Virginia Journal of International Law*, Vol. 42 (2001), p. 107; Alexander Orakhelashvili, *Peremptory Norms in International Law* (OUP, 2006), p. 288; Adeno Addis, "Imagining the International Community: The Constitutive Dimension of Universal Jurisdiction," *Human Rights Quarterly*, Vol. 31 (2009), pp. 142–144.

12 *Prosecutor v. Furundžija*, Judgment, IT-95-17/1-T, ICTY, Trial Chamber, 10 December 1998, para. 153.

13 *Ibid.*, para. 156.

way, there are two distinct questions relevant here: whether—and how—an individual can be an addressee of *jus cogens* norms, and, if so, whether this will entail that every State is entitled to punishment.

As to the first question, it may be answered in the affirmative, because it has been established that since WWII, individuals can be held liable in the international sphere by committing certain crimes, even if they acted on behalf of the organs of the State they belong to,[14] and because these crimes have been declared a violation of *jus cogens* norms on a number of occasions.[15]

In contrast, the second question seems problematic: while this can be seen as a reflection of constitutionalist ideas of jurisdiction, that is, to resemble the *jus cogens* norms to "a constitution that define the competence of all public actors,"[16] it is suggested that the breach of *jus cogens* does not necessarily entail corresponding procedures to attach a particular effect to that breach.[17]

In this regard, the *Eichmann* case has been heavily relied on as an authoritative precedent to support that the ground of universal jurisdiction is inferred from the peremptory nature of the prohibitions, although it was the interest of the international community on which the notion of *jus cogens* has been built, and not the *jus cogens* norms as such, that the Supreme Court of Israel invoked. In *Eichmann*, the Supreme Court observed, by using an analogy of piracy and war crimes, that it had been established as a principle of international law that an individual who committed crimes that "damage vital international interest," "impair the foundations and security of the international community," or "violate the universal moral values and humanitarian principles," must account for his or her own conduct.[18] It was thus confirmed that an individual could be held accountable on the international plane. The court then submitted that

---

14   Pierre-Marie Dupuy, "International Criminal Responsibility of the Individual and International Responsibility of the State," in Antonio Cassese, Paola Gaeta, and John R.W.D. Jones eds., *The Rome Statute of the International Criminal Court: A Commentary*, Vol. II (OUP, 2002), p. 1086.
15   *Affaire des activités armées sur le territoire du Congo (nouvelle requête: 2002) (République Démocratique du Congo c. Rwanda)*, arrêt du 3 février 2006, *C.I.J. Recueil 2006*, pp. 31–32, para. 64; *Al-Adsani v. The United Kingdom*, App. no.35763/97, European Court of Human Rights, Judgment, 21 November 2001, para. 61; *Prosecutor v. Kupreškić et al.*, Judgment, IT-95-16, ICTY, Trial Chamber II, 14 January 2000, para. 520.
16   Jean d'Aspremont, "Multilateral versus Unilateral Exercises of Universal Criminal Jurisdiction," *Israel Law Review*, Vol. 43 (2010), p. 310.
17   James Crawford, "Multilateral Rights and Obligations in International Law," *Recueil des Cours*, Tom. 319 (2006), p. 456.
18   The *Eichmann* case, Judgment of the Supreme Court of Israel, 29 May 1962, *International Law Reports*, Vol. 36, pp. 291–293.

the harmful and murderous effects of these crimes were "so embracing and widespread as to shake the international community to its very foundation" and that every State, including Israel, that had not existed at the time of the commission of the crimes was entitled to try the offender. In this case, the State trying the offender was regarded as acting "in the capacity of a guardian of international law and an agent for its enforcement."[19] The entitlement of Israel to act on this basis was later confirmed by the U.S. Court of Appeals for the Sixth Circuit in the *Demjanjuk* case. According to the court, in the case of exercising universal jurisdiction, "neither the nationality of the accused or the victim(s), nor the location of the crime is significant. The underlying assumption is that the crimes are offences against the law of nations or against humanity and the prosecuting nation is acting for all nations."[20]

It should be pointed out here that the Supreme Court of Israel in *Eichmann* admitted that there was no procedure of criminalization and allocation of powers as such in the decentralized system of international law.[21] Rather, it was the very lack of this procedure that was alleged to authorize the States to exercise their jurisdiction on behalf of the international community. Thus, the notion of community interest in the *Eichmann* case, in itself, may not be equated to the rules of distributing jurisdiction. In addition, Israel was a Jewish State that could be considered as the most convenient, as well as the most legitimate, place to conduct the trial, either because the great majority of the witnesses and the greater part of the evidence were concentrated there[22] or because it could be regarded as a State of victims that would have a legitimate interest in prosecution under the passive personality principle.[23]

---

19   *Ibid.*, p. 304.
20   Demjanjuk v. Petrovsky, 776 F. 2d 571 (USCA 6th Circuit 1985); cert. den. 475 US 1016 (1986), 628 F. Supp. 1370; 784 F. 2d 1254 (1986).
21   The court provides: "It is true that international law does not prescribe explicit and scaled criminal sanctions; that there still does not exist either an International Criminal Court or even international penal machinery." The Eichmann case, *supra* note 18, pp. 291–292. For the lack of criminalizing powers in the international society, *see* Robert Cryer, "The Doctrinal Foundations of International Criminalization," in M. Cherif Bassiouni ed., *International Criminal Law, Vol. 1: Sources, Subjects, and Contents* (3rd ed., Brill, 2008), p. 118.
22   The *Eichmann* case, *supra* note 18, p. 302.
23   M. Cherif Bassiouni, "The History of Universal Jurisdiction and Its Place in International Law," in Stephen Macedo ed., *Universal Jurisdiction* (University of Pennsylvania Press, 2004), p. 52. But *see* Diane F. Orentlicher, "Universal Jurisdiction: A Pragmatic Strategy in Pursuit of a Moralist's Vision," in Leila Nadya Sadat and Michael P. Scharf eds., *The Theory and Practice of International Criminal Law: Essays in Honor of M. Cherif Bassiouni* (Martinus Nijhoff, 2008), p. 137.

While the significance of the *Eichmann* case as a precedent is thus rather limited, the substance of its jurisprudence—that is, the community interest having an impact of *transcending* sovereignty, making the scope of jurisdiction of one State reach an individual who is otherwise subject only to the territorial jurisdiction or the jurisdiction of his or her own State—has been followed by the "case law," gradually generated in the 1990s. Indeed, it was this case law that would actually become the driving force of the promotion of universal jurisdiction.

The first and foremost follower was Belgium, where the most advanced basis of universal jurisdiction had once been established under the Act of 1993/1999,[24] and the Court of First Instance of Brussels took advantage of this transcending effect in *Re Pinochet*. In this case, the court was faced with the question of whether it had jurisdiction to try a crime against humanity that had not been explicitly included in its domestic law at that time. In order to deal with this deficiency, it first distinguished *jus cogens* crimes, which had an unspeakable and unacceptable nature, from "any others;" the former is subject to the exercise of universal jurisdiction, even in the absence of any treaty requirement, because "all States in the world can be considered as having a legal interest in ensuring that such crimes are punished;" in contrast, the latter "[does] not transcend national boundaries and [its] punishment is to be left to the discretion of each State."[25] The jurisdiction of the Belgian courts was confirmed based on the findings that the crime against humanity belongs to the former.

Interestingly enough, the transcending effect of *jus cogens* has also been invoked by the international criminal tribunals. For example, in the *Prosecutor v. Tadić*, the Appeal's Chamber of the ICTY was faced with the plea of sovereign equality raised by the appellant, who alleged that no State could assume jurisdiction to prosecute crimes committed on the territory of another State

---

24   Loi du 16 Juin 1993 relative à la répression des infractions graves aux conventions internationals de Genève du 12 août 1949 et aux protocols I et II du 8 juin 1988, additionales à ces conventions, Moniteur belge, 5 août 1993, p. 17751; Loi du 10 février 1999 relative à la répression des violations graves du droit international humanitaire, Moniteur belge, 23 mars 1999, p. 9286. Having been "the most progressive of its kind," the Act of 1993/1999 not only established universal jurisdiction over the listed crimes, not all of which were subjected to the principle of *aut dedere aut judicare* provided in the relevant treaties. It also contained several rules derogating from the general principles of criminal law, such as the inapplicability of any statute of limitations or amnesties and the rejection of immunity attached to an official capacity of a person.

25   *Re Pinochet*, Court of First Instance of Brussels, 6 November 1998, *International Law Reports*, Vol. 119, p. 356.

without any justification by a treaty or customary international law.²⁶ Based on this proposition, the appellant argued that the same requirement applied to the exercise of jurisdiction of an international tribunal, in light of which the principle of State sovereignty would have been violated in that case. The Appeal's Chamber rejected this plea, relying on the nature of the crime, with explicit reference to the jurisprudence of the *Eichmann* case. According to the Appeal's Chamber, the primacy of the international tribunal over a domestic court can be confirmed with regard to the crime, which was "universal in nature, well recognized in international law as serious breaches of international humanitarian law, and *transcending* the interest of any one State [emphasis added]."²⁷

Similarly, the Special Court for Sierra Leone was faced with the challenge to its jurisdiction in the *Prosecutor v. Kallon & Kamara*, in light of the amnesty granted in the Lomé agreement. In rejecting this allegation, the Court, while admitting that "the grant of amnesty or pardon is undoubtedly an exercise of sovereign power,"²⁸ submitted that the grant of amnesty would not amount to depriving another State of its jurisdiction where it is universal. Whether or not the crimes are crimes susceptible to universal jurisdiction depends on the nature of the crimes. Thus, "[o]ne consequence of the nature of grave international crimes against humanity is that States can, under international law, exercise universal jurisdiction over such crimes."²⁹

To sum up, the transcending effect of community interest, though its origin is somewhat blurred, seemed to succeed in obtaining a status of "principle" with regard to universal jurisdiction. It served to promote the assertion of universal jurisdiction by having been repeatedly referred to in the judgments of international and domestic courts. Indeed, these "case laws" are regarded to establish a customary rule,³⁰ or at least to be highly influential in "interpreting and clarifying international criminal law."³¹ In fact, when Lord Brown-Wilkinson

---

26   *Prosecutor v. Tadić*, Decision on the Defence Motion for Interlocutory Appeal on Jurisdiction, IT-94-1-AR 74, ICTY, Appeals Chamber, 2 October 1995, para. 55.
27   *Ibid.*, para. 59.
28   *Prosecutor v. Kallon and Prosecutor v. Kamara*, Decision on Challenge to Jurisdiction, SCSL-2004-15-AR 72 (E) and SCSL-2004-16-AR 72 (E), Special Court for Sierra Leone, Appeals Chamber, 13 March 2004, para. 67.
29   *Ibid.*, para. 70.
30   Andreas Zimmermann, "The Exercise of Universal Jurisdiction in Criminal Matters," in Christian Tomuschat and Jean-Marc Thouvenin eds., *The Fundamental Rules of International Legal Order* (Martinus Nijhof, 2006), p. 339.
31   R. Cryer, *supra* note 21, p. 119.

stated in *Pinochet (No. 3)* in the House of Lords that "[t]he *jus cogens* nature of the international crime of torture justifies States in taking universal jurisdiction over torture wherever committed,"[32] he did not seem to feel obliged to make detailed arguments, but merely referred to *Furundzija* and *Demjanjuk*.

2   Resistance from Sovereignty

The assertion of universal jurisdiction thus promoted, however, has raised strenuous protests from the State where the crime took place (territorial State) or the national States of the perpetrator (national State). They tend to allege that the exercise of universal jurisdiction in the absence of treaty or customary rule would violate "the principles of legal equality among states and of the nonintervention in the domestic affairs of other countries."[33] For these States, the incident that took place in their territory or was caused by their nationals should be deferred to their treatment, and their consent should be given, at least *in abstracto*, when other States assert their jurisdiction over it.[34] In practice, these States have exerted their influence, both directly and indirectly, or formally and informally, in order to challenge the exercise of universal jurisdiction, which has often led to the "fall"[35] or "death"[36] of the assertion of universal jurisdiction. It is the way in which this "resistance" from sovereignty has been taken that this section focuses on.

(1)   Direct Way of Resistance

The most direct and formal way of raising an objection is to bring a lawsuit against the State exercising jurisdiction. For instance, the Democratic Republic of the Congo initiated legal proceedings against Belgium before the International Court of Justice, alleging that the issuance of an arrest warrant for its incumbent minister constituted "violation of the principle that a State may not exercise its authority on the territory of another State and of the principle of sovereign equality," along with "violation of the diplomatic immunity of the

---

32   R. v. Bow Street Metropolitan Stipendiary Magistrate, Ex parte Pinochet Ugarte (No. 3) [1999], 2 All E.R. 97 [1999], 2 W.L.R. 827 (H.L.).

33   Joint declaration of the Mercosur countries (Brazil, Argentina, Paraguay, Uruguay) and Bolivia and Chili, Rio de Janeiro, 9 December 1998 (condemning the Spanish and British actions with regard to Pinochet), reproduced in Luc Reydams, *Universal Jurisdiction* (OUP, 2003), p. 72.

34   For the modalities of the way in which a consent is given, J. d'Asprement, *supra* note 16, p. 325.

35   L. Reydams, *supra* note 9, p. 337.

36   Steven R. Ratner, "Belgium's War Crimes Statute: A Postmortem," *American Journal of International Law*, Vol. 97 (2003), p. 888.

Minister for Foreign Affairs of a sovereign State."[37] Based on this allegation, it requested the Court to declare that Belgium would annul the arrest warrant. Likewise, the Republic of Congo sought to introduce proceedings before the International Court of Justice against France in the case of *Certain Criminal Proceedings in France*, seeking the annulment of the investigation and prosecution measures taken by French judicial authorities. It alleged that unilateral attribution of universal jurisdiction in criminal matters and arrogating to itself the power to prosecute and try the Minister of the Interior of a foreign state constituted a violation of the principle of sovereign equality.[38]

It should be noted that in the above cases, the issues concerning the illegality of the exercise of universal jurisdiction and the legal consequences thereof have not been fully addressed by the Court. In the *Arrest Warrant* case, the Democratic Republic of Congo dropped the allegation regarding universal jurisdiction at a later stage of the proceedings and invoked only the violation of the immunities of the Minister for Foreign Affairs, which allowed the court to focus only on the legality of the issuance and circulation of the arrest warrant in light of the principle of immunity.[39] In the case of *Certain Criminal Proceedings in France*, the Republic of Congo later withdrew its application, which resulted in the removal of the case from the list of the Court.[40] Nevertheless, the initiation of legal proceedings by a State itself sends a strong message to the other party that the exercise of jurisdiction is a source of dispute and may deteriorate relations between them. This may serve to induce the other party—especially its executive branch—to reconsider its way of exercising jurisdiction. It may be recalled that in the *Certain Criminal Proceeding in France*, the agent and the counsel of France stated during the oral proceedings at the stage of provisional measures that France in no way denied that President Nguesso enjoyed immunities from jurisdiction, both civil and criminal, and the Court took them as grounds to decide there was no

---

37 Requête introductive d'instance, enregistrée au Greffe de la Cour le 17 octobre 2000, mandat d'arrêt du 11 avril 2000 (République Démocratique du Congo c. Belgique).

38 Requête introductive d'instance, enregistrée au Greffe de la Cour le 9 décembre 2002, certaines procédures pénales en engagées en France (République du Congo c. France).

39 *Mandat d'arrêt du 11 avril 2000 (République démocratique du Congo c. Belgique)*, arrêt du 14 fevrier 2002, *C.I.J. recueil 2002*, p. 19, paras. 45–46. The court found that the issue of the arrest warrant and its international circulation constituted violations of the immunity from criminal jurisdiction and the inviolability which the incumbent foreign minister could enjoy, and thus the arrest warrant must be cancelled by means of which Belgium would choose. *Ibid.*, p. 32, para. 76.

40 ICJ Press Release 2010/36.

risk of irreparable prejudice.⁴¹ Although it was made as a statement of law and not as a commitment,⁴² it seems crucial that those statements were made *before* the French domestic court actually decided the case, and that the International Court of Justice gave them some weight in making its findings.

There is also a way of expressing objection by exerting political or diplomatic pressure, which is a less formal but often more effective way of resistance. For instance, Israel withdrew its ambassador to Belgium in protest of the decision of the Court of Cassation of Belgium in which the court allowed the investigation against Amos Yaron to proceed.⁴³ Similarly, Rwanda cut its diplomatic ties with France in protest against French judicial authorities' issuance of international arrest warrants to three Rwandan officials and also their sending of request to the United Nations Secretary-General for President Paul Kagame of Rwanda to stand trial at the International Criminal Tribunal for Rwanda.⁴⁴

One of the most successful examples of exerting pressure was the U.S. reaction to Belgium in protest of the several criminal complaints filed against U.S. officials under the law of 1993/1999. In response to the complaints filed in March 2003 against former U.S. President George H.W. Bush and several of his advisers for allegedly committing war crimes during the 1991 Gulf war, Secretary of State Colin Powell warned that Belgium risked losing its status as the host State of the North Atlantic Treaty Organization (NATO) by allowing investigations of those who might travel to Belgium.⁴⁵ Belgium reacted immediately by amending the law (effective May 7, 2003)⁴⁶ to the effect that the decision to initiate proceedings was deferred to federal prosecutors if the violation had

---

41   *Certaines procédures pénales en engagées en France (République du Congo c. France)*, ordonnance du 17 Juin 2003, *C.I.J. recueil 2003*, pp. 109–110, paras. 33–35.
42   If a statement made by an agent of a state party during the proceedings is a commitment, it will bind the state as a legal obligation to act in conformity with the commitment. *See* e.g., *Barbados/Trinidad Tobago*, Arbitral Award of 11 April 2006, *International Legal Materials*, Vol. 45 (2006), p. 848, para. 291.
43   *H.S.A. et al. v. S.A. et al.*, Court of Cassation, 12 February 2003. English translation and original French version are reproduced in *International Legal Materials*, Vol. 42 (2003), pp. 596–605. Yaron was alleged to have been involved in the 1982 massacre of Palestinian refugees when he was the general in charge of the Beirut sector.
44   BBC News, "Rwanda Cuts Relations with France," at http://news.bbc.co.uk/2/hi/6179436.stm (as of September 24, 2014).
45   Sean D. Murphy, "Contemporary Practice of the United States Relating to International Law," *American Journal of International Law*, Vol. 97 (2003), p. 985.
46   Loi modifiant la loi du 16 jin 1993 relative à la répresttion des violations graves du droit international humanitaire et l'article 144*ter* du Code judiciaire, *Moniteur Belge*, 7 mai 2003, p. 24846.

no link with Belgium.[47] Moreover, the prosecutor may refuse to proceed if the matter should be brought either before international tribunals or before a tribunal of States that have links with the offense, as long as this tribunal is competent, independent, impartial, and fair. However, this amendment did not prevent another complaint from being filed against U.S. General Tommy Franks for alleged war crimes during the invasion of Iraq in March 2003. On June 12, 2003, Secretary of Defense Donald Rumsfeld announced that the United States would oppose any further spending for construction of a new NATO headquarters unless Belgium repealed its law, stating that "Belgium appears not to respect the sovereignty of other countries."[48] Belgium again reacted through parliamentary legislation, this time by renouncing the basis of universal jurisdiction.[49]

(2) Indirect Way of Resistance

In many cases, with regard to the exercise of jurisdiction over an extraterritorial event, the cooperation of territorial or national States is crucial, especially in terms of collecting evidence or obtaining custody of the accused.[50] This being the case, the refusal of cooperation by these States can effectively block the exercise of jurisdiction. It seems useful to distinguish two cases in light of the place where an alleged perpetrator is found.

If the alleged perpetrator stays in the territory of his or her own national State, the refusal of these States to extradite the individual gives a crucial blow to the exercise of universal jurisdiction, because trial *in absentia* is not allowed

---

47   S. Ratner, *supra* note 36, p. 891.
48   News Transcript: Secretary of Defense Rumsfeld at NATO Headquarters, quated by Ratner, *ibid.*, p. 891.
49   Loi modifiant law loi du 16 juin 1993 relative à la repression des violations graves du droit international humanitaire et l'article 144ter du Code judiciaire, 23 avril 2003, *Moniteur Belge*, 7 août 2003, p. 40506. As for the substantive aspect, the loi 5 Août 2003 limits the scope of the jurisdiction of Belgian courts to the case that the perpetrator is a Belgian national, or the person has a principal residence in Belgium, or the victim is a Belgian national or a person who has resided in Belgium for at least three years. In addition, the new amendment recognizes immunity on the basis of international law or binding treaty law and for persons staying in Belgium on the invitation either of Belgian authorities or of an international organization established in Belgium and with which Belgium has concluded a headquarter agreement (Article 13). As for the procedural aspect, the new amendment stipulates that the prosecution may only be undertaken at the request of the federal prosecutor (procureur fédéral), which means that the mechanism of constitution de partie civile will not be applied. Moreover, this decision of the federal prosecutor may not be appealed.
50   Robert Cryer *et al.*, *An Introduction to International Criminal Law and Procedure* (2nd ed., Cambridge University Press, 2010), p. 85.

in most of the countries.[51] This is usually the most expected reaction, even if there is an extradition treaty between the relevant parties. For instance, in the Guatemala Genocide case, the Guatemalan Constitutional Court faced the request of extradition from Spain that was grounded on the assertion of universal jurisdiction over the alleged massacre of indigenous people committed by Guatemalan officials during its civil war. The court interpreted whether that request fell within the realm of "competent authority" provided in the extradition treaty between them. According to the court, the assertion of this sort of jurisdiction inevitably involves a unilateral assessment of the judicial capacity of another State—that is, an assessment of the unwillingness or inability to investigate and prosecute, which cannot be accepted because it constitutes a violation of other States' sovereignty.[52] As a consequence, the Spanish request was rejected.

On the other hand, even if the State exercising universal jurisdiction succeeds in obtaining custody of the perpetrator, the refusal of cooperation from territorial or national States would still hamper the following proceedings, especially in terms of evidence and witnesses who are, in most cases, located in territorial States. For instance, although France succeeded in obtaining custody of Rose Kabuye on November 9, 2008, one of the nine Rwandan officials accused by a French judge in connection with the fatal April 1994 attack on President Juvenal Habyarimana's plane, she was released in April 2009, due to the fact that no proof had been found to determine her guilt.[53] It is not hard to imagine that French authorities could not receive any judicial cooperation from Rwanda to bring forward evidence against her because of the break of diplomatic ties caused by the issuance of the arrest warrant. Ironically, the French inquiry team was allowed to visit the scene of the attack after the two countries recovered their diplomatic relations, and they eventually concluded that it was not Mr. Kagame and his allies, but Hutu extremists that killed Mr. Habyarimana.[54]

---

51   Damien Vandermeersch, "La compétence universelle," dans Antonio Cassese et Mireille Delmas-Marty (dir.), *Juridictions nationales et crimes internationaux* (PUF, 2002), p. 606.

52   Constitutional Court (Corte de Constitucionalidad), Decision on Jurisdiction of Spanish Courts, 10 December 2007 (Original Spanish text file with author). *See also*, Naomi Roht-Arriaza, "Making the State Do Justice: Transnational Prosecutions and International Support for Criminal Investigations in Post-Armed Conflict Guatemala," *Chicago Journal of International Law*, Vol. 9 (2008), p. 79.

53   BBC News, "France Releases Rwandan Official", at http://news.bbc.co.uk/2/hi/7797024.stm (as of September 24, 2014).

54   BBC News, "Rwanda Genocide: Kagame 'Cleared of Habyarimana Crash'," at http://www.bbc.co.uk/news/world-africa-16472013 (as of September 24, 2014).

II   Interaction between Community Interest and Sovereignty

1   *Emergence of Dialogue*

As has been shown in the previous chapter, the assertion of universal jurisdiction underpinned by community interest has been met by strenuous "resistance" from sovereignty. It is ironic that the measures that are allegedly taken in order to protect community interest give rise to tensions between members of that very community.

However, it can be argued that there has already been an embryo of dialogue in the dialectic; confrontation may serve to make States realize the existence of other parties as obstacles to their claims and also to bring into relief the difference between parties, which may provide a ground for entering into a dialogue to reconcile the conflicting claims.

On the one hand, while the promotion of universal jurisdiction has indeed contributed to the establishment of individuals being held responsible for the breach of *jus cogens* norms, it has not succeeded in creating a new obligation on the States where alleged perpetrators or evidences are found to cooperate with the States exercising universal jurisdiction. In fact, each State monopolizes the physical power within its borders, and without their cooperation, the assertion of universal jurisdiction would lack its effectiveness. On the other hand, while territorial States may still refuse to cooperate, they may no longer deny that the third States have interest in the serious violations of human rights that occur in their territory when those violations give rise to the breach of *jus cogens* norms. In fact, many of the former opponent States have made a public recognition that the basis of universal jurisdiction in relation to these crimes is validly established while still expressing their concerns about its abusive use.[55]

Given the above, the so-called subsidiarity principle has increasingly gained support as a guiding principle for the exercise of universal jurisdiction, not only in the literature[56] but also in the international instruments[57] and in the

---

55   See e.g., UN Doc. A/63/PV.105 (Tanzania, on behalf of the African States), 18 September 2009, p. 9.

56   Antonio Cassese, "Is the Bell Tolling for Universality? A Plea for a Sensible Notion of Universal Jurisdiction," *Journal of International Criminal Justice*, Vol. 1 (2003), p. 593; Claus Kreß, "Universal Jurisdiction over International Crimes and the *Institute de Droit International*," *Journal of International Criminal Justice*, Vol. 4 (2006), p. 579; Fannie Lafontaine, "Universal Jurisdiction—The Realistic Utopia," *Journal of International Criminal Justice*, Vol. 10 (2012), pp. 1286–1291.

57   Institut de droit international, Resolution on Universal criminal jurisdiction with regard to the crime of genocide, crimes against humanity and war crimes (2005), at http://www.idi-iil.org/idiE/resolutionsE/2005_kra_03_en.pdf (as of September 24, 2014); AU-EU

statement of governments.[58] Premised on the idea that the entity closer to the stakeholders should be secured its own freedom of action based on its own free will and judgment, while other entities may intervene in order to support the former when there is a limitation to the former's ability,[59] the principle of subsidiarity as applied to the exercise of universal jurisdiction provides that, given the priority accorded to the territorial jurisdiction, universal jurisdiction may only be exercised when the territorial State is unwilling or unable to institute criminal proceedings.[60]

Nevertheless, there is some difficulty in applying the principle of subsidiarity in the actual context. In fact, the application of this principle is conditioned on the unwillingness and inability of the territorial States, which inevitably involves an assessment of the administration of criminal justice of the territorial State, and it would be regarded by the latter as an intrusion on its sovereignty.[61] Thus, while the territorial States would no longer be opposed to the assertion of universal jurisdiction, they would still condemn its actual exercise as abusive, alleging that it is incompatible with the principle of sovereign equality or that of nonintervention. This seems to give rise to another resistance from sovereignty. Is there any means to reconcile this apparent conflict between the interest of prosecution on the part of States asserting universal jurisdiction and that of self-determination on the part of territorial States?

    Expert Report, *supra* note 7; African Union Model National Law on Universal Jurisdiction over International Crimes (2012), EXP/MIN/Leal/VI.

58   Those statements are made in the discussion in the Sixth Committee. *See* NZ (on behalf of the Canada, Australia, and NZ [CANZ]), UN Doc. A/C.6/67/SR.12, para. 15 (2012); Chile, UN Doc. A/C.6/67/SR.12, para. 36 (2012); Norway, UN Doc. A/C.6/67/SR.12, para. 61 (2012); Argentina, UN Doc. A/C.6/67/SR.12, para. 65 (2012); South Africa, UN Doc. A/C.6/67/SR.13, para. 3 (2012); Sri Lanka, UN Doc. A/C.6/67/SR.13, para. 20 (2012); Brazil, UN Doc. A/C.6/67/SR.13, para. 33 (2012); Azerbaijan, UN Doc. A/C.6/67/SR.13, para. 40 (2012); Malaysia, UN Doc. A/C.6/67/SR.13, para. 43 (2012).

59   Paolo G. Carozza, "Subsidiarity as a Structural Principle of International Human Rights Law," *American Journal of International Law*, Vol. 97 (2003), p. 28; Isabel Feichtner, "Subsidiarity," *Max Planck Encyclopedia of Public International Law* (2012), at www.mpepil.com (as of September 24, 2014).

60   Article 3(c) of the Resolution of the Institut de droit international; Recommendation 10 of the AU-EU Expert Report; Article 4 (2) of the African Union Model National Law on Universal Jurisdiction over International Crimes.

61   Stephen D. Krasner, *Sovereignty: Organized Hypocrisy* (Princeton University Press, 1999), p. 20. *See also* Brad R. Roth, *Sovereign Equality and Moral Disagreement* (OUP, 2011), pp. 58–59.

2   *The Obligation to Prosecute as a Mediator for Dialogue*

In considering the question of conflict of relevant interests, it seems, as a first step, useful to address the *Ould Dah* case in the European Court of Human Rights.[62] In this case, a Mauritanian applicant complained that his conviction for torture in application of French law was in breach of the principle of legality under Article 7 of the European Convention of Human Rights, as the 1993 Act of Mauritania amnestied any acts of armed groups from 1989 to 1992, and its validity should not be denied by the application of French law. Thus, the court was faced with the question of the validity of amnesty law of the territorial State vis-à-vis the State exercising universal jurisdiction.

It is important to note here that the Court could not invoke the European Convention or the Convention against Torture vis-à-vis Mauritania, in order to justify the exercise of universal jurisdiction initiated in 1999 by French authorities, as Mauritania was not party to the European Convention nor had been to the Convention against Torture before 2004. Nevertheless, the Court proceeded into the question of the relation between amnesty laws and the assertion of universal jurisdiction. First, it noted that the prohibitions of torture have been established as *jus cogens* norms and observed that amnesty laws are generally incompatible with the duty to investigate acts such as torture. It then continued:

> It is certain that, in general, one could not exclude the possibility of a conflict between, on the one hand, the necessity to prosecute the crimes committed, and, on the other hand, the need to reconcile the social structure of the country. In any case, no process of reconciliation of this kind was put in place in Mauritania. However, as the court has already pointed out, the prohibition of torture holds a core place in all international instruments relevant to the protection of human rights and is one of the core values of democratic societies. One could not therefore question the obligation to prosecute such actions by allowing impunity to the perpetrator through adoption of an amnesty law, susceptible of being abusive with regard to international law.

And it further noted:

> ...[international law] does not exclude the conviction of a person granted amnesty in his state of origin prior to being tried by another state, which derives for example from Article 17 of the Statute of the International

---

62   *Ould Dah c. France*, requête no.13113/03, CEDI, décision sur la recevalibité, 14 mar 2009.

Criminal Court, whose list that enumerates inadmissible cases does not include this type of situation.

Thus, the court relied on the obligation to prosecute as a key concept to coordinate the conflict between the interest of States exercising universal jurisdiction and that of territorial States. It should, however, be noted that the court merely examined whether the application of French law was in breach of the principle of legality under Article 7 of the Convention, and the status of the obligation to prosecute in this context was not entirely clear. Moreover, further consideration is needed as to how the exercise of universal jurisdiction is related to that obligation.

As for the status of the obligation to prosecute, there has been a consensus that under current or emerging customary international law, there is a duty to bring to justice perpetrators of flagrant violations of human rights, such as genocide, crimes against humanity, and war crimes, "at least with respect to crimes committed on the State's territory or by its nationals."[63] Admittedly, there has been an argument that measures short of prosecution—such as establishment of an investigative commission that specifically identifies perpetrators and victims, noncriminal sanctions against responsible officials and military personnel, and judicial redress for victims—would be adequate to discharge the duty to ensure human rights.[64] However, as international practice and jurisprudence have matured, they have gradually generated that States owe a duty to ensure *judicial remedy*—and measures short of prosecution are not sufficient for this purpose—for the violation of non-derogable rights recognized by international human rights.[65]

The enactment of amnesty law has been regarded as being incompatible with that obligation, mainly due to the fact that it sweepingly denies the possibility of criminal proceedings, which leads to impunity for those responsible for grave violations of human rights, thereby eroding the basis for the rule of

---

63   Darryl Robbinson, "Serving the Interests of Justice: Amnesties, Truth Commission and the International Criminal Court," *European Journal of International Law*, Vol. 14 (2003), p. 491. See also Diane F. Orentlicher, "Setting Accounts: The Duty to Prosecute Human Rights Violations of a Prior Regime," *Yale Law Journal*, Vol. 100 (1990–1991), pp. 2551–2594.
64   Michael P. Scharf, "The Letter of the Law: The Scope of the International Legal Obligation to Prosecute Human Rights Crimes," *Law and Contemporary Problems*, Vol. 59, No.4 (1996), p. 61.
65   *Barrios Altos (Chumbipuma Aguirre et al. v. Peru)*, 2001 IACtHR (ser. C) No. 75, 14 March 2001, para. 41; *Almonacid Arellano et al. v. Chile*, 2007 IACtHR (ser. C) No. 154, 26 September 2006, para. 99.

law.⁶⁶ Thus, it could be argued that, as far as the nonaction of a territorial State constitutes the nonperformance of the obligation to prosecute, it may not be justified as the exercise of discretion in administrating criminal justice. In this case, territorial States would no longer be able to oppose to the exercise of universal jurisdiction, by recourse to their priority.

If the conditions of the exercise of universal jurisdiction is structured like this, it gives rise to the second question as to how it works in the actual confrontation between States. In this regard, there are commentators who designate the exercise of universal jurisdiction as a means of reparation or remedy for the violation of the obligation to prosecute. For instance, de Hoogh argues that "the punishment of culprits by the author State is necessary to have it perform its obligation" and that because of the fundamental importance of the obligations concerned, this gives rise to a rule endowing each and every State with universal jurisdiction.⁶⁷ Van der Wilt reformulates de Hoogh's argument, suggesting that the exercise of universal jurisdiction is "a correlative right of the international community" for the failure of those States that assume a responsibility to bring perpetrators of international crimes to justice.⁶⁸ He concludes:

> ...if the state most responsible for suppressing international crimes flouts its obligations, other states, as trustees of the international community, are at least allowed to redress the situation. In this way, the claim of universal jurisdiction gains legitimacy, because it is directly tagged to, and originates from, original sovereign rights that have been turned into obligations and contribute to a watertight system of international criminal law enforcement.⁶⁹

This argument appears plausible, but it is problematic as far as it may be understood as an invocation of the responsibility of territorial States generated from a breach of an international obligation. In fact, States do not have a right to unilaterally decide other States' legal status. As Gross observed, each State has a right to interpret the law, but this "autointerpretation" is "not a 'decision'

---

66   In fact, the necessity to fight against impunity has been emphasized in terms of maintaining the rule of law. Vienna Declaration and Programme of Action, UN Doc. A/CONF.157/23 (1993), para. 60.
67   André de Hoogh, *Obligation Erga Omnes and International Crimes* (Kluwer, 1996), p. 165.
68   Harmen van der Wilt, "Universal Jurisdiction under Attack," *Journal of International Criminal Law*, Vol. 9 (2011), p. 1050.
69   *Ibid.*, p. 1051.

and is neither final nor binding upon the other parties."⁷⁰ Thus, the question still remains as to if and how an exercise of universal jurisdiction that inevitably involves an assessment of the administration of criminal justice of other States can be located in the international legal system.

Regarding this, it seems useful as a first step to draw a comparison with the case law under human rights conventions on the consideration of possible human rights violations within a context of extradition.⁷¹ Indeed, in the field of extradition, there has been an established jurisprudence that it would be a violation of human rights for a State to surrender a fugitive under its custody to a State where he or she would be in danger of being subjected to human rights abuses.⁷² It is important to note that it is the liability of a sending State, and not a receiving State, that is at stake in this context, whereas, at the same time, the decision regarding it apparently involves an assessment of the administration of justice in the receiving State. Nevertheless, it has been regarded that "there is no question of adjudicating on or establishing the responsibility of the receiving country, whether under general international law, under the Convention or otherwise."⁷³ In fact, an assessment of this kind is an interpretation of the factual situation in order to determine the liability of the sending State and should not be seen as a binding decision on the receiving State or as an intervention on its internal affairs.

---

70   Leo Gross, "States as Organs of International Law and the Problem of Autointerpretation," *Selected Essays on International Law and Organization* (1993), p. 386. *See also* Georges Abi-Saab, "'Interpretation' et 'Auto-Interpretation': Quelques réflexions sur leur rôle dans la formation et la résolution du différend international," hrsg. von Ulrich Beyerlin *et al.*, *Recht zwischen Umbruch und Bewahrung: Völkerrecht, Europarecht, Staatsrecht: Festschrift für Rudolf Bernhardt* (1995), p. 9.

71   *See* Maja Munivrana Vajda, "The 2009 AIDP's Resolution on Universal Jurisdiction—An Epitaph or a Revival Call?" *International Criminal Law Review*, Vol. 10 (2010), p. 343.

72   *Soering v. the United Kingdom*, App. no. 14038/88, European Court of Human Rights, Judgment, 7 July 1989, para. 91. *See also Saadi v. Italy*, App. no. 37201/06, European Court of Human Rights, Judgment, 28 February 2008, para. 138; *Kaboulov v. Ukraine*, App. no. 41015/04, European Court of Human Rights, Judgment, 19 November 2009, para. 107. *See* in general, John Dugard and Christine Van den Wyngaert, "Reconciling extradition with human rights," *American Journal of International Law*, Vol. 92 (1998), p. 187; Harmen van der Wilt, "Après Soering: The Relationship between Extradition and Human Rights in the Legal Practice of Germany, the Netherland and the United States," *Netherlands International Law Review*, Vol. XLII (1995), p. 53.

73   *Al-Saadoon and Mfudhi v. the United Kingtom*, App. no. 61498/08, European Court of Human Rights, Judgment, 2 March 2010, para. 124. *See also Drozd and Janousek v France and Spain*, App. no. 12747/87, European Court of Human Rights, Judgment, 26 June 1992, para. 110.

This observation has a great implication on the matter of universal jurisdiction. It can be argued that an assessment of the administration of justice in the territorial State is an interpretation of the factual situation as far as the exercise of jurisdiction is concerned, and it does not determine the breach of the obligation on the part of the territorial State or invoke the latter's responsibility. It should be recalled that, in the *Ould Dah* case, the European Court was cautious not to assess directly the legality or validity of Mauritanian amnesty law. Rather, the Court suggested that the enactment of amnesty law was regarded as *abusive* in light of the obligation to prosecute and that it would not be able to exclude the assertion of universal jurisdiction. In fact, it is the liability of individuals that is to be directly incurred in the exercise of universal jurisdiction, and this liability is distinguished from that of the State on behalf of which those individuals acted. Thus, the territorial State would not be disadvantaged other than having to recognize the fact that it does not administer its own apparatus adequately to meet the obligation to prosecute.

Moreover, this assessment may lead to a dialogue between relevant parties due precisely to the fact that it does not involve a final decision and leaves some room for the territorial State to recover its primacy by showing its own ability and willingness to prosecute. The following example of interaction between Spanish and Argentine authorities seems to provide a good example of this.

In the *Cavallo* case, Argentine amnesty laws played a key role in establishing Spanish jurisdiction in the beginning and also in extinguishing it later. At an early stage, the Spanish Audiencia Nacional confirmed the "inaction" of the Argentine authority due to the existence of the Ley de Punto Final (Full Stop Law) and the Ley de Obediencia Debida (Due Obedience Law), which had been a major obstacle in Argentina to conducting criminal proceedings against offences committed during its "dirty war" period in the 1980s. Thus, with its basis of universal jurisdiction confirmed in light of the principle of subsidiarity, the Spanish authority then issued an arrest warrant, circulated it internationally, and eventually obtained an extradition of Cavallo in 2003 from Mexico, where he had been found. When the Spanish authority finished an investigation and reached the stage of deciding whether to initiate public prosecution in 2005, however, the Argentine Supreme Court declared those two amnesty laws to be null and void[74] in application of the established jurisprudence of the Inter-American Court of Human Rights, stating that enactment of amnesty

---

74   *Simón, Julio Héctor y otros s/privación ilegítima de la libertad, etc.*, Suprema Corte [Supreme Court], 14 June 2005. Original Spanish text is available at http://www.derechos.org/nizkor/arg/doc/nulidad.html (as of September 25, 2014).

laws would constitute a violation of the obligation to prosecute with regard to the serious violation of human rights.[75] In response, the Audiencia Nacional reviewed its proceedings and rendered a decision in 2006 in which it suggested that Argentine jurisdiction be preferred. According to the court:

> There is no doubt that Argentinean jurisdiction, under the leadership of the Public Prosecutor once the obstacle of the Ley de Punto Final and the Ley de Obediencia Debida had been removed, has been *acting effectively* in judging the acts that took place in the ESMA, thus responding [to] the expectation of the international community and, in particular, of their victims.[76] [emphasis added]

Despite the Spanish Supreme Court later repealing the above decision,[77] the Spanish government eventually decided on Cavallo's extradition to Argentina, which was implemented on March 31, 2008.

This series of events seems to show that the establishment and conceptualization of the obligation to prosecute allowed an objective assessment on whether or not the territorial States are responding to "the expectation of the international community," which would be the grounds for judicial dialogue between relevant parties. Indeed, one of the judges who constituted the majority opinion of the Argentinean Supreme Court observed that universal jurisdiction became operational when a State did not exercise its sovereign power, whereas he also maintained that the amnesty laws had been declared null and void now, and there would be no room for other States to step in.[78] This statement suggests that there was an ongoing judicial dialogue between

---

75 *Barrios Altos (Chumbipuma Aguirre et al. v. Peru)*, 2001 IACtHR (ser. C) No. 75, 14 March 2001, para. 41; *Almonacid Arellano et al. v. Chile*, 2007 IACtHR (ser. C) No. 154, 26 September 2006, para. 119. In fact, Article 75.22 of the Argentine Constitution of 1994 provides the primacy of international rules over domestic rules, in which the American Convention on Human Rights is listed as one of those international rules, and the domestic courts have actually applied the jurisprudence of the American Courts of Human Rights as an authoritative interpretation of the Convention.

76 Audiencia Nacional, Criminal Chamber, 20 December 2006. English Translation is reproduced in *Yearbook of International Humanitarian Law*, Vol. 9 (2006), pp. 556–557.

77 The Supreme Court of Spain, Decision, 18 July 2007. English translation is reproduced in *Yearbook of International Humanitarian Law*, Vol. 10 (2007), pp. 430–431.

78 *Simón, supra* note 74, Voro del senor Ministro Doctor Don E. Raul Zaffaroni, para.37. Some commentators, however, express concerns as to whether the annulment of amnesty laws would result in the actual exercise of jurisdiction.

the relevant parties as to if and how effective criminal proceedings can be conducted.

Concluding Remarks

As has been overviewed, the discourse surrounding universal jurisdiction has developed from a dialectic between sovereignty and community interest into a dialogue on the function of sovereignty to implement community interest. Focusing on how the opposing concepts are confronted makes it possible to bring out this panoptic overview, and we should admit how much we owe to Professor Ida's vision.

On the other hand, this article also tried to explore the normative ground that allowed for dialogue between parties. It can be argued that the obligation to prosecute has played a key role in the change of the function of sovereignty. Indeed, there is a consensus that the territorial States may no longer justify their inaction by invoking sovereignty, as far as this inaction is considered as nonperformance of the obligation to prosecute, and accordingly, the exercise of universal jurisdiction can be structured as a reaction to that nonperformance.

Be that as it may, this is not an end to this universal jurisdiction saga but merely brings about more and harder challenges. Indeed, there are a growing number of territorial or national States—former opponents of universal jurisdiction—that have started instituting criminal proceedings by themselves, yet some of the proceedings can be contested in terms of their fairness or impartiality. For instance, there are cases where the accused was acquitted of the alleged offence, but that decision appears to be made in order to shield the accused from other jurisdictions. These cases may fall within the scope of the "unwillingness" to prosecute that triggers the exercise of universal jurisdiction,[79] yet this would present another seed of confrontation; unlike the case of enactment of amnesty, the case of acquittal involves an assessment of the genuineness of the manner of conducting prosecution, and it can be taken as particularly intrusive on their sovereignty by those who are conducting proceedings.

---

79   In this regard, *see* Harmen van der Wilt & Sandra Lyngdorf, "Procedural Obligations under the European Convention on Human Rights: Useful Guidelines for the Assessment of 'Unwillingness' and 'Inability' in the Context of the Complementarity Principle," *International Criminal Law Review*, Vol. 9 (2009), p. 39ff.

However hard these challenges might be, though, we should not turn back to take a relatively easy path to support either side of the opposing claims. We should continue to open eyes on an ongoing dialectic between them and try to discern from this dynamism a normative implication, if any, which would provide a foundation for dialogue—that is, after all, what I have learned from a dialogue with Professor Ida and his works.

PART 2

Effectiveness: Formality of Law and Amorphous Reality

∴

CHAPTER 6

Running Many FTAs is Like Balancing between Many Bicycles: A Multidimensional Comparison of Institutional Provisions in Japan's FTAS

Tomohiko Kobayashi

> Life is like riding a bicycle. To keep your balance you must keep moving.
> ALBERT EINSTEIN

⁝

I   Introduction

Regional trade agreements (RTAs)[1] serve as the building blocks that facilitate world trade, especially under the framework of the World Trade Organization (WTO). Concluding RTAs such as free trade agreements (FTAS) and customs unions is therefore not by itself a goal. If the prevailing conditions permit, countries would rather create broader and deeper frameworks of regional integration that would ultimately replace or incorporate their existing RTAs. In this sense, all RTAs have a limited life-span to accomplish their purposes. Therefore, a country that has more than one RTA must keep them all running smoothly despite their diverse lifecycles and characteristics. The more RTAs a country seals, the more difficult it is to manage them simultaneously, in a manner coordinate with one another.

Since the 1990s, WTO members have strived to conclude RTAs, not only in quantity (their number now exceeds 200) but also in quality. In this regard, WTO members have shifted their political centre of gravity toward RTAs.[2] For

---

1   In this chapter, we include preferential trade agreements (PTAS) among developing countries in this category, as well as free trade agreements (FTAS) and customs unions.
2   Consultative Board to the former Director-General Supachai Panitchpakdi, *The Future of the WTO: Addressing Institutional Challenges in the New Millennium* (2004), available at http://www.wto.org/english/thewto_e/10anniv_e/future_wto_e.pdf (as of February 1, 2014), p. 19.

Japan, the priority of regional economic integration in the Asia-Pacific region has risen under the frameworks of APEC (Asia-Pacific Economic Cooperation) and the Trans-Pacific Partnership (TPP).[3] On the other hand, however, the co-existence of RTAs has been described as a "spaghetti bowl" that may cause more harm than good to the functioning of each agreement,[4] setting aside the impacts on global trade as a whole. Thus, in order for any RTA to function effectively, setting up organizational mechanisms to streamline its regular operations and adjust to subsequent changes in circumstances is essential. This need for an organization mechanism is especially the case for FTAs, compared with customs unions that create common tariff systems.

Along with econometric surveys of the trade creation/diversion effects of regional trade liberalization, international trade lawyers have paid attention to the way in which substantive RTA provisions affect tariff reductions and domestic regulations. Further, many compelling studies have focused on dispute settlement procedures, rules of origin, and improvements in the business environment.[5] However, few attempts have been made to examine the role and design of the *institutional* provisions that govern the regular and orderly functioning of RTAs. This chapter focuses on such institutional arrangements in RTAs to take initial steps toward clarifying how they should be designed in the future.

From an institutional perspective, every RTA firstly needs a proper implementation structure, not only a dispute settlement mechanism, in order to ensure its effective operation. Indeed, the more the number of RTAs a country concludes, the more the burden on the government as well as private parties. Secondly, every RTA needs proper rules to clarify its jurisdiction relative to other international agreements including WTO Agreements, treaties of commerce, tax conventions, and other RTAs. Again, the greater the number of RTAs a country concludes, the higher is the risk of jurisdictional conflicts.[6]

---

3   For APEC, *see* Ryuichi Ida, "Sustainable Development in the APEC," in Friedl Weiss, Erik Denters and Paul de Waart eds., *International Economic Law with a Human Face* (Kluwer Law International, 1998), pp. 347–355.

4   Jagdish Bhagwati, "U.S. Trade Policy: The Infatuation with Free Trade Agreements," in Jagdish Bhagwati and Anne O. Krueger eds., *The Dangerous Drift to Preferential Trade Agreements* (AEI Press, 1995), p. 3.

5   For dispute settlement procedures, *see* e.g., Ryuichi Ida, "Second Report of the Committee on Regional Economic Development Law," *International Law Association Report of the Conference*, Vol. 68 (1998), pp. 545–546.

6   Joint Expert Group for Feasibility Study on EAFTA, *Towards an East Asia FTA: Modality and Road Map* (2006), available at http://www.thaifta.com/thaifta/Portals/0/eafta_report.pdf (as of February 1, 2014), p. 33.

Lastly, every RTA needs a proper mechanism through which it can adjust to subsequent changes in circumstances, given that all RTAS are imperfect in nature, established by a limited number of WTO members to achieve further, broader multilateral trade liberalization.

In this context, institutional arrangements are crucial for the effective functioning of RTAS now and in the future.[7] However, comprehensive research on the role and design of institutional arrangements within RTAS is scarce,[8] except for those few studies that have focused on specific RTAS such as the North American Free Trade Agreement (NAFTA), the European Union (EU), and the Association of South East Asian Nations (ASEAN) FTA.[9] Admittedly, it is hard to generalize because institutional mechanisms of RTAS highly depend on specific relationship between contracting parties. Also, institutional arrangements raise few questions about their consistency with WTO Agreements,[10] which are silent about how institutional arrangements should be formulated in RTAS in order to meet the requirements set forth in Article XXIV of the GATT and Article V of the GATS. Moreover, dispute settlement mechanisms have thus far attracted a disproportionate amount of research attention as the principal tool for enforcing RTA obligations, despite that recourse to dispute settlement procedures under the RTAS is rare in reality.

---

7   In this chapter, we define "institutional arrangements" as mechanisms within an RTA that govern its institutional functioning, other than dispute settlement mechanisms. *See also* Brigid Gavin & Luk van Langenhove, "Trade in a World of Regions," in Gary P. Sampson and Stephen Woolcock eds., *Regionalism, Multilateralism and Economic Integration: The Recent Experience* (United Nations University Press, 2003), p. 295.

8   A document issued in 1998 by the WTO Secretariat covers only part of these issues. *See* WTO Secretariat, *Inventory of Non-tariff Provisions in Regional Trade Agreements, Background Note by the Secretariat*, WT/REG/W/26 (5 May 1998).

9   *See* e.g., Joseph A. McKinney, *Created from NAFTA: The Structure, Function, and Significance of the Treaty's Related Institutions* (M.E. Sharpe, 2000); Zakir Hafez, *The Dimensions of Regional Trade Integration in Southeast Asia* (Transnational Publishers, 2004).

10 An enormous amount of research is devoted to the consistency of RTAS with WTO Agreements. *See* e.g., Lorand Bartels & Federico Ortino eds., *Regional Trade Agreements and the WTO Legal System* (Oxford University Press, 2006); James H. Mathis, *Regional Trade Agreements in the GATT/WTO: Article XXIV and the Internal Trade Requirement* (Asser Press, 2002).

Assuming that there are no established analytical methods to address institutional arrangements of RTAs, this chapter tries to widen our perspectives toward the possible role and design of institutional arrangements in RTAs setting aside those of dispute settlement mechanisms. Since WTO Agreements do not set overarching criteria, negotiators of each RTA have ample room of discretion with regard to the institutional arrangements in RTAs. This analysis aims to provide RTA negotiators with useful insights into how institutional arrangements should be designed in accordance with the specific features of a given RTA.

The remainder of this chapter is organized as follows. Section II specifies the subject and methodology used in the present research. Section III presents a multidimensional comparison of RTAs, which is summarized in Section IV, the concluding section.

II   Methodology

1   Specification of the Subject

Our analysis focuses on the three major functions of institutional provisions in RTAS.

First of all, we divide structural problems that institutional arrangements are supposed to address into three categories, based on the time range they normally occur. Firstly, there are *short-term* problems, namely those that arise as soon as within a relatively short period after an RTA comes into force. They typically include regular communication, monitoring and decision-making in order to keep running the system. Secondly, *mid-term* problems relate to the conflicts or overlaps with other international agreements such as tax treaties and environmental agreements. This kind of problems would not occur shortly after the signing, because drafters try to avoid it. However, they may come up over time. Lastly, *long-term* problems concern the need to address subsequent changes in economic and political circumstances.

Needless to say, no bright lines exist between these categories. In some cases, for example, structural changes may be required immediately after the RTA entered into force.

Corresponding to these three types of problems, institutional arrangements in RTAs have three major functions, namely, external, internal, and interstitial functions. Firstly, it is the *external* function that coordinates relationships with other international agreements to ensure the integrity of the

RTA. Typically, this function addresses the mid-term problems. Secondly, *internal* function involves orderly functioning within an RTA that addresses short-term problems. And lastly, *interstitial* function involves adjustment of RTA provisions and structures to subsequent changes in circumstances that most typically addresses long-term problems.

Given the categorizations above, our analysis covers three types of provisions in RTAs. Firstly, we focus on provisions relating to the *institutional structure* of the RTA for the orderly functioning of RTA mechanisms, including the organization and procedures of communication and decision-making between contracting parties. We then focus on provisions relating to the *relationships with other agreements* to streamline relationships with other trade-related agreements, such as WTO Agreements, multilateral environmental agreements (MEAs), tax treaties, and other RTAs. Lastly, we focus on provisions relating to *subsequent modifications* to RTAs, including their amendment, accession, and termination, to adjust to subsequent changes in circumstances.

In sum, the coverage of this chapter is as follows: (1) provisions relating to institutional structure that involves internal function to addresses short-term problems; (2) provisions relating to the relationship with other agreements that involves external function to address mid-term problems; and (3) provisions relating to later modifications that involves interstitial function to address long-term problems. Covering these provisions that have three different functions should allow us to illustrate a balanced overview of the overall function of institutional arrangements within the RTA.[11] By so doing, we shed light on the roles of institutional arrangements in RTAs as part of the world trading system.

2   *Comparison Method*

Evaluating whether institutional arrangements work well in the future RTAs requires a careful analysis of different agreements that display sufficiently diverse objectives, structures, and contracting parties. It is not meaningful to compare the provisions in one RTA such as NAFTA with those in the MERCOSUR, since these RTAs have different purposes, different structures, concluded by different parties. To ensure an accurate comparison, we focus on a specific

---

11   Note that this chapter deals with system-wide provisions that cover the whole of the given RTA across the board, leaving provisions that apply only to specific chapters within the RTA outside the scope of the present study.

country as the axis of comparison in order to highlight the salient features of the RTAs in question.

(1)   Three-Dimensional Comparisons

In this study, we evaluate the roles of the three groups of provisions presented above by using the three-dimensional comparison technique. This approach consists of three comparisons (1) comparison among the RTAs concluded by the target country X with different countries Y (Y: Y_1, Y_2, Y_3, ...) (hereinafter Target Country RTAs); (2) comparison between the RTAs concluded between a country Y and third countries Z (Z: Z_1, Z_2, Z_3, ...) (hereinafter Partner RTAs) and Target Country RTAs; and (3) comparison of the RTA and other trade-related treaties, which are the target country X concluded with a country Y (hereinafter Parallel Agreements).

The first comparison evaluates consistency and diversity of the drafting policy of that country; the second comparison explains the background reasons behind any dependency on a partner country; and the third comparison illustrates the characteristics of the RTAs compared with other trade agreements.

The comparison of Target Country RTAs is a good starting point since the trade policies of each partner country significantly affect the feature and design of these RTAs. As shown in Figure 6.1, this comparison allows us to find the commonalities of RTAs concluded by the target country based on the characteristics of the counterpart countries. However, the mere comparison of Target Country RTAs does not tell us what such differences mean or what brought about those differences.

Thus, secondly, we assess the features of Partner RTAs and compare them with the characteristics of Target Country RTAs, as shown in Figure 6.2. This comparison allows us to evaluate how the institutional arrangements in R(X, Y) are influenced by the negotiating policy of Country Y. Provisions in Target Country RTAs that are unknown to Partner RTAs indicate something characteristic of the former.

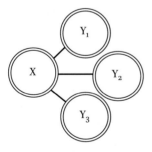

FIGURE 6.1 *Target country RTAs*

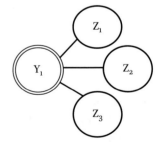

FIGURE 6.2 *Partner RTAs*

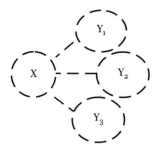
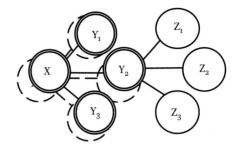

FIGURE 6.3 *Parallel agreements*   FIGURE 6.4 *Three-dimensional comparison*

Lastly, we compare Parallel Agreements, as shown in Figure 6.3. This comparison explains which features are specific to RTAs compared with other treaties such as commerce agreements, tax conventions, and bilateral investment treaties (BITs) and it is especially fruitful for understanding those institutional arrangements that are more or less necessary in any kind of modern trade-related agreement, whether domestic or international. A summary of this three-dimensional comparison is illustrated in Figure 6.4.

(2)   Selection of the Target Country

Theoretically, the above three-dimensional comparison that focuses on a particular target country could also be compared to another three-dimensional comparison of a different target country. However, we concentrate herein on comparing the RTAs concluded by a specific target country. Through this three-dimensional comparison process, we anticipated to extract (1) the variety of RTAs concluded by the target country, (2) the degree of partner dependency, and (3) the features specific to the institutional arrangements in RTAs.

We chose Japan as the target country of the presented research. Among the world's major economic powers, Japan is a relatively new user of RTAs, and it concluded its first FTA with Singapore in 2002. Since then, its accelerating FTA negotiations have resulted in 13 FTAs as of December 2013, namely with Switzerland, Peru, Mexico, India, Chile, and the seven members of ASEAN as well as ASEAN itself. Although these FTAs cover less than 20% of Japan's trade volume, it should be a good start to compare these agreements to find insights into the possible designs for future RTAs, such as trilateral FTA projects with Korea and China, and broader frameworks such as its on-going TPP negotiations. In addition, experience of Japan, a relatively new user of RTAs, will indicate the recent trends in the design of institutional arrangements in RTAs.

Firstly, the subjects of the first-level comparison (i.e. Target Country RTAS) are the 13 FTAS that Japan has already concluded. Secondly, seven out of these 13 partners, namely Singapore, Mexico, Malaysia, Chile, Thailand, Brunei, and ASEAN,[12] already had bilateral RTAS with third-party countries, which therefore become the subject of the second-level comparison (i.e. Partner RTAS). Lastly, we choose the most recent Friendship, Commerce, and Navigation (FCN) treaties concluded between Japan and its FTA partners after 1947, if applicable, for the subject of the third-level comparison (i.e. Parallel Agreements). In particular, we refer to the FCN treaties concluded by Japan with Thailand (1958), India (1958), Malaysia (1960), Peru (1961), Indonesia (1961), Mexico (1969), and the Philippines (1979).[13]

III Comparison of Japan's RTAS

1 *Institutional Structure*

(1) Comparison

In this first subsection of Section III, we examine the provisions in Japan's RTAS that govern internal administration. With regard to the characteristics of their organizational mechanisms, Japan's FTAS are almost identical, as shown in Table 6.1.

Every FTA concluded by Japan has an overarching governing and decision-making body that reviews the implementation of these agreements and discusses any issues between the parties involved, while daily operations are administered by the administrative agencies of each party. No FTAS have a standing secretariat, but rather these agreements ask parties to designate contact points in order to foster regular communication. In addition, the governing body typically has the power to monitor the operation of FTAS, discuss the issues raised by parties in order to mitigate trade disputes,

---

[12] While all RTAS concluded by ASEAN are, technically speaking, the bundle of bilateral RTAS concluded by each ASEAN member, we count each ASEAN-wide RTA as one on the grounds that institutional arrangements apply across the board equally to all contracting parties.

[13] FCN treaties are described herein as a traditional type of international agreement (other than RTAS) that covers trade. They include treaties of amity, commerce and navigation, agreements on commerce, and treaties of commerce and navigation.

RUNNING MANY FTAS IS LIKE BALANCING BETWEEN MANY BICYCLES 123

TABLE 6.1 *Provisions relating to the institutional structure of Japan's FTAs*

Partner	Organization		Function	
	Governing body	Composition	Competence	Frequency
Singapore (2002) Article 8	Supervisory Committee	Co-chaired by ministers or senior officials	Review implementation; discuss issues of interest; proactively improve the business environment; establish and review subsidiary organs; recommend ways of making improvements; and other functions as agreed	Once a year
Mexico (2004) Article 165	Joint Committee	Government representatives	Review implementation; recommend amendments; serve as part of the dispute settlement mechanism; adopt minor modifications/interpretations; supervise subsidiary organs; adopt operational rules; and other functions as agreed	Upon the request of either party
Malaysia (2005) Article 13	Joint Committee	Chaired by senior officials unless agreed at the ministerial level	Review implementation; recommend amendments; submit reports; recommend amendments; supervise subsidiary organs; adopt operational rules; and other functions as agreed	– On agreement – Can convene special meetings if either party requests
Philippines (2006) Article 13	Joint Committee	Government representatives	Review implementation; recommend amendments; supervise subsidiary organs; adopt operational rules; and other functions as agreed	Once a year, unless agreed otherwise

TABLE 6.1 *Provisions relating to the institutional structure of Japan's FTAs* (cont.)

Partner	Organization		Function	
	Governing body	Composition	Competence	Frequency
Chile (2007) Articles 189–191	Commission	Co-chaired by ministers or senior officials	Review implementation; recommend amendments; supervise subsidiary organs; modify Annex 15; adopt operational rules; and other functions as agreed	On agreement
Thailand (2007) Article 13	Joint Committee	Chaired by deputy minister (Japan) & deputy permanent secretary (Thai) or higher, unless agreed at the ministerial level	Review implementation; recommend amendments; supervise subsidiary organs; adopt operational rules; and other functions as agreed	N/A
Brunei (2007) Article 11	Joint Committee	Government representatives	Review implementation; recommend amendments; supervise subsidiary organs; adopt operational rules; and other functions as agreed	On agreement
Indonesia (2007) Article 14	Joint Committee	Government representatives	Review implementation; recommend amendments; supervise subsidiary organs; adopt operational rules; and other functions as agreed	On agreement
ASEAN (2006) Article 11	Joint Committee	Government representatives	Review implementation; submit reports; recommend amendments; supervise subsidiary organs; adopt operational rules; and other functions as agreed	On agreement

Vietnam (2008) Article 11	Joint Committee	Government representatives	Review implementation; recommend amendments; supervise subsidiary organs; adopt operational rules; and other functions as agreed	On agreement
Switzerland (2009) Article 148	Joint Committee	Co-chaired by senior officials	Review implementation; recommend amendments; supervise subsidiary organs; endeavour to resolve disputes; adopt & amend operational rules; and other functions as agreed	– Every two years – If a party requests a special meeting, the parties make every effort to hold it within 30 days
India (2011) Article 14	Joint Committee	Government representatives	Review implementation; recommend amendments; supervise subsidiary organs; adopt operational rules; and other functions as agreed	Once a year or upon request by either party
Peru (2012) Article 14	Commission	Co-chaired by ministers or senior officials	Review implementation; recommend interpretations; endeavour to resolve disputes; supervise subsidiary organs; and other functions as agreed	Once a year, unless agreed otherwise

adopt operational procedures, establish and supervise subsidiary bodies, and recommend amendments to governments.[14]

Having characterized Japan's FTAs through the first-level comparison above, we now move onto the second-level comparison, namely the comparison with Partner RTAs. We begin with Singapore, with which Japan sealed its first FTA. The recent RTAs concluded by Singapore such as the EFTA–Singapore RTA (2002), Singapore–Jordan FTA (2004), and original TPP (P4) (2005).[15] Agreement are similar to the Japan–Singapore FTA in terms of organization and decision-making, whereas the majority of Singaporean RTAs concluded in the 1990s have no decision-making body. The Mexico–Japan FTA has a similar organization to Mexican RTAs such as the EFTA–Mexico FTA (2000) as well.[16] The Korea–Chile FTA asks each party to assign a competent national body as its own secretariat rather than as an integrated secretariat.[17] Over the past decade, however, Japan has aimed to pursue its own path in order to ensure flexibility, characteristic of the subsequent FTAs that involve Japan, which do not require, for example, regularly holding governing body meetings at the ministerial level. Further, some of the articles in the Japan–Chile and Philippines–Japan FTAs show a degree of compromise because the respective partners pushed for more stable channels of communication.

Lastly, the third-level comparison with Parallel Agreements shows marked differences between the FTAs and FCN treaties with regard to organization and decision-making, since FCN treaties do not have organs to review or supervise their implementation because of the contractual nature of the rights and obligations set forth in such treaties. This fact shows the institutional nature of the rights and obligations in RTAs, which require continuous management compared with traditional treaties on commerce.

---

14   Each FTA has its own way terminology. For example, the Joint Committee of the Mexico–Japan FTA aims to serve "as a forum of consultation" between the parties, that is as the first stage for settling bilateral trade disputes.

15   See the EFTA–Singapore FTA, Article 55(6); the Singapore–Jordan FTA, Article 8.1(5); the P4 Agreement, Article 17.1.

16   See the EFTA–Mexico FTA, Article 70.

17   See the Chile-Korea FTA, Article 18.2. In some bilateral RTAs, secretarial bodies for upper-level umbrella RTAs serve as the secretariat of the subsidiary RTAs as well.

(2)   Evaluation

The comparative analysis above showed significant consistency in Japan's FTAs with regard to the rank of representatives and frequency of meetings in contrast with Partners' RTAs.[18] This is not to say that Japan's FTAs deserve extraordinary attention or that representatives' rank and meeting frequency are of significant importance for the operation of RTAs. However, as the number of RTAs increases, so does the administrative burden of the parties to keep them operating properly. From this viewpoint, the concerns of Japanese negotiators about overloading organizational arrangements have merit.

It should be noted that Japan's FTAs are marked by "flexibility" in the composition of the highest decision-making body and its meeting frequency. Firstly, the level of the members of the highest decision-making body is lower than those in Partner RTAs. The majority of Partner RTAs set forth that members of the highest decision-making body must be at the ministerial level for both parties. On the contrary, few of Japan's FTAs require the presence of ministers or senior officials at the meeting of the highest decision-making body. Secondly, few of Japan's FTAs require the Joint Committee or sub-committees to be held at regular intervals, except for the Japan–Singapore and Japan–Philippines FTAs, which demand that Joint Committee meetings be held at least once a year.

This degree of flexibility is no coincidence. Japan's FTAs are designed that way following specific requests on the Japanese side. Japan has consistently demanded not to specify the rank of representatives and meeting frequency in order to ensure the flexibility of communication and of the decision-making process. According to one Japanese negotiator, routine meetings at the senior official level, let alone the ministerial level, are not always necessary to ensure the effective operation of FTAs.[19] Thus, despite the clear stipulation for holding periodic meetings, the Joint Committee in the Japan–Singapore FTA has been held only sporadically (in 2002, 2006, and 2007) since its entrance into force in 2002. Assuming, however, that organs for communication and decision-making help improve cooperation among the contracting parties by fostering orderly communication among

---

18   This approach is common in Japan's recent BITs as well.
19   Interview with an anonymous government officer in Tokyo, Japan, on 23 February 2007.

them,[20] the said flexibility in Japan's FTAs may reduce the stability of the communication channels.

2   Relationships with Other Agreements

(1)   Comparison

The provisions in RTAs concerning relationships with other international agreements closely relate to the suitable functioning of the given RTA as an international institution. Before moving onto the multidimensional comparison of these relations, let us first clarify the role of the provisions that govern relationships with other agreements. These kinds of provisions mainly aim to prevent or reconcile "conflict" between the RTA and other agreements.[21] For instance, the risk of conflict between the provisions in RTAs and the WTO Agreements remains problematic even if the given RTA as a whole was approved as consistent with Article XXIV of the GATT,[22] while negotiators usually pay careful attention to avoid potential conflict with other agreements including the WTO Agreements. Conflict between RTAs and the WTO Agreements may arise when the latter is amended after the conclusion of a given RTA.[23] In addition, the provisions that govern this relationship may affect the interpretation of the provisions in other similar RTAs.[24] The comparison of Japan's FTAs in Table 6.2 shows the overarching provisions that cover relationships with other agreements.

---

20   Robert Keohane, *After Hegemony* (Princeton University Press, 1984), p. 89; J. McKinney, *supra* note 9, p. 16, p. 22.

21   According to Pauwelyn, "two norms are in a relationship of conflict if one constitutes, has led to, or may lead to, a breach of the other". Joost Pauwelyn, *Conflict of Norms in Public International Law: How WTO Relates to Other Rules of International Law* (Cambridge University Press, 2003), pp. 175–176. *See also* C. Wilfred Jenks, "The Conflict of Law-Making Treaties," *British Year Book of International Law*, Vol. 30 (1953), p. 426.

22   Appellate Body Report, *Turkey—Restrictions on Imports of Textile and Clothing Products*, WT/DS34/AB/R, adopted 19 November 1999, para. 60. Geraldo Vidigal, "From Bilateral to Multilateral Law-Making: Legislation, Practice, Evolution and the Future of Inter Se Agreements in the WTO," *European Journal of International Law*, Vol. 24 (2013), pp. 1043–1044.

23   C.W. Jenks, *supra* note 21, at 403. *See also* Tomohiko Kobayashi, "Changing the Legal Text of the WTO Agreement: Practicable Ways to Implement the Doha Round Negotiation Results," *Kokusaiho-gaiko-zasshi*, Vol. 105, No. 3 (2006), p. 89.

24   *See* Locknie Hsu, "Applicability of WTO Law in Regional Trade Agreements: Identifying the Links," in L. Bartels and F. Ortino eds., *supra* note 10, p. 550.

TABLE 6.2 *Provisions relating to the relationships with other agreements*

Partner	Agreements that all parties are party to	Other agreements that only some of the parties are party to	
		Partners' RTAs	Other agreements
Singapore (2002)	– Consult in the case of inconsistency with other agreements – Consult if the WTO is amended – Tax conventions[25] and the UN Charter prevail in the case of inconsistency	N/A	– Tax conventions prevail
Mexico (2004) Articles 167 & 170	– Reaffirm WTO rights/obligations – WTO countermeasures are not precluded by this FTA – Terminate existing Convention on Commerce between the parties – Tax conventions prevail in the case of inconsistency	N/A	– Tax conventions prevail

25 This provision did not exist in the original text agreed in 2002, but it was inserted through the amendment in 2007.

TABLE 6.2 *Provisions relating to the relationships with other agreements* (cont.)

Partner	Agreements that all parties are party to	Other agreements that only some of the parties are party to	
		Partners' RTAs	Other agreements
Malaysia (2005) Article 11	– Reaffirm the rights/obligations of other agreements – WTO rights/obligations prevail in case of inconsistency – Consult if inconsistent with non-WTO agreements – Tax conventions prevail in the case of inconsistency	N/A	– Tax conventions prevail
Philippines (2006) Articles 10–11	– Reaffirm rights/obligations under other agreements – WTO rights/obligations prevail in case of inconsistency – Consult in the case of inconsistency – If other agreements are amended, treaty law principles apply, but parties must be consulted if necessary – Tax conventions prevail in the case of inconsistency – Prevails over Treaties of Commerce	N/A	– Tax conventions prevail
Chile (2007) Articles 3 & 194	– Reaffirm rights/obligations under other agreements – Does not affect tax conventions	N/A	– Does not affect tax conventions

Thailand (2007) Articles 9 & 11	– Reaffirm rights/obligations under other agreements – WTO obligations prevail in case of inconsistency – Tax conventions prevail in the case of inconsistency	N/A	– Tax conventions prevail
Brunei (2007) Articles 7 & 9	– Reaffirm rights/obligations under other agreements – Consult if inconsistent with other agreements [No reference to tax conventions]	N/A	N/A
Indonesia (2007) Articles 10–12	– Reaffirm rights/obligations under other agreements – WTO rights/obligations prevail in case of inconsistency	N/A	N/A
ASEAN (2008) Articles 6 & 10	– Reaffirm rights/obligations under other agreements, no derogations from more favourable treatments – WTO rights/obligations prevail in case of inconsistency – Consult if inconsistent with non-WTO treaties – Tax conventions prevail in the case of inconsistency	Consult if inconsistent with agreements that two or more parties are party to	Tax conventions prevail

TABLE 6.2 *Provisions relating to the relationships with other agreements* (cont.)

Partner	Agreements that all parties are party to	Other agreements that only some of the parties are party to	
		Partners' RTAs	Other agreements
Vietnam (2008) Articles 7, 9, & 22	– Reaffirm rights/obligations under other agreements – WTO rights/obligations prevail in case of inconsistency – Consult if inconsistent with non-WTO treaties – Tax conventions prevail in the case of inconsistency – Incorporate BIT 2003 – Incorporate ASEAN–Japan FTA (22)	N/A	
Switzerland (2009) Articles 6, 7, 88, & 130	– Reaffirm rights/obligations under other agreements – Consult if inconsistent with other agreements – Tax conventions prevail in case of inconsistency – Amended GPA applies once both parties have been ratified – More favourable RTA treatments do not apply	N/A	– Tax conventions prevail, but consult if a party considers it affects the functioning of the FTA rules

India (2011) Articles 10 & 12	– Reaffirm rights/obligations of other agreements – Consult if inconsistent with other agreements – Tax conventions prevail in case of inconsistency	N/A
Peru (2012) Articles 2 & 12	– Reaffirm rights/obligations under other agreements – Consult if inconsistent with other agreements – Tax conventions prevail in case of inconsistency – Incorporate BIT 2008	N/A

First, Japan's FTAs can be classified into two groups with regard to their relationships with WTO Agreements: (a) those that explicitly recognize that WTO Agreements prevail over FTAs if they are not consistent with each other and (b) those that do not have explicit references to how inconsistency with WTO Agreements will be treated. Based on this classification, seven FTAs, namely those concluded with Singapore, Mexico, Chile, Brunei, Switzerland, India, and Peru, are categorized into the latter group, whereas six FTAs (those with Malaysia, the Philippines, Thailand, Indonesia, ASEAN, and Vietnam) belong to the former.

The provisions in the former group have almost identical wording. In order to affirm the rights and obligations of the WTO Agreements, they clearly set forth that "[i]n the event of any inconsistency between the [FTA] and the WTO Agreements, the WTO Agreements shall prevail to the extent of the inconsistency".[26] By contrast, variations exist within the latter group. The Japan–Chile and Japan–Mexico FTAs, for example, only include a provision that affirms the rights and obligations under the WTO Agreements.[27] The Japan–Singapore and Japan–Brunei FTAs further set forth that contracting parties must consult with each other in such a case of inconsistency, "with a view to finding a mutually satisfactory solution, taking into consideration [the] general principles of international law".[28]

Secondly, the provisions in Japan's FTAs that relate to other (non-WTO) agreements share common elements, which can be summarized thus: to the extent that both parties to a given RTA are party to other agreements, Japan's RTAs affirm the existing rights and obligations under these other agreements. Moreover, parties must consult in the case of inconsistency, while tax conventions always prevail over the RTA.

In contrast to Japan's FTAs, a major proportion of the Partner FTAs concluded by Mexico and Chile set forth that FTA provisions prevail over other international agreements in the case of inconsistency.[29] In addition, some Partner FTAs reaffirm the obligations or basic principles of the WTO Agreements.[30]

---

26   See e.g., the Japan–Malaysia FTA, Article 11(2); the Japan–Philippines FTA, Article 11(2); the Japan–Thailand FTA, Article 11(2); the Japan–Indonesia FTA, Article 12(2); the ASEAN–Japan FTA, Article 10(3).

27   See e.g., the Japan–Chile FTA, Article 3; the Japan–Mexico FTA, Article 167(2).

28   See e.g., the Japan–Singapore FTA, Article 6(1); the Japan–Brunei FTA, Article 9(2).

29   See e.g., the Chile-Mexico FTA, Article 1-03(2); the Chile-Korea FTA, Article 1.3(2).

30   See e.g., the Chile–EC FTA, Article 2(4)(d); the Australia–Singapore FTA, Article 1.1(d); the Singapore–US FTA, Article 1.1.2; the Chile–US FTA, Article 1.3; the Australia–Thailand FTA, Article 102(b).

Moreover, while all of Japan's FTAs were notified to the WTO Secretariat, some seem to ensure consistency with the WTO, whereas others do not. To examine the degree of coherence among Japan's FTAs, we move onto the next two levels of comparisons. Firstly, Partner RTAs can be classified into three groups, namely (1) those that affirm the rights and obligations under the WTO Agreements and direct parties to consult with each other in the case of inconsistency,[31] (2) those that prohibit derogation from multilateral agreements including the WTO Agreements,[32] and (3) those that declare the superiority of the RTA over the WTO Agreements to an extent incompatible with the given RTA.[33]

Secondly, some Partner RTAs also explicitly refer to certain MEAs as overarching provisions, particularly the Convention on International Trade in Endangered Species of Wild Fauna and Flora, the Montreal Protocol on Substances that Deplete the Ozone Layer, and the Basel Convention on the Control of Transboundary Movements of Hazardous Wastes and their Disposal.[34] Certain Partner RTAs even contain provisions that refer to other RTAs to which either of the parties is party.[35] Although these kinds of provisions are foreign to Japan's FTAs, its FCN treaties in the past used to refer to the non-extension of the rights and obligations under other preferential agreements in order not to haunt other FCN treaties.[36]

Lastly, with regard to Parallel Agreements, all Japan's FCN treaties concluded before 1994 provide that they must not be construed to derogate from the rights and obligations under the GATT 1947.[37]

---

31   *See* e.g., the Chile–US FTA, Article 1.3; the NZ–Singapore FTA, Article 80; the EFTA–Singapore FTA, Article 4; the Australia–Singapore FTA, Article 17.5; the Australia–Thailand FTA, Article 1906; the Korea–Singapore FTA, Article 1.3.

32   *See* e.g., the EFTA Convention, Article 49(1); the New Zealand–Singapore FTA, Article 80; the EFTA–Singapore FTA, Article 4; the P4 Agreement, Article 18.2.

33   *See* e.g., NAFTA, Article 103.2; the Canada–Chile FTA, Article A-03.2; the Chile–Mexico FTA, Article 1-04; the Mexico–Uruguay FTA, Article 1-03; the Chile–Korea FTA, Article 1.3(2); the Mexico–Nicaragua FTA, Article 1-05; the Chile–Mexico FTA, Article 1-04; the Israel–Mexico FTA, Article 1-04.2.

34   *See* e.g., the Canada–Chile FTA, Article A-04; the Chile–Mexico FTA, Article 1-06.

35   *See* e.g., the New Zealand–Singapore FTA, Article 81; the EFTA–Mexico FTA, Article 22; the Chile–EC FTA, Article 56(2).

36   *See* e.g., the Protocol to the Indonesia–Japan Treaty of Friendship and Commerce, para. 8; the Malaysia–Japan Treaty of Commerce, Article 1(5); the Philippines–Japan FCN Treaty, Article 13(a).

37   *See* e.g., the Malaysia–Japan Treaty of Commerce 1960, Article 8; the Indonesia–Japan Treaty on Friendship and Commerce 1961, Article 8; the Protocol to the Mexico–Japan

(2) Evaluation

The design of RTA provisions that govern relationships with other agreements varies since principles of general international law are of limited application with regard to consecutive treaties concluded with different parties.[38] WTO members have long discussed a way in which to allocate jurisdiction between the WTO Agreements and RTAS.[39] However, no consensus has been reached so far. Thus, as shown in the previous subsection, we find significant varieties with regard to the status of the WTO Agreements in FTAS. In addition, countries have their own preferences.

Against this background, provisions in six of Japan's FTAs have been marked by explicit deference to the WTO Agreements in cases of conflict, and such provisions are considered Japanese inventions. Japan's insistence on the superiority of the WTO Agreements comes partly from its ambition to adhere to multilateral trade rules and partly from concerns that FTAS that contain WTO-minus provisions may erode the integrity of the rights and obligations under the WTO Agreements.

Nevertheless, provisions that indicate Japan's policy preference toward multilateralism were not inserted into more recent FTAS such as those with Chile, Brunei, Switzerland, India, and Peru. They are silent about how parties address conflicts between FTA provisions and WTO provisions. Whether this is just a coincidence or reflects a shift in Japan's trade policy toward regionalism and whether this has any real impacts with regard to the interpretation of FTA provisions is to be seen.

In addition, Japan's FTAS can also be characterized by the treatment of the WTO, tax conventions, and other agreements. Except for the WTO Agreements and tax conventions, for example, Japan's FTAS do not specifically refer to other agreements (i.e. MEAS and third-party RTAS). This is not because Japanese negotiators are unconcerned about them, but because they wish to avoid drafting a long and time-consuming list of relevant agreements. How-

---

Convention on Commerce 1969, para. 1; the Protocol to the Philippines–Japan Treaty on Friendship and Commerce 1979, para. 9.

38 Thomas Cottier & Marina Foltea, "Constitutional Functions of the WTO and Regional Trade Agreements," in L. Bartels and F. Ortino eds., *supra* note 10, pp. 54–55.

39 *See* Frederick M. Abbott, "The North American Integration Regime and Its Implications for the World Trading System," in Joseph H.H. Weiler ed., *The EU, the WTO, and the NAFTA: Towards a Common Law of International Trade?* (Oxford University Press, 2000), pp. 177–178; Frederick M. Abbott, *Law and Policy of Regional Integration: The NAFTA and Western Hemispheric Integration in the World Trade Organization System* (Martinus Nijhoff, 1995), p. 107.

ever, this approach has somewhat muddied the scope of Japan's FTAs, partly explaining why the country has to exchange a special note with Thailand, the Philippines, and Brunei for them to reaffirm the rights and obligations under MEAs, as a side letter at the time of recognizing the entry into force of the FTA.[40]

3   Subsequent Adjustments

(1)   Comparison

RTAs may have legal arrangements that provide the contracting parties with several options to change current provisions in accordance with changes of circumstances following the conclusion of those agreements. There are three types of such arrangements: (1) amendment to RTAs; (2) accession to RTAs; and (3) termination of RTAs. As the first-level comparison, Table 6.3

TABLE 6.3   *Provisions relating to subsequent modifications*

Partner	Amendment		General periodic review	Accession	Termination
	Amending process	Other forms of changing text			
Singapore (2002) Article 10	On agreement	By exchange of notes to modify goods schedules	Every five years	N/A	One year prior notice
Mexico (2004) Articles 8, 37, 174, & 176	On agreement, effective 30 days after the exchange of notes	By exchange of notes to modify goods schedules & HS codes	N/A[41]	N/A	One year prior notice
Malaysia (2005) Articles 155–159	On agreement	By exchange of notes to modify goods schedules & HS codes	Every five years, unless agreed otherwise	N/A	– One year prior notice – The other party may request consultation

---

40   Letters exchanged by the Foreign Ministers of Japan and Thailand on 3 April 2007; Letters exchanged by the Foreign Ministers of Japan and the Philippines on 22 May 2007, available at http://www.mofa.go.jp/region/asia-paci/philippine/epa0609/letter.pdf (as of 30 May 2008).
41   As an exception, bilateral safeguard mechanisms are subject to review 10 years after their entry into force in accordance with Article 53(13) of the Mexico–Japan FTA.

TABLE 6.3 *Provisions relating to subsequent modifications* (cont.)

Partner	Amendment		General periodic review	Accession	Termination
	Amending process	Other forms of changing text			
Philippines (2006) Articles 161–165	On agreement	By exchange of notes to modify goods schedules and HS codes etc.	Every five years, unless otherwise agreed	N/A	One year prior notice through diplomatic channels
Chile (2007) Articles 197–199	On agreement	By exchange of notes to modify goods schedules & HS codes, on the part of Chile as an executive agreement	N/A	N/A	One year prior notice
Thailand (2007) Articles 169–173	On agreement	By exchange of notes to modify Annex goods schedules and HS codes etc.	Every 10 years, unless agreed otherwise	N/A	One year prior notice
Brunei (2007) Articles 119–122	On agreement, upon notifications of the completion of domestic approval by Japan & one or more ASEAN member	By exchange of notes to modify goods schedules & HS codes	Every five years, unless otherwise agreed	N/A	– One year prior notice – Consult if the other party requests
Indonesia (2007) Articles 151–154	On agreement	By exchange of notes to modify Annexes 2 & 3	Every five years	N/A	One year prior notice

Partner	Amendment		General periodic review	Accession	Termination
	Amending process	Other forms of changing text			
ASEAN (2008) Articles 77–80	On agreement	By exchange of notes to modify goods schedules and HS codes etc.	Every five years	N/A	One year prior notice
Vietnam (2008)	On agreement	By exchange of notes to modify goods schedules & HS codes	N/A[42]	N/A	One year prior notice
Switzerland (2009) Articles. 25, 60, & 102	On agreement	By exchange of notes to modify goods schedules and HS codes etc.	Only for goods chapter, five years after entry into force[43]	N/A	One year prior notice
India (2011)	On agreement	By exchange of notes to modify goods schedules & HS codes	N/A[44]	N/A	One year prior notice
Peru (2012)	On agreement	By exchange of notes to modify goods schedules and HS codes etc.	N/A[45]	N/A	One year prior notice

---

42 For the government procurement chapter, the parties must start renegotiations when India expressed its intentions to join the GPA, in accordance with Article 113.
43 The wording of Article 25 indicates that the general review of goods chapter is conducted only once, five years after the entry into force.
44 In accordance with Article 23, the bilateral special safeguard mechanism is subject to review 10 years after the entry into force of the agreement.
45 In accordance with Article 36, the bilateral special safeguard mechanism is subject to review 10 years after the entry into force of the agreement.

shows that Japan's FTAs are almost identical in terms of making subsequent changes.

First, with reference to the amendment of RTAs, Japan's FTAs do not specify any procedural requirements necessary in this regard; amendments to a given RTA simply enter into force conditional on the domestic approval process in each party. For certain provisions including rules of origin set forth in agreements,[46] amendments can become effective through an exchange of notes without parliamentary approval, which is required for normal treaty amendments. In addition, most of Japan's FTAs provide an opportunity for periodic general reviews. Second, none of Japan's FTAs allows third parties to accede to existing FTAs. Lastly, most of Japan's FTAs provide that either party can terminate the agreement by giving one year's advance notice in writing to the other party. Exceptions include Japan's FTAs with Malaysia and Brunei, for which one party can request a consultation to discuss the matters that would arise from the termination.[47]

For the second-level comparison, Partner RTAs allow only normal treaty amendment, although a number do permit the accession of third parties subject to the consent of all parties.[48] With regard to termination, the required period of advance notice is generally shorter (approximately six months) than those in Japan's FTA. In addition, only the Malaysia–Pakistan FTA (2007) and Singapore–Panama FTA (2006) provide an option for consultations before the termination.

Finally, Parallel Agreements, particularly traditional FCN treaties, are almost silent about amendment and accession, since they have limited durations in the first place and require periodic renewal or renegotiation in order to last longer. Finally, three to six months of advance notice is required to terminate FCN treaties. For example, in the FCN treaties with the Philippines, Malaysia, Indonesia, and India, either party can terminate the treaty after three years (two years for the treaty with India) from entry into force by providing six months of advance notification.[49] The FCN treaties with Mexico last three

---

46   Implementing agreements are classified as executive agreements in Japan whose amendment does not require diet approval.

47   The Malaysia–Japan FTA, Article 159(2); the Brunei–Japan FTA, Article 122(2).

48   *See* e.g., the Australia–Thailand FTA, Article 1905; the Singapore–US FTA, Article 21.6; the Australia–Singapore FTA, Article 17.4; the New Zealand–Singapore FTA, Article 79; the EFTA–Singapore FTA, Article 70; the EFTA–Mexico FTA, Article 82; the Israel–Mexico FTA, Article 12-04; the Mexico–Uruguay FTA, Article 21-06; the Mexico–Nicaragua FTA, Article 22-05; the Bolivia–Mexico FTA, Article 21-06.

49   The Philippines–Japan FCN treaty (1979), Article 17(3); the Malaysia–Japan FCN treaty (1960), Article 11(2); the Indonesia–Japan FCN treaty (1963), Article 11(3); the India–Japan FCN treaty (1958).

years, and are automatically renewed for another year thereafter. However, either party can terminate the treaty by providing three months of advance notice.[50] Similarly, the FCN treaty with Peru (1960) is renewed automatically every three years unless either party notifies the other of its intention to seek a termination 90 days before the renewal.[51] This means the treaty can be terminated only once every three years.

(2)   Evaluation

Japan's FTAs are characterized by flexible options in making amendments. Indeed, their simplified procedures may help parties adjust the given RTA to changes in situations that have occurred since the conclusion of the original RTA. By contrast, accession terms are far from flexible. It is true that every RTA is an outcome of the tailored negotiations that do not always suit extension to third parties. However, the mere incorporation of provisions for accession does not seem to open the door to a flood of applications to accede to existing RTAs or force present parties to approve applications. Rather, an option for accession helps RTAs serve as a building block toward open regionalism.[52] Moreover, amendment to the substance of RTAs and accession of third parties to existing RTAs may have a similar function in the sense that the former serves as a later adjustment *materiae* to existing RTAs, while the latter serves as a later adjustment *personae*. Thus, although bilateral RTAs rarely allow third parties to join,[53] the positive aspects of inserting provisions concerning accession must not be overlooked.

Finally, Japan consistently demands one year's advance notice before the termination of an FTA, which is longer than Parallel Agreements and Partner RTAs (typically six months) and thus generally serves to improve predictability. However, preventing accidental termination caused by miscommunication is relatively more important. Opportunities to consult with each other about the consequences of termination, such as whether the cooperation framework under an FTA will last after its expiry, are useful not only for ensuring orderly backlogging, but also for preventing the impatient issuance of the notice of termination. For example, the Malaysia–Japan and Brunei–Japan FTAs include provisions to provide at least an opportunity for consultation between parties before the termination is carried out.

---

50   The Mexico–Japan FCN treaty (1969), Article 8(2).
51   The Peru–Japan FCN treaty (1960), Article 9(2).
52   Jagdish Bhagwati, *The World Trading System at Risk* (Harvester Wheatsheaf, 1991), p. 77.
53   WTO Secretariat (1998), *supra* note 8, para. 22.

IV   Conclusion

This chapter explored a new analytical approach by examining the institutional arrangements of RTAs in Japan. It shed light on the provisions in RTAs that govern relationships with other agreements and subsequent changes to RTAs as well as their institutional structures, all of which have distinct functions to ensure proper functioning of RTAs as international institutions.

The multidimensional comparisons presented herein allowed us to draw a number of conclusions. First, we showed that the institutional structures of Japan's FTAs are characterized by simplicity and flexibility, leaving most of potential issues open to consultation among the contracting parties. While this approach may allow flexible response to address unexpected future challenges on the one hand, it increases communication cost between the parties, which could hinder the orderly management of the given FTAs, on the other.

Secondly, with regard to the relationships with other agreements, we found that almost a half of Japan's FTAs include provisions that explicitly defer to WTO Agreements in cases of inconsistency. This type of provisions is rare in non-Japanese RTAs and will help avoid future disputes over the conflict with WTO rights and/or obligations. By contrast, considerable ambiguity remains in Japan's RTAs with regard to relationships with non-WTO agreements. Further comparison with more target countries, more Partner RTAs, and a wider range of Parallel Agreements would enable us to explore the "family resemblance" among RTAs of different countries in terms of institutional designs.

Third and lastly, with regard to subsequent adjustments to original agreements, we showed that Japan's FTAs are characterized by the contrast between flexibility toward amending texts and a lack of flexibility in opening the door for accession. We were not able to find strong reasons for this contrast. The administrative cost to admit accession of third parties may be lower than the cost of writing a separate agreement with them from the scratch, to the extent that existing parties can agree that a specific accession does not cause significant harm to the system. Thus, Japan's consistent reluctance to inserting accession clauses is less plausible.

Finally, integrating three different aspects of comparison into one analytical method enabled us to understand the systematic problems in running multiple RTAs. Needless to say, the present research has a number of limitations that should be noted. In particular, its scope is limited to a kind of RTAs, i.e., FTAs, concluded by one target country, i.e., Japan, and compared with a narrow range of trade agreements such as FCN treaties. Nevertheless, this chapter has proven that a multidimensional comparison provides useful insights for the future design of institutional provisions in RTAs. Keep trying to innovate is one of the most important lessons I learned from Professor Ida, to whom this chapter is dedicated.

CHAPTER 7

Provisional Measures in Investor-State Dispute Settlement: Reappearance of *Community of Investment Interests*?

Dai Tamada

Introduction

The investor-State arbitration (ISDS), established under international investment agreements (IIAs), is generally considered to be functioning as a *forum* for protecting the investors' interests. However, some academics have pointed out that the ISDS is not only a means of protecting investments, but also a means of distributing and balancing the interests of both parties, i.e., claimants (investors) and defendants (host States), and thus realising a *community of investment interests* between the two sides.

Professor Ryuichi Ida made some important remarks as to this issue in his analysis of ISDS, especially on the matters of compensation and damages awards. First, he pointed out the existence of the mechanism of balancing the investor's interest and the host State's interests. Second, he noted that this mechanism is based on the arbitrator's effort to effectively resolve the investment disputes.[1] Third and finally, Professor Ida characterised this process as based on a *community of investment interest*.[2]

After large-scale development of ISDS in recent years, it becomes more important and necessary to examine the applicability of this *community* thesis to the present-day ISDS. In this context, this research focuses on the procedure of provisional measures. This is because Ida's analysis was based on the damages awards rendered by the sole arbitrators, i.e., ISDS in the pre-IIA era, in which the arbitrators exercise a wide range of discretion. Under the provisional measures, on the other hand, this kind of discretion of arbitrators is not so

---

[1] Ryuichi Ida, "Nationalisation pétrolière en droit international du développement" (1993), pp. 222–223.
[2] Ryuichi Ida, "Effective Settlement of Nationalization Disputes" (1997), p. 387. Here, he stated that "it is possible to say, extremely, that, through the law application process of arbitration, there seems to be established, unconsciously, something like a community of investment interests between the investors and the developing countries, which are at first sight contradictory".

wide and consequently it seems difficult to recognise a community of investment interests even in the provisional measures procedure. It should also be noted that the provisional measures are generally ordered in the form of an injunction, which normally requires the host States, for example, to suspend ongoing judicial procedures or administrative procedures. This means that provisional measures may be functioning as a severe restraint on the sovereign power of the host States. In the *Perenco* case, for instance, the Defendant State, Ecuador, alleged that "it was more important that the test [for the grant of provisional measures] was fully satisfied if a sovereign State were to be restrained from implementing its validly enacted laws".[3] Thus, the provisional measures procedure is an ideal material of research on the issue of whether the ISDS is generally based on an idea of *community of investment interests*.

Our analysis is divided into two parts. First, as to the requirement of investor's merits rights, the applicable standard established by the International Court of Justice (ICJ) is that of *plausibility* test. In the ISDS, on the other hand, the investor's substantive rights to specific performance have been in dispute in many cases and the ISDS tribunals have instead applied the *proportionality* test, i.e., investors do not have the right to specific performance if the demanded measures would excessively constrain the sovereignty or regulatory power of the host States. Here, it seems possible to conclude that arbitrators give weight to the sovereignty of host State.

Second, as to the requirement of investor's damage, the applicable standard established by the ICJ is that of the *irreparable damage* and the *compensability* test. It is apparent, however, that this standard cannot be applied directly to the investment dispute to the extent that all of the investment damage is monetarily compensable. The ISDS tribunals therefore established the *going-concern* test, i.e., the last interests of investors (represented by the investment's ability to earn) is to be protected even if they are monetarily compensable. It seems possible to conclude that the ISDS arbitrators give weight to the investor's ultimate interests.

To conclude, the interests of both parties of ISDS are fairly balanced in such a way that they could not be excessively damaged. As far as this can be affirmed, it might be possible to recognise the reappearance of *community of investment interests* which is the foundation of effective settlement of investment disputes. In this regard, it is important to refer to some new phenomena in the

---

3   *Perenco Ecuador Ltd. v. The Republic of Ecuador and Empresa Estatal Petróleos del Ecuador (PetroEcuador)*, Decision on Provisional Measures (8 May 2009), ICSID Case No. ARB/08/6, para. 29.

recent ISDS, such as the establishment of escrow accounts which manifestly aim to balance the interests between the parties.

I   Requirement of Investor's Rights

The international courts and tribunals have established some requirements for ordering, indicating or recommending the provisional measures. In the case of the ISDS, claimant is required to prove that they have either substantive or procedural merit rights at the time of submitting an application before the tribunal. This requirement is essentially rooted in the balance of interests in provisional measures, i.e., the balance between the urgent character of provisional measures and the purpose of protecting merit rights. On the one hand, the provisional measures procedure is instituted for preserving the merit rights, the violation of which constitutes the subject matter of a dispute. It is natural therefore to require claimants to show their merit rights at this stage of the proceeding. On the other hand, this procedure aims at preserving these rights in urgent situations. Thus, a profound and lengthy examination of merit rights at this stage may render the procedure useless or purposeless.

1   *The Applicable Standard of Investor's Rights*
According to the jurisprudence recently established by the ICJ, the test for examining this requirement is the *plausibility* of claim, i.e., whether the claimant's merits rights would likely be admitted by the Court in the merit phase. In the *Belgium v. Senegal* case, the ICJ stated that "the power of the Court to indicate provisional measures should be exercised only if the Court is satisfied that the rights asserted by a party are *at least plausible* (emphasis added)".[4] Taking into consideration of some differences of legal nature between the ICJ and the ISDS (and between their legal foundations), requiring the latter to adopt and apply the same test of plausibility would be strict.

(1)   The *Existing-Rights* Test
In some cases, the International Centre for Settlement of Investment Disputes (ICSID) tribunals require the presence of *existing rights* in order to recommend provisional measures. This means that a hypothetical right alleged by a

---

4   *Questions relating to the Obligation to Prosecute or Extradite* (Belgium v. Senegal), Request for the Indication of Provisional Measures, Order of 28 May 2009, *I.C.J. Reports 2009*, para. 57. This is the first time that the Court clarified this requirement as applicable to the provisional measures, and actually applied it in a concrete case.

claimant is not sufficient to deserve protection via provisional measures. In the *Maffezini* case, for example, the respondent State, Spain, requested the use of provisional measures and demanded the payment of arbitration procedure fees in the form of security. Responding to this request, the Tribunal stated that "[r]ule 39 (1) [of the ICSID Arbitration Rules] specifies that a party may request '...provisional measures for the preservation of its rights....' The use of the present tense implies that such rights *must exist* at the time of the request, *must not be hypothetical, nor are ones to be created in the future*."[5] Here, it is clarified that, as a requirement of provisional measures, the alleged rights must exist at the moment of requesting provisional measures. As a result, we can call this requirement the *existing-rights test*.

The tribunal applied this test in the *Maffezini* case and ultimately dismissed the claim for provisional measures on the ground that such a claim "contains several hypothetical situations".[6] The same test was adopted in other cases, such as the *Phoenix* case, in which the claimant requested, as a provisional measure, the release of funds frozen by the respondent State. The tribunal dismissed this claim on the ground that "[t]he rights that the Claimant can purport to protect through provisional measures must be rights that the Claimant *did possess* at one moment or another".[7] Thus, it is clear that the ICSID jurisprudence has established the *existing-rights* test as an applicable requirement for the provisional measures.

However, the *existing-rights* test necessarily provokes a procedural problem. First, a decision on this point at the provisional measures phase necessarily prejudges the merit award.[8] As is confirmed by the tribunal in the *Occidental* case, the "decision [on the provisional measures] is without prejudice to all substantive issues in dispute and should not be considered as prejudging any issue of fact or law concerning jurisdiction or the merits of this case".[9] If the tribunal should avoid prejudging the merit award at the provisional measures phase, the *existing-rights* test should not be regarded as a requirement for it. Second, the *existing-rights* test requires the arbitrators to examine profoundly and lengthy the existence of merit rights and, as a result, makes the procedure

---

5   *Emilio Agustín Maffezini v. Kingdom of Spain*, Procedural Order No. 2 (28 October 1999), ICSID Case No. ARB/97/7, paras. 12–13 (emphasis added).
6   *Ibid.*, para. 16.
7   *Phoenix Action, Ltd. v. The Czech Republic*, Decision on Provisional Measures (6 April 2007), ICSID Case No. ARB/06/5, para. 36 (emphasis added).
8   *Ibid.*, paras. 37, 38, 40.
9   *Occidental Petroleum Corporation, Occidental Exploration and Production Company v. The Republic of Ecuador*, Decision on Provisional Measures (17 August 2007), ICSID Case No. ARB/06/11, para. 101.

of provisional measures longer. As the provisional measures procedure is essentially an urgent procedure, this expansion of time, which is contrary to its original purpose and function, should be avoided.

(2)   The *Plausibility* Test and the *Theoretical Existence* Test

Recently, however, the recent ICSID jurisprudence tends to mitigate the *existing-rights* test in the sense that the tribunals require, not the *existence* of merits rights, but only the *plausibility* of the claimant's rights. This change of attitude was clearly manifested in the *Pey Casado* case, in which the tribunal stated that "it has to consider on the basis of *hypothesis* that the rights, which the arbitral award *could admit* to one or the other parties, may face to danger or destruction in the absence of provisional measures".[10] Here the tribunal applies the *plausibility* test, instead of *existing-rights* test. More symbolic was the criticism of the *Pay Casado* case tribunal against the *Maffezini* decision. According to the former, the latter's requirement of *existing rights* is the "expression which may produce a misunderstanding (expressions susceptible de prêter à malentendu)"[11] and "such position is wrong and is founded on a misunderstanding of the very system of ICSID on the provisional measures (cette position est erronée et repose sur un malentendu quant au système des mesures conservatoires de la Convention)".[12]

The criticism on the precedent significantly influenced the following findings. First, in the *Occidental* case, the tribunal stated that "the right to be preserved only has to be asserted as a theoretically existing right, as opposed to exist in fact".[13] Second, in the *Burlington* case, the tribunal made clear that "at the outset, one notes the Parties" concurrent view that the Tribunal must examine the existence of rights under a *prima facie* standard.... It cannot

---

10   *Víctor Pey Casado c. La République du Chili*, CIRDI/ARB/98/2, Décision sur les mesures conservatoires sollicitées par les Parties (le 25 septembre 2001), para. 46 (emphasis added). In original: « Il [Tribunal] doit donc raisonner, à ce stade préliminaire de la procédure arbitrale, sur la base non pas de « présomption » mais d'hypothèses [...] où les droits que la sentence arbitrale pourrait reconnaître à l'une ou à l'autre des Parties en cause risqueraient d'être mis en danger ou compromis par l'absence de mesures conservatoires ».

11   *Ibid.*, para. 47.

12   *Ibid.*, para. 80.

13   *Occidental* [2007], *supra* note 9, para. 64. The remaining problem is that the Tribunal's criterion of "theoretical existence" is not clear enough to identify its fulfilment. In this case, the subject matter in dispute was whether the claimant's right to specific performance exists or not. The Tribunal examined whether "a strongly arguable right" was proved or not. *See Occidental* [2007], *ibid.*, para. 68.

require actual proof, but must be satisfied that the rights exist *prima facie*".[14] These cases clearly show that the tribunals are now adopting the *theoretical existence* test or the *prima facie* rights test, instead of the *existing-rights* test. In other words, at the provisional measures phase, the real existence of rights is not any more required by tribunals and consequently there is no substantial difference between the *plausibility* test, established in the ICJ's jurisprudence, and the *theoretical existence* test or the *prima facie* test, established in the ISDS jurisprudence.

2   *The Issue of the Right to Specific Performance*

During the drafting process of the ICSID Convention, there was a discussion on the nature and the kind of right to be preserved by the provisional measures, but it did not result in any final disposition.[15] As a result, the scope of the right was deliberately left open to be subsequently identified by the arbitral jurisprudence. In this context, there remain some problems that should be resolved; one of which is whether "the right to specific performance" can be a right that should be preserved by provisional measures. This problem has occurred, for example, in a case where the host State, by enacting its law or regulation order, has modified, terminated, or suspended the investor's rights, which were previously admitted by an investment contract between parties. In such a case, a dispute arises as to whether the investor is entitled to claim, at the future merit stage, the performance of the investment contract by the host State.

Serious problems can arise if a tribunal admits such a right to the investor, because with this right, the investor could be entitled to suspend, or at least restrain, the exercise of the sovereign right of the host State, i.e., the sovereign power to legislate and execute laws in its territory. Thus, the host State firmly alleged, in this example case, that investors do not have the right to specific performance and consequently cannot be protected by the provisional measures.

(1)   The *Contract* Test

In some cases, the ICSID tribunals determined that the right to specific performance must be examined on the basis of whether the contract between the Parties remained valid or not (thus, hereinafter, we call it the *contract* test).

---

14   *Burlington Resources Inc. and Others v. Republic of Ecuador and Empresa Estatal Petróleos del Ecuador (PetroEcuador)*, Procedural Order No.1 on Burlington Oriente's Request for Provisional Measures (29 June 2009), ICSID Case No. ARB/08/5, para. 53.

15   Christoph H. Schreuer, with Loretta Malintoppi, *The ICSID Convention: A Commentary* (2nd ed., Cambridge University Press, 2009), p. 779.

In the *Occidental* case, the participation contract between the parties was terminated by the Ecuadorian government and the investor requested provisional measures for the execution of that contract. The respondent (Ecuador) alleged that "there is no right to specific performance of a natural resources concession agreement that has been terminated or cancelled by a sovereign State; the lawful remedy in the event of wrongful or illegal action by the State is payment of monetary compensation. Accordingly, Claimant has no right to obtain 'restitution' in the form of an order reinstating the Participation Contract and returning the Block 15 oil field to Claimants".[16] The tribunal in this case admitted the allegation of the respondent, ultimately denying the investor's right to specific performance on the following grounds. First, the tribunal confirmed the confusion of terminology, in that "*restitutio in integrum* is in fact sometimes used as meaning full reparation, and sometimes used as meaning restitution in kind",[17] and asserted that the tribunal "will use the expression 'specific performance' in relation to the Claimant's request for the reinstatement of their rights in Block 15".[18] Second, according to the tribunal, "[s]pecific performance is, of course, a conditional right, as it is precisely conditioned on the possibility of performance, and consequently hindered by its impossibility".[19] Thirdly, after confirming that "the Tribunal is not aware of any case where an ICSID tribunal has granted the kind of specific performance against a State that the Claimants seek in the present arbitration",[20] it concluded that "[i]t is well established that where a State has, in the exercise of its sovereign powers, *put an end to a contract or a license*, or any other foreign investor's entitlement, specific performance must be deemed legally impossible".[21] Here, the tribunal's finding that the right to specific performance cannot be admitted was based on the termination of contract by the respondent and it is thus clear that this finding adopts the test of whether a valid contract remains or not.

On the other hand, when the contract between the parties remains valid, the right to specific performance can be recognized, at least *prima facie*, as a right to be preserved by provisional measures. In the *Burlington* case, the tribunal stated that "the PSCs [production sharing contracts] *are in force* which

---

16   *Occidental* [2007], *supra* note 9, paras. 42–43.
17   Ibid., para. 72. The *Burlington* Tribunal, on the other hand, held that the specific performance is included in the restitution in the meaning of Article 35 of the ILC Articles on State Responsibility. *Burlington* [2009], *supra* note 15, para. 70.
18   *Occidental* [2007], *supra* note 9, para. 74.
19   Ibid., para. 75.
20   Ibid., para. 78.
21   Ibid., para. 79 (emphasis added).

makes it unnecessary to consider that view [of the *Occidental* Tribunal]",[22] ultimately admitting the *prima facie* existence of the right of the claimant to specific performance.[23] This reasoning was followed by the tribunal in the *Perenco* case, in which the parties disputed an Ecuadorian law and the enforcement order issued under that law. On this point, the tribunal concluded that "irrespective of whether the Occidental Tribunal was correct in this view, on which this Tribunal takes no position, ...there having been no such termination or cancellation, the principle invoked by the *Occidental* Tribunal is inapplicable".[24]

Among the three cases cited above, there is a sharp difference of opinion on whether the right to specific performance can be admitted or not. The right was rejected in the *Occidental* case, but admitted in the last two cases. There is, however, no difference in the criteria applied in all three cases, i.e., the *contract* test. According to this test, the right to specific performance depends on the validity or continuity of the investment contract between the parties.[25]

Even though the *contract* test makes it easy for arbitrators to draw a conclusion about whether a claimant has the right to specific performance or not, it cannot dissolve the substantive problem of why the unilateral termination of a contract by the host State must always result in the negation of the right to specific performance. In theory, it is always possible to admit such a right of investors, even after the unilateral termination of a contract. On this point, it is necessary to take into account the remedy for an internationally wrongful act in international law of responsibility, which consists of restitution in kind and monetary compensation.[26] First, if the breach or termination of a contract is

---

22 *Burlington* [2009], *supra* note 14, para. 70 (emphasis added). In this paragraph, the Tribunal indirectly criticized and departed from the reasoning of the *Occidental* award. Before the cited sentence, the *Burlington* Tribunal referred to the *Occidental* Tribunal's view, stating that "the view has been expressed that the right to specific performance is not available under international law where a concession agreement for natural resources has been terminated or cancelled by a sovereign State". Therefore, the "view" mentioned here is that of the *Occidental* Tribunal.

23 *Ibid.*, para. 71. The Tribunal's reasoning here is based on the *prima facie* test: "at first sight at least, a right to specific performance appears to exist".

24 *Perenco* [2009], *supra* note 3, para. 48.

25 J.A. Rueda-Garcia, "Provisional Measures in Investment Arbitration: Recent Experiences in Oil Arbitrations against the Republic of Ecuador," *Transnational Dispute Management*, Vol. 6, No. 4 (2009), pp. 17–18.

26 In the ISDS, "satisfaction" is rarely demanded by claimants and therefore such a remedy is deemed irrelevant to the investment remedy. Pierre-Yves Tschanz & Jorge E. Vinuales, "Compensation for Non-expropriatory Breaches of International Investment Law," *Journal*

deemed as a wrongful act by the host State, the claimant's right to specific performance as a form of restitution cannot theoretically be excluded. Second, if there are not many cases in which a claimant investor demands restitution or specific performance as a merit claim, this does not mean that claimants are legally prohibited from doing so.

(2)   The *Proportionality* Test

It is clear that the *contract* test is clear-cut but, at the same time, highly formalistic as a requirement of provisional measures. Taking this into consideration, it is necessary and possible to read differently the above cited findings of tribunals.

The tribunal in the *Occidental* case did not exactly apply the *contract* test, but its reasoning was grounded on the consideration of whether the interference into the sovereign rights on the basis of the right to specific performance was *proportional* or not. In this regard, the tribunal referred to Article 35 of the Articles of State Responsibility[27] and concluded that the right to specific performance does not satisfy the condition of restitution and therefore this claim must be replaced by the payment of monetary damages. According to the tribunal, when restitution is impossible or disproportionate, monetary compensation may be ordered in place of restitution in kind.[28] In fact, the tribunal held that "[t]o impose on a sovereign State reinstatement of a foreign investor in its concession, after a nationalization or termination of a concession license or contract by the State, would constitute a reparation *disproportional* to its

---

of *International Arbitration*, Vol. 26 (2009), p. 732. However, there remains the possibility of monetary compensation for "moral damages". In the *Desert Line* case (*Desert Line Projects LLC v. The Republic of Yemen*, Award (6 February 2008), ICSID Case No. ARB/05/17), the Claimant made a rare demand for compensation for the "moral damage", including the loss of reputation (para. 286). On this claims, the ICSID tribunal noted that "even if investment treaties primarily aim at protecting property and economic values, they do not exclude, as such, that a party may, in exceptional circumstances, ask for compensation for moral damages. It is generally accepted in most legal systems that moral damages may also be recovered besides pure economic damages. There are indeed no reasons to exclude them" (para. 289). In effect, the tribunal awarded Desert Line US $1 million in moral damages (para. 291).

27   Article 35 of the ILC Articles on State Responsibility stipulates, as to the restitution, that: "A State responsible for an internationally wrongful act is under an obligation to make restitution, that is, to re-establish the situation which existed before the wrongful act was committed, provided and to the extent that restitution: (a) is not materially impossible; (b) does not involve a burden out of all proportion to the benefit deriving from restitution instead of compensation".

28   *Occidental* [2007], *supra* note 9, para. 82.

interference with the sovereignty of the State when compared to monetary compensation".[29] The conclusion of the tribunal was that "the Claimants have not established a strongly arguable case that there exists a right to specific performance where a natural resources concession agreement has been terminated or cancelled by a sovereign State", and that "at this stage of the proceedings…no such right exists".[30] If it is true that the tribunal finally denied the right to specific performance, this conclusion was not based on the simple *contract* test, but rather on the *proportionality* test under which the right to specific performance as a restitution claim must be proportional to its interfering effect on the sovereignty of the host State. In the same way, the *Burlington* Tribunal interpreted Article 35 of the ILC Articles to mean that "it provides for restitution which includes specific performance *unless it is materially impossible or wholly disproportionate*".[31]

As is clear from the above findings as to the right to specific performance, the ISDS tribunals did not apply directly the *contract* test, but were applying the *proportionality* test instead. The latter requires proportionality between the claimant's right to specific performance of investment contract by the host State on the one hand and the sovereign power of the host State to enact its laws and to implement them on the other.

Note that the rights to be preserved by provisional measures are not limited to *substantive* rights, but they include *procedural* rights. In effect, in the ISDS, the claimants sometimes request the preservation of their *procedural* rights by way of provisional measures. Note also that in this case, the criteria of whether the procedural right could be admitted or not is also that of *proportionality*. There is no difference between the two kinds of rights in so far as their protection could infringe the sovereign power of the host States.

In the *Quiborax* case, in effect, the tribunal applied the *proportionality* test in order to justify the restraint of the host State's sovereignty. First, the Tribunal confirmed the sovereign power of the host State (Bolivia) to prosecute and investigate suspects in its territory. At the same time, however, it noted that "such powers must be exercised in good faith and respecting Claimants rights, including their prima facie right to pursue this arbitration".[32] This means that the sovereign power of the host State can be restrained or moderated by the

---

29   *Ibid.*, para. 84 (emphasis added).
30   *Ibid.*, para. 86.
31   *Burlington* [2009], *supra* note 14, para.70 (emphasis added).
32   *Quiborax S.A., Non Metallic Minerals S.A. and Allan Fosk Kaplún v. Plurinational State of Bolivia*, Decision on Provisional Measures (26 February 2010), ICSID Case No. ARB/06/2, para. 123.

opposite procedural right of investors to pursue investment arbitration. Second, the tribunal applied the *proportionality* test to this case with regard to the limitation of sovereignty, stating that "the Tribunal must thus balance the harm caused to Claimants by the criminal proceedings and the harm that would be caused to Respondent if the proceedings were stayed or terminated".[33] Here, the tribunal examines the balance of *harms* between the Parties. Third, the tribunal concluded that "a mere stay of the criminal proceedings would not affect Respondent's sovereignty nor require conduct in violation of national law. ...the harm that such a stay would cause to Bolivia is *proportionately less* than the harm caused to Claimants (emphasis added)".[34] Here the tribunal obviously applied the *proportionality* test for making balance between the harms of both parties and for examining the issue of whether the right in dispute could *plausibly* be admitted in the merit phase (the *plausibility* test). It is also clarified by the tribunal that the provisional measures are purported to preserve not only the *substantive* rights of investors, but also the *procedural* rights.

From the above examination, it is now possible to draw some conclusions on the issue of the requirement of claimant's rights in the provisional measures procedure. First, the *plausibility* test is established in the ISDS jurisprudence. In other words, the ISDS tribunals examine whether the claimant's rights, alleged to be in danger of irreparable violation in near future, have been *prima facie* established at the time that provisional measures are recommended.

Second, when applying this *plausibility* test, the tribunals are faced with the typical question of whether either a right to specific performance or a right to restitution in kind can be admitted on the basis of the *prima facie* case or not. As to this problem, the ISDS tribunals seem to have applied the *contract* test. A careful reading of the tribunals' decisions, however, enables us to conclude that these tribunals adopted and applied the *proportionality* test. Note that this test is applied also to cases in which the claimants' *procedural* rights, rather than their *substantive* rights, are in dispute. The adoption of the *proportionality* test by tribunals means that the claimant's merit rights cannot be preserved by provisional measures when such measures would risk excessive restraint on the sovereign power of the host States, including the power to legislate, execute its laws, and apply its laws in its territory. In other words, the *proportionality* test will be able to function for protecting the host States' sovereign power.

---

33   Ibid., para. 158.
34   Ibid., para. 165.

Third, the protection of sovereign power by way of limitation of the claimant's rights to specific performance or to restitution reflect the trend of IIAs which were recently concluded by a variety of States. Some IIAs actually stipulate that the arbitral tribunal is authorized only to render an award of monetary damages, excluding the possibility of an award of restitution. Representative of this type is the USA Model BIT (2012).[35] As another example, the Canada-Ecuador BIT (1996) provides in Article 13 (9) that: "a tribunal may award, separately or in combination, only: (a) monetary damages and any applicable interest; (b) restitution of property, in which case the award shall provide that the disputing Contracting Party may pay monetary damages and any applicable interest in lieu of restitution".[36] The same type of article can be found in non-American BITs, such as the India-Japan Comprehensive EPA (IJCEPA) (2011), which stipulates in Article 96 that: 'The award rendered by the arbitral tribunal shall include: (b) a remedy if there has been such breach. The remedy shall be limited to one or both of the following: (i) payment of monetary damages and applicable interest; and (ii) restitution of property, in which case the award shall provide that the disputing Party may pay monetary damages and any applicable interest in lieu of restitution'.[37] These IIAs clearly show that the contracting States tend to admit only monetary damages awards and seek to avoid restitution awards by the ISDS tribunals.

II   Requirement of Investor's Damage

The jurisprudence of the ICJ, as well as that of the Permanent Court of International Justice, on the indication of provisional measures requires the demanding party to establish that, in the absence of provisional measures, an *irreparable prejudice* or *harm* would be caused to their rights or interests before

---

35 The U.S. Model BIT of 2004 stipulates in Article 34 (Awards) that: "1. Where a tribunal makes a final award against a respondent, the tribunal may award, separately or in combination, only: (a) monetary damages and any applicable interest; (b) restitution of property, in which case the award shall provide that the respondent may pay monetary damages and any applicable interest in lieu of restitution". This article was maintained in the U.S. Model BIT of 2012.

36 Agreement between the Government of Canada and the Government of the Republic of Ecuador for the Promotion and Reciprocal Protection of Investments, available at http://unctad.org/sections/dite/iia/docs/bits/canada_ecuador.pdf (as of September 25, 2014).

37 Comprehensive Economic Partnership Agreement between Japan and the Republic of India, available at http://www.mofa.go.jp/region/asia-paci/india/epa201102/pdfs/ijcepa_ba_e.pdf (as of September 25, 2014).

a merit judgment will be rendered.[38] This requirement is satisfied in cases, for example, in which an ongoing armed conflict between parties is continuing,[39] or an execution of the death penalty by the defendant State is imminent.[40] In other words, the standard of *irreparable prejudice* was easily satisfied when human lives or health were in danger.[41]

On the other hand, where the prejudice alleged by the applicant could be monetarily compensated by the final judgment of the Court, this prejudice was considered as *reparable*. In this regard, the ICJ made clear, in the *Aegean Sea* case, that "the alleged breach by Turkey of the exclusivity of the right claimed by Greece to acquire information concerning the natural resources of areas of continental shelf, if it were established, is one that might be capable of reparation by appropriate means; and whereas it follows that the Court is unable to find in that alleged breach of Greece's rights such a risk of irreparable prejudice to rights in issue before the Court as might require the exercise of its power under Article 41 of the Statute to indicate interim measures for their preservation".[42] From the cases cited above, it becomes clear that the requirement of *irreparable prejudice* means that the alleged prejudice shall not be monetarily compensable by the merit judgment of the Court.

---

38   *Aegean Sea Continental Shelf Case* (Greece/Turkey), Request for the Indication of Interim Measures of Protection, Order of 11 September 1976, *I.C.J. Reports 1976*, p. 9, para. 25. In this case the Court stated that "the power of the Court to indicate interim measures under Article 41 of the Statute presupposes that irreparable prejudice should not be caused to rights which are the subject of dispute in judicial proceedings and that the Court's judgment should not be anticipated by reason of any initiative regarding the matters in issue before the Court".

39   *Frontier Dispute* (Burkina Faso/Republic of Mali), *I.C.J. Reports 1986*, p. 10, para. 21; *Application of the Convention on the Prevention and Punishment of the Crime of Genocide* (Bosnia and Herzegovina v. Serbia and Montenegro), *I.C.J. Reports 1993*, p. 19, para. 34; *Land and Maritime Boundary between Cameroon and Nigeria* (Cameroon v. Nigeria: Equatorial Guinea intervening), *I.C.J. Reports 1996*, p. 21, para. 35.

40   *LaGrand* (Germany v. United States of America), *I.C.J. Reports 1999*, p. 15, para. 24; *Avena and Other Mexican Nationals* (Mexico v. United States of America), *I.C.J. Reports 2003*, p. 91, para. 55.

41   *Nuclear Tests* (New Zealand v. France, Australia v. France), *I.C.J. Reports 1973*, p. 105, paras. 29–30; *United States Diplomatic and Consular Staff in Teheran* (United States of America v. Iran), *I.C.J. Reports 1979*, p. 20, para. 42. In the latter case, the ICJ stated that "continuance of the situation the subject of the present request exposes the human beings concerned to privation, hardship, anguish and even danger to life and health and thus to a serious possibility of irreparable harm".

42   *Aegean Sea Continental Shelf* (Greece v. Turkey), *I.C.J. Reports 1976*, p. 11, para. 33.

1   *The* Irreparable Damage *Test and the* Compensability *Test*

The ICSID tribunals follow the ICJ's standard. First, the ICSID tribunals have established the requirement of *irreparable harm or prejudice* for the recommendation of provisional measures.[43] In the *Tokios Tekeles* case, the tribunal cites the Order of the ICJ in the *Aegean Sea Continental Shelf* case, stating that 'the international jurisprudence on provisional measures indicates that a provisional measure is necessary where the actions of a party "are capable of causing or of threatening irreparable prejudice to the rights invoked".[44] Note also that the ICSID tribunals sometimes use the term *irreversible damage* instead of *irreparable prejudice*.[45] Second, the ICSID tribunals adopt the standard of compensability for examining the requirement of *irreparable damage*. In the *Plama* case, in fact, the tribunal stated that it "accepts Respondent's argument that harm is not irreparable if it can be compensated for by damages".[46] Also in the *Occidental* case, the tribunal stated that "any prejudice suffered as a result of the termination of the Block 15 contracts, if subsequently found illegal by the Tribunal, can readily be compensated by a monetary award".[47]

As is shown by other cases, the ICSID tribunals have already established a jurisprudence on the *compensability* test for examining whether the requirement of *irreparable damage* is satisfied or not.[48] However, even though the *compensability* test is firmly established as the ICSID jurisprudence, it can hardly be applied to the provisional measure procedure in the framework of ISDS without any modification.

First, in the ISDS, the claimant's final submissions normally consist of the demand of payment of some amount of money in the form of compensation, pecuniary reparation or damages. In other words, claimants rarely demand specific performance or restitution in kind by the host State.[49] Consequently,

---

43   *Plama Consortium Limited v. Republic of Bulgaria*, Order (6 September 2005), ICSID Case No. ARB/03/24, para. 38; *Phoenix* [2007], *supra* note 7, para. 33; *Occidental* [2007], *supra* note 9, para. 59.
44   *Tokios Tokelès v. Uklaine*, Order No.3 (18 January 2005), ICSID Case No. ARB/02/18, para. 8.
45   *Railroad* [2008], para. 34.
46   *Plama* [2005], *supra* note 43, para. 46.
47   *Occidental* [2007], *supra* note 9, para. 92.
48   *Perenco* [2009], *supra* note 3, para. 43; *Burlington* [2009], *supra* note 14, para. 79; *Quiborax* [2010], *supra* note 32, para. 156.
49   P.-Y. Tschanz & J.E. Vinuales, *supra* note 26, p. 732. This is partly because Article 54(1) of the ICSID Convention requires each Contracting State to *"enforce the pecuniary obligations imposed by that award* within its territories as if it were a final judgment of a court in that State" (*emphasis added*).

the damages which the investors allege for the merit judgment is always *compensable*. Should the tribunals apply unconditionally the *compensability* test to the investors' requests for provisional measures, those requests must be always rejected, since the prejudice alleged by claimants is *compensable*.

This problem already occurred in some cases. In the *Phoenix* case, for example, the Respondent—Czech Republic—alleged that "as the Claimant had not requested specific performance in its Request for arbitration, it cannot request a provisional measure to obtain it, as it was satisfied in its Request for arbitration to receive monetary compensation, which is not put in jeopardy if the provisional measure is not granted".[50] Similarly, in the *Paushok* case, the Respondent (Mongolian Republic) affirmed that "when the dispute only relates to a claim for damages, as in this case, there is no place for provisional measures, as damages can always be compensated with the payment of money".[51] These allegations by respondents became the position of the tribunal itself in the *Plama* case, in which the claimant claimed only the monetary damages. On the claim of claimant, the tribunal stated that "claimant has not sought restitution or any other relief from this Tribunal which would permit it to continue to operate the Nova Plama refinery"[52] and thereafter it concluded that if Nova Plama is placed into bankruptcy, sold to another investor or liquidated, and has its assets distributed to its creditors, such course of action "is not an issue in the ICSID arbitration".[53] Here, restitution or other relief was not took into consideration by the ICSID tribunal in the provisional measures procedure.

Second, the *compensability* test raises another problem. Even in the case where the amount of monetary compensation would extremely increase during the procedure of provisional measures, the tribunal has to deny the existence of *irreparable damage* if it applies the *compensability* test. In the *CEMEX* case, for example, the claimant requested provisional measures to cease the seizure of vessels by the Venezuelan government and to prevent an increase in claimant's damages by force of that seizure. However, the tribunal concluded that "the only consequence for them [Claimants] of those seizures would be a financial loss. Such a loss could be readily compensated by a damages award. Thus, the alleged harm is not 'irreparable' and there is neither necessity, nor

---

50 *Phoenix* [2007], *supra* note 7, para. 25.
51 Sergei Paushok, CJSC *Golden East Company*, CJSC *Vostokneftegaz Company v. The Government of Mongolia*, under the Rules of UNCITRAL, Order on Interim Measures (2 September 2008), para. 64.
52 *Plama* [2005], *supra* note 43, para. 47.
53 *Ibid.*, para. 47.

urgency to grant the requested provisional measures".⁵⁴ It is clear that the *compensability* test should not be applied directly to the provisional measures procedure where the claimants' claims generally consist of the payment of monetary compensation by the respondent.⁵⁵

2   Modification of the Compensability Test

It is apparent that the *compensability* test is not applicable to some cases in which the amount of eventual damages would extremely increase during the proceeding. Without any provisional measures, the increase of loss may finally cause the bankruptcy or liquidation of the investors, where investors cannot continue their investment activities. This means the disappearance and extinction of investment which is in issue before the ISDS. From the economic point of view, it is obviously more expensive to allow the continuation of the alleged acts of respondent which will be followed by subsequent recovery through a damages award, than to terminate or suspend the alleged act of respondent by provisional measures and maintain the *status quo*⁵⁶ Therefore, in some cases, the ISDS tribunals have modified and enlarged the notion of *irreparability* in order to avoid these potential problems.

(1)   The *Substantial Damage* Test

As an example of enlarging the notion of *irreparable damage*, the tribunal in the *Paushok* case adopted the *substantial damage* test. Based on the *Behring* case⁵⁷ before the Iran-U.S. Claims Tribunal, the *Paushok* Tribunal considered that "in international law, the concept of 'irreparable prejudice' does not

---

54   *CEMEX CARACAS Investments B.V. and CEMEX CARACAS II Investments B.V. v. Bolivarian Republic of Venezuela*, Decision on the Claimants' Request for Provisional Measures (3 March 2010), ICSID Case No. ARB/08/15, para. 58. *See also Occidental* [2007], *supra* note 9, para. 59, 98; *Plama* [2005], *supra* note 43, para. 64.

55   Naoki Idei, Kokka no Rippo Koui Oyobi Kyosei Shikko ni Taisuru Chusaitei no Zanteisochi [Provisional Measures of Arbitral Tribunals vis-à-vis the host State's legislation and enforcement,] *JCA Journal*, Vol. 57 (2010), p. 23. This author appropriately appreciated the problem in issue: "It is too narrow to consider that it is not necessary to protect the investments because they can be finally covered by the claims for damages. [...] Even if the Claimants' claims can be transformed to the damages claims, the amount of which can increase to be too huge. [...] We should take into consideration the fact that it is difficult to execute the monetary credit toward the host State".

56   *Ibid.*, p. 23.

57   *Behring International, Inc. v. Islamic Republic of Iranian Air Force, Iran Aircraft Industries, and The Government of Iran*, Award No. ITM/ITL 52-382-3 (21 June 1985), Iran-U.S.C.T.R., Vol. 8, p. 276.

necessarily require that the injury complained of be not remediable by an award of damages".[58] In quoting the opinion of Mr. K.P. Berger, the tribunal concluded that "this requirement [of irreparable damage] is satisfied if the delay in the adjudication of the main claim caused by the arbitral proceedings would lead to a 'substantial' (but not necessarily 'irreparable' as known in common law doctrine) prejudice for the requesting party".[59] It should be noticed, however, that this finding was based on the UNCITRAL Arbitral Rules and that the UNCITRAL Model Law uses in Article 17A the term of "harm not adequately reparable",[60] which may be different from the notion used by ICSID tribunals.

(2)   The *Extinction of Right* Test

In other cases, the *irreparable damage* test was modified to mean that where some rights may be definitively lost, the harm can be considered as *irreparable*. In the *Phoenix* case, for example, the tribunal stated that "it is common understanding that provisional measures should only be granted in situations of absolute necessity and urgency, in order to protect rights that could, absent these measures, be definitely lost".[61] This finding was followed by the *Occidental* Tribunal without any modification.[62] In the same way, in the *Quiborax* case the claimants demanded that the tribunal preserve their procedural rights—the access to the evidence—and the tribunal concluded that "any harm caused to the integrity of the ICSID proceedings, particularly with respect to a party's access to evidence or the integrity of the evidence produced could not be remedied by an award of damages".[63] These cases clearly show that if the claimants' rights would be "definitely lost" before the merit award, the supposed damage to the claimant's right should be considered as *irreparable* because such damage cannot be remediated monetarily by the subsequent award of damages. Note however that this standard was applied to cases where the procedural right was in dispute.

(3)   The *Going-Concern* Test

The applicability of the two modifications, examined above, is limited, i.e., they are applicable only in the UNCITRAL procedure or only to the procedural right.

---

58   *Paushok* [2008], *supra* note 51, para. 68.
59   *Ibid.*, paras. 67–68.
60   *Ibid.*, para. 69.
61   *Phoenix* [2007], *supra* note 7, para. 32.
62   *Occidental* [2007], *supra* note 9, para. 59.
63   *Quiborax* [2010], *supra* note 32, para. 157.

In addition to those modifications, some other tribunals have shown another important trend of enlarging the notion of *irreparability* by using the *going-concern* test.

According to the World Bank's Guideline on Foreign Investment, the *going-concern* means "an enterprise consisting of income-producing assets which has been in operation for a sufficient period of time to generate the data required for the calculation of future income and which could have been expected with reasonable certainty, if the taking had not occurred, to continue producing legitimate income over the course of its economic life in the general circumstances following the taking by the State".[64] *Going-concern* means, briefly, the future profitability of company and therefore the investment business itself.

In the *Perenco* case, in which the Claimant company demanded a provisional measure to cease the compulsory seizure of investment by the Ecuadorian government, the tribunal stated that "if Perenco's business in Ecuador were effectively brought to an end in this way, such injury could not, in the Tribunal's judgment, be adequately compensated by an award of damages should its claim be ultimately upheld".[65] Here, in summary, the tribunal considered that the "end of investor's business" constituted an *irreparable damage* for the purpose of provisional measures. *Business* in this context is equal to the *going-concern* as defined by the World Bank's Guideline.

In the same way, in the *Burlington* case,[66] the tribunal stated that "the risk here is the destruction of an ongoing investment and of its revenue producing potential which benefits both the investor and the State. ...There is also an obvious economic risk that it [investor] will cease operating altogether".[67] Here, too, the tribunal employed the notion of "revenue producing potential", i.e., *going-concern* of Burlington, as criteria for examining the *irreparability* of damage.

Finally, following the above two cases, the *CEMEX* tribunal made a distinction between (a) situations where the alleged prejudice can be readily compensated by awarding damages and (b) situations where there is a serious risk of destruction of a going-concern that constitutes the investment.[68] Here, the

---

64 World Bank, "Report to the Development Committee and Guidelines on Treatment of Foreign Investment," *International Legal Materials*, Vol. 31 (1992), p. 1366.
65 *Perenco* [2009], *supra* note 3, para. 46.
66 It should also be taken into consideration that the tribunal in this case adopted the standard of "harm not adequately reparable by an award of damages", which is admitted in the UNCITRAL Model Law. *Burlington* [2009], *supra* note 14, para. 82.
67 *Ibid.*, para. 83.
68 *CEMEX* [2010], *supra* note 54, para. 55.

tribunal makes clear that the *going-concern* test is generally applicable to the examination of *irreparability*. Similar reasoning can be found and applied in the non-ICSID arbitration. For example, in the *Paushok* case, based on the UNCITRAL Model Law, the tribunal stated that "immediate payment of the WPT [Windfall Profit Tax] allegedly owing to Mongolia would likely lead to the insolvency and bankruptcy of GEM (Mongolia's second largest gold producer) and the complete loss of Claimants' investment in that company"[69] and, because of such "unique circumstances of this case", the tribunal admitted that the requirement of proving damages had been fulfilled.

From the ISDS cases examined above, it becomes possible to draw conclusions. First, the *going-concern* test is already established in the ISDS jurisprudence as the applicable test for examining whether there is or is not an *irreparable* damage to claimants. In the process of applying this test, tribunals take into consideration such matters as the potential profitability of investment, the possible destruction or termination of investment, and whether the claimants are necessarily forced to cease the investment activity or to return its investments to their home States, or to a third State. Therefore, the ultimate goals and functions of the *going-concern* test is to protect the essential interest of investors and to preserve their investments.

Second, the purpose of the *going-concern* test is not only to preserve the essential interests of investors, but also to preserve and realize the mutual interests of both parties. On this point, the *Burlington* tribunal clearly stated that "an ongoing investment and...its revenue producing potential...benefit *both the investor and the State*",[70] and that "the consequences of the end of the investment relationship would affect the investor as well as the State".[71] Thus, the *going-concern* test largely rests on the idea that the going-concern or investment itself should be regarded as a common interest for both investors and host States, which should be consequently preserved by provisional measures.

Conclusions

It is possible to draw some conclusions with regard to the provisional measures in the ISDS. First, as to the requirement of investors' right, the ISDS tribunals have established the jurisprudence of applying the *plausibility* test for examining whether the claimant has a right or not at the merit phase. In some cases,

---

69   *Paushok* [2008], *supra* note 51, para. 77.
70   *Burlington* [2009], *supra* note 14, para. 83 (emphasis added).
71   *Ibid.*, para. 84.

tribunals are faced with the difficult problem of whether the right to specific performance of investors is *plausible* or not. Even though the ISDS tribunals seemingly apply the *contract* test, they adopt in reality the *proportionality* test, in order not to restrain excessively the sovereign power of the host States. This means that the requirement of investor's rights operates for preserving the host State's sovereign power.

Second, as to the requirement of investors' damage, the ISDS tribunals have established the jurisprudence of applying the *irreparable* damage test for examining whether the claimant would suffer serious damage from the host State's interference, which could not be remedied by the tribunal's merit award. The *compensability* test has been adopted by the ICJ in this regard. However, this test cannot be directly applied in the ISDS, as far as the investment damage is almost always *compensable* by the monetary award. Consequently, in the place of the *compensability* test, the ISDS tribunals have established the *going-concern* test. This means that the tribunals aim to preserve the essential interests of the investors, in other words, the profitability of the investor company itself.

Third, as to the question of whether the *community of investment interests* can be found also in the provisional measures procedure, it is possible to conclude that such a "community" exists as far as the ISDS tribunals make efforts to preserve the right and interests of both sides of parties, i.e., investors and host States. As we saw, the ISDS tribunals avoid imposing excessive burden on one of the parties, in that tribunals tend not to order provisional measures in favour of one party.[72] In this sense, both the *proportionality* test and the *going-concern* test play a role of balancing the interests of the parties. In this regard, the *Burlington* tribunal stated that "[t]he consequence of the end of the investment relationship would affect the investors as well as the State. ... This last observation shows that provisional measures are in the interest of both sides if they are adequately structured..."[73] In the same meaning, the *Saipem* tribunal stated that "the Tribunal considers that under Article 47 of the Convention a tribunal enjoys a broad discretion when ruling on provisional measures, but should not recommend provisional measures lightly and should weigh the parties' divergent interests in the light of all the circumstances of the case".[74] The tribunal in this case concluded that "[s]uch a recommendation

---

72 C.H. Schreuer, *supra* note 15, p. 802.
73 *Burlington* [2009], *supra* note 14, para. 85.
74 *Saipem S.p.A v. The People's Republic of Bangladesh*, Decision on Jurisdiction and Recommendation on Provisional Measures (21 March 2007), ICSID Case No. ARB/05/07, para. 175.

[of provisional measures] strikes a fair balance between the parties' interests".[75] Thus, "a fair balance" between interests of parties is of importance also in the provisional measures procedure.

Fourth and finally, it is necessary to examine whether the interests of parties can be common interests equivalent to a "community". In this regard, it is not useless to point out that investment itself is aimed to make benefits for both parties or, in other words, to establish a win–win relationship between parties. Here, it becomes clear that the notion of "community of investment interests" is largely based on the common interests of parties, i.e., investment itself. The ISDS tribunals, faced with the request for provisional measures, have taken into consideration the common interests of parties in order that this win-win relationship should continue.

---

75   *Ibid.*, para. 184.

CHAPTER 8

New Relationship between the United Nations and Regional Organizations in Peace and Security: A Case of the African Union

Hironobu Sakai

I Introduction

Since the end of the Cold War, the United Nations (UN) Security Council (SC) has energetically exercised its functions, particularly in the field of international peace and security. The mandate authorized by the SC in accordance with Chapter VII of the UN Charter, involving the use of force, has usually been implemented through a Member State or Member States, as the UN does not have its own proper instrument to conduct the military enforcement measures stipulated under Chapter VII.[1] Moreover, in addition to such a group of Member States, there are some regional or sub-regional organizations that have been admirably active in implementing the mandate from the UN.[2]

The African Union (AU) has largely contributed to UN operations for the purpose of supporting peace and security on the African continent, especially since the beginning of the 21st century.[3] However, whenever the AU takes any action in accordance with its own constitution, it should also be required to pay attention to decisions taken by the UNSC and follow them under Chapter VIII of the UN Charter if the action involves the use of force. The more involved the AU seeks to be and the more autonomously it takes action related to the peace and security in the region, the greater the tension may be regarding power between the AU and UN.

African nations began for reinforcing their solidarity when they established the AU in 2002, after considering the ever unsatisfactory practices of the Organization for African Unity (OAU), the predecessor of the AU. One of the most striking features of the AU's institutional developments is that it may

---

[1] Danesh Sarooshi, *The United Nations and the Development of Collective Security. The Delegation by the UN Security Council of its Chapter VII Powers* (Oxford University Press, 1999), pp. 27–32.
[2] Hilaire McCoubrey and Justine Morris, *Regional Peacekeeping in the Post-Cold War Era* (Kluwer Law International, 2000), p. 36.
[3] On the outline of the AU at the aspect of peace and security, Rodrigo Tavares, *Regional Security. The Capacity of International Organizations* (Routledge, 2010), pp. 21–34.

intervene in a Member State for particular reasons, even with force, under its Constitutive Act. This demonstrates a shift in attitude on the part of the African countries, from a reluctance to take action to aggressiveness to engagement not only in conflicts between Member States but also in humanitarian disasters or genocidal affairs within a Member State.[4] The result has been that the AU's autonomy has become greater and more intense than that of the OAU, so that it is possible that the AU, when performing its mandate on the African continent, may clash with the UN, in particular the SC, which has "primary responsibility for the maintenance of international peace and security" under Article 24 of the UN Charter.

This chapter considers the practices and procedures of the AU as well as UN practices related to the AU, in examining the AU's characteristics and how the mature of this organization influences its conduct, for the purpose of clarifying the relationship between the two organizations. Thus this chapter, first, examines relevant provisions of the constituent instruments of the AU and actual UN practices in cooperation with the AU and, second, closely considers the AU–UN partnership. Finally, some potential relationships between the UN and the regional organizations derived from a dialectical perspective.[5]

II AU's Relation to the UN in Its Constitutive Act and the UN's Responses

1 *The AU as a Regional Agency within the Meaning of Chapter VIII of the UN Charter*

(1)   Transition from the OAU to the AU and Its Effects

In July 2002, the AU was officially launched in Durban, South Africa, after the Constitutive Act of the AU was adopted at the 36th OAU summit in Togo in July 2000, and came into effect on 26 May 2001.

This Act consists of 33 Articles, and enshrines the objectives of the AU (Article 3) and principles in accordance with which it shall function (Article 4). The Act also specifies the organs of the AU (Article 5) and powers and

---

[4] For the transition from the OAU to AU and its effects to the African security problems, Solomon Gomes, "The Peacemaking Role of the OAU and the AU: A Comparative Analysis," in John Akokpari, Angela Ndinga-Muvumba and Tim Murithi eds., *The African Union and Its Institutions* (Fanele, 2008), pp. 113–130.

[5] Such a dialectical perspective should be suggested by Professor Ryuichi Ida's idea on the relationship between International Organization and its Member States. Ryuichi Ida, "L'O.N.U. et la souveraineté" (1991), pp. 435–481.

functions of each of those organs (Articles 6–23). At first glance, the AU appears to take over many important functions from the OAU. The Act, however, introduces some competences of the AU that are completely different from those of the OAU, such as the right of the AU to intervene in a Member State.[6]

As for its relation to the UN, the OAU has no express provisions in its Charter. Considering, however, that the Secretary-General of the OAU has been repeatedly invited to sessions of the UN General Assembly as well as to meetings of the UNSC, and that the Secretary-General of the OAU was asked to prepare a report under Article 54 of the UN Charter, and also that the objectives of the OAU are not viewed as conflicting with the UN Charter, it is safe to say that the OAU has been recognized as a regional agency within the meaning of Chapter VIII of the UN Charter.[7] Although, during the period of the OAU, there were some arguments against its status as a UN Chapter VIII regional organization because there was no basis for it either in the OAU Charter nor in its subsequent practice.[8]

In contrast, while the Constitutive Act of the AU similar to the OAU Charter, it contains no express provision on AU's relation to the UN, except for Article 3(e), which refers to the UN Charter, the AU can naturally be regarded as a regional agency under Chapter VIII of the UN Charter as well, on the assumption that the AU should be virtually a successor of the OAU. Adjusting and renewing itself to the new post-colonial globalized order, the Act still provides that the AU shall "achieve greater unity and solidarity between the African countries and the peoples of Africa" and shall "promote peace, security, and stability on the continent", which is consistent with the provisions under Chapter VIII of the UN Charter literally.

In addition, most crucial on this matter is the intention of the Member States of the AU, which, though not addressed in the Constitutive Act, has been clearly expressed in the Protocol relating to the Establishment of the Peace and SC of the AU. This Protocol contains relatively detailed provisions on the relationship between the AU and UN, referring to Chapter VIII of the UN Charter, as will be seen in the following section.

---

6 For the background of the adaptation of the Constitutive Act and the overview of its provisions, Corinne A.A. Packer and Donald Rukare, "The New African Union and Its Constitutive Act," *American Journal of International Law*, Vol. 96 (2002), pp. 366–377.

7 Waldemar Hummer & Michael Schweitzer, "Article 52," in Bruno Simma ed., *The Charter of the United Nations. A Commentary. Vol. I* (2nd ed., Oxford University Press, 2002), p. 830.

8 S. Azadon Tiewul, "Relations between the United Nations Organization and the Organization of African Unity in the Settlement of Secessionist Conflicts," *Harvard International Law Journal*, Vol. 16 (1975), pp. 278–286.

(2) Supremacy of the UN Over the AU

An objective of the Protocol relating to the Establishment of the Peace and Security Council of the AU is to establish the Peace and Security Council (PSC), which is responsible for the formulation and implementation of the main political decisions involving conflict prevention, peacekeeping, peace building or problematic humanitarian intervention.[9] The PSC, one of the main organs of the AU, particularly in the field of peace and security, was not created through the AU Constitutive Act. Rather, it has grown out of an ad hoc process to reform the Mechanism for Conflict Prevention, Management and Resolution, which was adopted by the OAU Assembly of Heads of States and Government in June 1993.[10] The outcome of this process resulted in the adoption of the Protocol in Durban on 9 July 2002, and it finally came into force on 26 December 2003. The circumstances that led to the establishment of the PSC were mainly political; therefore, its functions may be said to include—promoting peace, security and stability in Africa; anticipating conflicts and undertaking preventive diplomacy; and making peace through the use of good offices, mediation, conciliation and enquiry. However, it may, unlike its predecessor, exercise the power to decide whether to intervene in a Member State, pursuant to Article 4(j) of the Constitutive Act.

As for the AU's relations with the UN, Article 17 of the Protocol explicitly deals with the Relationship with the United Nations and Other International Organizations. This Article clearly expresses two points with regard to the AU's relation to the UN. First, the AU may ask the UN to provide any financial, logistical and military support for its own activities in the promotion and maintenance of peace, security and stability in Africa in the capacity of a regional organization within the meaning of Chapter VIII of the UN Charter.[11] That is to say, it is presumed in Article 17 of the Protocol that the AU's peace operations

---

9   One of reasons why the PSC was not provided in the AU Constitutive Act may lie in some hesitancy among the AU membership to establish the PSC, which arguably represents a struggle between notions of communal authority tarnished by a past history of paralysis and a current globalized demand on and within Africa to establish a continental locus of binding authority able to use military means for better continental governance. Henry Richardson, "The African Union and the New Pan-Africanism: Rushing to Organize or Timely Shift: The Danger of Oligarchy within the Pan-Africanist Authority of the African Union," *Transnational Law & Contemporary Problems*, Vol. 13 (2003), p. 272.

10 Paul. D. Williams, "The Peace and Security Council of the African Union: Evaluating an Embryonic International Institution," *Journal of Modern African Studies*, Vol. 47 (2009), pp. 604–607.

11 Abdou Yéro Ba, "La contribution de l'Union africaine au maintien de la paix," *Revue de Droit International et de Droit Comparé*, Tom. LXXXIII (2006), p. 209.

belong under Chapter VIII of the UN Charter, where the concrete forms of cooperation between these organizations, as the AU expects, lie mainly in the UN's financial, logistical and military support, not in command and control within the UN. Second, the AU Member States recognize that the UNSC should have the primary responsibility for the maintenance of international peace and security, and that they cooperate and closely work with it through the PSC to promote and maintain peace, security and stability in Africa. Therefore, the states, while confirming the supremacy of the UN over the AU in the field of international peace and security, stick to their own principle, "African Solutions for African Problems", which means that the AU should take primary responsibility for peace and stability in Africa.

On the last point, however, such dichotomy may be barely formed on the delicate balance to be maintained between the two elements: the UN's superiority in international peace and security, and the AU's superiority in African peace and stability. Therefore, the relationship between the two organizations could deteriorate and be in danger if this balance were significantly upset by the increasing domination of one organization over the other or by one organization's ignoring the voice of the other. The African leaders have, at the launching of this new African organization, aimed to give it more dominant power in some ambitious provisions of the relevant documents, such as a famous provision, Article 4(h) of the AU Constitutive Act.

2 AU's Attempts to Bypass UN Control under Chapter VIII of the UN Charter

(1) Implications of the Right of the AU to Intervene in Its Member States

The AU Constitutive Act refers to its right to intervene in a Member State in Article 4(h), which provides for "the right of the Union to intervene in a Member State pursuant to a decision of the Assembly in respect of grave circumstances, namely: war crimes, genocide and crimes against humanity". A similar provision is not found in the OAU Charter, and therefore the most significant differences between the AU Constitutive Act and the OAU Charter concern this intervention.[12] It is clear, based on the insertion of this provision into the Act, that the leaders of the AU decisively determined to move away

---

12 Jonathan D. Rechner, "From the OAU to the AU: A Normative Shift with Implications for Peacekeeping and Conflict Management, or Just a Name Change?" *Vanderbilt Journal of Transnational Law*, Vol. 39 (2006), p. 562. Osenga Badibake says that this right is recognized only as an exception of the Non-interference Principle. Thérèse Osenga Badibake, *Pouvoir des organisations internationales et souveraineté des États* (L'Harmattan, 2010), p. 99.

from the position of the OAU, in which traditional legal rules dominated, such as the principle of non-intervention. Thus, African leaders have renounced their long-established policy and decided to promote a new interventionist approach to African problems within the framework of the AU.

The leaders of the African continent have bestowed on the AU the right to intervene through the AU's Constitutive Act for several reasons. Among them, the most convincing is that the incorporation of that right into the Act derived from the concern about the would-be failure of a new organization to intervene to stop gross and massive human rights violations, which Africa has often faced in the past. As the leaders were concerned about the potential inability of the AU to prevent such violations, such as the genocide that occurred in Rwanda in 1994, they have sought to establish in the Act a legal basis by which the AU may take action to halt any cruel and inhuman conduct.[13]

In addition to these concerns, it should also be highlighted that most African states have refused to cooperate with the OAU's peacekeeping and peacemaking efforts. It is natural that the consent of the parties to a conflict should be indispensable to the implementation of engagement by the OAU. However, the heads of African states, at least some of them, realized that the AU needed to be ensured of the possibility of taking action without the consent of any parties to a conflict, when its Member States are faced with humanitarian disasters or immense human rights violations and when the AU cannot expect any cooperation from the parties to be forthcoming.

The move to give the AU stronger teeth further motivated African leaders to amend Article 4(h) to extend it to situations, in which the AU would be able to intervene in its Member States. In February 2003, the Heads of States and Government of the AU, meeting in their first extraordinary session, adopted many changes to the Constitutive Act, one of which was an amendment to Article 4(h). This amendment adds, at the end of the sub-paragraph of this provision, the words "as well as serious threat to legitimate order to restore peace and stability to the Member State of the Union upon the recommendation of the Peace and Security Council". In other words, it extends the right of the AU to intervene in a Member State to include situations in which the legitimate order is under threat. The Amendment is not yet in force, but there are some doubts as to whether such an extension of the AU's powers would be consistent with the other grounds for intervention, which purport to protect Africans from grave violations of human rights when their governments are

---

13   Ben Kioko, "The Right of Intervention under the African Union's Constitutive Act: From Non-interference to Non-Intervention," *International Review of the Red Cross*, Vol. 85 (2003), pp. 812–815.

unable or unwilling to do so,[14] as well as to reject unconstitutional changes of the government to safeguard the legitimate order.[15]

Thus, Article 4(h) of the AU Constitutive Act in conjunction with Article 4(j) turns the AU into a more powerful organization with robust mandate, by which it may intervene in its Member State to stop the commission of war crimes, crimes against humanity and genocide, or to prevent the establishment of an illegal regime in a Member State through a military coup, as long as the AU Assembly authorizes it to do so. Article 4(h) is meant for grave circumstances in collapsed states, such as Somalia, which has no structure to protect civilians from devastations that accompany those collapses, while Article 4(j) is meant to assist weak states that cannot protect their citizens from imminent danger. Therefore, these Articles have been hailed as marking a far-reaching departure from the OAU's non-interference principle.[16]

The point here is that the African nations have changed their attitude, literally, towards African conflicts which arise between nations or within a single nation, and that the AU has a plan to take the lead in resolving them, which is a completely different approach from the OAU's reluctant stance. According to the Constitutive Act and the Protocol, the AU may exercise its functions and perform its mandate with force, apparently even without authorization from the UNSC.[17]

Consequently, the Constitutive Act and the Protocol provided the AU with a legally substantial basis for its military operations in a Member State. The next problem for the AU, however, was how it may accomplish its objectives, and particularly how it may intervene militarily in a Member State. What the African leaders determined first, is that the AU should establish its proper force to be deployed in disputed districts, although this does not exclude the

---

14   Evarist Baimu & Kathryn Sturman, "Amendment to the African Union's Right to Intervene. A Shift from Human Security to Regime Security?" *African Security Review*, Vol. 12, No. 2 (2003), pp. 41–42.
15   Jeremy I. Levitt, "Pro-democratic Intervention in Africa," in *idem* ed., *Africa. Mapping New Boundaries in International Law* (Hart Publishing, 2008), p. 139.
16   Samuel M. Makinda & F. Wafula Okumu, *The African Union. Challenges of Globalization, Security, and Governance* (Routledge, 2008), p. 38.
17   Jeremy I. Levitt, "The Peace and Security Council of the African Union and the United Nations Security Council: The Case of Darfur, Sudan," in Niels Blokker and Nico Schrijver eds., *The Security Council and the Use of Force. Theory and Reality—A Need for Change?* (Martinus Nijhoff Publishers, 2005), pp. 229–236. To emphasize "exceptionnalism dans le cadre du continent africain" in the right to intervene by the AU in accordance with Article 4(h), Laurence Boisson de Chazournes, "Les relations entre organisations regionals et organisations universelles," *Recueil des Cours*, Tom. 347 (2010), p. 295.

possibility that the AU would authorize Member States to dispatch their own troops to a conflict area on its behalf.

(2)   Establishment of an African Standby Force

Having faced many brutal conflicts that the OAU did not prevented in the years prior to the early 21st century, many African leaders have continued to desire that a new organization should be equipped with strong weapons for the implementation of peacekeeping missions, that is, an African Standby Force (ASF). This plan was expressed in Article 13(1) of the PSC Protocol in 2002, which also lays down the role of the Member States to establish national standby contingents for the ASF as well as the areas where the ASF shall perform its functions, including intervention in a Member State in accordance with Article 4(h) and (j) of the Constitutive Act.

What should be noted particularly in this Protocol is Article 17, which, as mentioned above, governs the relationship between the AU, in particular the PSC, and the UN in the field of maintaining peace and security. The Article states that, in the fulfilment of its mandate to promote and maintain peace, security and stability in Africa, the PSC shall cooperate and closely work with the SC, and it also recognizes the SC as having the primary responsibility for the maintenance of international peace and security. Because this provision makes specific reference to Chapter VIII of the UN Charter, the PSC is obliged to cooperate and closely work with the SC, and the ASF missions are mandated by the PSC within the framework of the UN, in particular under authorization by the SC in the case of the use of force.

With regard to the relationship between the AU and the UN in this field, while the UN Charter as well as the Protocol confirms that the UNSC assumes primary responsibility for the maintenance of international peace and security, it should be recalled that Article 3(f) of the AU Constitutive Act clearly states that the AU has primary responsibility for the promotion of peace, security and stability in Africa. Thus, while the primary responsibility of the SC is recognized in the Protocol, the ASF mandate is approved by the PSC, and ASF missions are primarily under the AU command and control on the African continent in accordance with the Constitutive Act. Apparently, then, the AU has superiority over the UN, at least in peace operations in the African region, unless they involve the use of force inconsistent with the UN Charter.[18]

---

18   Cilliers & Sturman say that the AUPSC can authorize the deployment of peacekeepers as a regional organization in terms of Chapter VIII of the UN Chapter though ideally the ASF would be deployed under a mandate from the UN. Jakkie Cilliers & Kathryn Sturman,

The original intention by the African leaders was that African troops under the control of the AU would operate effectively enough to implement its mandate relating to regional security, including even military intervention in a Member State for humanitarian reasons, and part of this objective has been realized in the establishment of the ASF in the Protocol. Therefore, the Constitutive Act lays the groundwork for conferring on the AU the authority to intervene in a Member State with the AU's troops, namely the ASF, which is established by the Protocol. It has been presumed from the outset in these documents of the AU that, if that were the case, a conflict would necessarily result between the competences of the two organizations, the AU and the UN. Moreover, the AU has been expected to take over from the UN responsibilities in the area of peace and security on the African continent, even when the mandate approved by the AU involves the use of force, and when the ASF could use such force without any prior authorization by the SC, for example, for humanitarian intervention. In any case, nothing in the AU Constitutive Act or the PSC Protocol explicitly requires the AU to seek prior authorization from the SC before authorizing or launching such interventions.[19]

This ambitious plan may undermine the long-established legal framework of the relationship between the UN and regional organizations, including the AU, within the UN Charter, especially in Chapter VIII. How has the UN dealt with this problem as it has confronted these initiatives by the AU to strengthen its own capacities for regional security?

3   UN's Efforts in the Construction of a Partnership with the AU

Within the SC, discussions on the relationship between the UN and regional organizations have occurred many times, and more often, in particular, since the publication of "Agenda for Peace" in 1992. This has resulted in the adoption of some resolutions or presidential statements since the establishment of the AU in 2002. Among these statements was the SC's first presidential statement on its relationship with the AU, on 19 November 2004, in which it welcomed the establishment of the PSC and recognized "the importance of strengthening

---

"Challenges Facing the AU's Peace and Security Council," *African Security Review*, Vol. 13, No. 1 (2004), p. 98.

19   Jeremy I. Levitt, "The Peace and Security Council of the African Union: The Known Unknowns," *Transnational Law & Contemporary Problems*, Vol. 13 (2003), p. 125. However, it is said that the composition of the ASF expected under the AUPSC Protocol is quite different from that provided by the Memorandum of Understanding between the AU and African sub-regional organizations. Ademola Abass, "African Peace and Security Architecture and the Protection of Human Security," in *idem* ed., *Protecting Human Security in Africa* (Oxford University Press, 2010), pp. 262–264.

cooperation with the African Union in order to help build its capacity to deal with collective security challenges, including through the African Union's undertaking of rapid and appropriate responses to emerging crisis situations, peacekeeping and peace-building". This statement, citing the examples of the African missions in Sudan and Burundi, expressed appreciation for the strengthening of practical cooperation between the UN and AU, and invited the UN Secretary-General to explore new means of cooperation between these organizations, "especially taking into consideration the expanded mandate and the new Organs of the African Union".[20]

The 2005 World Summit Outcome, adopted on 16 September 2005, is notable in terms of expressing the relationship between the UN and the AU in the area of peace and security. The UN General Assembly, having already referred to the cooperation between the UN and the AU, and having highlighted the need to enforce the institutional capacity of the PSC in its Resolution 59/213 on 20 December 2004, recognized in the Outcome, "the important contribution to peace and security by regional organizations as provided for under Chapter VIII of the Charter and the importance of forging predictable partnerships and arrangements between the United Nations and regional organizations", and noted "in particular, given the special needs of Africa, the importance of a strong African Union".[21] Since then, following the actions of the General Assembly, the SC has regularly adopted resolutions or presidential statements that not only confirm this part of the World Summit Outcome but also stress the importance for the UN of developing the regional organization's ability to deploy peacekeeping forces rapidly in support of UN operations.[22]

In particular, concerning its relations with the AU, the UN has had a serious concern from the beginning about the AU's ability to engage in peacekeeping on the African continent. Thus, the UN Secretary-General, in his report on 1 September 2004, referred to the assistance provided by the UN in the setting up of the PSC,[23] and, in November of the same year, estimated that "[T]he African Union will not be able to implement its multifaceted agenda without the sustained support of the international community".[24] In July 2006, the Secretary-General also explored the possibility that increased regional capacity for effective action, undertaken within the framework of the SC's

---

20   UN Doc. S/PRST/2004/44, 19 November 2004.
21   UN Doc. A/RES/60/1, 24 October 2005, para.93.
22   UN Doc. S/RES/1631 (2005), 17 October 2005, pre.para. 3, op.para. 3; UN Doc. S/RES/1809 (2008), 16 April 2008, pre.para. 8, op.para. 4.
23   UN Doc. A/59/303, 1 September 2004, paras. 4–5.
24   UN Doc. A/59/591, 30 November 2004, para. 13.

primary responsibility for peace and security, should be promoted at a time of sustained peacekeeping demand, particularly in Africa, and he has supported the idea that the AU should develop an African stand-by force to ensure more equal ability between the UN and AU in maintaining peace and security.[25]

Therefore, the signing of the Declaration on "Enhancing UN–AU Cooperation: Framework for the Ten-Year Capacity Building Programme for the African Union", on 16 November 2006, was a significant landmark for both of these organizations. In this Declaration, the UN and AU, recalling the 2005 World Summit Outcome and reaffirming that the evolving Framework should cover all aspects of the cooperation between them, agreed to give special emphasis to enhancing the AU's capacities in the following areas: (a) institution-building, human resources development and financial management; (b) peace and security; (c) human rights; (d) political, legal and electoral matters; (e) social, economic, cultural and human development; (f) food security and environmental protection.[26] Immediately after the signing of this Declaration, the SC welcomed the AU in its presidential statement, and invited further collaboration with the PSC to help build the AU's capacity to undertake rapid and appropriate responses to emerging situations, and to develop effective strategies for conflict prevention, peacekeeping and peacebuilding. In the same statement, the SC also recognized that "in some cases, the AU may be authorized by the Security Council to deal with collective security challenges on the African continent", and in this connection, encouraged the increased exchange of information and sharing of experiences, best practices and lessons learned between the SC and the AU as well as other relevant organizations.[27]

Thus, as observed, the SC has regularly adopted certain resolutions and presidential statements on the relations between the UN and AU. These documents have certain points in common.

First, they mostly include the term "Chapter VIII of the UN Charter".[28] They also sometimes remind the Member States of the importance of there being a stronger relationship between the UN and the AU 'consistent with the principles laid down in Articles 52 and 53 of the United Nations Charter'.[29] In these words, the SC confirms that the relationship between the UN and AU should

---

25 UN Doc. A/61/204-S/2006/590, 28 July 2006, paras. 38, 56.
26 UN Doc. A/61/630, 12 December 2006, Annex.
27 UN Doc. S/PRST/2007/7, 28 March 2007.
28 UN Doc. S/RES/1631 (2005), 17 October 2005; UN Doc. S/RES/1809 (2008), 16 April 2008; UN Doc. S/PRST/2006/39, 20 September 2006; UN Doc. S/PRST/2007/42, 6 November 2007.
29 UN Doc. S/PRST/2004/27, 20 July 2004; UN Doc. S/PRST/2004/44, 19 November 2004.

be regulated within the framework of Chapter VIII of the UN Charter. This conveys that the SC has always shown a fixed determination to secure closer coordination between the UN and AU, and, in the case of the use of force, to take control over any AU military operations, in accordance with the UN Charter.[30]

Second, the SC, while stressing Chapter VIII of the UN Charter as the core for regulating the UN's relation with the AU, has constantly envisaged this relation as being connected—particularly to conflict prevention, peacekeeping or peacebuilding, not to enforcement action. In other words, the SC avoids placing excessive emphasis on the superiority of the UN over regional organizations, including the AU, but rather stresses mutual cooperation between them in the field of non-enforceable action. In such a practical way, the SC is attempting to reduce unnecessary tensions between the UN and AU with regard to the competence of military actions, although these records always affirm the SC's primary responsibility for the maintenance of international peace and security.

Third, as the discussion above, one of the primary targets for cooperation between the two organizations that is set out in these documents is the improvement of the AU's capacity for conflict prevention, peacekeeping or peacebuilding in African conflicts. Behind this target setting lies the idea that Africa should settle African problems with its own hands. This notion may derive from the increasing independence and expectations of the African nations that they should deal with their own problems in place of the UN, as well as from what the UN views as an opportunity, as it has been concerned about the expansion of conflicts and been unwilling to bear the heavy and continuous burden of containing conflicts, and keeping peace on the African continent.

Thus, both sides have shared in the construction of a new relationship between them related to ensuring peace and security in the region, and more specifically, to formulating a mode of peacekeeping missions to coordinate two requirements: what type of missions the AU engages in and how the UN provides support for them. Some practical forms of cooperation between the two organizations have gradually appeared as their practices have developed in the field of peace and security on the African continent.

---

30 This practice may derive from the UN's idea that the role of the AU should be strengthened as "Chapter VIII Regional Agency." Mutoy Mubiala, "Cooperation between the United Nations, the European Union and the African Union for Peace and Security in Africa," *Studia Diplomatica*, Vol. LX (2007), pp. 119–120.

III   Possibility of New Development in the AU–UN Partnership

1   *Two Types of Cooperation between the AU and the UN in Peace Operations*

The main peace operations launched by the AU thus far are as follows: the AU Mission in Burundi (AMIB),[31] the AU Mission in the Sudan (AMIS)[32] and the AU Mission in Somalia (AMISOM),[33] of which the first two are closely related to UN peacekeeping operations.[34] The role of peacekeeping forces from the AU and UN should be discussed here within the overarching architecture of international peace and security in the respective regions.

Initially, as seen in these cases, it should be acknowledged that the AU has not yet achieved the establishment of the ASF system in the context of its peace missions. Thus, as the ASF has not been available, the AU has been obliged in each case to ask its Member States to provide troops so that it could form a force for implementing the peace mission mandate. These ad hoc AU forces are surely a convenient tool based on a realistic approach, as a substitute for the as yet unavailable ASF, and are suitable and even more appropriate for the decentralized structure of the AU organization. However, this does not mean that they are not deficient in fulfilling their mandate. They have poor equipment and little training for peace missions; they lack unity in standards of conduct; there is a permanent shortage of participating troops in AU missions due to the increasing number and enlarged scale of conflicts, as well as to the uneasiness of their own countries and so on. These weaknesses of ad hoc AU forces may not be entirely corrected by the AU itself; therefore, effective solutions require that the AU obtain solid and continuous help from outside. The UN is undoubtedly the most likely and pragmatic choice to play this role, thus, the ways in which the UN and AU can cooperate should be considered and elaborated on briefly and effectively here.

Empirically and practically, two types of cooperation may be confirmed between the UN and AU with regard to peace missions in these African conflicts. One is that the institution and deployment of the AU mission precedes a UN mission, and that the latter has replaced or would be supposed to replace the AU mission immediately after it has accomplished and completed its

---

31   AU Doc. Central Organ/MEC/AMB/Comm.(XCI), 2 April 2003.
32   AU Doc. PSC/AHG/Comm.(X), 25 May 2004; AU Doc. PSC/PR/Comm.(XVII), 20 October 2004.
33   AU Doc. PSC/PR/Comm.(LXIX), 19 January 2007.
34   Christian Walter, "Article 52," in Bruno Simma *et al.* eds., *The Charter of the United Nations. A Commentary. Volume II* (3rd ed., Oxford University Press, 2012), p. 1460.

mandate. The transition from the AMIB to the UN Operation in Burundi (ONUB)[35] or the plan to shift from the AMIS to the UN Mission in the Sudan (UNMIS)[36] are examples. The AMISOM, which is to be replaced by a UN peace operation, may be also included in this group.[37] This cooperation may be called the "transition model". This type of military cooperation has been observed in some cases of multinational forces in African conflicts, because it has been quite useful in suppressing disturbances and maintaining order in several respects.

First, the "transition model" is supposed to operate so quickly that an AU peace mission would be able to tackle a conflict in its very early stages. It stands to reason that the earlier a mission started, the more successful it would be in completing its objectives. Because an AU mission, if well organized, should be able to access African conflicts geographically and psychologically more easily than the UN, it is reasonable and appropriate for it to attempt to deal with them first, with the aim of minimizing damage and preventing extended hostilities. Moreover, following an AU mission to manage conflict, a UN mission can then enter and work for peacekeeping, peacebuilding, national conciliation and so on. Second, such a role may serve to promote the efficient use of resources. It is clear that the AU cannot deploy its missions in local regions for a long period from the perspective of personnel and finances. Therefore, a UN mission, which UN Member States as a whole may provide with personnel and financial support, would be more suitable for a state rebuilding project, the completion of which would require much more time and a higher cost. Contrary to these positive aspects, however, it should be noted out that the AU has sometimes shown an inability to protect civilians. Moreover, it must be

---

35   UN Doc. S/RES/1545 (2004), 21 May 2004; UN Doc. S/2004/210, 16 March 2004, paras. 100–102. Mutoy Mubiala, "Peacekeeping Operations: The Examples of Burundi and Sudan," in Abdulqawi A. Yusuf and Fatsah Ouguergouz eds., *The African Union: Legal and Institutional Framework. A Manual on the Pan-African Organization* (Martinus Nijhoff Publishers, 2012), pp. 362–365.

36   UN Doc. S/RES/1590 (2005), 24 March 2005. The transition from AMIS to UNMIS was not realized, because the Government of the Sudan rejected the deployment of UNMIS to the Darfur region. Thus, the AU and the UN, considering that intention by the Government of the Sudan as well as the expectation by the AU of the transition from AMIS to UNMIS due to the financial and logistic burden, have invented a new architecture, UNAMID. Mutoy Mubiala, "Les operations de maintien de la paix de l'Union Africaine: Etudes de cas (Burundi et Soudan)," in Abdulqawi A. Yusuf et Fatah Ouguergouz, dir., *L'Union Africaine: Cadre juridique et institutionnel. Manuel sur l'organisation panafricaine* (Pedone, 2013), pp. 319–322.

37   UN Doc. S/RES/1744 (2007), 20 February 2007, op.para. 9.

added that the AU would lose its own primary responsibility in managing African conflicts when the UN took over an AU mission, as the SC would take primary responsibility in its operation.

Another type of operation may be named the "hybrid model", which means that both the AU and UN provide the personnel for a single mission. Typical is the AU/UN Hybrid Operation in Darfur (UNAMID).[38] This sort of the cooperation can be viewed as a revision of the "transition model", so that some faults of the latter may be corrected through AU–UN collaboration.[39]

This type of mission greatly improves the ways of sharing and making effective use of the limited resources between the AU and UN. Both organizations, facing shortages in their budgets and difficulty in constantly providing troops for peace missions, have experienced problems and been reluctant to undertake their respective independent missions. These concerns, if only some of them, may be relieved if the AU and UN collaborated on sending personnel and providing logistical and financial support for a single mission, thus sparing their respective resources.[40] Additionally, it could be expected that the standards of equipment and conduct and the quality of training of troops, mainly from African states, would be developed and equalized in a mission as a whole through the UN's participating in it. Also important may be that the political will of the international community would be expressed if the UN became directly involved in African conflicts by participating in a peace mission.[41]

---

38 UN Doc. S/RES/1769 (2007), 31 July 2007. Robert P. Barnidge, Jr., "The United Nations and the African Union: Assessing a Partnership for Peace in Darfur," *Journal of Conflict & Security Law*, Vol. 14 (2009), pp. 103–104.

39 It is also to be noted that "the hybrid structure of UNAMID was a specific reaction to the refusal of the Sudanese Government to accept a robust UN mission". Christian Walter, "Hybrid Peacekeeping: Is UNAMID a New Model for Cooperation between the United Nations and Regional Organizations?" in Holger P. Hestermeyer *et al.* eds., *Coexistence, Cooperation and Solidarity. Liber Amicorum Rüdiger Wolfrum. Volume II* (Martinus Nijhoff Publishers, 2012), p. 1340.

40 But, in fact, UNAMID has struggled to get the required armoured vehicles and helicopters to conduct patrols, which has largely depended on the UN budgetary assessment. In this sense, a hybrid mission is suggested not necessarily to be a panacea to the AU's peacekeeping challenges. Timothy Murithi, "The African Union's Foray into Peacekeeping: Lessons from the Hybrid Mission in Darfur," *Journal of Peace, Conflict and Development*, Vol. 14 (2009), p. 15.

41 In the "hybrid model", the AU and the UN seek to assemble a force that would represent a predominantly "African Character", while retaining both the impartiality and the competency required to undertake the challenging mission. Theo Neethling, "Whither Peacekeeping in Africa: Revisiting the Evolving Role of the United Nations," *African Security Review*, Vol. 18, No. 1 (2009), p. 16.

This may, however, produce other serious problems with respect to the AU Member States and the AU itself. As for the former, an AU Member State, hostile to the UN, may refuse to accept the deployment of such a hybrid mission, in which the UN participated with the AU, within its own territory, although the Member State may be willing to cooperate with the AU in the implementation of a similar mandate.[42] Concerning the latter, this type of cooperation may lead the AU to mitigate its main responsibility for African problems, or even worse, to feel excluded from the indispensable work of peace operations on the African continent if the UN were to mismanage this type of cooperation.

2 *Need for Ownership and Its Restricted Significance*

The final point is related to the ambiguous and difficult relations between the two organizations in the field of peace and security in the region, as the AU has primary responsibility for the promotion of peace, security and stability in Africa under its Constitutive Act, and the SC also assumes primary responsibility for the maintenance of international peace and security under the UN Charter. These organizations have been so aware of this problem that their own organs issued a communiqué in 2007, in which the PSC and SC expressed their commitment to the development of a stronger and more structured relationship between their respective institutions, and also agreed to remember that in taking the initiative for the promotion of peace and security in Africa, the AU was acting on behalf of the UN and international community consistent with Chapter VIII of the UN Charter.[43] The above-mentioned 2006 Declaration on Enhancing UN-AU Cooperation may also be seen as a response to this problem.

In parallel with such development of the various AU–UN cooperation practices related to the maintenance of peace and security, the UN Secretary-General, in his report issued in April 2008, which was based on his review of conflict prevention in Africa,[44] stressed the importance of the type and division of responsibilities between the UN and regional organizations under Chapter VIII of the UN Charter, and recommended many specific solutions related to the UN's relationship to them.[45] These recommendations, which are

---

42 For example, the Government of the Sudan, though supporting the strengthening of AMIS, questioned the need for a transition from the AU mission to a UN operation. UN Doc. S/2006/591, 28 July 2006, para. 20.
43 UN Doc. S/2007/421, 11 July 2007, Annex II.
44 UN Doc. S/2008/18, 14 January 2008.
45 UN Doc. S/2008/186, 7 April 2008.

useful but limited to the practical and operational level, are unsatisfactory in terms of coordinating the legal relationship between the AU and UN concerning their competence.

Regarding this subject, the Report of the AU–UN Panel on Modalities for Support to AU Peacekeeping Operations, published in December 2008, is also particularly noteworthy. The Panel, which consisted of six experts as an independent status, was established on the basis of the UN Secretary-General's proposal to consider the modalities of how to support peacekeeping operations under UN mandate, in particular start-up funding, equipment and logistics, and to contemplate lessons from past and current AU peacekeeping efforts.[46] Interestingly, this report, recognizing the primacy of the SC in the maintenance of peace and security, confirms the need for developing a more effective relationship between the PSC and the SC, and underlines that the objective is "to establish a division of responsibility based on the African Union's comparative advantages". Moreover, in defining the division of responsibilities, it denies that the UN is subcontracting peacekeeping to the AU, and, rather, emphasizes that "[T]he objective should be to maximize the African Union's strengths in terms of its contribution to conflict prevention, mediation, its ability to address smaller-scale requirements [...], and, finally, its capacity to act as the first response to large-scale United Nations missions".[47]

Similarly, the UN Secretary-General Report, which was published in September 2009 to provide an assessment of the recommendations of this Panel and propose practical ways in which the UN can assist the AU in enhancing its effectiveness in the development and management of peacekeeping operations, has basically followed the conclusions offered by the Panel. The Report states that it is the responsibility of AU Member States to provide the necessary resources for the AU's peacekeeping interventions, and stresses the importance of strategic and operational coordination, as well as consultation between the respective organs of these two organizations, but does not express a way in which to compromise on the possible conflicts between the two organizations' powers. It simply confirms that the AU has assumed on responsibilities in complex political environments with the authorization of the SC.[48]

In sum, the UN has attempted through its studies to organize its relations with the AU in the field of the maintenance of peace and security in the following ways.

---

46   UN Doc. S/RES/1809 (2008), 16 April 2008, op. para. 16.
47   UN Doc. A/63/666-S/2008/813, 24 December 2008, paras. 6, 39.
48   UN Doc. A/64/359-S/2009/470, 18 September 2009, para. 67.

First, the UN has recognized and even yielded to the relative superiority of the AU over the UN itself, at least with regard to African continental problems. The expression "a division of responsibility based on the African Union's comparative advantages" should be understood as such, and the UN has taken into consideration the truism that the AU has primary responsibility for the promotion of peace, security and stability in Africa. The UN has taken this step because it has realized theoretically that Africa's ownership—Africa itself must deal with African problems—is crucial to the management of African conflicts, and also, practically, that the UN has not had much energy—logistic and financial—to spare for many African problems that have simultaneously occurred.

Second, and related to the first point, AU–UN cooperation is supposed to be limited to activities on the practical and operational levels: the carrying on of constant and close dialogue between the respective organs of the two organizations, the affording of logistic and financial support, as well as the providing of useful information by the UN to the AU and so on. There is no doubt that seeking such strategic cooperation makes it possible to mitigate any conflict between the legal competences of both the AU and UN, to avoid interfering with the legal relationship between them, and therefore practically to maintain the compatibility of the two propositions: the SC assumes primary responsibility in the maintenance of international peace and security, on the one hand, and the AU has primary responsibility for the promotion of peace, security and stability in Africa, on the other hand.

Third, these arrangements between two bodies have been entirely organized within the framework of Chapter VIII of the UN Charter. They have been constructed particularly in the context of the implementation of peace operations by the AU. This is quite logical, as it is Chapter VIII, not Chapter VII, of the UN Charter that governs the relation between the UN and regional organizations. Moreover, most of the cases undertaken by the UN that have involved the AU and African conflicts, for which research should be carried out and discussions should take place among the UN Member States, have been in the area of conflict prevention, peacekeeping, or peacebuilding activities.

Surely, greater weight should be placed on the roles and burdens of the African countries in particular for the purpose of their having conscious ownership of the events that occur on their continent.[49] This is why the UN has recognized and stressed the comparative advantages of the AU in the

---

49   Charles Riziki Majinge, "The Future of Peacekeeping in Africa and the Normative Role of the African Union," *Göttingn Journal of International Law*, Vol. 2 (2010), p. 497.

division of responsibility between the AU and UN. Simultaneously, however, it must not be forgotten that the AU's ownership stands in sharp contradiction to the funding and implementation capacities that are available to it; therefore, the AU will prove effective only if donors are prepared to fund its policies.[50]

Furthermore, the UN's notion of its relation to the AU is so carefully stated as being restricted mainly to the realm of peacekeeping that it remains to be seen what relationship may be formed between these two organizations in other areas, especially in the case of the AU's being involved in activities related to the use of force without any authorization by the SC. Even in the case of peace operations, it should be recalled that, since the first decade of this century, many "robust" peacekeeping efforts have appeared, which were permitted to use force beyond self-defence, under Chapter VII of the UN Charter.[51]

3   Acting under Chapter VII or without Authorization by the UN

Current practices suggest that most collaborative operations between the AU and UN have been placed within the framework of Chapter VIII of the UN Charter, on the premise that the UN has undertaken to construct a scheme of cooperation between these organizations. The UN, by restricting its cooperation with the AU mainly to peacekeeping and encompassing it within a type of Chapter VIII operation, may make certain that the SC assumes its primary responsibility in the maintenance of international peace and security, while taking into account the AU's ownership of African problems. Nevertheless, under Chapter VIII, the SC has control over regional organizations, the operations of which would involve the use of force.

It is true that a Chapter VII operation would not be called into question if the AU held and clarified its mandate in consultation with the UN and implemented it with the consent of the parties concerned under Chapter VIII of the UN Charter in SC resolutions. Legally speaking, it is the AU Member States as UN Member States or a UN mission that includes them, not the AU itself, to which the SC would authorize a Chapter VII operation. As a matter of fact, the

---

50   Stephan Klingebiel, "Africa's New Peace and Security Architecture. Converging the Roles of External Actors and African Interests," *African Security Review*, Vol. 14 (2) (2005), p. 41.

51   For the recent tendency to combine UN peacekeeping with Chapter VII of the UN Charter, Hironobu Sakai, "Legitimization of Measures to Secure Effectiveness in UN Peacekeeping: The Role of Chapter VII of the UN Charter," in Teruo Komori and Karel Wellens eds., *Public Interest Rules of International Law. Towards Effective Implementation* (Ashgate, 2009), pp. 119–139.

SC has typically authorized most UN peacekeeping missions, which sometimes became AU peacekeeping missions, to act under Chapter VII, not Chapter VIII, because other UN Member States than the AU Member States have been able to participate in UN missions in African conflicts for the purpose of filling troop quotas.

However, the above-mentioned UN plan, according to which the AU's activities should be contained to Chapter VIII operations, does not provide any clear answer to the question, whether the AU can take its own initiative in deploying its troops to a conflict area to use force in accordance with its Constitutive Act and the PSC Protocol, such as exercising the right of intervention, when the UNSC gives it no authorization under Chapter VII nor Chapter VIII. As long as the formula "African Solutions for African Problems" is rigidly adhered to, and the AU has the primary responsibility for African conflicts, there would be no barrier to the AU's actions involving the use of force, in particular, if the SC were to adopt no resolutions and nor make any presidential statements to officially express its position.

Furthermore, another question may come up even when the AU has launched its own peacekeeping operations to address African problems, which do not necessarily require authorization by the SC. Recent peacekeeping operations have covered various dimensions, from the supervision of cease-fires to the maintenance of order to national conciliations; therefore, they have been permitted to use force to implement their mandate beyond self-defence. In the case of UN peacekeeping operations, the SC has authorized them to act and use force under Chapter VII of the UN Charter, for example, to protect civilians under the imminent threat of physical violence. However, is it necessary for the AU to ask the SC to authorize AU peace missions under Chapters VII or VIII when the AU gives a similar mandate to its peace missions? Or is the AU entitled to establish its own robust peacekeeping operations, which could, if necessary, use force to enforce a mandate, even without SC authorization?

Unfortunately, no clear and definitive responses to these points can be found in the practices of the AU and UN. Therefore, it may be argued that should the SC fail to act, the AU can determine the grounds for intervention and no longer need a SC determination of threat to the peace under Chapter VII of the UN Charter to intervene in its Member State.[52] It is also contended that the effect of Article 4(h) of the AU Constitutive Act is ultimately to

---

52   Abdulqawi Yusuf, "The Right of Intervention by the African Union: A New Paradigm in Regional Enforcement Action?" *African Yearbook of International Law*, Vol. 11 (2003), p. 19.

empower the AU to act without authorization from the SC.[53] Nevertheless, there is no evidence from the actual practices of the AU that it has yet done this, and thus it may be premature to express too much concern about this.[54]

It is theoretically possible that the SC would applaud an AU mission involving the use of force at a later stage, thereby approving the legality of the AU's actions retroactively. However, it is unlikely that the SC would justify them *ex post* under a Chapter VII resolution without having given the AU any prior authorization for the mission, unless the situation had completely changed. The UN's recent practices testify to this, as the SC approved only the existing state of affairs after intervention by the UN Member States, without regard to its legality under international law, in cases such as the North Atlantic Treaty Organization's intervention in Yugoslavia and the adoption of SC resolution 1244 after that incident.[55]

Some have sought "humanitarian intervention" or "responsibility to protect" as the legal basis of the AU's action without authorization by the SC. They have regarded Article 4(h) of the AU Constitutive Act as a good example of "humanitarian intervention" or "responsibility to protect" from the outset of its adoption.[56] It cannot be denied that this provision would have one aspect of possible justification if it were taken literally and separated from the others. However, when Article 4(h) is interpreted in light of this Act and the PSC Protocol as a whole, in particular Article 17 of the Protocol on its relations to the UN, it is not so easy for the AU to justify "humanitarian intervention" through this provision only. What is more, the status of the concepts "humanitarian intervention" or "responsibility to protect" is still ambiguous under international

---

53   Ademola Abass, *Regional Organizations and the Development of Collective Security. Beyond Chapter VIII of the UN Charter* (Hart Publishing, 2004), pp. 162–171.

54   Gary Wilson, "Regional Arrangement as Agents of the UN Security Council: Some African and European Organisations Contrasted," *Liverpool Law Review*, Vol. 29 (2008), p. 200.

55   For the contention that the UNSC Resolution 1244 cannot be regarded as justifying lawfully the NATO's conducts in Yugoslavia, Marcelo Kohen, "L'emploi de la force et la crise du Kosovo: Vers un nouveau désordre juridique international," *Revue belge de droit international*, Tom. 32 (1999), pp. 128–129.

56   Timothy Murithi, "The Responsibility to Protect, as Enshrined in Article 4 of the Constitutive Act of the African Union," *African Security Review*, Vol. 16, No. 3 (2007), pp. 14–25; Kwesi Aning & Samuel Atuobi, "Responsibility to Protect in Africa: An Analysis of the African Union's Peace and Security Architecture," *Global Responsibility to Protect*, Vol. 1 (2009), pp. 90–113; Jeremy Sarkin, "The Role of the United Nations, the African Union and Africa's Sub-Regional Organizations in Dealing with Africa's Human Rights Problems: Connecting Humanitarian Intervention and the Responsibility to Protect," *Journal of African Law*, Vol. 53, No. 1 (2009), pp. 17–20.

law, and the legality of military intervention for alleged humanitarian reasons is also highly controversial,[57] although the decision by a regional organization regarding such conduct may be more legitimate than unilateral actions by a state,[58] due to its collectivity and proximity.[59] Arguably, whether the AU has the right of intervention without authorization from the SC largely depends upon the maturity of these concepts in international law.[60]

It rather seems from ongoing practice that the UN and AU have jointly taken or have sought to take a more pragmatic approach on this issue to avoid disputable solutions. By developing closer cooperation and partnership between the respective operational counterparts and building up the UN's financial, logistical and military support for the AU, these organizations have worked hard together to avoid any risk that the AU's activities may be contrary to the relevant provisions of the UN Charter and the rules of general international law, and simultaneously balancing two seemingly contradictory ideas: the AU has primary responsibility for the promotion of peace, security and stability in Africa, and the SC assumes primary responsibility in the maintenance of international peace and security. Certainly, the conceptual device for this compromise is composed of the AU's "ownership" or "a division of responsibility based on the AU's comparative advantages", which is too vague to apply to an actual situation. Therefore, the AU–UN cooperation has deliberately concentrated on working at the business and—operational levels, that is, through the exchange of information, making any decisions with prior informal consultation, and with the UN's providing material, personnel and financial support for the AU, within the framework of Chapter VIII of the UN Charter. Moreover, where necessary, a political decision by the SC would bring the AU's mission under Chapter VII, surely with the result of prior consultation between the AU and UN. Thus, to promote greater effectiveness of their operations in the field of peace and security in Africa, these two organizations, maintaining their own principles concerning the relationship between them, have managed to

---

57 For the overall consideration on these concepts, James Pattison, *Humanitarian Intervention & The Responsibility to Protect* (Oxford University Press, 2010).

58 For the interpretation of Article 4(h) by the AU, The Common African Position on the Proposed Reform of the United Nations: "The Ezulwini Consensus," AU Doc. Ext/Ex. CL/2(VII), 7–8 March 2005, p. 6.

59 Dace Winther, *Regional Maintenance of Peace and Security under International Law. The Distorted Mirrors* (Routledge, 2014), p. 72.

60 On the relationship between Article 4(h) and responsibility to protect, Dan Kuwali, *The Responsibility to Protect. Implementation of Article 4(h) Intervention* (Martinus Nijhoff Publishers, 2011).

endorse so much more practical connections in this field that the AU need not invoke any use of force without authorization from the SC.

It goes without saying that such an effort to make gradual and steady progress in the relationship between the AU and UN is important and highly desirable for the construction of its system. Nevertheless, it is also correct that this pragmatic approach cannot be a decisive solution to this issue when, for example, the SC fails to operate in a humanitarian emergency in Africa. Hence, the possibility might exist that the AU alone could invoke Article 4(h) of the Constitutive Act to intervene in its Member State for the purpose of preventing genocide or humanitarian disasters, and it remains to be seen whether the AU's action without prior authorization from the SC would be lawful under international law. However, it should also be noted that the legitimacy of a regional organization in undertaking peacekeeping and security actions depends upon whether it has the capacity to implement such actions,[61] and if so, this pragmatic approach, which may contribute to the capacity-building of the AU, is much more advantageous.[62]

IV   Concluding Remarks

Some conclusions may be derived from the above considerations. First, both the AU and UN have in practice shown respect for each other's competences in their respective fields of peace and security. Particularly for the AU, although it is entitled to intervene in its Member States under the Constitutive Act, it, in practice in close consultation with the UN, has refrained from invoking such intervention without authorization from the SC, and, rather, has acted on the basis of the consent of the parties concerned in the conflict, as well as under Chapter VIII of the UN Charter, or where necessary, with authorization under Chapter VII by the SC. Otherwise, the AU's action may have challenged and rejected the authority and control of the SC over the use of force by UN Member States, which would have entailed the danger of undermining the UN

---

61 Nishkala Suntharalingam, "The UN Security Council, Regional Arrangements, and Peacekeeping Operations," in Hilary Charlesworth and Jean-Marc Coicaud eds., *Fault Lines of International Legitimacy* (Cambridge University Press, 2010), p. 228.

62 Thus, "there is no generic model for cooperation between the two organizations that can be applied to any situation", and "each situation requires innovative solutions". UN Doc. S/2011/805, 29 December 2011, para. 64. The strategic vision of the Partnership between the AU and UN in this Report was confirmed by SC Resolution 2033 (2012). UN Doc. S/RES/2033 (2012), 12 January 2012, op.para. 5.

collective security system.⁶³ The UN also has entrusted the AU with African problems to the extent that the AU's action would be consistent with the UN Charter, and has provided it with multifaceted assistance so that the AU mission may implement its mandate.

Second, in parallel with such respect for each other's principles, workable solutions for coordinating likely conflicts between the two principles with— the AU having primary responsibility for peace and stability in the African continent, and the UN, in particular the SC, assuming primary responsibility in the maintenance of international peace and security—have been pursued not in the legal but rather in the practical sphere of activities.⁶⁴ The chief merit of this pragmatic approach lies in the fact that the increasingly operational cooperation between the two organizations has become their regular routine for sharing their values in the field of, international or regional, peace and security without impairing their respective principles. As the AU is, legally speaking, not bound by the UN Charter, and is subject to it *de facto* or indirectly through the AU Member States bound by the UN Charter as UN Member States, a new binding document would be legally required to govern their relationship, which would be less effective from the viewpoint of a cost-benefit analysis. Rather, the establishment of the AU–UN partnership and its operations on the practical level may contribute most to constructing the guiding principles in their relations. Moreover, setting up such norms governing a link of these two organizations, in parallel with establishing operational organs in the respective organizations, is needed for the system of their relationship to work more effectively.⁶⁵

As a matter of course, it should be noted that there are some particularities of Africa and the African countries, which may serve the formation and application of this pragmatic approach. While many armed conflicts or humanitarian disasters have occurred on the African continent, the AU and its Member

---

63   In this sense, Article 4(h) of the AU Constitutive Act is legally effective only within the AU to attribute it the explicit competence for military actions as legal rules of the international organization, and does not intend to modify any rules under the UN Charter or general international law. Olivier Corten, *Le droit contre la guerre. L'interdiction du recours à la force en droit international contemporain* (Pedone, 2008), pp. 525–526.

64   Thus, the principle of subsidiarity within the meaning of Article 53(1) of the UN Charter seems to be similar to the idea of cooperation between the AU and the UN in this case. Ana Peyró Liopis, *Force, ONU et organisations regionales. Répartition des responsabilités en matière coercitive* (Bruylant, 2012), pp. 363–364.

65   For the effectiveness of a system to be operated, especially within the UN economic cooperation, Ryuichi Ida, "La coopération économique et sociale dans le système des Nations Unies" (1989), pp. 32–33.

States have been relatively poor in human, logistical and financial resources to deal with these problems, and have had to ask the international community to provide assistance so that the AU could deploy its missions in its Member States and work hard for conflict prevention, peacekeeping, peace establishment and so on. Thus, the reality is that the AU's principle, "African Solutions for African Problems", which is indeed advanced and cannot be denied by anyone, would not be applied and realized, as the AU itself has recognized, without support from outsiders, in particular the UN. Against this background, a pragmatic approach has been generally adopted in the construction of the AU–UN relationship.

However, a more crucial point in the practice of AU–UN cooperation is that two dimensional compatibilities, between the respective principles of the AU and UN, on the one hand, and the autonomy of the AU and the political control by the UN over the military conduct of the AU, on the other hand, would both be ensured through institutional dialogue between them. This can suggest how to regulate the relationship between the UN and regional organizations in general. Because the autonomy of regional organizations is usually built into their constitutions, and the UN conveniently entrusts them with tasks related to peace and security due to share the burden and endorse the promotion of their autonomy, it is not realistic that a prior agreement would be concluded between the UN and regional organizations to restrict their autonomy, which would be unavoidable if they sought to agree on their relationship in a legal document, despite the fact that both parties usually recognize the superiority of the UN in the maintenance of peace and security. In this sense, the pragmatic approach appears useful for other regional organizations in their relations with the UN and, as discussed above, as many UN Secretary-General's Reports have suggested, it is worthwhile to emulate the relationships between the UN and other regional organizations. The lessons from the practices of the AU and UN are equally valuable for others, and this usefulness is not limited to these two organizations. Both the UN and regional organizations have dealt with crises through common actions or a combination of efforts between them.[66] They need each other and must assume shared responsibility for resolving security problems in the future.[67]

---

66   Christian Dominicé, "Co-ordination between Universal and Regional Organizations," in Niels M. Blokker and Henry G. Schermers eds., *Proliferation of International Organizations. Legal Issues* (Kluwer Law International, 2001), p. 83.

67   Fredrik Söderbaum and Björn Hettne, "Regional Security in a Global Perspective," in Ulf Engel and João Gomes Porto eds., *Africa's New Peace and Security Architecture. Promoting Norms, Institutionalizing Solutions* (Ashgate, 2010), p. 30.

PART 3

*Law-Making: International Law Catching
Up with the Globalizing Community*

∴

CHAPTER 9

International and Domestic Laws in Collaboration: An Effective Means of Environmental Liability Regime-Making

Akiho Shibata

I   Introduction: The Concept of Effectiveness in Law-Making

Professor Ryuichi Ida argued that, in order to examine how international law adapts to and effectively copes with new challenges posed by scientific and technological innovations and changing values in the international community,[1] one must be able to depict the dynamic process of norm evolution from its inception to actual implementation. "Thus, one may need to conceptualise the law as a process."[2] Within this dynamic process of norm-creation, the normativity of international law in the broader sense depends on its effectiveness, meaning the degree to which international law is actually complied with through its implementation at international, national, and even private actors' levels.[3] In his recent studies of international law on bioethics, a field where the life and health of individuals are at stake, Professor Ida has been increasingly focusing on the theoretical and practical approaches in which a collaboration of international and domestic laws can be attained in order to strengthen the effectiveness of the international law on bioethics.[4]

According to Professor Ida, international law as a complete process of its creation and implementation both at international and national levels has become an important forum to confirm the fundamental values shared by the community as well as an important forum to garner the compliance consciousness amongst its members based on their good faith.[5] The structure, procedure, and outcome of "normative diplomacy" would be important indicators regarding

---

1   Ryuichi Ida, "Norm Making Process in the Contemporary International Law" (1999), pp. 378–379; Ryuichi Ida, "Science, Technology and International Protection of Human Rights" (2001), pp. 207–208.
2   Ryuichi Ida, "Qu'est-ce que le 'Soft Law'? (2)" (1985), p. 9.
3   Ryuichi Ida, "Le droit international et la bioéthique" (2005), p. 89.
4   Ryuichi Ida, "Un suivi de la Déclaration universelle sur le génome humain" (2000), pp. 53–62.
5   Ryuichi Ida, "The Significance of Soft Law as Standards of Medical Practice" (2005), p. 96; Ryuichi Ida, "Le droit international et la bioéthique" (2005), p. 89.

whether such consciousness emerged, so that the norms created could be expected to be effective.⁶ "The bioethics as social norms shall be created by the discussion and agreement of all relevant members of the society, that is, scientists, doctors, patients, and the general public. In other words, such social norms must emerge from the society, therefore, the process of agreement through open discourse in the society would be important [for its effectiveness]."⁷

Thus, Professor Ida suggests that the concept of effectiveness in law-making necessitates the examination of both the legal design of international law that intends to promote collaboration between international and domestic laws in its implementation phase, and how the legal design contributed to the garnering of compliance consciousness of relevant actors during its normative diplomacy.⁸

Adopting this suggestion by Professor Ida as an analytical framework, my contribution examines a recently adopted environmental liability regime that addresses environmental damage arising from the use of genetically modified organisms (GMOs). The Nagoya-Kuala Lumpur Supplementary Protocol on Liability and Redress to the Cartagena Protocol on Biosafety (Supplementary Protocol),⁹ adopted in October 2010, is a perfect case study for such an examination, as it reflects an evolution of international environmental law catching up with new technologies that greatly benefit human society but with potential risks to human health and to the environment.¹⁰ The Supplementary Protocol provides for operator liability for damage to biological diversity, the effective implementation of which necessarily involves the domestic legal system of the parties to the Supplementary Protocol. The use of GMOs as crops and in industry

---

6   Ryuichi Ida, "International Lawmaking Process in Transition?" (1996); Ryuichi Ida, "La mutation de la formation des norms internationals" (1999); Ryuichi Ida, "Norm Making Process in the Contemporary International Law" (1999).

7   Ryuichi Ida, "Development of Life Science and Respect for Human Dignity and Human Rights" (2004), p. 601.

8   Thus, this approach does not enter into the doctrinal debate over the relationship of validity between international and domestic legal orders as such. Professor Ida had shown very little interest in this debate.

9   Nagoya-Kuala Lumpur Supplementary Protocol on Liability and Redress to the Cartagena Protocol on Biosafety (Supplementary Protocol), adopted by decision BS-V/11 in its Annex on 15 October 2010, UNEP/CBD/BS/COP-MOP/5/17 (29 November 2010), pp. 68–75. As of 31 March 2015, thirty-one (31) Parties deposited their instruments of ratification, acceptance, approval and accession. According to its Article 18(1), the Supplementary Protocol needs forty (40) ratifications, etc to enter into force.

10 *See generally* Akiho Shibata ed., *International Liability Regime for Biodiversity Damage: The Nagoya-Kuala Lumpur Supplementary Protocol* (Routledge, 2014).

processes is now ubiquitous, but their potential impacts on biodiversity are still politically controversial. Since their development in the 1970s through the field trials in the 1980s, to their first sales in the 1990s, and to the current date, the GMOs that were intentionally introduced into the environment have gone through rigorous risk assessments and have not caused scientifically confirmed cases of environmental damage or human health problems. The political controversy revolves around the possibility of GMOs being unintentionally, accidentally, or illegally introduced into the environment without proper risk assessment; their social and economic impacts; and the emotional resistance amongst some of the populace towards new technologies.[11] The international law-making process addressing GMOs and their impacts invariably encompasses conflicting interests of States and the societal values of their citizens.

Moreover, the extensive referencing to the domestic law of the parties in the Supplementary Protocol has been criticised by some as "subordinating" international law to domestic law, questioning the "international" character of the rules and principles established in the treaty.[12] It is true that there are eighteen references to domestic law within nine of the Supplementary Protocol's twenty-one articles. However, the legal effect of these referencing provisions varies and needs to be carefully examined in order to assess whether some of them may undermine, rather than strengthen, the effectiveness of the international liability regime for biodiversity damage.

II The Supplementary Protocol: Innovative Approach to Environmental Liability

As Professor Ida accurately argued in his recent studies of international law on bioethics, the theoretical examination of the potential collaboration between international law and domestic law in international environmental law requires delving into both aspects of implementation and law-making. The first encompasses the concept of domestic implementation of international environmental law, the discipline that has been recognised as an important area of study for its effectiveness. The international liability regimes have been

---

11 See generally Mark A. Pollack & Gregory C. Shaffer, *When Cooperation Fails: The International Law and Politics of Genetically Modified Foods* (Oxford University Press, 2009).

12 Worku Damena Yifru & Kathryn Garforth, "Chapter 10: The Supplementary Protocol: A Treaty Subject to Domestic Law?" in A. Shibata, *International Liability Regime*, supra note 10, pp. 150–166.

particularly identified as those types of multilateral environmental agreements (MEAs) that clearly require domestic legislative measures to implement the international rules contained therein.[13] The Nagoya-Kuala Lumpur Supplementary Protocol is no exception, as it obliges its Parties to establish under their domestic legal systems the liability of operators to take appropriate response measures in the event of damage to biodiversity and its enforcement scheme.[14] In addition, international systems of reporting, monitoring, and capacity-building, as established in MEAs, usually play supporting and strengthening role in States' endeavours to the domestic implementation of these international obligations.[15] The Supplementary Protocol recognises the importance of international review of domestic implementation by its State Parties. Article 13 on Assessment and Review mandates the Conference of the Parties serving as the meeting of the Parties to the Cartagena Protocol on Biosafety (COP-MOP) to undertake a review of the effectiveness of the Supplementary Protocol based on the information provided by the Parties.

The aspect of law-making has a direct impact on the examination of domestic implementation of international environmental obligations. The concepts of and the distinction between "obligations of means" and "obligations of result", for example, have a direct bearing on the issue. It is often argued that most of the obligations under the MEAs remain soft obligations of result, respecting the States' sovereign freedom regarding the nature and substance of their domestic legal systems.[16] The concepts of and the distinction between "principles" and "rules" are other examples of law-making jargon that pertains to their implementation.[17] The law-making techniques of "framework treaties, later supplemented by protocols" and "the use of soft instruments and soft laws" have already been extensively examined, including their relation to domestic implementation.[18] These law-making concepts and techniques, affecting

---

13   Catherine Redgwell, "National Implementation," in Daniel Bodansky, Jutta Brunnée, and Ellen Hey eds., *The Oxford Handbook of International Environmental Law* (Oxford University Press, 2007), p. 930.
14   Articles 5 and 12 of the Supplementary Protocol.
15   Philippe Sands & Jacqueline Peel, *Principles of International Environmental Law* (3rd ed., Cambridge University Press, 2012), pp. 138–144.
16   Yoshiro Matui, *Kokusai Kankyoho no Kihon Gensoku* [*International Law of the Environment: Its Fundamental Principles*] (Toshindo, 2010), p. 53 (in Japanese).
17   Ulrich Beyerlin, "Different Types of Norms in International Environmental Law: Policies, Principles, and Rules," in D. Bodansky *et al.* eds., *Oxford Handbook, supra* note 13, pp. 425–448.
18   Ryuichi Ida, "Un suivi de la Déclaration universelle sur le génome humain" (2000), pp. 46–47. Akiho Shibata, "International Environmental Lawmaking in the First Decade of the

the intrusiveness of international law upon the domestic legal systems of States, can be assessed from their acceptability by the addressees. This perception of acceptability can be considered as an important element of compliance consciousness garnered during normative diplomacy, as suggested by Professor Ida.

Thus, the legal challenges encountered by the Supplementary Protocol in establishing an effective environmental liability regime for biodiversity damage are formidable. It must ensure the acceptability amongst the negotiating State Parties and the interested groups[19] of an international regime that penetrates deeply into the domestic legal systems of States and affects directly the activities of their citizens, while addressing a still politically controversial issue of the use of biotechnology and its possible impacts on the environment. In response to these challenges, the Supplementary Protocol introduced various types of collaboration between international law and domestic law, demonstrating nuanced differences in their intention and legal effects. It is the author's argument that the above criticism of the Supplementary Protocol did not appropriately appreciate such nuances.

In essence, the Supplementary Protocol obliges its State Parties to establish a domestic legal system that effectively addresses biodiversity damage caused by GMOs[20] by requiring the operator who has the control of the GMOs at issue to take response measures to prevent, minimise, contain, and mitigate such damage, and restore the damaged biological diversity (Articles 12(1) and 5(1)).[21] In this process, the Supplementary Protocol mandates the competent authority of the State Parties to identify the operator, evaluate the damage, and determine which response measures should be taken by the operator. Further, it allows the competent authority of the parties to implement appropriate response measures if the circumstances so require, and to

---

Twenty-First Century: The Form and Process," *Japanese Yearbook of International Law*, Vol. 54, Year 2011 (2012), pp. 28–61.

19   On the participation of NGOs and industry representatives in the negotiations of the Supplementary Protocol and their influence on the final outcome, see René Lefeber & Jimena Nieto Carrasco, "Chapter 3: Negotiating the Supplementary Protocol: The Co-Chairs' Perspective," in A. Shibata ed., *International Liability Regime*, supra note 10, pp. 52–70.

20   Technically, the Supplementary Protocol deals with living modified organisms (LMOs) as defined in the Cartagena Protocol. However, for the purpose of this contribution, the technical differences between GMOs and LMOs will not be important.

21   The following is based on Akiho Shibata, "Chapter 2: A New Dimension in International Environmental Liability Regimes: A Prelude to the Supplementary Protocol," in A. Shibata, ed., *International Liability Regime*, supra note 10, pp. 17–51.

obtain reimbursement of the costs from the liable operator (paras. 2, 4, and 5 of Article 5).

The legal regime of the Supplementary Protocol is premised on the following four normative features. First, it addresses damage to biodiversity, and not traditional damage to persons, property, or economic interests. The Supplementary Protocol addresses damage that is defined as "an adverse effect on conservation and sustainable use of biological diversity, taking also into account risks to human health" (Articles 2(2)(b) and 2(3)). Second, the content of liability, namely the legal consequences of causing such damage, shall be for the operator to take response measures to contain and mitigate such damage, and to restore the damaged biological diversity to its original condition or to its nearest equivalent, in lieu of monetary compensation. Third, the liability of the operator is incurred in relation to the administrative organ of the government, rather than in relation to the victim of such damage. As such, the obligation of the operator will be pursued largely by utilising the administrative apparatus and procedures, rather than in the courts. And fourth, liability is imposed on the operators, usually private actors involved in the development, export, import, marketing, or use of GMOs, instead of territorial States where such activities take place.

Having all these features, the Supplementary Protocol is the first international treaty of global applicability that adopts an administrative approach to liability for biodiversity damage. In addition, this is the first-ever global treaty that defines "biodiversity damage" and establishes legal consequences arising from such damage. Such a "paradigm evolution"[22] in international liability regime-making was only possible with extensive reference to the domestic law of the State Parties implementing as well as supplementing, in certain cases, the international regime.

III   Various Types of Collaboration between International and Domestic Laws

It is essential to state the fundamental principle of the international community: States come to a negotiating forum, in good faith, to collectively solve a problem of common concern and genuinely endeavour to reach a solution by

---

22   See René Lefeber, "Chapter 4: The Legal Significance of the Supplementary Protocol: The Result of a Paradigm Evolution," in A. Shibata ed., *International Liability Regime, supra* note 10, pp. 73–91.

adopting a treaty.²³ Once such a treaty comes into force for the States, they shall perform the obligations contained therein in good faith.²⁴ The sovereign States comprising the international community do not need to participate in such a law-making forum, nor are they obliged to ratify a treaty resulting from it. This sovereign freedom underlies the consequential obligations of the States that voluntarily participate in the negotiations and in the resulting treaty to act in good faith.²⁵ The extensive references to domestic law in the Supplementary Protocol should be examined in light of this fundamental principle of good faith, and not on the presumption of bad faith²⁶ such as where States intend to avoid or deviate from the collective endeavour to achieve a common objective. The Supplementary Protocol's stated objective is "to contribute to the conservation and sustainable use of biological diversity...by providing *international* rules and procedures in the field of liability", "*recognising the need* to provide for appropriate response measures where there is damage or sufficient likelihood of damage".²⁷

In light of the prevailing academic discussion on "referencing" domestic law in international law, we can examine three types of referencing in the Supplementary Protocol, without being exhaustive in characterising all the provisions that explicitly refer to domestic law.²⁸ The purpose of this examination

---

23   The States have the good faith obligation "to conduct themselves [so] that the negotiations are meaningful, which will not be the case when [any of them] insists upon its own position without contemplating any modification of it". *North Sea Continental Shelf Cases* (Germany/Denmark, Germany/Netherlands), *ICJ Reports 1969*, para. 85(a).

24   "Every treaty in force is binding upon the parties to it and must be performed by them in good faith." Article 26, Vienna Convention on the Law of Treaties (VCLT).

25   The author believes this good faith foundation of international law comprises what Professor Ida calls "the common fundamental values of international community, without which norm creation would be difficult". Ryuichi Ida, "Le droit international et la bioéthique" (2005), p. 90.

26   "(1)l est un principe general de droit bien établi selon lequel la mauvaise foi ne se presume pas." *Lac Lanoux*, 1957, *Report of the International Arbitral Awards*, Vol. 12, p. 305.

27   Article 1(Objective) and the fourth preambular paragraph of the Supplementary Protocol (emphasis added).

28   There is another category of referencing domestic law in many environmental treaties, namely an authorisation to impose more environmentally protective domestic measures within the State's jurisdiction, but this is almost always in accordance with relevant international obligations. An example is Article 2(4) of the Cartagena Protocol on Biosafety. Article 10 on Financial Security under the Supplementary Protocol may be examined in this category, as well as its controversial Article 12 on civil liability. The unique phrase in Article 10 "retain the right" and the perplexed and sweeping references to international law in Articles 10(2) and 16(4) all require separate examination.

is to exemplify the different intentions and legal effects of some of those provisions, and to argue that the criticism of the "subordination" of international law to domestic law is a misleading oversimplification of the legal situation brought about by those provisions.

1 International Obligations of Result and Specific Domestic Rules to Achieve Them

Again, the core obligation of State Parties under the Supplementary Protocol is to establish rules and procedures under their domestic laws to address damage to biodiversity caused by a GMO by requiring the operator in control of that GMO to take appropriate response measures, defined as reasonable actions to prevent, minimise, contain, mitigate, or otherwise avoid such damage, and to restore biological diversity to the original condition, or by other means. This clear obligation of result is established by Articles 12(1), 5(1), 2(2)(c) and 2(2)(d) of the Supplementary Protocol as read together. The Supplementary Protocol, however, leaves broad discretion as to specific rules and procedures within the domestic legal system that establishes an administrative approach to liability. The negotiating Parties were discreet in prescribing the details of such an innovative approach to liability. Even the European Union (EU) that had already established in 2004 a legal framework premised on an administrative approach to liability for environmental damage[29] was reluctant to "export" its system because of a lack of actual experience under the new framework.[30] The EU Environmental Liability Directive itself had several flexible provisions.[31] Some negotiating Parties explicitly demanded discretion under its domestic

---

Although these provisions raise an interesting issue of "trade vs environment" on the *international law plane*, this category of referencing domestic law is less relevant to the possible collaboration between international and domestic laws or the possible "subordination" of the former by the latter. See Rodrigo C.A. Lima, "Chapter 9: Trade and the Supplementary Protocol: How to Achieve Mutual Supportiveness," in A. Shibata ed., *International Liability Regime, supra* note 10, pp. 131–149.

29   Mai Fujii, "EU Kankyo Shirei niokeru Gyousei teki Approach: Sono Kokusaihou eno Shisa [The Administrative Approach in the EU Environmental Liability Directive]," Kokusai Kyoryoku Ronshu [*Journal of International Cooperation Studies*], Vol. 17, No. 2 (2009), pp. 137–160 (in Japanese).

30   Alejandro Lago Candeira, "Chapter 5: Administrative Approach to Liability: Its Origin, Negotiation and Outcome," in A. Shibata ed., *International Liability Regime, supra* note 10, pp. 92–104.

31   Directive 2004/35/EC of 21 April 2004 on Environmental Liability with regard to the Prevention and Remedying of Environmental Damage, OJ L 143/56 (30 April 2004). Edward H.P. Brans & Dorith H. Dongelmans, "Chapter 12: The Supplementary Protocol and the EU

legal system regarding the specific methods of constructing such a new approach to liability.

For example, under the Supplementary Protocol, the question of what kind of exemptions to operator's liability, if any, would be provided in the domestic law is left for the State Parties to determine (Article 6 of the Supplementary Protocol).[32] There is no question that the details of exemption clause under the implementing domestic laws of a State Party have profound implication on the potential GMO operators intending to do business in that country. In fact, the biotech industries have made it clear that a permit defence, that is, an exemption or mitigation of liability for a realisation of risk (damage) that was explicitly assessed and authorised by the State, must be available in order for them to accept the liability for biodiversity damage caused by their GMOs.[33] On the other hand, the industries do not consider the state-of-the-art exemption necessary. The developing country Parties, lacking the necessary capacity to evaluate and determine the acceptability of such risk when making the decision to import GMOs, may find it problematic to provide the permit defence in its implementing legislation. In developed countries like Japan, and as one of the largest importers of GMOs in the world, it is suggested that, under its existing domestic legal system, the permit defence as claimed by the industry may only be allowed if combined with the concept of "latest scientific knowledge", a concept that is usually connected with the state-of-the-art defence.[34] These considerations demonstrate the need, when constructing a specific legal design of domestic laws to implement the Supplementary Protocol, to take into account the particularities of each State Party's legal system and culture, and to balance relevant interests within the context of that State's particular situation regarding the use of GMOs and biodiversity. In providing such discretion, the overriding concern at the international law level is

---

Environmental Liability Directive: Similarities and Differences," in A. Shibata ed., *International Liability Regime*, supra note 10, pp. 180–200.

32 Article 6(Exemptions): 1. Parties may provide, in their domestic law, for the following exemptions: (a) Act of God or *force majeure*; and (b) Act of war or civil unrest. 2. Parties may provide, in their domestic law, for any other exemptions or mitigations as they may deem fit. *See also* Article 7 on time limits, Article 8 on financial limits, and Article 4 on causation.

33 J. Thomas Carrato, John Barkett & Phil Goldberg, "Chapter 14: The Industry's Compact and Its Implications for the Supplementary Protocol," in A Shibata ed., *International Liability Regime*, supra note 10, pp. 218–239.

34 Eriko Futami & Tadashi Otsuka, "Chapter 13: A Japanese Approach to the Domestic Implementation of the Supplementary Protocol," in A. Shibata ed., *International Liability Regime*, supra note 10, pp. 201–217.

whether a State Party implementing the Supplementary Protocol has made efforts in good faith to address the biodiversity damage caused by GMOs by establishing an administrative approach to the liability of the operators.

Thus, the discretion as to specific methods under domestic laws of State Parties to achieve the international obligations under the Supplementary Protocol was inserted deliberately to deal with this innovative liability approach, which did not yet have much experience in its domestic implementation. For negotiating Parties, such discretion was considered necessary in order to allow them to design the implementing domestic laws that best accommodated their particular legal systems and interests. For global GMO producers and exporters doing business in several jurisdictions, the difference in the details regarding State Parties implementing domestic laws may pose some difficulties, but they considered the legal design of the Supplementary Protocol as an acceptable outcome coming of extremely complex negotiations.[35] Therefore, this type of collaboration between international and domestic laws was considered necessary and acceptable by the relevant interested parties under the Supplementary Protocol.

Article 5(8) of the Supplementary Protocol provides that the "(r)esponse measures shall be implemented in accordance with domestic law". This provision has been particularly criticised as "subjecting the provision on response measures to domestic law".[36] It is true that the core obligation of the Supplementary Protocol is to require the operators to take appropriate response measures as defined in Article 2(2)(d). Except for a typical "reasonableness" criterion, Article 2(2)(d) of the Supplementary Protocol provides very precisely the specific actions required, including their sequence. The concern expressed above, therefore, is that with the insertion of Article 5(8), "the Parties are free either to adopt or set aside the requirements of the Supplementary Protocol related to response measures to the extent implementation at the domestic level justifies such action".[37]

In fact, a stipulation providing for international obligations to be "implemented in accordance with domestic law" can be found in many treaties, including environmental treaties, and its legal effect has already been the subject of extensive discussion.[38] For example, the 1998 Aarhus Convention on

---

35   J. Thomas, Carrato et al., supra note 33, pp. 222–223.
36   W.D. Yifru & K. Garforth, supra note 12, p. 159.
37   Ibid.
38   This issue now takes on an extended dimension into customary international law. The International Court of Justice declared that the obligation to undertake an environmental impact assessment "may now be considered a requirement under general international

Access to Information, Public Participation in Decision-Making and Access to Justice in Environmental Matters, reflecting its sovereign-intrusive nature, contains several phrases such as "in accordance with its national law" or "within the framework of national legislation" in its key provisions establishing specific obligations of result on the State Parties.[39] According to the Convention's *Implementation Guide* published in 2000, there was a suggestion, through these phrases, to "introduce flexibility, not only in the means of implementing obligations, but also as to the scope and/or content of the obligations themselves".[40] However, this interpretation, according to the *Implementation Guide*, was found to be "more problematic".[41] Although it is indeed true that these phrases were inserted to express the Convention's respect for various legal traditions amongst State Parties, according to the *Implementation Guide*, the State Parties still need to make adjustments even to their basic legal framework, if necessary, to meet the obligations of the Convention. The Convention utilising phrases like "in accordance with national legislation" should be read, instead, as setting the "floor" or minimum standard rather than the "ceiling," and it is hoped that "as the international law on the subject evolves and Parties assist each other in implementation an upward harmonisation can take place".[42]

Thus, Article 5(8) of the Supplementary Protocol cannot be interpreted to "set aside" the requirements under the Supplementary Protocol to require the liable operator to take all "reasonable actions" as specifically set forth in Article 2(2)(d). It is only the ways in which to implement such an obligation that can be susceptible to some discretion of the State Parties utilising their particular domestic legal systems. An example of the discretion permitted in implementing response measures has already been explained elsewhere.[43] The effectiveness of such implementation of international obligations through the means

---

law", but "it is for each State to determine in its domestic legislation...the specific content of the environmental impact assessment required in each case". *Case Concerning Pulp Mills on the River Uruguay* (Argentina v. Uruguay), Judgment, *ICJ Reports 2010*, paras. 204–205.

39   For example, Article 4(1) on Access to Environmental Information of the Aarhus Convention provides that: "Each Party shall ensure that...public authorities, in response to a request for environmental information, make such information available to the public, within the framework of national legislation...".
40   Economic Commission for Europe, *The Aarhus Convention: An Implementation Guide* (United Nations, 2000), p. 30.
41   *Ibid.*, p. 31.
42   *Ibid.*
43   Akiho Shibata, "Chapter 15: Conclusion: Beyond the Supplementary Protocol," in A. Shibata, ed., *supra* note 10, p. 243.

of domestic rules of State Parties shall be assessed and reviewed in accordance with the international law criteria of good faith, namely, whether such implementation promotes the object and purpose of the Supplementary Protocol. Such assessment and review shall be conducted in COP-MOP in accordance with Article 13 of the Supplementary Protocol. Thus, the domestic implementation of international obligations "in accordance with domestic law" is under the overarching control of international law and its processes.

2   Domestic Law at the Service of the Implementation of International Law[44]

The rule on channelling liability comprises one of the core elements in designing an environmental liability regime. Most environmental liability treaties in existence today are based on strict civil liability for a particular hazardous activity, and the liability is channelled to a clearly identifiable entity, for example, the ship owner in the oil pollution liability regime.[45] The Nagoya-Kuala Lumpur Supplementary Protocol, in Article 2(2)(c), defines the liable operator as: "any person in direct or indirect control of the (GMO) which could, as appropriate and as determined by domestic law, include, *inter alia*, the permit holder, person who placed the (GMO) on the market, developer, producer, notifier, exporter, importer, carrier or supplier". This provision is again criticised as adding ambiguity and giving more discretion to the implementer.[46] Although there are scientific and legal rationales, as well as an element of politically oriented compromise behind this provision, the effectiveness of such a law-making technique must be carefully examined in light of the prevalent international legal theories.

It is important to state the well-known principles of international law. "It is to rules generally accepted by municipal legal systems..., and not to the municipal law of a particular State, that international law refers".[47] Unless a rule of domestic law obtains the status of a generally accepted norm, "(f)rom the

---

44   This section has been inspired by Pierre-Marie Dupuy, "Chapter 15: Relations between the International Law of Responsibility and Responsibility in Municipal Law," in James Crawford *et al.* eds., *The Law of International Responsibility* (Oxford University Press, 2010), pp. 173–183.

45   Article III, International Convention on Civil Liability for Oil Pollution Damage, as amended (1992), *United Nations Treaty Series*, Vol. 973, p. 3 and Vol. 1956, p. 255.

46   Dire Tladi, "Chapter 11: Challenges and Opportunities in the Implementation of the Supplementary Protocol: Re-interpretation and Re-imagination," in A. Shibata ed., *International Liability Regime, supra* note 10, pp. 175–176.

47   *Case concerning Barcelona Traction, Light and Power Company, Limited* (New Application: 1962) (Belgium v. Spain), Second Phase, Judgment, *ICJ Reports 1970*, p. 38, para. 50.

standpoint of international law…, municipal laws are merely facts which express the will and constitute the activities of States, in the same manner as do legal decisions or administrative measures".[48] Thus, it is the principle of international law that a domestic law of a State or a decision in accordance with such law is, under international law, merely a fact and does not establish a norm justifiable at the international law plane.

At the same time, international law often refers to the determination of domestic law, like in the case of defining "State organ" within the context of the law of State responsibility. Article 4(1) of the ILC's Articles on Responsibility of States provides that "[t]he conduct of any State organ shall be considered an act of that State under international law". Article 4(2) provides that "(a)n organ includes any person or entity which has that status in accordance with the internal law of the State." As to the legal nature of this reference to domestic law, it is argued that "(i)t does so not as an admission of (international law's) dependence with respect to one or the other domestic law, but to ensure implementation of its own legal mechanism: the international responsibility of the State".[49]

How independent the international law is from the domestic law determination, however, is a matter of degree. For example, Article 5 of the ILC's Articles on Responsibility of States provides that "[t]he conduct of a person or entity which is…empowered by the [domestic] law of that State to exercise elements of governmental authority shall be considered as an act of the State under international law". In this case, although it is the international law that ultimately controls the determination whether "an element of governmental authority" is exercised or not, a more minute analysis of the domestic law elements applied in the case would be necessary to reveal the reality of the legal situation specific to the entity in question.[50]

The definition of "operator" under the Nagoya-Kuala Lumpur Supplementary Protocol can be examined in the same theoretical light. It is the Supplementary Protocol that controls the criteria of "direct or indirect control" in order for an entity to be identified as an appropriate liable person under the treaty. It is, again, the Supplementary Protocol that uses the fact as determined by domestic law as to which entity has control in specific cases of damage caused by GMOs. In this sense, the domestic laws of the State Parties that identify an operator are at the service of implementing the environmental liability regime

---

48   *Certain German Interests in Polish Upper Silesia* (Germany v. Poland), Judgment of 8 February 1928, PCIJ Series A, No. 7, p. 19.
49   P.-M. Dupuy, *supra* note 44, p. 180.
50   *Ibid.*, pp. 181–182.

established by the Supplementary Protocol. In fact, the rule on channelling liability is such a fundamental element for an effective operation of the regime, the domestic rule to that effect has become an essential part of the international regime. Its substantive content and effectiveness have become a legitimate interest of the State Parties to the Supplementary Protocol, as well as the relevant non-state actors involved in activities relating to GMOs. As such, the domestic law on channelling liability would become an important subject matter for assessment and review under Article 13 of the Supplementary Protocol.

It is also true that, while Supplementary Protocol remains free in its treatment of facts as determined by domestic rules, "it owns up to the relative dependence in which domestic law keeps it".[51] In other words, as long as its determination is within the general international criterion of "direct or indirect control", the domestic rule on channelling liability would be drafted and applied by the State Party in accordance with its own domestic legal and policy considerations. The facts incorporated by the Supplementary Protocol when operationalising its environmental liability regime are, in reality, dependent on these domestic legal and policy considerations of State Parties.

While not subjecting international law to domestic law, such dependence was considered necessary during the negotiations within the specific context of the Supplementary Protocol that addresses biodiversity damage characterised by the long-term, latent, and cumulative nature of damage caused by GMOs.[52] Such dependence was also considered appropriate in a liability regime based on the administrative approach to liability, as it is the competent national authority, rather than the victim of damage, that would identify the operator using the channelling rules in the first place.[53] Thus, the definition of operator in Article 2(2)(c) was considered acceptable to the negotiating Parties and interested non-State actors.

3   Scope of International Protection Supplanted by Domestic Criteria

The Nagoya-Kuala Lumpur Supplementary Protocol is epoch-making in providing the first-ever internationally-agreed upon definition of damage to biological diversity and establishing legal consequences as a liability for causing such damage. However, Article 3(6) provides as follows: "Parties may use criteria set out in their domestic law to address damage that occurs within the limits of their national jurisdiction."

---

51   Ibid., p. 183.
52   Reynaldo Ariel Alvarez-Morales, "A Scientific Perspective on the Supplementary Protocol," in A. Shibata ed., *International Liability Regime, supra* note 10, pp. 105–106.
53   A. Shibata, "Chapter 2," *supra* note 21, pp. 39–40.

This provision was proposed by the EU during the late stages of negotiations. The intention of the original EU proposal[54] was clear: the core obligation under the Supplementary Protocol to require the operators to take response measures in relation to biodiversity damage may be implemented by applying the domestic laws of State Parties that provide the "criteria" or "components of biological diversity" in establishing the liability of operators. The initial reactions from other negotiating Parties were indeed generally negative, as the proposal seemed to bring the domestic definition of damage into and superior to the agreed upon text of the international definition of damage to the conservation and sustainable use of biological diversity. However, its proposal finally made it into Article 3, basically retaining its original intention. There are reasons to be sceptical about Article 3(6) as subjecting the scope of protection under international law to the conditions defined by domestic law.

Under the jurisprudence of international investment arbitrations, a similar issue has been raised as to the interpretation of a provision in bilateral investment treaties (BITs) that defines the scope of its protection as "investment in accordance with the host State law". With such a provision, it was questioned whether the scope of protection under the treaty would be conditioned by the domestic law of the host State. In the famous *Salini* case, the host State, Morocco, argued that it was the Moroccan Law that should define the notion of investment, and that, applying its domestic rule, the transaction in question should be characterised as a contract for service, rather than as an investment.[55] However, the arbitral tribunals have been consistent in rejecting such arguments, restricting the flexibility provided by domestic law to the implementation phase of

---

54 EU proposal of 8 February 2010: To be introduced at the end of Article 2.2(d) (on "damage"): "Parties may use criteria set out in their domestic law in order to establish liability for any damage that falls within the scope of this Supplementary Protocol where such damage occurs within the limits of their national jurisdiction." OR New Article 7, para. 9 (on Response measures): "9. In implementing this Article, Parties may, in order to ensure conservation and sustainable use of biological diversity, establish in their domestic legislation which components of biological diversity are covered by the obligation to undertake domestic response measures." *See Report of the Group of the Friends of the Co-Chairs on Liability and Redress in the Context of the Cartagena Protocol on Biosafety on the Work of Its Second Session*, UNEP/CBD/BS/GF-L&R/2/3 (14 February 2010), p. 14.

55 *Salini Costruttori S.P.A. and Italstrade S.P.A. v. Kingdom of Morocco*, Decision on Jurisdiction (July 23, 2001), ICSID Case No. ARB/00/4, *International Legal Materials*, Vol. 42, No. 3 (2003), pp. 618–619, paras. 36–38. A similar attempt was made by Pakistan in *Bayindir Insaat Turizm Ticaret ve Sayayi A.S. v. Islamic Republic of Pakistan*, Decision on Jurisdiction (14 November 2005), ICSID Case No. ARB/03/29, paras. 106–107. Available at <http://italaw.com/> (accessed 29 September 2014).

treaty obligations. In the reasoning of the tribunals, the term "investment" would be defined in its generic concept under the BITs and be determined by international law, but the State Parties are required to implement domestically the obligation to protect such investments only in so far as they are made in conformity with their respective domestic laws.[56] When understood as such, as Dolzer and Schreuer conclude, even with the provision referring to domestic law, "the final ruling [on the scope of investment] falls into the responsibility of the international tribunal."[57] This interpretation is indeed to retain the control of international law over the reference to domestic laws.

While international law controls the scope of protection by defining the term "investment", the domestic law is relevant in supplanting the precise conditions for its protection when a State Party is implementing the treaty obligation. Thus, as another arbitral tribunal declared: "[p]lainly, as indicated by these four provisions [referring to the domestic laws of the Parties], economic transactions undertaken by a national of one of the Parties to the BIT had to meet certain legal requirements of the host State in order to qualify as an "investment" and fall under the Treaty".[58]

The same logic should be applied to the legal effect of Article 3(6) in relation to the definition of damage as provided in Article 2(2)(b) of the Supplementary Protocol. It is the definition of biodiversity damage as provided in Article 2(2)(b) that determines the scope of protection under the Supplementary Protocol. The precise condition, or criteria, for State Parties to address such damage, namely to implement the international obligation of protection, may be provided by the domestic laws of those States. This supplanting effect by the domestic law would be particularly useful when international rules themselves do not provide such conditions for implementation. Indeed, this is the case for the concept of biodiversity damage as provided by the Supplementary Protocol for the first time in the history of binding international instruments.

The Convention on Biological Diversity (CBD) contains the phrase "damage to biological diversity" (Article 14(2)), whereas, within the context of GMOs, both the CBD and the Cartagena Protocol on Biosafety (CPB) use the phrase

---

56 *Salini, supra* note 55, pp. 620–621, paras. 45–46.
57 Rudolf Dolzer & Christoph Schreuer, *Principles of International Investment Law* (Oxford University Press, 2008), p. 65. *See also* Masao Sakata, "Toushi Kyotei no 'Kokunaihou ni sitagatta Toushi' Joukou wo meguru Kaishaku Tairitsu no Igi [The Meaning of 'Investments in Accordance with the Laws of the Host State']," *Shinsedai Houseisakugaku Kenkyu* [*Hokkaido Journal of New Global Law and Policy*], Vol. 4 (2009), p. 360 (in Japanese).
58 *Fraport AG Frankfurt Airport Services Worldwide v. Republic of the Philippines*, Award (16 August 2007), ICSID Case No. ARB/03/25, para. 340. *See also* UNCTAD, *Bilateral Investment Treaties in the Mid-1990's* (United Nations, 1998), p. 36.

"adverse effects on the conservation and sustainable use of biological diversity" (CBD Article 19(3), CPB Article 1). The term "biological diversity" is defined generally and abstractly in Article 2 of the CBD as "variability among living organisms from all sources...[and] this includes diversity within species, between species and of ecosystems". The term "sustainable use" is defined in the same Article, again very generally, as "the use of components of biological diversity in a way and at a rate that does not lead to the long-term decline of biological diversity". Yet, terms like "damage" or "adverse effects" have not been legally defined. Under the CBD, certain studies have been carried out on these and similar concepts, such as "biodiversity loss",[59] but no agreement has yet been reached on the methods and/or benchmarks to evaluate such loss.[60]

Article 2(2)(b) of the Supplementary Protocol goes on to define the damage in terms of measurability and significance of the adverse effects. In other words, it defines damage in relation to the qualitative and quantitative characteristic of the effects on the conservation and sustainable use of biological diversity. The Supplementary Protocol, however, does not fully specify the adverse nature of such effects in relation to the specific content and scope of the object being affected, namely the conservation and sustainable use of biological diversity. As Michael Bowman suggests,[61] since the concept of damage can be conceptualised in terms of a diminution in value, the nature (cf. instrumental, inherent, and/or intrinsic) and the locus (cf. each individual organism, species, and/or ecosystems) of values must be ascertained in order to have a workable definition of damage. Article 2(3) of the Supplementary Protocol does provide a few hints,[62] but as a whole, Articles 2(2)(b) and 2(3) leave many of these issues open.

---

59 CBD decision VII/30 (2004), para. 2 defines "biodiversity loss" as "the long-term or permanent qualitative or quantitative reduction in components of biodiversity and their potential to provide goods and services, to be measured at global, regional and national levels." UNEP/CBD/COP/DEC/VII/30 (2004).

60 *Report of the Workshop on Liability and Redress in the context of the Convention on Biological Diversity*, UNEP/CBD/WS-L&R/3 (29 June 2001); *Synthesis report on technical information relating to damage to biological diversity and approaches to valuation and restoration of damage to biological diversity, as well as information on national/domestic measures and experiences*, UNEP/CBD/COP/9/20/Add.1 (20 March 2008).

61 Michael Bowman, "Biodiversity, Intrinsic Value, and the Definition and Valuation of Environmental Harm," in Michael Bowman and Alan Boyle eds., *Environmental Damage in International and Comparative Law: Problems of Definition and Valuation* (Oxford University Press, 2002), pp. 41–61.

62 *See* Yumihiko Matsumura, "Kankyo Songai nitaisuru Sekinin Seido no Zentei Jouken [Preconditions for a Liability Regime for Environmental Damage]," *Kankyo Kanri* [*Environmental Management*], Vol. 42, No. 12 (2006), p. 66 (in Japanese).

Thus, the definition of damage under the Supplementary Protocol must be supplanted by the domestic law of the State Party when it applies and implements the concept of damage in concrete contexts, with the understanding that the concept of damage itself is defined by the treaty. Article 3(6) can be considered as an explicit authorisation for its State Parties to use their domestic law criteria of damage to biological diversity in implementing its obligations so long as such criteria meet the internationally-agreed upon requirements of damage. Such supplanting effect by a particular domestic law of State Party may also be a temporary phenomenon. A further development and refinement of the specific content of damage under Article 2(2)(b) of the Supplementary Protocol could occur through both the domestic implementing practice and international standard-setting endeavours. Such a process may establish a subsequent agreement (VCLT Article 31(3)(a)) on the interpretation of Article 2(2)(d), effectively narrowing the discretion left for domestic law in addressing such damage as authorised under Article 3(6).[63] Again, the gap-filling function by the domestic law is within the overall control of international law.

IV Conclusion

Domestic laws are relevant only as to the methods and designs through which to implement international obligations. In this context, international law is not subordinate to domestic law.

> International law and domestic law should not be allowed to combine, ...to form a hybrid in which the content of domestic law directly controls the content of an international legal obligation. This would create unacceptable uncertainty in international affairs. Specifically, it would allow a State to make fluctuating, uncertain and un-notified assertions about the content of its domestic law, after a dispute has already arisen. Such a State, ... would be bound by nothing but its own whims and would make a mockery of the international legal agreement to which it chose to subject itself.[64]

---

63 The ICJ recognised explicitly the possibility of non-binding resolutions adopted by consensus in treaty bodies, like the COP, may comprise a subsequent agreement and/or a subsequent practice within the meaning of Article 31(3)(a) and (b) of the Vienna Convention on the Law of Treaties. *Whaling in the Antarctic* (Australia v. Japan, New Zealand intervening), Judgement of 31 March 2014, *ICJ Reports 2014*, paras. 46 and 83.

64 PCA Case No. AA 227, in the Matter of an Arbitration before a Tribunal constituted in accordance with Article 26 of the Energy Charter Treaty and the UNCITRAL Arbitration

This admonition in the *Yukos* award has been repeatedly confirmed, for example, in the *Implementation Guide* when interpreting the phrase "within the framework of national legislation" in the Aarhus Convention, and in the *Salini* award when interpreting the phrase "investment in accordance with the host State law". It is the international law that controls the extent of referencing to domestic law, either through the good faith obligation in achieving the object and purpose of a treaty, or by establishing internationally-defined concepts and definitions, only within which the domestic conditions can be take into account. In other instances, facts as determined by domestic laws of States may be utilised in operationalising an international regime: the domestic law at the service of international law. The relative dependence on the domestic law varies depending on the specific stipulation, but it is still the international law that ultimately controls the extent of such utilisation.

The same *Yukos* award, however, continued:

> The Tribunal recognises...that Parties negotiating a treaty enjoy drafting freedom and could (using clear and unambiguous language) overcome the "strong presumption of the separation of international from national law". Indeed, Parties to a treaty are free to agree to any particular regime.[65]

International regimes deliberately incorporating such interaction between international law and domestic law are in fact numerous.[66] The legal nature and the extent of such interaction, of course, depend on the particular regimes. This contribution endeavoured to examine the nature of this interaction as reflected in the Nagoya-Kuala Lumpur Supplementary Protocol providing an international liability regime for biodiversity damage caused by GMOs. In doing so, the author adopted an analytical framework of Professor Ida's concept of effectiveness in law-making that necessitates the examination of both the legal design of international law that intends to promote collaboration between international and domestic laws in its implementation phase, and how such legal design contributed to the acceptability of the regime by interested parties.

Rules 1976, between Yukos Universal Limited (Isle of Man) and the Russian Federation, Interim Award on Jurisdiction and Admissibility, 30 November 2009, para. 315.

65   *Ibid.*, para. 320.

66   Luigi Ferrari-Bravo, "International and Municipal Law: The Complementarity of Legal Systems," in R. St. J. Macdonald and Douglas M. Johnston eds., *The Structure and Process of International Law* (1986), pp. 721–722.

This all contributes to the strengthening of "implementation force (jisshi ryoku)"⁶⁷ of international law.

In light of the prevalent practice and jurisprudence on the role of domestic law in international law (as summarised above),⁶⁸ the references to domestic law in the Supplementary Protocol, although extensive and far-reaching, does not support a general criticism that international rules under the Supplementary Protocol are subordinate to the domestic laws of State Parties. Most of these references relate to the core international obligation of result to establish an innovative administrative approach to liability of operators to take response measures when a GMO under their control causes biodiversity damage. It is indeed typical in international environmental law to provide obligations of result that are of a "soft nature", as a large part of specifics in the legal design of an administrative approach to liability would be determined by the domestic laws of State Parties, including the rules on exemption and financial limits, and the methods of demonstrating a causal link between the damage and the GMOs. Notwithstanding, the State Parties are under a good faith obligation to establish an effective domestic system of liability that ensures "appropriate response measures where there is damage or sufficient likelihood of damage" (preamble of the Supplementary Protocol). The effectiveness of such a domestic system will be assessed and reviewed in the international scheme established by Article 13 of the Supplementary Protocol.

The Nagoya-Kuala Lumpur Supplementary Protocol is unique, on the other hand, in incorporating domestic law determinations and criteria in relation to the very core elements of the liability system, namely the channelling of liability and the damage that it attempts to address. These relate to Article 2(2)(c) as regards the definition of operator "as determined by domestic law", and Article 3(6) referring to the "criteria set out in [the] domestic law" in relation to the biodiversity damage. A careful reading of these provisions, however, does not support a simple claim to the effect that the determination of these elements will be totally subjected to the domestic laws of State Parties. International law controls the utilisation of those domestic determinations by providing a legal framework of "control", or an internationally-agreed upon definition of damage to biological diversity. Only within such international legal constraints can domestic law determinations be effectuated. Some discretion is allowed under the domestic laws (hence certain differences in domestic implementation of the Supplementary Protocol), and it was positively accepted by the negotiating

---

67 Ryuichi Ida, "Le droit international et la bioéthique" (2005), p. 89.
68 *See also* Carlo Santulli, *Le statut international de l'ordre juridique étatique : étude du traitement du droit interne par le droit international* (Pédone, 2001).

States and interested non-State actors because of the technical nature of biodiversity damage caused by GMOs, the legal nature of the Supplementary Protocol based on an administrative approach to liability, and the lack of internationally-agreed upon criteria and methods to operationalise the concept of biodiversity damage.

The incorporation of domestic law determinations in the international rules on channelling liability and damage in the Supplementary Protocol has far-reaching international legal implications beyond the typical "soft" obligations of result, as described above. Since these determinations comprise the essential elements for the operationalisation of the international liability regime established by the Supplementary Protocol, the existence and the proper application of the relevant domestic laws are *sine qua non* for its effectiveness. As such, the substantive content of such laws has become a legitimate common concern of its State Parties. Having an appropriate domestic law to channel the liability to an operator has become an obligation of the State Parties to effectuate the international liability regime[69] as established by the Supplementary Protocol. Having certain domestic law criteria to address biodiversity damage, although not a "hard" obligation under the Supplementary Protocol, would be necessary in order for the liability regime to work effectively. International endeavours on capacity-building as envisioned by the negotiating Parties[70] will become important in this context. Indeed, the legal situation brought about by these provisions referring to domestic law is far from the characterisation that "the Supplementary Protocol establishes minimum and minimal international norms and subjects these to domestic law".[71]

---

69   On "obligation of maintenance" as distinct from obligations of result or conduct, *see* Shinya Murase, "Perspective from International Economic Law on Transnational Environmental Issues," *Recueil des cours*, Vol. 253 (1995), pp. 419–420.

70   Section C on Complementary Capacity-Building Measures, Decision BS-V/11: *International rules and procedures in the field of liability and redress for damage resulting from transboundary movements of living modified organisms*, adopted on 15 October 2010, by the 5th Meeting of COP-MOP, Cartagena Protocol on Biosafety.

71   W.D. Yifru & K. Garforth, *supra* note 12, p. 150.

CHAPTER 10

New Perspectives on Soft Law: Towards More Effective Regime Governance

Tatsuya Abe

Introduction

Discussion on soft law has been revived since in the middle of the 1990s. In response to issues of worldwide importance, such as the protection of the global environment, the prevention of international terrorism, the promotion of universal human rights, and the non-proliferation of weapons of mass destruction, soft law has been widely and frequently used as a useful instrument to address these issues and is thus attracting the attention of contemporary commentators again.

Soft law was a matter of discussion in the 1970s–80s. At that time it was mostly international law scholars who were involved in the discussion. Some writers favoured soft law; however, the majority of authors were more or less critical or even negative about soft law. Professor Ryuichi Ida was one of the international law scholars who contributed to the discussion, with his articles "Qu'est-ce que le 'Soft Law'?"[1] and "Formation des normes internationales dans un monde en mutation—Critique de la notion de soft law—"[2] in which he pointed out that "as an instrument of legal analysis, the concept of soft law lacks clarity."[3] In that period, most international law scholars attempted to confine the legal implications of soft law to the minimum within a limited context. This attempt was successful and, before long, discussion on soft law was thus virtually exhausted. Nevertheless, it has regained momentum in the latter half of the 90s. Contemporary international lawyers who are familiar with the concept of international relations have led the debate. Their approach to soft law is quite different from that taken by the majority of international law scholars in the 1970s–80s. They highlight the positive elements in soft law as a flexible and useful means to maintain and strengthen the continuous effectiveness of a specific

---

1 Ryuichi Ida, "Qu'est-ce que le 'Soft Law'?" No. 1 (1985), pp. 1–26; Ryuichi Ida, "Qu'est-ce que le 'Soft Law'?" No. 2 (1985), pp. 1–21.
2 Ryuichi Ida, "Formation des normes internationales dans un monde en mutation" (1991), pp. 333–340.
3 *Ibid.*, p. 340.

international treaty regime, and discuss sociological topics such as reasons to choose soft law instead of hard law, the practical effects of soft law and so on. Although the current arguments are valuable for understanding soft law phenomena from various angles, a fundamental *legal* question that has already been identified by international law scholars in the 1970s–80s still remains unanswered: what *legal* effects does soft law have?[4]

Against this background, this article aims to revisit this *legal* question. In the following sections, the author will first outline the development of the academic discussion on soft law and identify new general perspectives on soft law (I). It is curious that contemporary international lawyers who are familiar with the concept of international relations have paid more attention to soft law since the middle of the 1990s. Is this because soft law itself has changed? Is this because soft law itself has become diverse? Is this because soft law has gained new features? Based on these findings, the author will then analyse two arms control regimes that offer many examples of soft law and illustrate its *legal* effects (II).

I Discourse on Soft Law

There has been no well-established definition of soft law. A lack of a common definition has made discussion on soft law difficult and even complicated because different arguments have been based on different understandings from different perspectives. This was particularly the case in the early phase of discussion. In fact, at that time commentators engaged in serious discussion on the usefulness of soft law at a terminological or conceptual level. However, as the discussion progressed, most authors tended to use the term "soft law" with more or less the same meaning. Therefore, it seemed that a minimal understanding of the concept of soft law emerged. For the purpose of this article, the author will use soft law as "any international instrument other than a treaty that contains principles, norms, standards, or other statements of expected behaviour."[5] The point is that soft law is not legally binding, but has certain implications.

---

4   Professor Ida pointed out that the precise and exact concept of soft law should be considered based on the development of international law (Ryuichi Ida, "Formation des normes internationales dans un monde en mutation" (1991), p. 340). However, he did not suggest *what* the precise and exact concept of soft law is.

5   Dinah Shelton, "Normative Hierarchy in International Law," *American Journal of International Law*, Vol. 100 (2006), p. 319. *See also* Andrew T. Guzman & Timothy L. Meyer, "International Soft Law," *Journal of Legal Analysis*, Vol. 2, No. 1 (2010), p. 172.

1 Traditional Discussion in the 1970s–80s

(1) Background

It was in the 1970s–80s that legally non-binding soft law documents were most frequently adopted, although this phenomenon had also been recognized after World War II.[6]

In the 1960s, newly independent developing States, taking full advantage of their automatic and numerical majority in the international forum, in particular in the United Nations General Assembly, speculated on the utilization of soft law instruments, such as resolutions, declarations and recommendations, with a view to modifying a number of traditional rules and principles of the international legal order.[7] In an attempt to achieve a radical change in the traditional international legal system that had been set up at a time when they were not sovereign States, they focused on establishing an international economic order that was favourable to them. These efforts resulted in three important UN General Assembly Resolutions: the 1962 Permanent Sovereignty over Natural Resources;[8] the 1974 Declaration for the Establishment of a New International Economic Order;[9] and the 1974 Charter of Economic Rights and Duties of States.[10] Developing States claimed that some of these non-legal instruments had acquired legal force and had even become norms of *jus cogens*, though this argument provoked negative reactions from their counterparts, i.e. developed States, because it departed from the traditional law-making process based on voluntarism.

At this juncture, it was not only the field of international economy that was the subject of regulation by soft law. The rapid progress of science and technology and the interdependence among States required the international community as a whole to tackle in an expeditious manner such important topics as the regulation of outer space activities, the control of deep seabed mining, the protection of the human environment, and the

---

6   The 1948 Universal Declaration on Human Rights was one of the early soft law documents adopted at the United Nations General Assembly, which made a list of human rights with the intention of exploring possibilities for a legally binding treaty in the future.

7   C.M. Chinkin, "The Challenge of Soft Law: Development and Change in International Law," *International and Comparative Law Quarterly*, Vol. 38 (1989), p. 853; Pierre-Marie Dupuy, "Soft Law and the International Law of the Environment," *Michigan Journal of International Law*, Vol. 12, No. 2 (1991), p. 421.

8   UN Doc. A/RES/1803 (XVII), dated 14 December 1962.

9   UN Doc. A/RES/S-6/3201, dated 1 May 1974.

10 UN Doc. A/RES/3281 (XXIX), dated 12 December 1974. For detailed analysis *see* Ryuichi Ida, "The Legal Structure of the New International Economic Order" (1982).

realisation of general disarmament. Several key, legally non-binding documents in these areas were drawn up: the 1963 Declaration of Legal Principles Governing the Activities of States in the Exploration and Use of Outer Space;[11] the 1970 Declaration of Principles Governing the Seabed and the Ocean Floor, and the Subsoil Thereof, beyond the Limits of National Jurisdiction;[12] the 1972 Declaration of the United Nations Conference on the Human Environment (Stockholm Declaration);[13] the 1978 Final document of First Special Session of the General Assembly devoted to Disarmament and the 1982 Concluding document of the Second Special Session of the General Assembly devoted to Disarmament.[14] Furthermore, soft law was used in a regional context as well. An example was the 1975 Helsinki Final Act.[15]

In any event, the usefulness of soft law was generally and widely shared among States as indicated through international practice. Soft law was recognized as a useful means to overcome the difficulties of the traditional law-making process and its formality. In this regard, standing institutions such as the United Nations and other inter-governmental organisations played an indispensable role in producing numerous soft law instruments.[16]

(2)   Academic Arguments
(a)   *Terminological/Conceptual Level*

The frequent adoption of soft law documents in international practice has prompted academic discussion on soft law since the 1970s. Initially, the commentators focused on its terminology and concepts. This was not without reason, for there was (and remains) no clear-cut definition of soft law.

---

11   UN Doc. A/RES/1962 (XVIII), dated 13 December 1963.
12   UN Doc. A/RES/2749 (XXV), dated 17 December 1970.
13   UN Doc. A/CONF.48/14/Rev.1 (1973).
14   UN Doc. A/S-10/2, dated 30 June 1978; A/S-12/32, dated 10 July 1982.
15   Final Act of the Conference on Security and Cooperation in Europe, dated 1 August 1975. The inclusion of the phrase of "...this Final Act, which is not eligible for registration under Article 102 of the Charter of the United Nations..." implies the legally non-binding status of the Final Act (R.R. Baxter, "International Law in 'Her Infinite Variety'," *International and Comparative Law Quarterly*, Vol. 29 (1980), p. 558).
16   P.M. Dupuy, *supra* note 7, pp. 420–421. The fact that the delineation of treaties and the modality of treaty-making were established by the Vienna Convention on the Law of Treaties would provide states with guidance on the policy choice between a legally binding treaty and a legally non-binding document (*See* C.M. Chinkin, *supra* note 7, p. 860).

Two different connotations of soft law were put forward.[17] One understanding was that soft law is a weak and ambiguous stipulation in legally binding instruments. As Pierre-Marie Dupuy pointed out, "an increasing number of treaty provisions can be found in which the wording used is so "soft" that it seems impossible to consider them as creating a precise obligation or burden on States parties."[18] The other depicted it as a legally non-binding instrument. According to Baxter, "[s]tates have on a number of occasions undertaken the preparation of instruments which deliberately do not create legal obligations but which are intended to create pressures and to influence the conduct of States and to set the development of international law in new courses."[19] The problem was that sometimes these connotations were not clearly distinguished from each other.[20] Consequently, several authors expressed a critical view that the term "soft law" was not appropriate because it created much terminological confusion.[21] Given that "the very nature of 'soft' law lies in the fact that it is not in itself legally binding," it is important to distinguish clearly between the *substance* and *form*, since they are not necessarily in perfect accordance with one another.[22] However, even if "soft law" was understood in the latter meaning, this concept encountered other strong criticisms. Sztucki claimed that "the term is inadequate and misleading" based on the position that "[t]here are no two levels or 'species' of law; something is law or is not law" and that "the concept is counter-productive or even dangerous" because "[o]n the one hand, it creates illusory expectations of (perhaps even insistence on) compliance with what no one is obliged to comply with; and on the other hand, it exposes binding legal norms for risks of neglect, and international law

---

17 R.R. Baxter, *supra* note 15, pp. 553–560; Ryuichi Ida, "Qu'est-ce que le 'Soft Law'?" No. 1 (1985), pp. 1–26; Jerzy Sztucki, "Reflections on International 'Soft Law'," in Jan Ramberg, Ove Bring, and Said Mahmoudi eds., *Festskrift till Lars Hjerner: Studies in International Law* (Norstedts, 1990), pp. 551–556; Ryuichi Ida, "Formation des normes internationales dans un monde en mutation" (1991), pp. 333–348. cf. C.M. Chinkin, *supra* note 7, p. 851.

18 P.M. Dupuy, *supra* note 7, p. 429.

19 R.R. Baxter, *supra* note 15, p. 557.

20 This problem is still seen in a recent work. *See* Vassilis Pergantis, "Soft Law, Diplomatic Assurances and the Instrumentalisation of Normativity: Wither a Liberal Promise?" *Netherlands International Law Review*, Vol. 56, No. 2 (2009), p. 142.

21 Michel Virally, "La distinction entre texts internationaux de portée juridique et texte internaitonaux dépourvus de portée juridique (à l'exception des textes émanant des organizations internationals): Rapport provisoire," *Annuaire de l'Institut de droit international, Session de Cambridge* (1983), p. 246. *See also* Chris Ingelse, "Soft Law?" *Polish Yearbook of International Law*, Vol. 20 (1993), p. 82.

22 P.M. Dupuy, *supra* note 7, p. 429.

as a whole for risks of erosion, by blurring the threshold between what is legally binding and what is not."[23] Behind these criticisms, the traditional binary character of law can be observed. Those authors who were negative about the terminology or concept of soft law took the position that there must be a sharp and rigid distinction between law and non-law, and did not accept anything in the middle.[24]

Furthermore, developing States' controversial arguments on soft law were questioned not only by developed States but also by academia. The attempt of developing States to create their favourable legal norms through quickly adopted soft law documents was nothing more than an introduction of a *new* method of law-making and would lead to "a revolutionary change in the structure of the system itself."[25] It was thus clear that this *new* method of law-making was neither supported nor endorsed by scholars who held a positivistic view of international law.

(b)   *Substantive Level*

The fact that sceptical and critical views were expressed at both terminological and conceptual levels did not necessarily mean that international law scholars found nothing substantive in soft law. On the contrary, virtually all international law scholars acknowledged the possibility that a soft law rule could be transformed into a hard law rule in the context of the dynamic process of law-making. It was evident that "a substantial part of 'soft' law today, in an impressionistic way, describes part of the 'hard' law of tomorrow."[26]

There are two ways for transformation to occur: adopting a soft law rule as a treaty hard law and crystallizing it into a customary hard law. The former may occur when the preceding soft law rule provides the basis of diplomatic negotiation among interested States and, as a result, ends up being reflected in legally binding instruments. A typical example is the 1948 Universal Declaration

---

23   J. Sztucki, *supra* note 17, pp. 550–551. See also Francesco Francioni, "International 'Soft Law': A Contemporary Assessment," in Vaughan Lowe and Malgosia Fitzmaurice eds., *Fifty Years of the International Court of Justice, Essay in Honour of Sir Robert Jennings* (Cambridge University Press, 1996), p. 167; Jan Klabbers, "The Redundancy of Soft Law," *Nordic Journal of International Law*, Vol. 65, No. 2 (1996), p. 182: "The Undesirability of Soft Law," *Nordic Journal of International Law*, Vol. 67, No. 2 (1998), p. 391.

24   Gaetano Arangio-Ruiz, *The United Nations Declaration on Friendly Relations and the System of the Sources of International Law* (BRILL, 1979), p. 29; Prosper Weil, "Towards Relative Normativity in International Law?" *American Journal of International Law*, Vol. 77 (1983), p. 417. See also C. Ingelse, *supra* note 21, p. 79, p. 88.

25   C.M. Chinkin, *supra* note 7, p. 856.

26   P.M. Dupuy, *supra* note 7, p. 433. See also C. Ingelse, *supra* note 21, p. 83.

on Human Rights, which served as the foundation for the 1966 International Covenants on Civil and Political Rights and on Economic, Social and Cultural Rights. The latter may happen when a soft law rule constitutes an evidence of *opinio juris*, which is one of the two requirements for creating a customary rule. In the case of Military and Paramilitary Activities in and against Nicaragua, the International Court of Justice (ICJ) admitted that "*opinio juris* may, though with all due caution, be deduced from, *inter alia*, the attitude of the Parties and the attitude of States towards certain General Assembly resolutions."[27] Soft law was thus generally recognized as "an important factor of the law-creating process in international relations,"[28] "an important *stage* in the process of elaborating international norms,"[29] and "a significant element of development of customary international law."[30]

The academic argument about soft law described above indicates that international law scholars have been successful in limiting the scope of discussion to traditional law-making theory. This delineation was fully acceptable to and even comfortable for them, particularly those who took a positivistic stance, because it was firmly grounded in the traditional theory on the sources of international law. International law scholars, intentionally or unintentionally, dealt with nothing more than the issue of one-way transformation of a soft law rule into a hard law rule; in other words, the issue of whether a non-legally binding rule X *becomes* legally binding or not.[31] As a consequence, virtually no attention was paid to the relation between soft law and hard law. However, if soft law is different from, but related to and dependent on hard law, the former must have *some* legal effects on the latter.

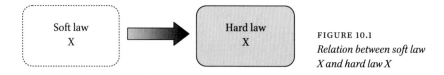

FIGURE 10.1
Relation between soft law X and hard law X

---

27   Military and Paramilitary Activities in and against Nicaragua (Nicaragua v. United States of America), Judgment, *I.C.J. Reports* 1986, pp. 99–100, para. 188; Legality of the Threat or Use of Nuclear Weapons, Advisory Opinion, *I.C.J. Reports* 1996, pp. 254–255, para. 70.
28   Michael Bothe, "Legal and Non-legal Norms—A Meaningful Distinction in International Relations?" *Netherlands Yearbook of International Law*, Vol. XI (1980), p. 79.
29   P. Weil, *supra* note 24, p. 417.
30   Remigiusz Bierzanek, "Some Remarks on 'Soft' International Law," *Polish Yearbook of International Law*, Vol. 17 (1988), p. 31.
31   *See* Ryuichi Ida, "Formation des normes internationales dans un monde en mutation" (1991), p. 334.

2 Contemporary Debate Since the Middle of the 1990s

(1) Background

Since the middle of the 1990s soft law has been more widely used than ever. This is mainly because of the development of certain matters in the international community. Needless to say, it was the end of the Cold War that removed the main political obstacle to reaching agreements among States and paved the way for the international community to achieve common interests such as the protection of specific human rights and the elimination or control of specific weapons. Moreover, increasing cross-border and global activities, not only of States but also of non-State actors, due largely to the rapid developments in science and technology, drew the attention of the international community to the need to regulate these activities with a view to promoting free trade, protecting the global environment and combating terrorism. The development of these matters led to the introduction of new and additional regulations. Although the international community, as a matter of principle, normally seeks to adopt legally binding treaties, non-legally binding instruments have also become more pervasive and diverse in the international regulatory landscape than ever.[32]

Admittedly, there remains the traditional type of soft law which incorporates general substantive norms and guidelines for States activities on specific topics.[33] However, contemporary soft law documents also accommodate procedural and institutional mechanisms to implement these norms and guidelines with a view to enhancing their effectiveness. Since establishing substantive norms as such does not guarantee compliance with them, it is widely recognized that, for these norms to be effective, a monitoring mechanism is required.[34] In the post-Cold War era, the prevalence of this type of instrument gradually increased. The 1993 Vienna Declaration and Programme of Action, the 1995 Beijing Declaration, the 1997 Universal Declaration on Human Genome and Human Rights, and the 2007 United Nations Declaration on the Rights of Indigenous Peoples dealt with the protection of human rights. The 1991 United Nations Register of Conventional Arms and the 2001 United Nations Programme of Action to Prevent, Combat and Eradicate the Illicit Trade in Small Arms and Light Weapons in All Its Aspects covered conventional weapons. The 2000 United Nations Millennium Declaration focused on the issue of the social and economic development. The 2006 United

---

32 Timothy L. Meyer, "Soft Law as Delegation," *Fordham International Law Journal*, Vol. 32 (2009), p. 890.

33 The 1992 Rio Declaration on Environment and Development is a good example.

34 Ryuichi Ida, "Making of International Norms on Bioethics" (2004), pp. 173–198.

Nations Global Counter-Terrorism Strategy addressed actions against international terrorism.

In the meantime, even hard law regimes have also relied on soft law measures. Many contemporary international treaties that established their own regimes have in fact made efforts to enhance and strengthen their effectiveness through soft law measures that were subsequently adopted by international monitoring organs. Several international treaties embarked on such efforts in the 1970s. For instance, the 1966 International Covenant on Civil and Political Rights has been monitored by the Human Rights Committee since 1976. This Committee is mandated to submit legally non-binding comments and observations. In the area of the global environment, the 1985 Vienna Convention for the Protection of the Ozone Layer and its 1987 Montreal Protocol on Substances that Deplete the Ozone Layer began a treaty organ process which plays a key role in implementing the provisions through annual or biennial discussion among States Parties with the assistance of its secretariat, and this process has proliferated in many other areas in the same field since the middle of the 1990s. Another area that features soft law measures within hard law regimes is disarmament and arms control. Both the 1968 Nuclear Non-Proliferation Treaty and the 1972 Biological Weapons Convention (BWC) have relied on political documents adopted by their own treaty organ—a Review Conference—held almost every five years. In both cases, specific legally non-binding measures have been introduced with a view to enhancing and strengthening the regime. This process drew more attention after the end of the Cold War. In addition to these two treaties, the 1993 Chemical Weapons Convention (CWC) is also a hard law regime that has been developed through soft law measures. Due to a number of decisions taken by a newly established full-fledged international organization, the Organisation for the Prohibition of Chemical Weapons (OPCW), the CWC regime has become one of the most complicated international hard law regimes.

In any event, the tendency to use soft law instruments has been accelerated by movements to institutionalize the international community and to establish specific regimes which attach great importance to continuous and increasing their effective operation through collaborative activities among States Parties, international monitoring organs and other stakeholders, including the private sector and civil society.

(2)   Academic Arguments

The quantitative and qualitative expansion of soft law instruments illustrated above has facilitated a revival of discussion on soft law since the middle of the 1990s, mainly led by contemporary international lawyers who are familiar with the concept of international relations. Their perceptions of soft law are quite different from those of international law scholars in the 1970s and 80s. In general, they are rather positive about soft law.

It is true that contemporary international lawyers share almost the same views as previous international law scholars on several topics. They have more or less the same understanding of soft law. Guzman and Meyer argue that "soft law is most commonly defined to include hortatory, rather than legally binding, obligations."[35] They also discuss soft law in the context of law-making. According to Hillgenberg, soft law "can be 'subsequent practice' as defined in Article 31(3)(b) of the Vienna Convention on the Law of Treaties, to be taken into account in interpreting a treaty."[36] However, they have extended the scope of the discussion to reasons for choosing soft law instead of hard law, and the advantages of soft law over hard law. This goes beyond the delineation successfully established by international law scholars in the previous decades.

Contemporary international lawyers are attracted by the flexibility of soft law in terms of its procedures, commitment and implementation. Regarding the procedures, soft law instruments are easy to adopt because they can avoid constitutional and other domestic legal requirements for entry into force;[37] they are more adaptable to an unexpected change of situation, in particular to technical matters that may need rapid or repeated revision;[38] and, they can be drafted and signed by parties that are not entitled to participate in treaty negotiation or conclude a treaty under international law.[39] As to the commitment, the very fact that soft law is non-binding makes it easier to induce reluctant States to become a party, and overcomes concerns that they might be committing themselves to a course of conduct when future circumstances are hard to foresee.[40] Finally, in regard to the implementation, soft law documents provide

---

35   A. Guzman and T. Meyer, *supra* note 5, p. 172.
36   Hartmut Hillgenberg, "A Fresh Look at Soft Law," *European Journal of International Law*, Vol. 10, No. 3 (1999), pp. 513–514.
37   Richard L. Williamson Jr., "Hard Law, Soft Law, and Non-law in Multilateral Arms Control: Some Compliance Hypotheses," *Chicago Journal of International Law*, Vol. 4, No. 1 (2003), p. 63; Andrew T. Guzman, "The Design of International Agreements," *European Journal of International Law*, Vol. 16, No. 4 (2005), p. 592; D. Shelton, *supra* note 5, p. 322.
38   Charles Lipson, "Why Are Some International Agreements Informal?" *International Organization*, Vol. 45 (1991), p. 500; H. Hillgenberg, *supra* note 36, p. 501; D. Shelton, *supra* note 5, p. 322.
39   H. Hillgenberg, *supra* note 36, p. 501; D. Shelton, *supra* note 5, p. 322; V. Pergantis, *supra* note 20, pp. 161–164; Mauro Barelli, "The Role of Soft Law in the International Legal System: the Case of the United Nations Declaration on the Rights of Indigenous Peoples," *International and Comparative Law Quarterly*, Vol. 58, No. 4 (2009), pp. 964–968.
40   R. Williamson Jr., *supra* note 37, p. 63; A. Guzman, *supra* note 37, p. 593.

States with a wide margin of discretion as to national implementation, which enables them to accommodate divergent national interests.[41] It should also be pointed out that soft law norms have the same effect on the domestic order as hard law norms if they are incorporated as domestic "hard" regulations by States or by private business bodies. Consequently, almost all contemporary international lawyers share the view that when dealing with a matter of considerable uncertainty, an essential factor is flexibility.[42]

The fundamental differences between the traditional debate and the contemporary argument lie in the focus of interest as well as the context of discussion. On the one hand, international law scholars in the 1970s-80s concentrated on the topic of possible transformation of a soft law into a hard law in the very limited context of the traditional law-making theory. On the other hand, contemporary international lawyers today regard soft law as one of the most useful means to maintain and strengthen the effective operation of a specific international regime, and even recognize the coexistence and convergence of hard law and soft law in a wide context of more effective global governance.[43] Emerging soft law measures within hard law regimes in this wide context raise a question about the relation between soft law and hard law. If soft law measures are useful for hard law regimes, the former must have some *legal* effects on the latter from a legal point of view.[44]

In this regard, a useful perspective is offered by a contemporary international lawyer. Dinah Shelton categorizes soft law into two types: "primary soft law" and "secondary soft law."[45] "Primary soft law" is a legally non-binding instrument declaring general principles and guidelines on certain topics, as often seen in previous decades. Such an instrument is addressed to the entire membership of the international community or of international institutions, and is sometimes intended to be a potential basis for a future legally binding

---

41 C. Lipson, *supra* note 38, p. 500; Kenneth W. Abbott & Duncan Snidal, "Hard and Soft Law in International Governance," *International Organization*, Vol. 54, No. 3 (2000), p. 445.

42 H. Hillgenberg, *supra* note 36, p. 501; K. Abbott & D. Snidal, *supra* note 41, pp. 441–444; A. Guzman, *supra* note 37, p. 591; Kal Raustiala, "Form and Substance in International Agreements," *American Journal of International Law*, Vol. 99 (2005), pp. 592–593, p. 599, pp. 612–613.

43 John J. Kirton & Michael J. Trebilcock, *Hard Choices, Soft Law: Voluntary Standards in Global Trade, Environment, and Social Governance* (Ashgate, 2004), p. 5.

44 cf. Professor Ida emphasizes positive aspects of soft law instruments in the field of international bioethics. (Ryuichi Ida, "Science, Technology and International Protection of Human Rights," (2001), p. 214).

45 D. Shelton, *supra* note 5, p. 70.

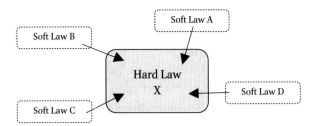

FIGURE 10.2   *Relation between soft law A to D and hard law X*

treaty. "Secondary soft law" is a legally non-binding complementary measure implementing an existing hard law regime. This type of soft law is no longer recognized as "a precursor" of hard law but is combined with and supplemental to the hard law regime with a view to enhancing its effectiveness.[46] The decisions, recommendations, and resolutions of international supervisory organs as well as the comments, views and findings of independent monitoring bodies are classified in this category. Secondary soft law has expanded, largely as a consequence of the proliferation of multilateral treaty regimes and the creation of their monitoring institutions supervising the compliance with treaty obligations.[47] Until recently this type of soft law has hardly been subject to concrete examination. Therefore, its extensive analysis should shed fresh light on contemporary features of soft law.

II   Secondary Soft Law

Secondary soft law has been practiced in a variety of ways in many contemporary international treaties. Among them, the present author picks up two legal disarmament regimes: the 1972 Biological Weapons Convention (BWC)[48] and the 1993 Chemical Weapons Convention (CWC).[49] As mentioned briefly above, in both cases, international monitoring organs are the main vehicles for the production of a wide range of secondary soft law. While the BWC regime has been strengthened through the measures adopted at the Review Conferences

---

46   cf. Ryuichi Ida, "Making of International Norms on Bioethics" (2004), pp. 173–198.
47   D. Shelton, *supra* note 5, p. 70.
48   The Convention on the Prohibition of the Development, Production, and Stockpiling of Bacteriological (Biological) and Toxin Weapons and on Their Destruction, 1015 UNTS 163 (No. 14860).
49   The Convention on the Prohibition of the Development, Production, Stockpiling and Use of Chemical Weapons and on Their Destruction, 1974 UNTS 317 (No. 33757).

held seven times since 1980, the CWC regime has been enriched by the measures adopted by the Organisation for the Prohibition of Chemical Weapons (OPCW) operational since 1997. It should be noted that these two institutions have different organizational structures. On the one hand, the Review Conference of the BWC is an *ad hoc* treaty organ; on the other hand, the OPCW is a standing international organization. In the following sections, the present author first illustrates the various types of secondary soft law adopted under the two regimes and then attempts to analyse multiple *legal* effects of secondary soft law on hard law regimes.

1 Practice of the Biological and Chemical Weapons Conventions Regimes

(1) Biological Weapons Convention (BWC) Regime

The BWC regime aims at prohibiting and getting rid of biological weapons. In order to achieve this goal, the BWC includes fifteen articles covering both substantive obligations such as the prohibition of military activities (Articles I and III), the destruction of biological weapons (Article II) and the national implementation measures (Article IV) as well as procedural provisions such as consultation and cooperation (Article V) and complaints to the UN Security Council (Article VI). The operation of the BWC has been reviewed every five years by the "Review Conference," an *ad hoc* treaty organ, which has produced a number of secondary soft law measures.

States Parties have agreed to the interpretations, definitions and/or elaborations of the provisions. There have been understandings on substantive obligations under Articles I, II, III and IV.[50] For instance, the Third and Fourth Review Conferences reaffirmed that *the Convention prohibits the development, production, stockpiling, other acquisition or retention of microbial or other biological agents or toxins harmful to plants and animals, as well as humans, of types and in quantities that have no justification for prophylactic, protective or other peaceful purposes.*[51]

Secondly, a lack of its own verification system has been rectified through the introduction of additional measures, i.e. voluntary declarations as well as

---

50 BWC Doc. BWC/CONF.I/10, dated 21 March 1980, pp. 6–7; BWC/CONF.II/13, dated 30 September 1986, Part II, pp. 3–5; BWC/CONF.III/23 (1991), Part II, pp. 11–13; BWC/CONF.IV/9 (1996), Part II, pp. 15–18; BWC/CONF.VI/6 (2006), pp. 9–11; BWC/CONF.VII/7, dated 13 January 2012, pp. 10–12.

51 BWC Doc. BWC/CONF.III/23 (1991), Part II, p. 11; BWC/CONF.IV/9 (1996), Part II, p. 15, para. 2. *See also* BWC/CONF.VI/6 (2006), p. 10, para. 1; BWC/CONF.VII/7, dated 13 January 2012, p. 10, para. 1.

procedural and institutional mechanisms. With regard to the voluntary declarations, States Parties have been requested to provide information on the compliance with substantive obligations under Articles I, II, III and IV.[52] States Parties have also been encouraged to participate in an annual exchange of information, known as Confidence-Building Measures (CBMs) based on the agreement at the Second Review Conference in the context of consultation and cooperation among States Parties under Article V.[53] After the subsequent elaboration, the current scope of CBMs covers eight items.[54] All in all, due to the fact that the BWC has no obligation to make declarations on domestic activities, these two types of voluntary submission system have contributed to making the status of compliance visible to the international community and to enhancing the confidence and the transparency among States Parties, although wider participation is required in the future. As far as procedural and institutional mechanisms are concerned, various measures have been taken. The idea of a mechanism to allow any State Party to request an *ad hoc* meeting with a view to considering and resolving doubts about compliance with the BWC of another State Party was realized as "the Formal Consultative Meeting" in accordance with the measures taken by the Second and Third Review Conferences.[55] This overcomes the criticism that the Article VI procedure providing for the lodging of a complaint to the UN Security Council would be totally ineffective if an alleged State Party was one of the permanent members of the Security Council.[56] In addition, institutional deficiencies of the Review Conference were addressed by subsequent agreements, although this is a temporary solution.

---

52 BWC Doc. BWC/CONF.I/3, dated 2 January 1980, p. 4, para. 10; BWC/CONF.II/1, dated 5 May 1986, p. 4, para. 18; BWC/CONF.III/1, dated 15 April 1991, pp. 6–7, para. 23; BWC/CONF. IV/1, dated 1 November 1996, p. 4, para. 21; BWC/CONF.V/PC/1, dated 1 May 2001, p. 4, para. 22; BWC/CONF.VI/PC/2, dated 3 May 2006, p. 4, para. 22 (b); BWC/CONF.VII/PC/2, dated 26 April 2011, p. 4, para. 24. Approximately 20–35 States Parties have submitted to every session of the Review Conference their information which is compiled and distributed as an official document (BWC Doc. BWC/CONF.VII/INF.2, dated 23 November 2011; BWC/CONF.VII/INF.2/Add.1, dated 7 December 2011).

53 BWC Doc. BWC/CONF.II/13, dated 30 September 1986, Part II, p. 6.

54 BWC Doc. BWC/CONF.III/23 (1991), Part II, pp. 14–15. Around 60–70 States Parties have participated in the CBMs almost every year in the last interval of the Review Conferences, and a total of 112 States Parties have submitted information at least once since the introduction of the CBMs (BWC Doc. BWC/CONF.VII/INF.1, dated 28 September 2011, p. 8, para. 26. *See also ibid.*, pp. 26–31).

55 BWC Doc. BWC/CONF.II/13, dated 30 September 1986, Part II, pp. 5–6; BWC/CONF.III/23 (1991), Part II, pp. 15–16.

56 This mechanism was, in fact, invoked once by Cuba against the United States in 1997 (UN Doc. A/52/128, dated 29 April 1997).

Since 2003, the Meeting of States Parties, an annual inter-sessional meeting, has been held every year for the purpose of preparing the next session of the Review Conference. In the meantime, the Implementation Support Unit (ISU) that is an interim independent organ composed of three full-time staff members and functions in the role of secretariat was established in 2006 and renewed in 2011 by the decisions adopted at the Sixth and Seventh Review Conferences.[57]

These practices illustrate the important role that secondary soft law measures play in the BWC regime and its operation.

(2)   Chemical Weapons Convention (CWC) Regime

The CWC regime has the purpose of complete elimination of chemical weapons. For this purpose, substantive obligations such as the prohibition of military activities, the destruction of chemical weapons and chemical weapons production facilities (Articles I) as well as national implementation (Article VIII) are included and, in addition, an intrusive verification system based on declarations and inspections (Articles III, IV, V and VI and relevant Verification Annexes) is accommodated. In 1997 the CWC regime became operational under the supervision of the Organisation for the Prohibition of Chemical Weapons (OPCW), a standing international organization, which consists of three internal organs: the Conference of the States Parties (hereinafter "the Conference"), the Executive Council and the Technical Secretariat. It is the Conference and the Executive Council that have adopted a number of secondary soft law measures.

Firstly, decisions on the interpretation of specific provisions have been taken in order to clarify their scope or meaning. The Conference adopted relevant understandings on terms such as "buried by a state party on its territory" and "dumped at sea" (Article III, para. 2 and Article IV, para. 17);[58] "interpretation" (Verification Annex Part II, para. 26);[59] "end-use certificate" (Verification Annex Part VIII, para. 32 and Verification Annex Part VIII, para. 26);[60] "import" and "export." (Verification Annex Part VII, paras. 1, 8(b) and 8(c) and the Verification Annex Part VIII, para. 1)[61]

Secondly, recommendations to States Parties to take specific actions have also been adopted. For instance, States Parties are invited to inform, on a vol-

---

57   BWC Doc. BWC/CONF.VI/6 (2006), pp. 19–20, paras. 5–6; BWC/CONF.VII/7, dated 13 January 2012, pp. 25–26, paras. 31–36.
58   OPCW Doc. C-I/DEC.31, dated 16 May 1997.
59   OPCW Doc. C-II/DEC.9, dated 5 December 1997.
60   OPCW Doc. C-III/DEC.7, dated 17 November 1998.
61   OPCW Doc. C-13/DEC.4, dated 3 December 2008.

untary basis, that a facility of Schedule 2 or Schedule 3 chemicals has reduced its level of activities to below the declaration threshold.[62] States Parties are also requested to provide the Technical Secretariat with the full text of their national implementation legislation.[63]

Thirdly, decisions of policy-making organs can lead to the waiver of hard law obligations. With respect to the regulation of transfer[64] of Schedule 1 chemicals, the 30-day advance notification by both sending and receiving States Parties under the Verification Annex Part VI, paras. 3 and 5 was not required in the case of transfer of saxitoxin (a Schedule 1 chemical used for medical/diagnostic purposes) by the *interim* practical guideline adopted by the Executive Council,[65] which enabled States Parties to address emergency situations in which saxitoxin needs to be transferred at very short notice as a reference standard in field detection kits for paralytic shellfish poisoning.[66] In regard to the transfer of Schedule 2 and 3 chemicals to non-States Party, the prohibition of the former chemicals under the Verification Annex Part VII, para. 31 and the requirement for an end-user certificate from the recipient State under the Verification Annex Part VIII, para. 26 were waived in the cases of products containing a specified percentage or less of Schedule 2 and 3 chemicals as well as products identified as consumer goods packaged for retail sale for personal use or packaged for individual use in accordance with the decisions of the Conference.[67]

Fourthly, mandates of the Technical Secretariat have been controlled through secondary soft law measures. There are three examples. First, the inviolability of the papers of the inspection teams under the Verification Annex Part II, para. 11(c) was compromised by the guidance adopted by the Executive Council which seemed in favour of the right of the inspected State party to receive copies, at its request, of the information and data about its facility(ies) from the Technical Secretariat under the Verification Annex Part II, paras. 50 and 60.[68] Although some commentators were of the opinion that the inviolability of the inspectors' notebooks should be upheld, which would

---

62 OPCW Doc. C-I/DEC.38, dated 16 May 1997, para. 5.
63 OPCW Doc RC-1/5, dated 8 May 2003, para. 7.83(c); C-8/DEC.16, dated 23 October 2003, para. 14(c).
64 Transfer means export or import.
65 OPCW Doc. EC-XII/DEC.5, dated 9 October 1998.
66 OPCW Doc. RC-1/S/6, dated 25 April 2003, p. 55, para. 6.9.
67 OPCW Doc. C-V/DEC.16, dated 17 May 2000, para. 1; C-VI/DEC.10, dated 17 May 2001, para. 2.
68 OPCW Doc. EC-XII/2*, dated 9 October 1998, p. 8, para. 4.10.

ensure the unbiased and independent nature of inspection records,[69] this guidance clarifies the position of the policy-making organ composed of States Parties. Second, the discretion of the Technical Secretariat to update "approved equipment"[70] indicated in the Verification Annex Part II, para. 27[71] was effectively overruled by a subsequent measure of the policy-making organs. The Conference adopted procedures both for updating the list of "approved equipment" and for revising technical specifications of "approved equipment" which required the formal approval of the Conference and the Executive Council respectively.[72] Third, the consent of the Technical Secretariat not to conclude a Schedule 2 facility agreement stipulated in the Verification Annex Part VII, para. 24[73] does not seem to be required in accordance with the recommendation of the Executive Council.[74] Although the recommendation is not quite clear as regards whether it endorsed a *de facto* veto of a State Party or not, its context implied a preference for having fewer Schedule 2 facility agreements. It thus would become more difficult for the Technical Secretariat to persuade reluctant States Parties to conclude a Schedule 2 facility agreement.

2   *Multiple Effects of Secondary Soft Law*

The actual practice in the case of the BWC and CWC regimes proves that there are various types of secondary soft law measures. In the present author's view,

---

[69]   Daniel Feakes, "Progress in The Hague, Quarterly Review No. 21, Developments in the Organization for the Prohibition of Chemical Weapons," CBW *Conventions Bulletin*, No. 39 (1998), p. 15; Walter Krutzsch, "Article VI of the Chemical Weapons Convention: Past, Present and Future," *CBW Conventions Bulletin*, No. 50 (2000), p. 7.

[70]   Para. 1 of Part I of Verification Annex.

[71]   Para. 27 of Part II of Verification Annex states that the Technical Secretariat shall prepare and, as appropriate, update a list of approved equipment. *See* Walter Krutzsch & Ralf Trapp, *A Commentary on the Chemical Weapons Convention* (Martinus Nijhoff, 1994), p. 307.

[72]   OPCW Doc. C-7/DEC.20, dated 11 October 2002, para. 5; C-8/DEC.3, dated 22 October 2003, para. (c).

[73]   Para. 24 of Part VII of Verification Annex stipulates that [a] facility agreement...shall be concluded...unless the inspected State Party and the Technical Secretariat agree that it is not needed. The text suggests that the requirement for a facility agreement, although normally obligatory, can be circumvented if there is consent between the inspected state party and the Technical Secretariat (W. Krutzsch & R. Trapp, *supra* note 71, pp. 440–441.) and that neither side could exercise a veto over the conclusion of a Schedule 2 facility agreement.

[74]   OPCW Doc. EC-38/3, C-9/3, dated 12 October 2004, para. 2.60.

secondary soft law has three *legal* effects on hard law: (1) clarifying, (2) supplemental and (3) adapting ones.

(1) Clarifying Effect

Secondary soft law measures exercise a clarifying effect on ambiguous hard law provisions. Under international law, this effect can be understood in the context of interpretation of treaties. Article 31, para. 3(a) of the Vienna Convention on the Law of Treaties identifies "any subsequent agreement between the parties regarding the interpretation of the treaty or the application of its provisions" as one of the elements of treaty interpretation.[75] Shelton points out that "[u]sing non-binding texts to give authoritative interpretation to treaty terms is particularly useful when the issues are contentious and left unresolved in the treaty itself" and that "[o]ther non-binding instruments adopted by State parties similarly 'authoritatively interpret' the obligations contained in pre-existing treaty provisions."[76]

As demonstrated above, this type of soft law measure is common in the BWC and CWC regimes, though there are different backgrounds in terms of quantity and quality. On the one hand, the BWC has only fifteen Articles without any verification mechanism or a standing international body. Due to the relatively simple structure of the treaty, the secondary soft law measures focus on clarifying such fundamental obligations as the prohibition of biological weapons, the destruction of biological weapons as well as national implementation under Articles I–IV. On the other hand, the CWC contains a huge number of provisions consisting of twenty-four Articles and three Annexes. These Articles and Annexes not only provide substantive rules but also deal with the very detailed verification procedures and organizational matters of a fully-fledged international organization. The complexity of treaty provisions intrinsically and inevitably invites the Conference to address different interpretations among States Parties.

Is this practice consistent with Article 31, para. 3(a) of the Vienna Convention on the Law of Treaties? Aust argues that "[p]rovided the purpose is clear, the agreement can take various forms, including a decision adopted by a meeting of the parties."[77] Common understandings on interpretation have been reflected in

---

75 *See* Yearbook of the International Law Commission, 1966, Volume II, pp. 221–222, paras. (14)–(15).
76 D. Shelton, *supra* note 5, pp. 73–74.
77 Anthony Aust, *Modern Treaty Law and Practice* (2nd ed., Cambridge University Press, 2007), p. 239.

a final document of the BWC Review Conference[78] as well as a decision of the CWC Conference. The BWC Review Conference is a treaty-monitoring organ that is held every five years, while the CWC Conference is one of the internal organs of the OPCW which has general powers to consider, make recommendations, and take decisions on any questions, matters or issues within the scope of the CWC. Despite their different organisational modalities, both the BWC Review Conference and the CWC Conference are forums in which every State Party is entitled to participate. Their Rules of Procedure may allow the matter of substance to be decided by a two-thirds majority; however, in practice, all final documents of the BWC Review Conference and all but two decisions[79] of the CWC Conference have been adopted by consensus. This consensus-based approach ensures the authority of the agreement on interpretation and is thus consistent with Article 31, para 3(a) of the Vienna Convention on the Law of Treaties.

(2) Supplemental Effect

Secondary soft law measures can also act interstitially to supplement binding agreements[80] and thus have a supplemental effect on hard law regimes. For a supplemental effect to be viable, two conditions must be met in advance. First, shortcomings in the existing hard law regimes need to be identified. Second, ways to overcome such shortcomings should be found among the States Parties.

This effect is observed in the practice of both the BWC and CWC regimes. However, as was the case with the clarifying effect, the backgrounds of soft law measures in this regard are different. Regarding the BWC regime, the necessity for supplemental measures comes from the fundamental institutional deficiencies in substantive, procedural and organizational aspects. It has no mechanism to ensure compliance with obligations under the BWC. This fundamental limitation has been duly addressed among States Parties with the introduction of the Confidence-Building Measures (CBMs), the Formal Consultative Meeting, the Implementation Support Unit (ISU), and the annual Meeting of States Parties. When it comes to the CWC regime, the last-minute massive volume of agreement among negotiating States requires supplemental measures

---

78 A background information document showing the additional understandings and agreements reached by previous Review Conferences relating to each article of the Convention (BWC Doc. BWC/CONF.VI/INF.1, dated 11 July 2006; BWC/CONF.VII/INF.5, dated 28 September 2011).

79 One is the decision related to the tenure of the current Director-General of the Technical Secretariat (OPCW Doc. C-SS-1/5, dated 25 July 2002, para. 4.3); the other is the decision regarding the final extended deadline of 29 April 2012 (OPCW Doc. C-16/5, dated 2 December 2011, para. 9.4).

80 D. Shelton, *supra* note 5, p.73.

with a view to ensuring more effective implementation of the CWC. For instance, the obligation to submit information by States Parties is further strengthened with the introduction of "voluntary nil declarations" on peaceful chemical activities as well as the submission of the text of national implementation measures, as illustrated above.

There are both positive and negative sides to the supplemental effect. On the one hand, supplemental soft law measures have advantages in addressing specific issues in a quick and flexible manner. In theory, it is possible to add a legal obligation to an existing hard law regime in accordance with the relevant provisions on amendments; however, in reality, States Parties seem to be reluctant to use formal procedures once a hard law regime is fixed, probably because the process of amendment is lengthy and complicated, both at international and domestic levels. These difficulties can be almost completely avoided by soft law measures. On the other hand, supplemental soft law measures are fragile due to a lack of binding force. For instance, as a matter of fact, the number of States Parties participating in the Confidence-Building Measures within the framework of the BWC regime has not been encouraging. There are more than eighty States Parties, and fifty-seven percent of them do not provide any information.[81] The number of States Parties submitting voluntary nil declarations on peaceful chemical activities under the CWC regime has also been very low and remains in single figures.[82] This unsatisfactory status is, in fact, due to the fundamental lack of binding force and has not been addressed effectively even with the efforts by the international monitoring organs to continue to induce non-participating States Parties to submit information.

(3)   Adapting Effect

Finally, secondary soft law measures have an adapting effect on hard law rules. This effect has been witnessed in the practice of the CWC only. Having recognized that some detailed obligations and procedures are not functional, based on the experience gained after the entry into force, policy-making organs of the OPCW have relied on soft law measures which provide flexibility within the operation of hard law regimes, and adapt hard law provisions to meet the needs of the real world.

One example of this is the relaxation of regulations on the transfer of Schedule chemicals. The CWC deals with chemicals of a dual use nature,

---

81   BWC Doc. BWC/MSP/2010/2, dated 23 November 2010, p. 32.
82   OPCW Doc. S/867/2010, dated 24 September 2010, p. 19, paras. 7.10–7.11; S/869/2010, dated 24 September 2010, p. 20, paras. 7.10–7.11; S/963/2011, dated 22 September 2011, p. 21, paras. 7.10–7.11; S/1042/Rev.2, dated 19 December 2012, p. 22, paras. 7.9–7.10.

regulation of which requires a balance between the prohibition of military activities and the promotion of peaceful activities. In this context, the policy-making organs have been successful in adapting the regulations on the transfer of specific chemicals when it becomes clear that the CWC has placed an unnecessary burden on activities for legitimate purposes, as seen above. Another example is the deprivation of powers assigned to the Technical Secretariat. Both the Schedule 2 facility agreements and "approved equipment" of inspection are cases in which practical experience has proved the original idea of the delegation of specific powers to the Technical Secretariat to be wrong. The legal rationale seems to be that States Parties are interested in recovering powers that were delegated by States Parties themselves to the Technical Secretariat. All in all, the practice shows that the States Parties have agreed to adapt the existing provisions to the contemporary needs or demands identified by themselves through the operation and implementation of the CWC.

However, this adapting effect of secondary soft law is controversial from the viewpoint of the law of treaties. Why is it possible to adapt existing text by legally non-binding secondary soft law measures? Is adaptation different from (formal) amendments? Does it not bypass formal amendment procedures? The CWC Article XV stipulates two different procedures for modification of text: "amendments" that need to meet extremely strict conditions[83] and "changes" that can be made under more flexible "silent" procedures.[84] In any case, both modalities require formal procedures. How should we understand the practice of adapting secondary soft law measures that do not follow formal procedures on amendments or changes? Is this practice legally sound?

It could be argued that soft law measures make seemingly illegal or unauthorized conduct lawful in certain circumstances, and that this practice is not consistent with the relevant provisions on modification. However, this purely theoretical argument is not convincing when no objection has been raised among States Parties. Perhaps it may be possible to understand the adaption by secondary soft law in the context of the treaty interpretation under the law of treaties: either as "any subsequent agreement between the parties regarding the interpretation of the treaty or the application of its provisions" (Article 31, para. 3(a) of the Vienna Convention on the Law of Treaties)[85] or based on the so-called teleological approach. There are two reasons for this understanding.

---

83 Article XV, paras. 2–3. No amendment has been proposed since the entry into force of the CWC.
84 Article XV, paras. 4–5. Three changes have been proposed since the entry into force of the CWC. Two were agreed, while one was withdrawn.
85 See A. Aust, *supra* note 77, p. 239.

First, adapting secondary soft law measures limits the scope of the treaty or the powers of organs. These measures do not create a new or additional obligation but allow States Parties to be exempted from existing obligations or to regain delegated powers from the Technical Secretariat. Prohibitive provisions do not necessarily mean a complete and absolute ban, and there is always some room for interpretation. Although a relaxing measure should be taken carefully, if there is a sufficient need to adapt a provision to contemporary circumstances, this measure would be justified. Second, the decision to adapt hard law rule by secondary soft law measures is made by consensus among States Parties. Even if doubts about the legal soundness could be raised, the fact that there is no objection would give the adapted hard law indisputable authority and legitimacy from the viewpoint of positivism. In this regard, a collective will expressed as a decision of policy-making organ is *the* decisive factor.

Despite this possible legal explanation for adapting secondary soft law measures, it seems that States Parties have not been completely confident as to their soundness and have thus regarded them as exceptional. This attitude was particularly implied by a series of events regarding the prior notification rule on saxitoxin. At the adoption of the interim guideline, the Executive Council emphasized its interim status and recognized that this measure "does not constitute a precedent for other purposes."[86] Moreover, the States Parties came to the conclusion that this interim status should be followed and fixed by formal procedures. Before long, a change to the Verification Annex Part VI, para. 5 was formally requested by Canada in accordance with Article XV, para. 5. After a careful consideration, this request was endorsed by the Executive Council in January 1999 and a new paragraph, 5bis, was introduced.[87]

Conclusion

This article aims to revisit a fundamental *legal* question that was identified by international law scholars in the 1970s–80s but remains unanswered, i.e. what *legal* effects does soft law have? In order to answer this question, the present author first illustrated the traditional debate in the 1970s as well as the contem-

---

86   OPCW Doc. EC-XXII/DEC.5, dated 9 October 1998.
87   OPCW Doc. C-IV/1, EC-MV/2, dated 4 June 1999, para. 3.35. *See also* OPCW Doc. EC-XVII/DG.6, dated 10 November 1999, para. 1; cf. C.N.916.1999.TREATIES-7 of 11 October 1999. In the meantime it was also decided that the interim practical guideline would be extended for more than three months in order to fill a gap between its original application period and the entry into force of the change (OPCW Doc. EC-XV/DEC.5, dated 29 April 1999).

porary argument since the 1990s and then explored multiple effects of (secondary) soft law based on the evaluation of practice in the Biological and Chemical Weapons Conventions regimes. This analysis was inspired by positive views of contemporary international lawyers who are familiar with international relations on soft law as well as by the concept of "secondary soft law" suggested by Shelton. As a result of discussion, it became clear that secondary soft law instruments have (1) clarifying, (2) supplemental and (3) adapting effects on hard law rules and regimes.

The author concludes this article by describing four features of secondary soft law. First of all, secondary soft law presupposes, by its nature, an existing relevant hard law regime, and thus is always introduced as a subsequent measure in the process of its operation and implementation. In this regard, secondary soft law is quite different from primary soft law, which is regarded as a precursor of future hard law. Due to the expansion and proliferation of international regimes based on hard law in recent years, it is expected that secondary soft law will play a more significant role in enhancing the effectiveness of international regimes. Second, secondary soft law should be recognized as purpose-oriented measures rather than declaratory instruments. As illustrated, it has clarifying, supplemental and adapting effects on hard law rules and regimes. Since these objectives could also be achieved by hard law instruments, the difference between (secondary) hard law and secondary soft law is not absolute but relative, and the question of its binding or non-binding nature is almost irrelevant. Rather, it becomes more important for hard law regimes to make soft law measures functional. In this regard, consensus among States Parties is vital because it provides authority, legitimacy and integrity to regimes. This is the third feature. It is a policy-making organ that produces secondary soft law measures. As is often the case with the field of arms control, obtaining consensus has been the traditional practice in both BWC and CWC regimes.[88] This is mostly because the level of armament directly affects national security. As a rule, voting has been the last resort, and even if consensus is not attainable, voting is deferred for 24–48 hours with a view to achieving consensus. Only if these efforts are unsuccessful will voting take place.[89] Practice proves that this approach has been followed by States Parties. Last but not least, secondary soft law is not a perfect solution and has limitations. It cannot or will not address all issues identified through the operation and implementation of existing hard law regimes. It is true that secondary

---

88 As far as a policy-making body is concerned, it seems that differences between treaty organs and international organisations become blurred.

89 BWC Doc. BWC/CONF.VII//7, dated 13 January 2012, p. 49, Rule 28 of the Rules of procedure of Conference; CWC Article VIII, para. 18.

soft law plays a more flexible and efficient role in responding to new problems not recognized at the time of negotiation.[90] However, as indicated above, it functions within the scope of a hard law regime. If a hard law regime requires new obligations and mechanisms, a hard law measure is better than a soft law one. This is not only because there is a great risk of bypassing and thus damaging formal amendment procedures, but also because legally binding measures provide the undisputed normative foundation with the hard law regime.

These days, there are a variety of hard law regimes exploring universal values such as human rights, global environment and arms control.[91] Having accumulated various secondary soft law measures, each hard law regime evolves as a more functional, multilayered and complex system. Secondary soft law will continue to play an indispensable role in more effective regime governance as long as States Parties of the regime find it useful, desirable and appropriate.

---

90   cf. D. Shelton, *supra* note 5, p. 322.
91   *See* Geir Ulfstein ed., *Making Treaty Work* (Cambridge University Press, 2007), pp. 3–12.

CHAPTER 11

The Defence of Necessity as Customary International Law: The Fisheries Jurisdiction Case (Spain v. Canada) Re-examined

Takuhei Yamada

Introduction

The question as to whether "the defence of necessity" may be invoked by a State as a ground for justifying its otherwise internationally wrongful act has long been in controversy. Quite a few eminent writers have been opposed to or sceptical about the defence of necessity.[1] This is mainly because of the potential for its abuse as it being a pretext for wrongful conduct. Given the lack of enforceability of international legal norms, particularly within the boundaries of a sovereign State, this concern is understandable.

However, an objection can be raised against this opposition. It may sound paradoxical, but the defence of necessity is expected to operate to ensure the rule of law in case of emergency. Without the defence of necessity in international law, States in emergencies may, especially from the realist point of view,

---

1 Charles de Visscher, "La responsabilité des États," *Bibliotheca Visseriana Dissertationvm ivs Internationale Illvstrantivm*, Vol. 2 (1924), pp. 111–112; Arrigo Cavaglieri, "Règles générales du droit de la paix," *Recueil des cours de l'Académie de droit international de la Haye*, Vol. 26 (1929), pp. 557–560; Alfred Verdross, "Règles générales du droit international de la paix," *Recueil des cours de l'Académie de droit international de la Haye*, Vol. 30 (1929–V), pp. 489–490; Hans Kelsen, "Unrecht und Unrechtsfolge im Völkerrecht," *Zeitschrift für öffentliches Recht*, Vol. 12 (1932), p. 565; Jules Basdevant, "Règles générales du droit de la paix," *Recueil des cours de l'Académie de droit international de la Haye*, Vol. 58 (1936–IV), pp. 551–555; Claud Humphrey Waldock, "The Regulation of the Use of Force by Individual States in International Law," *Recueil des cours de l'Académie de droit international de la Haye*, Vol. 81 (1952), pp. 461–462; James Leslie Brierly, *Law of Nations* (6th ed., Clarendon Press, 1963), pp. 404–405; Eduardo Jiménez de Aréchaga, "International Responsibility," in Sørensen ed., *Manual of Public International Law* (St. Martin's Press, 1968), p. 543; Ian Brownlie, "The Use of Force in Self-defense," *British Year Book of International Law*, Vol. 37 (1961), pp. 184–191; Ian Brownlie, *Principles of Public International Law* (7th ed., 2008), p. 466; Sarah Heathcote, "Est-ce que l'état de nécessité est un principe de droit international coutumier?" *Revue belge de droit international*, 2007/1 (2007), pp. 53–89; Robert D. Sloane, "On the Use and Abuse of Necessity in the Law of State Responsibility," *American Journal of International Law*, Vol. 106 (2012), p. 451.

choose inevitably to make light of or ignore international legal rules which prohibit dealing with appropriate situations. In such cases, there is a danger that the maxim *"Necessitas non habet legem"* will turn into reality. Given this concern, quite a few scholars believe that an international rule of necessity is needed to ensure that States remain willing to adhere to rules of international law, even when in the midst of an emergency.[2]

As Professor Ryuichi Ida postulated, the normativity of international law in its broader sense depends on its effectiveness, that is, the degree to which States actually comply with international law.[3] He also argues that, for certain norms to be effective, compliance consciousness is extremely important. Combining these principles, Professor Ida would argue that a rule of necessity defence may actually contribute to the preservation of the purpose of international law, by incentivising States to comply, even during an emergency.

A recent and remarkable example of the development of the necessity defence is Article 25 of the *Articles on State Responsibility* adopted by the United Nations International Law Commission (ILC) in 2001.[4] Article 25 states:

Art. 25 Necessity
1. Necessity may not be invoked by a State as a ground for precluding the wrongfulness of an act not in conformity with an international obligation of that State unless the act:
   (a) Is the only way for the State to safeguard an essential interest against a grave and imminent peril; and
   (b) Does not seriously impair an essential interest of the State or States towards which the obligation exists, or of the international community as a whole.

---

2   Sarah Cassella asserts as follows: '[L]a souplesse premise par l'état de necessité constitue l'un des elements essentiels rendant possible le fonctionnement normal du système juridique international. ... Non seulement l'état de nécessité a une place en droit international, mais il y occupe même une place centrale. ...L'absence de législateur en droit international rend indispensable le recours à des mécanismes intersubjectifs afin d'éviter un coût social excessif issu de l'application du droit. ...[L]'effectivité des norms dépende en grande partie de mécanismes tells que l'état de nécessité, qui est adapté aux rapports intersubjectifs. ...Bien que l'effectivité ne constitue pas une condition de validité de la norme—une certaine ineffectivité étant présente dans tout ordre juridique—les risques d'inapplication du droit international sont particulièrement élevés'. Sarah Cassella, *La nécessité en droit international: De l'état de nécessité aux situations de nécessité* (Martinus Nijhoff Publishers, 2011), pp. 515–516.
3   See Ryuichi Ida, "Making of International Norms on Bioethics" (2004), p. 190.
4   Responsibility of States for internationally wrongful acts, UN Doc. A/RES/56/83 (2001).

2. In any case, necessity may not be invoked by a State as a ground for precluding wrongfulness if:
   (a) The international obligation in question excludes the possibility of invoking necessity; or
   (b) The State has contributed to the situation of necessity.

This article and its predecessor draft Article 33 have been recognised as reflecting customary law by international tribunals, in quite a few cases.[5]

Nevertheless, any articles adopted by the ILC are not of themselves binding legal documents, and the adoption thereof does not necessarily mean that all provisions stipulated reflect customary international law. To what extent a provision reflects customary law is answered on the basis of relevant international practice.[6] In addition, in recognising the necessity defence as customary law, international tribunals seem to have relied on the ILC's works more than "extensive and virtually uniform"[7] State practice.

Thus, the question we must consider is: Whether and to what extent has the defence of necessity been accepted by States? As part of this study, this paper will examine the dispute between Canada and Spain (and the EU), concerning Canadian enforcement action taken against a Spanish fishing vessel on the high seas, beyond Canada's 200-mile fishing zone. Little is known about the dispute's implication for a rule concerning necessity because, while the

---

5 Gabcíkovo-Nagymaros Project (Hungary/Slovakia), Judgment, *I.C.J. Reports 1997*, p. 40, para. 51 ("The Court considers, first of all, that the state of necessity is a ground recognized by customary international law for precluding the wrongfulness of an act not in conformity with an international obligation"); Conséquences juridiques de l'édification d'un mur dans le territoire palestinien occupé, avis consultatif, *C.I.J. Recueil 2004*, p. 195, para. 140; CMS Gas Transmission Company v. Argentina, Award (12 May 2005), ICSID Case No. ARB/01/8, para. 315; Enron Corporation and Ponderosa Assets, L.P. v. Argentina, Award (22 May 2007), ICSID Case No. ARB/01/3, para. 303; Sempra Energy International v. Argentina, Award (28 September 2007), ICSID Case No. ARB/02/16, para. 344; National Grid plc v. Argentina (UNCITRAL Arbitration), Award (3 Nov 2008), para. 256; Suez, Sociedad General de Aguas de Barcelona S.A., and InterAgua Servicios Integrales del Agua S.A. v. Argentina, Decision on Liability (30 July 2010), ICSID Case No. ARB/03/17, para. 236; Suez, Sociedad General de Aguas de Barcelona S.A., and Vivendi Universal S.A. v. Argentina, ICSID Case No. ARB/03/19; AWG Group Ltd. v. Argentina, Decision on Liability (30 July 2010), para. 258; Total S.A., v. Argentina, Decision on Liability (27 December 2010), ICSID Case No. ARB/04/1, para. 220; Impregilo S.p.A. v. Argentina, Award (21 June 2011), ICSID Case No. ARB/07/17, para. 344.

6 *See* David D. Caron, "The ILC Articles on State Responsibility: The Paradoxical Relationship between Form and Authority," *American Journal of International Law*, Vol. 96 (2002), p. 867.

7 North Sea Continental Shelf (Germany/Denmark, Germany/Netherlands), Judgment, *I.C.J. Reports 1969*, p. 44, para. 74.

dispute was filed with the International Court of Justice (ICJ), the Court did not adjudicate on its merits.

I Relevant Facts

1 Regime for Fisheries Management and Conservation in the Northwest Atlantic Region

The Convention on Future Multilateral Cooperation in the Northwest Atlantic Fisheries, signed on 24 October 1978 in Ottawa, came into force on 1 January 1979.[8] This Convention establishes the Northwest Atlantic Fisheries Organization (NAFO). The prime objective of NAFO is to contribute, through consultation and cooperation, to the optimum utilization, rational management, and conservation of the fishery resources of the Northwest Atlantic Region. The convention applies to the waters of the Northwest Atlantic north of 35°00' north latitude, which is designated as "the Convention Area" (Article 1(1)).[9] The portion of the Convention Area which lies beyond coastal States' fisheries jurisdiction is designated as "the Regulatory Area" (Article 1(2)).[10] The Convention Area is divided into seven "Subareas", and each Subarea consists of several "Divisions". For example, most of the waters off Newfoundland are designated as "Subarea 3", which has six Divisions (3K, 3L, 3M, 3N, 3O, and 3P) (Article 20 & Annex III).

The NAFO consists of four organs: General Council, Scientific Council, Fisheries Commission, and Secretariat (Article 2). In particular, the Fisheries Commission is responsible for the management and conservation of the fishery resources of the Regulatory Area (Article 11(1)). The commission adopts proposals for joint

---

8   The current contracting parties to the Convention are Canada, Cuba, Denmark (in respect of Faroe Islands and Greenland), the European Union (EU), France (in respect of Saint Pierre and Miquelon), Iceland, Japan, the Republic of Korea, Norway, the Russian Federation, Ukraine, and the United States of America. All but Ukraine were already NAFO members at the time of the *Estai* incident.

9   Article 1(1) "The area to which this Convention applies, hereinafter referred to as "the Convention Area," shall be the waters of the Northwest Atlantic Ocean north of 35°00' north latitude and west of a line extending due north from 35°00' north latitude and 42°00' west longitude to 59°00' north latitude, thence due west to 44°00' west longitude, and thence due north to the coast of Greenland, and the waters of the Gulf of St. Lawrence, Davis Strait and Baffin Bay south of 78°10' north latitude".

10 Article 1(2) "The area referred to in this Convention as "the Regulatory Area" is that part of the Convention Area which lies beyond the areas in which Coastal States exercise fisheries jurisdiction".

action by the Contracting Parties, designed to achieve optimum utilization of the fishery resources (Article 11(2)). It also adopts proposals for international measures of control and enforcement within the Regulatory Area, beyond coastal States' jurisdiction (Article 11(5)). Each proposal adopted by the commission becomes a measure binding on all contracting parties (Article 11(7)).[11]

2   Canadian Legislation Allowing Unilateral Enforcement Action on the High Seas

Canada was sceptical about the effectiveness of the NAFO for fishery conservation on the high seas beyond its 200-mile fishing zone for three reasons. First, a member State is not bound to a proposal adopted by the Fisheries Commission if the member presents an objection thereto.[12] Second, even when, without any objection, a proposal becomes a measure binding on all members, any enforcement action against a fishing vessel in the Regulatory Area remains in the hands of the vessel's flag State. Third, any vessels flying flags of non-member States, especially flag-of-convenience vessels, remain unregulated.

That being so, Canada considered it necessary, for the purpose of more effective fishery conservation, to take unilateral enforcement action against foreign vessels in the Regulatory Area. That is, on the high seas, beyond its 200-mile fishing zone. As a result, the Government of Canada presented Bill C-8 to

---

11   Article 11
   "1. The Fisheries Commission, hereinafter referred to as "the Commission," shall be responsible for the management and conservation of the fishery resources of the Regulatory Area in accordance with the provisions of this Article.
   2. The Commission may adopt proposals for joint action by the Contracting Parties designed to achieve the optimum utilization of the fishery resources of the Regulatory Area. In considering such proposals, the Commission shall take into account any relevant information or advice provided to it by the Scientific Council.
   5. The Commission may also adopt proposals for international measures of control and enforcement within the Regulatory Area for the purpose of ensuring within that Area the application of this Convention and the measures in force thereunder.
   7. Subject to the provisions of Article XII, each proposal adopted by the Commission under this Article shall become a measure binding on all Contracting Parties to enter into force on a date determined by the Commission."

12   Article 12(1) "If any Commission member presents to the Executive Secretary an objection to a proposal within sixty days of the date of transmittal specified in the notification of the proposal by the Executive Secretary, the proposal shall not become a binding measure until the expiration of forty days following the date of transmittal specified in the notification of that objection to the Contracting Parties. ...The proposal shall then become a measure binding on all Contracting Parties, except those which have presented objections, at the end of the extended period or periods for objecting."

Parliament in February 1994 and Bill C-29 on 10 May 1994. The two bills were adopted by Parliament and received Royal Assent on 12 May 1994. The objective of them is to amend the Criminal Code of Canada and the Coastal Fisheries Protection Act (CFPA). The amendments allow Canadian officers to take enforcement action, including use of force if necessary, against foreign vessels in the Regulatory Area.

Among the relevant new or amended provisions of the CFPA, the new Section 5.1 stipulates as follows:

> Parliament, recognizing
> (a)   that straddling stocks on the Grand Banks of Newfoundland are a major renewable world food source having provided a livelihood for centuries to fishers,
> (b)   that those stocks are threatened with extinction,
> (c)   that there is an urgent need for all fishing vessels to comply in both Canadian fisheries waters and the NAFO Regulatory Area with sound conservation and management measures for those stocks, notably those measures that are taken under the *Convention on Future Multilateral Co-operation in the Northwest Atlantic Fisheries,* done at Ottawa on October 24, 1978, Canada Treaty Series 1979 No. 11, and
> (d)   that some foreign fishing vessels continue to fish for those stocks in the NAFO Regulatory Area in a manner that undermines the effectiveness of sound conservation and management measures,

declares that the purpose of Section 5.2 is to enable Canada to take urgent action necessary to prevent further destruction of those stocks and to permit their rebuilding, while continuing to seek effective international solutions to the situation referred to in paragraph (d).[13]

As to "urgent action" necessary to prevent destruction of fisheries stocks, the new Section 5.2 provides as follows:

> No person, being aboard a foreign fishing vessel of a prescribed class, shall, in the NAFO Regulatory Area, fish or prepare to fish for a straddling stock in contravention of any of the prescribed conservation and management measures.

---

13   Coastal Fisheries Protection Act, R.S.C., ch. C-33 (1985)(Can.), amended by ch. 14, 1994 S.C. (Can.), *International Legal Materials,* Vol. 33 (1994), p. 1383.

Section 5.2 is clarified by Section 21.2 of Coastal Fisheries Protection Regulations (CFPR), as amended on 25 May 1994.[14] First, "a foreign fishing vessel of a prescribed class" is a vessel which does not have nationality or flies a flag of Belize, the Cayman Islands, Honduras, Panama, Saint Vincent and the Grenadines, or Sierra Leone. Second, "the prescribed conservation and management measures" include prohibitions against fishing, preparing to fish or catching and retaining straddling stocks.

In addition, an "urgent action" can include the use of force. In order to ensure compliance with the fishing prohibition, the new CFPA includes the right of inspection, arrest, and use of force necessary for arrest. Specifically, sections 7 and 8.1 of the CFPA state:

> 7. A protection officer may
> (a) for the purpose of ensuring compliance with this Act and the regulations, board and inspect any fishing vessel found within Canadian fisheries waters or the NAFO Regulatory Area; and
> (b) with a warrant issued under Section 7.1, search any fishing vessel found within Canadian fisheries waters or the NAFO Regulatory Area and its cargo.
>
> 8.1. A protection officer may, in the manner and to the extent prescribed by the regulations, use force that is intended or is likely to disable a foreign fishing vessel, if the protection officer
> (a) is proceeding lawfully to arrest the master or other person in command of the vessel; and
> (b) believes on reasonable grounds that the force is necessary for the purpose of arresting that master or other person.

In sum, as "urgent action[s]" is defined in Section 5.1, Canada prohibited fishing operations in the Regulatory Area by vessels which are stateless or flying a flag of convenience. Additionally, Canada entitled itself to unilateral enforcement actions against such vessels, including the use of force if necessary.

3 *Arrest of the* Estai

Despite Canada's attempts to regulate fishing in the Regulatory Area, overfishing by vessels of the EU countries, especially Spain and Portugal, was a

---

14   I.C.J. Pleadings, Fisheries Jurisdiction (Spain v. Canada), pp. 155–161; *see* Fisheries Jurisdiction (Spain v. Canada), Judgment, *I.C.J. Reports 1998*, pp. 441–442, para. 17.

problem.[15] The EU itself admitted that, while average catches from 1991 to 1993 of Greenland halibut by Canadian vessels were 3,400 tons, those of EU vessels were 37,000 tons, and over 40,000 tons were caught in 1994.[16]

To deal with the problem, Canada at first tried to make use of the NAFO. It was agreed, on Canada's initiative, to set the TAC (Total Allowable Catch) of 27,000 tons for Greenland halibut in the annual NAFO meeting held in September 1994. Having first proposed the TAC of 40,000 tons, the European Commission then accepted the TAC of 27,000 and raised no objections thereto.[17] However, the proposal adopted at the NAFO Fisheries Commission in January 1995 on the allocation of the TAC among the Contracting Parties was not accepted by the EU. While the Fisheries Commission formally adopted the following allocations Canada—60.37% (16,300 tons) and the EU—12.59% (3,400 tons), the European Commission lodged a formal objection to the NAFO quota on 3 March 1995, and set for itself a unilateral quota of 69% (18,630 tons).[18]

In response to this disagreement, Canada finally decided to extend the fishing prohibition to EU countries. On 3 March 1995, the same day as the EU's objection to the NAFO quota, Canada amended the CFPR, adding Portugal and Spain to "a prescribed class".[19] One of the 'prescribed conservation and management measures' against the two countries' vessels is a prohibition against fishing for Greenland halibut in Division 3 L, 3 M, 3 N, or 3O between 3 March and 31 December in any year.

On 9 March 1995, the *Estai*, a Spanish fishing vessel, was intercepted and boarded by Canadian Government vessels some 245 miles from the Canadian coast, in Division 3 L of the NAFO Regulatory Area.[20] The vessel was seized and its captain was arrested for violating the CFPA and CFPR. Although the captain was released on 12 March 1995, following the payment of bail, and the vessel was released on 15 March following the posting of a bond, Spain filed an

---

15 John Solomon (Regina-Lumsden), House of Commons Debates, Official Report (Hansard), Vol. 133, No. 68, 1st Sess., 35th Parl., 11 May 1994, p. 4219.
16 EU Press Release, MEMO/95/38, 10 March 1995, at http://europa.eu/rapid/press-release_MEMO-95-38_en.htm (as of October 25, 2014).
17 European Parliament, "Resolution on the Recent Agreement on NAFO Fisheries Quotas for 1995," B4-0430/94 (18 November 1994), OJ [1994] C341, p. 262.
18 *See* Counter-Memorial of Canada, para. 39, I.C.J. Pleadings, *supra* note 14, p. 230; *see* EU Press Release, MEMO/95/44, 14 March 1995, at http://europa.eu/rapid/press-release_MEMO-95-44_en.htm (as of October 25, 2014).
19 Memorial of Spain, Annex 19, I.C.J. Pleadings, *supra* note 14, pp. 162–167; *see* Fisheries Jurisdiction, Judgment, *supra* note 14, pp. 442–443, para. 18.
20 Fisheries Jurisdiction, Judgment, *supra* note 14, p. 443, para. 19.

Application instituting proceedings against Canada on 28 March with the ICJ. In its Application, Spain made the following requests:

> (A) that the Court declare that the legislation of Canada, in so far as it claims to exercise a jurisdiction over ships flying a foreign flag on the high seas, outside the exclusive economic zone of Canada, is not opposable to the Kingdom of Spain;
> (B) that the Court adjudge and declare that Canada is bound to refrain from any repetition of the acts complained of, and to offer to the Kingdom of Spain the reparation that is due, in the form of an indemnity the amount of which must cover all the damages and injuries occasioned; and
> (C) that, consequently, the Court declare also that the boarding on the high seas, on 9 March 1995, of the ship *Estai* flying the flag of Spain and the measures of coercion and the exercise of jurisdiction over that ship and over its captain constitute a concrete violation of the aforementioned principles and norms of international law.[21]

However, the Court, in its judgment of 4 December 1998, found that it had no jurisdiction to adjudicate upon the dispute brought by Spain. The reason for this decision was that the present dispute constituted a dispute for which reservations contained in Canadian declaration under Article 36(2) of the Court Statute excluded the Court's jurisdiction.[22]

4 Criticisms of Interested Parties

Although the ICJ regrettably did not adjudicate on the merits of the case, the interested parties criticized Canada for its legislation and actions.

First, Spain immediately condemned the Canadian action. On the day of the arrest, the Spanish Embassy in Canada sent two Notes Verbales to the Canadian Department of Foreign Affairs and International Trade. The second of them stated:

> The Spanish Government categorically condemns the pursuit and harassment of a Spanish vessel by vessels of the Canadian navy, in flagrant

---

21   I.C.J. Pleadings, *supra* note 14, p. 8.
22   One of the reservations in the Canadian declaration excluded the compulsory jurisdiction of the Court over "disputes arising out of or concerning conservation and management measures taken by Canada with respect to vessels fishing in the NAFO Regulatory Area …, and the enforcement of such measures". Fisheries Jurisdiction, Judgment, *supra* note 14, pp. 438–439, para. 14.

violation of the international law in force, since these acts take place outside the 200-mile zone.[23]

The Permanent Representative of Spain to the United Nations also criticized Canada in its letter to the Secretary-General, contending again that its action was a flagrant violation of international law:

> These actions, which constitute a flagrant violation by Canada of international law and of the Charter of the United Nations, have caused serious harm to Spanish citizens and in some cases have endangered their lives and physical integrity, a situation to which the Spanish Government has reacted by immediately making the relevant protests through the diplomatic channel, while fully reserving its rights and its claim to the corresponding compensation for the damage and injury sustained.[24]

In addition, the Spanish Government, in its Memorial submitted to the ICJ, enumerated the following principles and rules of international law which, in its view, Canada violated: freedom of navigation and fishing on the high seas, prohibition of threat or use of force, State's exclusive jurisdiction over ships flying its flag on the high seas, rules concerning the rights of visit and hot pursuit, non-possession of the high seas, obligation of pacific cooperation for conservation of living resources on the high seas, human rights to life and physical integrity, and obligation of pacific settlement of disputes.[25]

The European Union also condemned the Canadian action. In a Note Verbale of 10 March 1995 from the EC and its member States to the Canadian Department of Foreign Affairs and International Trade, it claimed as follows:

> The arrest of a vessel in international waters by a State other than the State of which the vessel is flying the flag and under whose jurisdiction it falls, is an illegal act under both the NAFO Convention and customary international law, and cannot be justified by any means. With this action

---

23 Note verbale n° 25, du 9 mars 1995, de l'ambassade d'Espagne au Canada au ministère des affaires étrangères et du commerce international du Canada, I.C.J. Pleadings, Fisheries Jurisdiction (Spain v. Canada), p. 11; see Fisheries Jurisdiction, Judgment, supra note 14, p. 443, para. 20.

24 Letter dated 31 March 1995, from the Spanish Permanent Representative to the United Nations, Yáñez-Barnuevo, addressed to the UNSG, UN Doc. A/50/98, S/1995/252, 31 March 1995, Spanish Yearbook of International Law, Vol. 4 (1995–1996), pp. 150–151.

25 Memorial of Spain, para. 23, I.C.J. Pleadings, supra note 14, p. 67.

> Canada is not only flagrantly violating international law, but is failing to observe normal behaviour of responsible States.[26]

Furthermore, in its press release on the same day, it stated:

> The unilateral measures adopted by the Canadian authorities, together with any action taken pursuant to them, are in clear contravention of the relevant international rules relating to the law of the sea. Customary international law and the international agreements which apply in respect of the high seas provide that no [S]tate may legitimately claim to submit any part of the high seas to its sovereignty.[27]

In addition, in the press release on 29 March 1995,[28] Emma Bonino, the EC Commissioner for fisheries, enumerated the following provisions of the United Nations Convention on the Law of the Sea (UNCLOS) which, in her view, the Canadian actions contravened: Articles 87 (Freedom of the high seas), 116 (Right to fish on the high seas), 89 (Invalidity of claims of sovereignty over the high seas), 92(1) (Flag State's exclusive jurisdiction over its ship on the high seas), and 63(2) (Obligation to attempt to agree upon the measures necessary for conservation between coastal States and fishing States). She also asserted the violation of Article 2(4) of the United Nations Charter.

In response to these criticisms, on what grounds did Canada try to justify its legislation and actions?

II Did Canada Invoke the Defence of Necessity to Legally Justify Its Actions?

Before turning to Canada's attempt at justification, a few remarks should be made. The UNCLOS, which came into effect in November 1994, was not binding on Canada at the time of the *Estai* incident. Canada did not ratify it until 2003. Despite that, the principle of the flag-State's exclusive jurisdiction over its vessels on the high seas, as laid down in Article 92 of the UNCLOS had been established under customary international law, and Canada did not unequivocally deny that its legislation and actions thereunder contravened the principle.

---

26 Fisheries Jurisdiction, Judgment, *supra* note 14, p. 444, para. 20.
27 EU Press Release, MEMO/95/38, 10 March 1995, *supra* note 16.
28 EU Press Release, IP/95/313, 29 March 1995, *at* http://europa.eu/rapid/press-release_IP-95-313_en.htm (as of October 25, 2014).

That being so, Canada was placed in the position of having to justify its actions. Accordingly, we may now turn to the real subject.

On 10 March 1995, the day after the arrest, the Canadian Department of Foreign Affairs and International Trade stated in its Note Verbale:

> The Minister [of Foreign Affairs and International Trade] recalls that the arrest of the *Estai* was necessary in order to put a stop to the overfishing of Greenland halibut by Spanish fishermen.[29]

Given that the Department did no more than stress the necessity of arresting the Spanish ship, it is not clear whether Canada was attempting to legally justify the arrest or invoke the defence of necessity.

Such uncertainty is also seen in Canada's arguments before the ICJ. The Government of Canada's Counter-Memorial, submitted to the ICJ in February 1996, reads as follows:

> The recent history of the Northwest Atlantic straddling stocks is one of crisis and decline. In the face of these conditions, it is clear that Canada's actions in May 1994 and March 1995 were *driven by the imperative of conservation.*[30] [italics added]

Further, having challenged the jurisdiction of the Court, Canada made the following submission, concerning the arrest itself:

> Faced with a conservation crisis, and unfortunately unable to persuade all States involved to control their vessels, the Canadian Government *felt compelled* to take special measures to conserve the fisheries. ...Since diplomatic approaches had failed to prevent this unilateral EU action, Canada *felt compelled* to take emergency actions to prevent the overfishing of Greenland halibut by Spain and Portugal. ...Canada therefore *felt compelled* to enforce its conservation and management measures against Spanish vessels in the NAFO Regulatory Area.[31] [italics added]

---

29   Note verbale du ministère des affaires étrangères et du commerce international du Canada à l'ambassade d'Espagne au Canada, I.C.J. Pleadings, *supra* note 14, pp. 15–16; *see* Fisheries Jurisdiction, Judgment, *supra* note 14, p. 443, para. 20.

30   Counter-Memorial of Canada, para. 45, I.C.J. Pleadings, *supra* note 14, p. 232.

31   Oral Argument of Blair Hankey, 11 June 1998, CR 98/11, paras. 73–74, 76, I.C.J. Pleadings, *supra* note 14, pp. 516–517.

Although Canada clearly insisted on the compelling need for the arrest, it is again not clear that there was an intention to invoke the defence of necessity, as a legal justification.

Thus, as far as we observe Canada's external statements, we cannot definitely conclude that it had the intention to invoke the defence of necessity as legal justification for its legislation and arrest of the *Estai*. That being so, in order to uncover Canada's real intention, we need to extend the observation into its internal documents.

On 19 April 1994, three weeks before the submission of Bill C-29 to the Parliament, the Legal Bureau at the Canadian Department of Foreign Affairs and International Trade expressed, in its memorandum, the following noteworthy opinions in respect of legal grounds for enforcement actions against foreign vessels on the high seas:

> An act that would otherwise constitute a breach of an obligation is not wrongful if taken in *a state of necessity*, where an essential interest of the [S]tate is threatened by a grave and imminent peril and there is no other means of averting it. The severe depletion of the fish stocks in the Northwest Atlantic is a grave and imminent peril threatening the livelihood of scores of thousands of Canadians and the economy of the Atlantic provinces. If the flag of convenience vessels are allowed to continue fishing, the fish stocks may be permanently wiped out. In the short term enforcement action on the high seas is the only way to stop the fishing and save the stocks.[32] [italics added]

What is immediately apparent in this memorandum is that the defence of "a state of necessity" as legal grounds for Canadian enforcement actions, against flag of convenience vessels on the high seas is mentioned. What is more, the memorandum also contains a detailed explanation of the necessity defence as follows:

> Unlike self-defence and countermeasures, which also preclude wrongfulness, the operation of *the doctrine of necessity* does not presuppose the existence of wrongful act committed by another State whose right is infringed by the State acting out of necessity. In circumstances of

---

[32] Memorandum written by the Legal Bureau at the Canadian Department of Foreign Affairs and International Trade, 19 April 1994, *Canadian Yearbook of International Law*, Vol. 32 (1994), p. 312; *see* Michael F. Keiver, "The Pacific Salmon War: The Defence of Necessity Revisited," *Dalhousie Law Journal*, Vol. 21 (1998), p. 420.

necessity, the other State may be innocent or guilty. What is required is that the State relying on the plea is acting in a situation of urgency, of "abnormal conditions of peril," of grave and imminent danger that threatens an essential or "vital" interest of the State. This vital interest need not be such that it threatens the very existence of the State, but it must be at the level of an economic calamity, something endangering the survival of at least a portion of the population, an ecological disaster, and so forth, that creates an imperative necessity to act. This act is a conscious deliberated choice. For the action adopted to avoid the taint of wrongfulness, it must be the only effective means of averting the imminent peril. If some other means is available that does not constitutes the breach of an international obligation, that means must be chosen.[33] [italics added]

In conclusion, the memorandum contains a list of the following four requirements for the defence of necessity:

(1) an "essential" interest of the State must be invoked (what is essential will depend upon the circumstances);
(2) the peril must be extremely grave and must have been a threat to the interest at the actual time, and the action complained of must definitively have been the only means of warding off the extremely grave and imminent peril;
(3) the State claiming the benefit of the state of necessity must not itself have provoked, either deliberately or by negligence, the occurrence of the state of necessity, and
(4) the interest of the State towards which the obligation existed must itself be a less essential interest of the State in question.[34]

The above passages make it clear that the memorandum referred to and used the defence of necessity to justify Canada's enforcement actions on the high seas. Furthermore, we can find that, with reference to the then progressing works in the ILC, it made a detailed explanation of the norm's contents.

In light of the statements cited above, the ambiguous external statements cited above might possibly be interpreted as implying a legal justification based on the necessity defence.

---

33 Memorandum, *supra* note 32, p. 312.
34 *Ibid.*, p. 313.

III Did Spain Deny the Defence of Necessity?

As discussed in section 1.4 above, the Spanish Government strongly condemned the arrest of the *Estai*. This position raises the question of whether Spain took the view that the defence of necessity is not established in international law.

Yet it should be noted that, while Spain did not accept the *Estai* incident as a precedent of the necessity defence, it did not oppose a proposed article on the defence (then draft Article 33 on first reading) itself. While, in the Sixth Committee of the United Nations General Assembly in 1999, the Spanish representative stated that "the case in question should not be mentioned in the commentary on article 33" since "the arrest of a Spanish vessel on the high seas and by force could in no way be justified by the state of necessity", it agreed with the draft article itself.[35] These statements show that Spain did not disagree with the defence of necessity in principle.

The question then arises about why, in Spain's view, the arrest of the *Estai* could not be justified by the necessity defence.

On 10 March 1995, the day after the arrest, the Ministry of Foreign Affairs of Spain stressed the violation of a customary rule (Flag State's exclusive jurisdiction over its ship on the high seas) by Canada before stating:

> The Spanish Government considers that the wrongful act committed by ships of the Canadian navy *can in no way be justified by presumed concern* to conserve fisheries in the area, *since it violates the established provisions of the* NAFO *Convention to which Canada is a party.*[36] [italics added]

The former part ("can in no way be justified by presumed concern") might, if interpreted differently, read as if a *certain* crisis could have justified the arrest. However, the whole passage should be considered. Then we notice that the reason of non-justification is mentioned in the sentence after "since". Specifically, the passage indicates that the arrest cannot be justified "since it violates the NAFO Convention". Another interpretation of this part might indicate that enforcement actions on the high seas are justifiable in international law, only if they are taken in accordance with the NAFO Convention. Then

---

35 UN Doc. A/C.6/54/SR.21 (1999), para. 21.
36 Note verbale n° 10 du ministère des affaires étrangères d'Espagne à l'ambassade du Canada en Espagne, I.C.J. Pleadings, *supra* note 14, pp. 12–14; *see* Fisheries Jurisdiction, Judgment, *supra* note 14, p. 443, para. 20.

NAFO Convention could be interpreted to exclude the possibility of invoking the necessity defence.

Whether this interpretation is persuasive or not, it is clear that Spain did not deny the necessity defence in principle in the passage cited. Spain's acknowledgement of the rule was also confirmed in its oral pleading before the ICJ. Before the ICJ, Spain's Counsel stated: "Canada even suggests the existence of a kind of state of environmental necessity or of also environmental preventive self-defence", and continued:

> As regards the suggestion of a hitherto unheard of preventive self-defence, or of a conservationist state of necessity, said in fact to be circumstances precluding wrongfulness, *that has nothing to do with Articles 33 and 34 of the draft of the International Law Commission*....[37] [italics added]

Again, although Spain rejected Canada's argument by saying that it "has nothing to do with Article 33", it did not reject the necessity defence in principle.

Consequently, it can be concluded that Spain accepts the defence of necessity in principle.

Concluding Remarks

Let me summarize the main points that have been made in this paper. As confirmed in section I above, Spain and the EU strongly criticized Canada for its enforcement actions, arguing that its legislation and the arrest of the *Estai* on the high seas constituted a flagrant violation of international law. Despite that, the Canadian Department of Foreign Affairs and International Trade, as demonstrated in section II, suggested the defence of necessity as legal justification for the legislation. In addition, as demonstrated in section III, Spain also accepted the defence of necessity in principle, although it categorically disagreed with any justification for the arrest of the *Estai*.

Given the foregoing, it can be concluded that, although the Canada/Spain Fisheries Jurisdiction case was not adjudicated on the merits in the ICJ, it can be regarded as a practice which would positively contribute to forming a customary rule of necessity defence, as far as we observe the attitudes of States concerned.

---

37   Oral Argument of Sánchez Rodríguez, 15 June 1998, CR 98/13, para. 6, I.C.J. Pleadings, *supra* note 14, p. 567.

As I mentioned at the beginning of this paper, the defence of necessity can play a role in maintaining the international legal order, even when States are in emergencies. When we consider Professor Ida's view again—the effectiveness and normativity of international law is based on a consciousness of compliance—we can also conclude that the case analysed in this paper provides evidence for the view that international law is developing in a manner that strengthens its own effectiveness and normativity.

CHAPTER 12

Catching Up with Society—What, How, and Why: The Regulation of the UN Security Council's Targeted Sanctions

*Machiko Kanetake**

I   Introduction

It is one of Professor Ryuichi Ida's favourite lines that law is, in a sense, a function of a given society.[1] This formula is broadly agreeable only because it is abstract enough to accommodate all the possible correlations between law and society, the complexity of which Professor Ida is too aware of. Yet the phrase still captures Professor Ida's basic understanding about law, namely, that law cannot be divorced from the society in which it exerts its regulatory force. Or perhaps more accurately, his conviction is that law, or more precisely, law-makers, *will* be catching up to a social change. For Professor Ida, the identity of "law" is the "substantive binding force". The substantive bindingness is sustained by social practice, deliberation, and understanding that a specific norm ought to be followed. In order not to lose its own identity, law cannot be distanced too much from social transitions.

The social dependency of law holds true especially with respect to formally non-binding standards which can be collectively called "soft law".[2] Here, I define the dichotomy of "hard" and "soft" according to whether a standard qualifies as

---

*   This chapter is built on Machiko Kanetake, "The Interfaces between the National and International Rule of Law: The Case of UN Targeted Sanctions," *International Organizations Law Review*, Vol. 9, No. 2 (2012), pp. 267–338.

1   Ryuichi Ida, "Science, Technology and International Protection of Human Rights,"(2001), p. 207. Professor Ida further observed that if scientific technologies have an impact on society, they necessarily affect law, which is a function of the society: *Ibid.*

2   There is voluminous literature on soft law: compare, for instance, Jan Klabbers, "The Redundancy of Soft Law," *Nordic Journal of International Law*, Vol. 65, (1996), pp. 167 et seq; Christine M. Chinkin, "The Challenge of Soft Law: Development and Change in International Law," *International & Comparative Law Quarterly*, Vol. 38, No. 04, (1989), pp. 850 et seq. The controversy surrounding "soft" law is inseparable from one's understanding about "law" or more precisely, its bindingness: *see* Joost Pauwelyn, "Is It International Law

one of the sources of international law,³ notably treaties, custom, and general principles.⁴ As contrasted with hard law, which retains formal binding force, the scope of standards which can be called soft law are much less cumbersome; neither the combination of *opinion juris* and State practice necessary for customary international law, nor the procedures for concluding treaties, are required. More fundamentally, soft law does not require State consent which sustains the binding force of hard law. Soft law is sustained, not by the formal binding force, but by social practice involving not only States but also non-State actors. Soft law is therefore, by definition, more responsive to social transitions than is hard law. To put it the other way around, the development of soft law could be one indicator to learn how a society has transformed itself.

This chapter attempts to apply Professor Ida's conviction and insights to a specific scenario. I analyse how social transitions accompany the development of international law—which is, in this chapter, broadly understood to include soft law—on the exercise of authority by international organisations, whose norm-making Professor Ida has extensively elaborated on. Among international organisations, the principles and rules governing the authority of the United Nations (UN) bear particular importance, as they have contributed to the development of common principles applicable to international organisations.⁵ Among the UN organs and bodies, this chapter focuses on the UN

---

or Not, and Does It Even Matter?" in Joost Pauwelyn, Ramses A. Wessel and Jan Wouters eds., *Informal International Lawmaking* (Oxford University Press, 2012), pp. 127–131. For those who see "law" as a binary, black-and-white matter, "law" cannot be "softened". If you accept "law" as a matter of degree, on the other hand, the combination the terms "soft" and "law" seems to be possible.

3   There are also other ways of defining the dichotomy of "hard" and "soft". For instance, one defines "soft" law based upon (i) the imperativity of certain provisions or (ii) judicial enforceability. For the details of the different meanings given to the "hard" and "soft" dichotomy, see Ryuichi Ida, "Formation des normes internationales dans un monde en mutation" (1990), pp. 333 et seq.

4   Statute of the International Court of Justice, 26 June 1945, *American Journal of International Law*, Vol. 39, Supp. 215 (1945) (entered into force on 24 October 1945) (1945) Article 38(1). The question as to whether the sources laid down in Article 38(1) exhaust the rules which render a norm binding under international law (see e.g., J. Pauwelyn, *supra* note 2) is beyond the scope of this chapter.

5   For instance, an *ultra vires* doctrine, the legal personality of international organisations, an implied power doctrine, and a series of rules on immunities and privileges, have developed in relation to the practice of the UN and international judicial decisions on the UN: see Elihu Lauterpacht, "The Development of the Law of International Organization by the Decisions of International Tribunals," Vol. 152, *Recueil des Cours* (1976), pp. 377 et seq; Dapo Akande,

Security Council's sanctions committees.⁶ I analyse the development of the principles of "fairness and transparency" that regulate the UN sanctions committees' decisions to designate specific individuals and entities as targets⁷ of restrictive measures, such as asset freeze. The case of targeted sanctions provides a good example to consider how formally non-binding principles emerge in response to judicial and political contestations that incrementally cast human rights law against the UN Security Council's decision-making.

The aim of this paper is a modest one; it by no means intends to provide any overall accounts for social transitions and corresponding legal development concerning the UN Security Council, much less any general observations on other UN organs or other international organisations. This chapter provides one scenario that supports the conviction and insights Professor Ida expressed through his works; namely, that international law, through soft law instruments, catches up with social transitions in international society. I first overview Professor Ida's general insights on law and society (Section II). I then situate his observations in the specific context of the UN Security Council's targeted sanctions, and analyse the following three inter-related questions: *what* transitions have international law and law-makers encountered in the context of the UN's targeted sanctions (Section III), *how* international law has caught up with social transitions (Section IV), and *why* it has done so (Section V). The analysis employed in this chapter has an obvious limit; it does not indicate what social transitions international law *ought* to catch up with. Yet this limit reflects the practice-oriented approach adopted by Professor Ida's works, which overall underscored the need for caution in not readily presuming a normative framework without foundation in society.

II   Catching Up with Society: The Three Insights from Professor Ida's Works

Professor Ida's extensive contributions to the ostensibly distinct areas of law—
le droit international de développement and international bioethics law—were

---

"International Organizations," in Malcolm D. Evans ed., *International Law* (4th ed., Oxford University Press, 2014), pp. 248 et seq.

6   On the development of sanctions regimes, *see* Jeremy Matam Farrall, *United Nations Sanctions and the Rule of Law* (Cambridge University Press, 2007).

7   Individuals and entities can be the specific objects of overall "strategic" targets of sanctions regimes themselves, and/or "tactical" targets of restrictive measures such as asset freeze and travel ban. "Targeted sanctions" in this paper is used in the latter, tactical, sense.

probably motivated by a common concern that existing international legal principles and rules encounter tremendous global-scale transitions. The broad proposition that law *will* be catching up with social transitions gives rise to three sets of questions: what transitions, how does international law catch up, and why?

The first question obviously depends on the fields of law and its specific legal rules at issue. With respect to *le droit international de développement*,[8] which caught Professor Ida's interest especially during the 1970–80s, the primary transitions that led to legal development were the dissatisfaction and demands raised by newly independent Asian and African States in the 1960–70s. They sought to qualify the way in which international law marginalised the problem of economic gaps between States. While the principle of self-determination under international law helped the decolonisation processes, it did not shed light on the economic inequality that many of the newly independent States had to encounter. Their dissatisfaction toward existing legal frameworks has generated the concept of "substantive equality", which was developed and institutionalised through a series of UN General Assembly resolutions.[9] In international law on bioethics,[10] which was pioneered by Professor Ida in the 1990s, the rapid progress in life sciences, such as embryo research, human genome research, and reproductive technologies, has increased national and international concerns over the ethicality of life science research and its application. These concerns have generated the international principles and rules on bioethics.

On the second question of *how* international law catches up with social transitions, in both spheres of law, Professor Ida situated soft law as a bridge between social transitions and hard law. The legislative or interpretive development of "hard" international law is often time-consuming and may not be best equipped for responding to transitions in social facts and values. Professor Ida therefore found the potential in formally non-binding standards. Professor Ida observed as follows:

> La notion de *soft law* est apparue comme une réponse face à la mutation de la société internationale de nos jours.... [L]e processus de formation

---

8   For the overview of Professor Ida's contribution in this area, *see* also Chapters 1 (Shotaro Hamamoto), 2 (Tomonori Mizushima), 3 (Zhian Wang) of this edited volume.

9   *See* Ryuichi Ida, "La revendication d'une réelle égalité (1)" (1974), pp. 34–63; Ryuichi Ida, "La revendication d'une réelle égalité (2)" (1975), pp. 63–103.

10 For the overview of Professor Ida's contribution in bioethics, *see* also Chapter 9 (Akiho Shibata) of this edited volume.

habituel des règles internationales, traités et coutumes, nécessite une durée considérable, de sorte que la droit ne peut rattraper l'évolution sociale. En revanche, les règles de *soft law*, surtout celles qui sont issues des résolutions, n'exigent pas un temps d'élaboration aussi long que les sources de droit traditionnelles.[11]

As encapsulated by this sentence, the flexibility of soft law better enables it to catch up with the rapid changes in international society and the demands for law. Although Professor Ida was in fact one of the critics who voiced dissent on the use of the blanket term "soft law",[12] his critical view was primarily based on the terminology. Professor Ida argued that the term "softness" ought to be more specified and be replaced by the alternative terms such as "droit programmatoire," "pré-droit", and "lex in statu nascendi" in order to distinguish the different meanings given to the broad term.[13] Professor Ida's criticism did not downplay the normative significance of non-binding standards and their roles in the development of hard law.

Non-binding standards and instruments played a significant role in *le droit international de développement* in formulating the concept of "substantive equality" as well as institutionalizing mechanisms to achieve it.[14] The instruments progressively challenged the traditional international law which, under the abstract concept of a State, treated all States with the formal equality while disregarding the substantive inequality. In *international bioethics law*, the guidelines of experts and the declarations of international organisations such as UNESCO[15] have filled the regulatory gaps in the practice of life science which has been rapidly transforming itself by the technological advancement.[16]

On the third question of *why* international law catches up with social transitions, for Professor Ida, the answer to this question is probably already given by

---

11   Ryuichi Ida, "Formation des normes internationales dans un monde en mutation" (1990), pp. 339–340.
12   Ryuichi Ida, "Qu'est-ce que le 'Soft Law?'" No. 1 (1985), pp. 1 et seq; Ryuichi Ida, "Qu'est-ce que le 'Soft Law?'" No. 2 (1985), pp. 1 et seq.
13   Ryuichi Ida, "Formation des normes internationales dans un monde en mutation" (1990), p. 340.
14   For this paragraph, Ryuichi Ida, "Statut juridique des pays en voie de développement" (1985), pp. 609 et seq.
15   See Ryuichi Ida, "Bioethics and International Law" (2003), pp. 370–371; Ryuichi Ida, "Nature juridique des normes internationals de la bioéthique"(2008), pp. 19 et seq.
16   For the roles of soft and hard law in life sciences in the national context of Japan, Ryuichi Ida, "The Significance of Soft Law as Standards of Medical Practice" (Kobundo, 2005), pp. 70 et seq.

the definition of "law", or more precisely, its bindingness. He understands law as part of "social norms" or "social codes of conduct"[17] which have substantive binding force within a society. In this vein, in Professor Ida's works, law and ethics are situated on a continuation of the same platform in that they are both codes of conduct developed in a given society.[18] Should law distance itself from social facts and values which generate social norms, law would lose its substantive binding force, and may lose its social regulatory identity.

The role of soft law in catching up with social transitions can be observed in many areas of international law, including the regulation of authority exercised by international organisations. Applying Professor Ida's analytical perspectives to a specific context, the following sections of this paper engage with the case study on the development of the principles of fairness and transparency for the regulation of the UN Security Council's targeted sanctions regimes. It illustrates how international law, through the formally non-binding standards, progressively catches up with human rights calls raised at the domestic and international levels.

III   Regulating the UN Security Council's Targeted Sanctions: What Changes?

What social transitions brought about changes to a particular legal framework must be assessed by a separate quantitative study. Yet one broad factor that could be identified is the development of human rights law both at the domestic and international levels. Human rights law is relevant to the UN's targeted sanctions in three respects: it first encouraged the transition of sanctions from comprehensive to targeted ones (as will be overviewed in the next section); human rights law was invoked as a basis to challenge the sanctions committees'

---

17   Ryuichi Ida, "Le droit international et la bioéthique" (2005) pp. 65–68.
18   *See* Ryuichi Ida, "Bioethics and International Law," (2003), p. 367. His conceptualization of bioethics as a social norm may appear contradictory to his reference to the concept of "human dignity" because the notion, at least at an abstract level, appears to inhere in humanity itself, rather than any being dependent on any "social" factors. Nevertheless, such a concern is perhaps eliminated by the fact that Professor Ida has been analyzing the existence, meaning, and application of bioethics standards applicable to the level of "human society", and, in search of the standards of human society, Professor Ida situates "international law" as a possible device to formulate and implement the standards applicable to the whole "human society". In discussing human dignity, he notes the fact that "[m]any international instruments took this word [of human dignity] as the basic value of the human community": Ryuichi Ida, *Ibid.*, p. 368.

decisions (Section III-2 below); and it has finally facilitated the development of normative and procedural developments regulating the sanctions committees' decisions (Section IV below).

1   *Human Rights Law as a Genesis of Targeted Sanctions*

The development of international human rights law is one of the key achievements of the UN.[19] The UN General Assembly played a crucial role in adopting the Universal Declaration of Human Rights[20] and major human rights conventions, including the International Covenant on Civil and Political Rights (ICCPR) and the International Covenant on Economic, Social and Cultural Rights (ICESCR).[21] The UN Security Council, by contrast, has little relevance to international human rights law, at least under the assumption of the drafters of the UN Charter. As an organ established in the aftermath of World War II, the Security Council was supposed to exercise its authority against States, and not against individuals.[22]

Yet comprehensive economic sanctions, such as those against Iraq in the 1990s, invited criticisms on both humanitarian and human rights grounds,[23] and required more targeted alternatives. Council Resolution 917 against Haiti,[24] adopted in May 1994, is the first Council resolution that enabled a sanctions committee to designate specific individuals and entities.

Under Resolution 917, the designation of the individuals was left in the hands of the Security Council's Sanctions Committee established earlier under

---

19 *See generally*, Louis B. Sohn, "The Human Rights Law of the Charter," *Texas International Law Journal*, Vol. 12 (1977), pp. 129 et seq.

20 Universal Declaration of Human Rights, A/RES/217A (III) (10 December 1948).

21 International Covenant on Civil and Political Rights, 16 December 1966, 999 UNTS 171 (1966); International Covenant on Economic, Social and Cultural Rights, 16 December 1966, 993 UNTS 3.

22 For instance, the targets of economic enforcement measures adopted by the Council were assumed to be member States. Article 41 of the UN Charter provides that measures not involving the use of armed force "may include complete or partial interruption of *economic relations* and of rail, sea, air, postal, telegraphic, radio, and other means of communication, and the severance of *diplomatic relations*": Charter of the United Nations, 26 June 1945, 1 UNTS XVI (entered into force 24 October 1945) (1945), Article 41. The wording in these examples, such as the phrases "economic relations" and "diplomatic relations", suggests that economic sanctions were assumed to be taken primarily against member States.

23 *See e.g.*, Sub-Commission on the Promotion and Protection of Human Rights, *The Adverse Consequences of Economic Sanctions on the Enjoyment of Human Rights: Working Paper Prepared by Mr. Marc Bossuyt*, E/CN.4/Sub.2/2000/33 (21 June 2000).

24 UN Doc. S/RES/917 (6 May 1994).

Resolution 841,[25] which was mandated to "maintain an updated list, based on information provided by States and regional organizations" of targeted persons, and to approve exceptions to the travel ban.[26] Since the Haiti sanctions, it has been a common practice for the Security Council to designate specific individuals and entities as targets of the asset freeze and travel ban. Between 1994 and May 2012, the Council instigated eighteen sanctions targeting specific individuals.[27] As noted above, the flourishing of these targeted sanctions is largely owed to the lessons learned from comprehensive economic sanctions which caused devastating humanitarian side effects. Targeted sanctions were thus devised as better alternatives from humanitarian and human rights perspectives.

---

25   UN Doc. S/RES/841 (16 June 1993).

26   UN Doc. S/RES/917, *supra* note 24, para. 3. All States are mandated to impose travel ban and asset freeze measures against a potentially wide range of individuals under the following three categories: (a) Haitian military/police officers (and their immediate families), (b) participants in the coup and the subsequent governments (and their immediate families), and (c) those employed by or acting on behalf of the Haitian military (and their immediate families): *Ibid.* paras. 3–4.

27   Between 1994 and May 2012, the Council instigated eighteen sanctions targeting specific individuals and entities. (i) Haiti: UN Doc. S/RES/917, *supra* note 24, paras. 3–4. (ii) Bosnian Serbs: UN Doc. S/RES/942 (23 September 1994) (1994), para. 14. The list was not drawn: *see* Final Report of the Security Council Committee Established Pursuant to Resolution 724 (1991) Concerning Yugoslavia, S/1996/946 (15 November 1996), para. 63. (iii) Angola: UN Doc. S/RES/1127 (28 August 1997), para. 4(a), para. 4(b); UN Doc. S/RES/1173 (12 June 1998), para. 11. (iv) Sierra Leone: UN Doc. S/RES/1132 (8 October 1997), para. 5; UN Doc. S/RES/1171 (5 June 1998), para. 5. (v) Al Qaeda and Taliban: UN Doc. S/RES/1267 (15 October 1999), para. 4; UN Doc. S/RES/1333 (19 December 2000), para. 8, para. 10, para. 11; UN Doc. S/RES/1390 (28 January 2002), para. 2. In June 2011, the sanctions regime was split into two: for Al Qaeda, UN Doc. S/RES/1989 (17 June 2011). For Taliban, UN Doc. S/RES/1988 (17 June 2011). (vi) Liberia; UN Doc. S/RES/1343 (7 March 2001), para. 7(a). (vii) Iraq: UN Doc. S/RES/1483 (22 May 2003), para. 23(b). (viii) Liberia, UN Doc. S/RES/1521 (22 December 2003), para. 4(a); UN Doc. S/RES/1532 (12 March 2004) para. 1. (ix) DRC: UN Doc. S/RES/1533 (12 March 2004), para. 13, para. 15; UN Doc. S/RES/1596 (18 April 2005); UN Doc. S/RES/1807 (31 March 2008). (x) Côte d'Ivoire: UN Doc. S/RES/1572 (15 November 2004), para. 9, para. 11. (xi) Sudan: UN Doc. S/RES/1591 (29 March 2005), para. 3. Cf. UN Doc. S/RES/1054 (26 April 1996), para. 3(b). (xii) Lebanon/Syria, UN Doc. S/RES/1636 (31 October 2005), para. 3. (xiii) North Korea: UN Doc. S/RES/1718 (14 October 2006), para. 8. (xiv) Iran: UN Doc. S/RES/1737 (27 December 2006), para. 10, para. 12. (xv) Eritrea/Somalia: UN Doc. S/RES/1844 (20 November 2008); UN Doc. S/RES/1907 (23 December 2009). (xvi) Libya: UN Doc. S/RES/1970 (26 February 2011). (xvii) Taliban: UN Doc. S/RES/1988 (2011). (xviii) Guinea-Bissau: UN Doc. S/RES/2048 (18 May 2012). For the summary and analysis of each sanctions regime, *see* J. Farrall, *supra* note 6.

2   Human Rights Law as a Challenge to Targeted Sanctions

While the use of targeted sanctions succeeded in avoiding widespread humanitarian effects, it has brought a new controversy with respect to its disrespect for the human rights of those individuals listed by the UN.[28] Criticisms have been particularly levelled against the sanctions regime imposed against Al Qaeda instigated by Security Council Resolution 1267,[29] under which the targets geographically proliferated across the globe.

An assets freeze certainly has a significant impact on the listed individuals' right to property,[30] and a person's privacy, reputation, and family rights.[31] Despite the scale of impact on human rights, when individuals were designated as specific targets, no hearing was conducted prior to or following the designation of targets, nor were they informed of the detailed grounds for listing.[32] No direct petition mechanisms had been institutionalised for the targeted individuals and entities claiming their non-involvement until the adoption of Council Resolution 1730 in late 2006.[33]

---

28   There are a number of human rights critiques regarding the Council-led sanctions. *See* e.g., August Reinisch, "Developing Human Rights and Humanitarian Law Accountability of the Security Council for the Imposition of Economic Sanctions," *American Journal of International Law*, Vol. 95, No. 4 (2001), pp. 851 et seq; Iain Cameron, "UN Targeted Sanctions, Legal Safeguards and the European Convention on Human Rights," *Nordic Journal of International Law*, Vol. 72, No. 2 (2003), pp. 159 et seq; Erika De Wet, *The Chapter VII Powers of the United Nations Security Council* (Hart Publishing, 2004) Chapter 6; Jose E. Alvarez, "The Security Council's War on Terrorism: Problems and Policy Options," in *Review of the Security Council by Member States* (Intersentia, 2003), pp. 119 et seq.

29   UN Doc. S/RES/1267 (15 October 1999). In December 2000, Resolution 1333 extended the reach of the assets freeze to members of Al Qaeda: UN Doc. S/RES/1333 (19 December 2000), para. 8(c). In January 2002, Resolution 1390 further expanded the targets of the assets freeze to those "associated with" members of Al Qaeda, and imposed a travel ban and arms embargo not limited to the territory of Afghanistan: UN Doc. S/RES/1390 (28 January 2002), para. 2. The sanctions regime was initially established against Al Qaeda and Taliban. The sanctions regime was split into two different sanctions regimes on 17 June 2011: for Al Qaeda, UN Doc. S/RES/1989 (17 June 2011); for Taliban, UN Doc. S/RES/1988 (17 June 2011).

30   Universal Declaration of Human Rights, *supra* note 20, Article 17.

31   ICCPR, *supra* note 21, Article 17. *See* I. Cameron, *supra* note 28, pp. 159–173; Peter Gutherie, "Security Council Sanctions and the Protection of Individual Rights," *New York University Annual Survey of American Law*, Vol. 60 (2004), pp. 499–511.

32   For the procedural improvement regarding the Al Qaeda sanctions regime, *see* Section IV-2 of this chapter; Machiko Kanetake, "The Interfaces between the National and International Rule of Law: The Case of UN Targeted Sanctions," *International Organizations Law Review*, Vol. 9, No. 2 (2012), Annex II.

33   UN Doc. S/RES/1730 (19 December 2006).

The lack of procedural safeguards led to criticism directed against the Council for failing to ensure the right to a fair hearing[34] and the right to an effective remedy for those who are targeted by the Council and its sanctions committees.[35] Individuals are entitled to a fair hearing if the asset freeze, the deprivation of property, amounts to a "criminal charge"[36] or if it involves the determination of a person's "rights and obligations in a suit at law".[37] Arguably, the longer a suspected individual remains on the list, the more likely it is that the effect of sanctions will resemble a criminal charge.[38] These human rights concerns have invited a series of domestic and international contestations against domestic and EU law which has implemented the decisions of the UN Security Council and its sanctions committees.[39]

The most well-known case is *Kadi* before the EU courts, which has also shaped the fate of other similar cases in EU courts and its member States. Extensive debates have been conducted with respect to the case,[40] and I will

---

34   ICCPR, *supra* note 21, Article 14.
35   *Ibid.*, Article 2(3).
36   *Ibid.*, Article 14(1). Compare, e.g., Erika De Wet, "The Role of Human Rights in Limiting the Enforcement Power of the Security Council: A Principled View," in Erika De Wet, André Nollkaemper and Petra Dijkstra eds., *Review of the Security Council by Member States* (Intersentia, 2003), pp. 15–16; Strengthening Targeted Sanctions through Fair and Clear Procedures: White Paper prepared by the Watson Institute Targeted Sanctions Project (Brown University), 30 March 2006, A/60/887–S/2006/331 (14 June 2006) (2006) at 14–18.
37   ICCPR, *supra* note 21, Article 14(1). See I. Cameron, *supra* note 28, p. 192, and fn. 91. Compare with Watson Report, *supra* note 36, pp. 14–15.
38   See J. Alvarez, *supra* note 28, p. 132, pp. 134–135; P. Gutherie, *supra* note 31, pp. 503–506. *See also* Report of the Special Rapporteur on the Promotion and Protection of Human Rights and Fundamental Freedoms while Countering Terrorism, A/63/223 (6 August 2008) (the Special Rapporteur, Martin Scheinin, observes that the indefinite freezing of the assets amounts to a criminal punishment due to the severity of the sanction).
39   *See* the list of judicial decisions, M. Kanetake, *supra* note 32, Annex I (The List of National, European and International Cases regarding UN Targeted Sanctions). A large number of studies have been carried out on sanctions-related cases and wider domestic court decisions contesting the exercise of authority by the Council and its subsidiary organs. For a useful overview, *see* Christina Eckes, "The Role of Judges Confronted with Norms form Different Origins: The Case of Counter-Terrorist Sanctions," in Knud Erik Jørgensen and Katie Verlin Laatikainen eds., *Routledge Handbook on the European Union and International Institutions: Performance, Policy, Power* (Routledge, 2013), pp. 171–184; August Reinisch ed., *Challenging Acts of International Organizations Before National Courts* (Oxford University Press, 2011), Chapters 2 (Hilpold), 3 (Tzanakopoulos), 4 (Wouters and Schmitt), 5 (d'Aspremont and Brölmann).
40   For a useful overview of literature on *Kadi*, *see* Sara Poli and Maria Tzanou, "The Kadi Rulings: A Survey of the Literature," *Yearbook of European Law*, Vol. 28, No. 1 (2009), pp. 533 et seq.

not reiterate the details of the decisions. The then Court of First Instance (CFI), which is now the General Court (EGC),[41] in September 2005 found itself structurally limited in carrying out the review ("*Kadi I*, CFI").[42] The Court of Justice (ECJ) in September 2008 ("*Kadi I*, ECJ") set aside the CFI's judgment and conducted the "full review" by upholding the autonomy of the EU legal order based upon the "rule of law".[43] The EGC in September 2010 ("*Kadi II*, EGC") then followed the ECJ's decision in *Kadi I* and conducted the "full and rigorous" review of the measures, although the EGC still voiced criticism on the formalistic divide adopted by the ECJ with respect to EU and UN legal orders.[44] The ECJ in July 2013 ("*Kadi II*, ECJ") intensified the level of "full review", and

---

[41] For the purpose of this paper, I continue to use the CFI (instead of EGC) as it would be convenient to distinguish *Kadi* decisions rendered in 2005 (by the CFI) and 2010 (by the EGC).

[42] Case T-315/01 *Yassin Abdullah Kadi v. Council of the European Union and Commission of the European Communities* [2005] ECR II-03649 (CFI) (Judgment of 21 September 2005, hereinafter Kadi I (CFI)). On the CFI judgment, *see* e.g., August Reinisch, "Introductory Note to Court of First Instance of the European Communities: Yassin Abdullah Kadi v. Council of the European Union and Commission of the European Communities," *International Legal Materials*, Vol. 45 (2006), pp. 77 et seq; Christian Tomuschat, "Case T-306/01, Ahmed Ali Yusuf and Al Barakaat International Foundation v. Council and Commission; Case T-315/01, Yassin Abdullah Kadi v. Council and Commission," *Common Market Law Review*, Vol. 43, pp. 537 et seq; Mielle Bulterman, "Fundamental Rights and the United Nations Financial Sanction Regime: The Kadi and Yusuf Judgments of the Court of First Instance of the European Communities," *Leiden Journal of International Law*, Vol. 19, No. 3 (2006), pp. 753 et seq; Christina Eckes, "Judicial Review of European Anti-Terrorism Measures— The Yusuf and Kadi Judgments of the Court of First Instance," *European law journal*, Vol. 14, No. 1 (2008), pp. 74 et seq.

[43] Cases C-402/05 P and C-415/05 P *Kadi and Al Barakaat International Foundation v. Council of the European Union and Commission of the European Communities* [2008] ECR I-06351 (ECJ) (Judgment of 3 September 2008, hereinafter Kadi I (ECJ)). On the ECJ judgment, *see* e.g., Deirdre Curtin and Christina Eckes, "The Kadi Case: Mapping the Boundaries between the Executive and the Judiciary in Europe," *International Organizations Law Review*, Vol. 5 (2008), pp. 365 et seq; Christina Eckes, *EU Counter-Terrorist Policies and Fundamental Rights* (Oxford University Press, 2009), Chapter 5; Paul James Cardwell, Duncan French and Nigel White, "European Court of Justice, Yassin Abdullah Kadi and Al Barakaat International Foundation v Council and Commission (Joined Cases C-402/05 P and C-415/05 P) Judgment of 3 September 2008," *International & Comparative Law Quarterly*, Vol. 58, No. 01 (2009), pp. 229 et seq; Gráinne de Burca, "The EU, the European Court of Justice and the International Legal Order after Kadi," *Harvard International Law Journal*, Vol. 51, No. 1 (2010), pp. 1 et seq.

[44] Case T-85/09 *Kadi v. European Commission and Council of the European Union* [2010] ECR II-05177 (EGC) (Judgment of 30 September 2010, hereinafter Kadi II (EGC)). See *ibid.*, para. 151 ("full and rigorous judicial review").

found itself tasked with two things:[45] whether one of the reasons (for listing) stated in the summary provided by the UN's Sanctions Committee was sufficiently detailed and specific,[46] and whether it is substantiated.[47] With regard to the former, the ECJ acknowledged that some of the reasons stated in the Sanctions Committee's summary were sufficiently detailed and specific.[48] Nevertheless, for the latter, the ECJ found that information or evidence which might have substantiated the reason for listing was absent,[49] and thereby annulled the contested EU regulation that implemented the decisions of the UN sanctions committees' decisions.[50]

The proliferation of the individuals' claims before national courts has succeeded in inviting the international calls for procedural reform. In 2004, the UN High-Level Panel made an unequivocal call for a reviewing process in relation to the Al Qaeda and Taliban sanctions regime, noting that "[t]he way entities or individuals are added to the terrorist list maintained by the Council and the absence of review or appeal for those listed raise serious accountability issues and possibly violate fundamental human rights norms and conventions".[51]

---

45   Joined cases C-584/10 P, C-593/10 P and C-595/10 P *Kadi v European Commission* (ECJ) (Judgment of 18 July 2013, hereinafter Kadi II (ECJ)), para. 130.
46   In *Kadi II*, the ECJ held that EU institutions owe not only the obligation to communicate the allegations, but also the "duty of careful and impartial examination": *Ibid.*, para. 115. This duty is part of the obligation to state reasons laid down in Article 296 of TEFU (*Ibid.*, para. 116.), and part of procedural safeguards established through the jurisprudence of EU courts (*see Ibid.*, para. 114.). The duty of careful and impartial examination requires EU institutions to assess the necessity of seeking the assistance of the UN Sanctions Committee and of member States in order to obtain the "disclosure of information or evidence, confidential or not": *Ibid.*, para. 115. In determining the compliance of the competent EU authority with the duty of careful and impartial examination, the courts determine "in particular, whether the reasons relied on are sufficiently detailed and specific": *Ibid.*, para. 118.
47   According to the ECJ, the right to effective judicial protection requires EU courts to ensure that the listing decision is "taken on a sufficiently solid factual basis": Kadi II (ECJ, 2013), *supra* note 45, para. 119. This means that judicial review "must concern whether those reasons, or, at the very least, one of those reasons, deemed sufficient in itself to support that decision, is substantiated": *Ibid.* When security considerations preclude the competent EU authority to disclose information requested by EU courts, the courts determine whether the grounds of non-disclosure are well founded, and if they are, strike an appropriate balance between the protection of the rights and that of the security: *Ibid.*, paras. 125–128.
48   Kadi II (ECJ, 2013), *supra* note 45, paras. 140–150.
49   *Ibid.*, paras. 151–163.
50   *Ibid.*, para. 164.
51   Report of the High-Level Panel on Threats, Challenges and Change, *A More Secure World: Our Shared Responsibility*, A/59/565 (2 December 2004), para. 152.

Individuals' claims before national courts were accompanied by diplomatic initiative to study the political and legal issues involved in the Council's targeted sanctions, including the human rights compatibility of the listing procedure.[52] In particular, the Watson Institute of Brown University's report entitled "Strengthening Targeted Sanctions Through Fair and Clear Procedures" addressed procedural guarantees to a greater extent,[53] and the report was presented to the Security Council and the General Assembly in June 2006.[54] The call for procedural safeguards was also echoed by a number of member States and the wider UN family.[55]

IV   How to Catch Up?

A question can then be posed as to how international law regulating the decisions of the UN Security Council's sanctions committees can absorb human rights contestations raised at both the domestic and international levels. International law regulating the authority of the UN Security Council's sanctions committees includes the UN Charter, the decisions of the UN Security Council, common rules and principles of international organisations, and possibly non-binding international standards. As pointed out by Professor Ida,[56] the rigidity of hard law leaves soft law to reflect on and absorb human rights contestations into regulatory frameworks.

---

52   The Swedish government took one of the first diplomatic initiatives, the so-called Stockholm Process, during 2001–2002, to invite governmental and non-governmental attention to the issue of procedural guarantees. *See* Peter Wallensteen, Carina Staibano and Mikael Eriksson eds., *Making Targeted Sanctions Effective: Guidelines for the Implementation of UN Policy Options—Results from the Stockholm Process on the Implementation of Targeted Sanctions* (Department of Peace and Conflict Research, Uppsala University, 2003), available at http://www.smartsanctions.se/ (as of 31 October 2014), para. 37, paras. 282–285. The report was presented to the Security Council: *see* UN Press Release, SC/7673 (25 February 2003); UN Doc. S/PV. 4713 (25 February 2003).

53   It recommended that an administrative focal point be designated within the UN Secretariat to which individuals may submit their delisting requests: Watson Report, *supra* note 36, pp. 43–44. It also proposed several options for review mechanisms accessible to individuals: *Ibid.*, pp. 46–51.

54   Watson Report, *supra* note 36.

55   For governmental and institutional contestations, *see* further Machiko Kanetake, "Enhancing Community Accountability of the Security Council through Pluralistic Structure: The Case of the 1267 Committee," *Max Planck Yearbook of United Nations Law*, Vol. 12 (2008), pp. 113 et seq.

56   *See* Section II of this chapter.

1   By Hard Law

The decisions of the UN and its organs are governed by the UN Charter as a constituent instrument. As the International Court of Justice (ICJ) affirmed this at the outset of the UN, the "political character of an organ cannot release it from the observance of the treaty provisions established by the Charter when they constitute limitations of its powers".[57] The same was reconfirmed by the Appeals Chamber of the International Criminal Tribunal for the former Yugoslavia (ICTY) in *Tadić* (1995), in which the Tribunal stated "neither the text nor the spirit of the Charter conceives of the Security Council as *legibus solutus* (unbound by law)".[58]

There are broadly two ways through which the UN Charter could catch up with social transitions; the formal amendment of the UN Charter, and interpretive development. As for the former, it is well-known that the amendment of the UN Charter is hampered by the complexity of political bargaining and the rigidity of the amendment procedures. The realistic possibility would therefore be to rely upon the interpretive development of the UN Charter. Just as with any other treaties, the interpretation of the UN Charter could change over time. The flexibility of interpretive rule for treaties allows one to take into consideration the UN Charter's "special characteristics"[59] that the instrument has not only conventional but also institutional dimensions.[60] Such characteristics could justify a greater emphasis on the purposes and subsequent practices among the interpretive elements contained in the Vienna Convention on the Law of Treaties.[61]

---

57   *Admission of a State to the United Nations (Charter, Article 4)*, Advisory Opinion, *I.C.J. Reports 1948*, p. 57, p. 64.

58   Case No. IT-94-1-AR72 *Prosecutor v. Duško Tadić, Appeals Chamber, Decision on Jurisdiction* (ICTY) (Decision of 2 October 1995) para. 28 (in relation to the Council's power under Article 39 of the UN Charter).

59   *Certain Expenses of the United Nations (Article 17, Paragraph 2, of the Charter)*, Advisory Opinion, *I.C.J. Reports 1962*, p. 151, p. 157.

60   *Legality of the Use by a State of Nuclear Weapons in Armed Conflict (WHO Request)*, Advisory Opinion, *I.C.J. Reports 1948*, p. 66, p. 75, para. 19.

61   For the interpretation of UN Charter provisions, see e.g., Georg Ress, "The Interpretation of the Charter," in Bruno Simma ed., *The Charter of the United Nations: A Commentary* (2nd ed., Oxford University Press, 2002), p. 13; Jose E. Alvarez, *International Organizations as Law-Makers* (Oxford University Press, 2005), pp. 65–108; Pollux, "The Interpretation of the Charter," *British Year Book of International Law*, Vol. 23 (1946), pp. 54 et seq; Oscar Schachter, "Interpretation of the Charter in the Political Organs of the United Nations," in Salo Engel ed., *Law, State and International Legal Order: Essays in Honor of Hans Kelsen* (University of Tennessee Press, 1964), pp. 269 et seq.

There is a divergence of views as to whether the UN Charter, particularly Article 1(3), imposes obligations, through Article 24(2), not only to "promote" respect for human rights, but also to "ensure" respect for human rights *strictu sensu*.[62] Among the elements of treaty interpretation,[63] the textual reading of Article 1(3) suggests that the UN organs are required to "promote" respect for human rights, but not to "ensure" respect for human rights.[64] The use of the reserved language, "promoting and encouraging", under Article 1(3) was deliberate. At the San Francisco Conference, a proposal was made to replace the terms with the words "to assure" or "to protect". However, it did not win support among delegates. According to the subcommittee I/1/A, to assure or protect fundamental rights and freedoms is "primarily the concern of each state",[65] and not of the UN. This is not surprising, inasmuch as the anticipated impact

---

62   One side observes that the compliance *strictu sensu* with human rights obligations, both under treaties and customary law, is not assumed by the Charter (i.e., obligation to promote): *see* Jochen Abr. Frowein and Nico Krisch, "Introduction to Chapter VII," in Bruno Simma ed., *The Charter of the United Nations: A Commentary*, (2nd ed., Oxford University Press, 2002), p. 711. The other side argues that Charter obliges the Security Council to comply with human rights established under customary law and those under major human rights treaties (i.e., obligation to ensure): *see* J. Alvarez, *supra* note 28 , pp. 125, 129–132 (with respect to the obligations established as customary international law); E. De Wet, *supra* note 36, pp. 8–14.

63   The basic formula of treaty interpretation is to give "ordinary meaning" to the treaty terms: Vienna Convention on the Law of Treaties, 23 May 1969, 1155 UNTS 311 (entered into force 27 January 1980) (1969), Article 31(1). An exception is when the parties have given a "special meaning" to a term: Article 31(4). Such ordinariness is nevertheless a highly relative notion, being sustained by multiple variables; namely, the terms' context, the treaty's object and purpose, and three other mandatory considerations, including subsequent practice: Vienna Convention on the Law of Treaties, *Ibid.*, Article 31(1), (2), (3). While the reference to the preparatory works is one of "supplementary" means for interpretation and not part of the mandatory variables, reference to preparatory works can be readily licensed by Article 32.

64   Under Article 1(3) of the UN Charter, it is one of the purposes of the UN "[t]o achieve international cooperation…in *promoting and encouraging* respect for human rights and for fundamental freedoms for all": Charter of the United Nations, *supra* note 14, Article 1(3) (emphasis added). *See* Frederic Mégret and Florian Hoffman, "The UN as a Human Rights Violator—Some Reflections on the United Nations Changing Human Rights Responsibilities," *Human Rights Quarterly*, Vol. 25 (2003), pp. 314 et seq.

65   *Documents of the United Nations Conference on International Organization, San Francisco, 1945*, (United Nations Information Organizations, 1945) Vol. 6, at 705 ("Report of Rapporteur, Subcommittee I/1/A", Doc. 723, I/1/A/19, 1 June 1945).

that the UN itself impinges upon the rights of individuals was significantly limited when the Charter was drafted.[66]

The subsequent development in practice indicates that the Security Council has increasingly narrowed its discretion in terms of how to take into account the respect for human rights when acting under Chapter 7 of the UN Charter. For instance, a range of measures to ameliorate the humanitarian and human rights-related impacts of sanctions have been implemented by the Security Council,[67] as exemplified by the Oil-for-Food Program for Iraq,[68] the provision of humanitarian exemptions,[69] the monitoring of humanitarian impact,[70] and more broadly, the methodological transition of the Security Council's sanctions from comprehensive ones to more targeted measures.[71] Yet subsequent practice, albeit providing greater guidance as to how the UN and its organs take into account human rights, does not go so far as to suggest that the organs are formally bound by human rights law. Also, the development of the Charter through subsequent practices must be done by the practice that "establishes the agreement of the parties regarding its interpretation".[72] To reinterpret UN Charter provisions requires member States' approval and compromise, which is probably time-consuming and favours the State-centric variables.

One may observe that the human rights obligation attaches *a priori* to the legal personality of international organisations, inclusive of the UN, enjoyed

---

66   In addition, with regard to Article 1(1) of the UN Charter, the Charter failed short of constraining the exercise of Chapter VII authority by the UN Security Council to the same degree as in Chapter VI by not referring to the "principles of justice and international law" in the first part of Article 1(1) of the UN Charter regarding collective measures. On the drafting history of Article 1(1) of the UN Charter, see Terry D. Gill, "Legal and Some Political Limitations on the Power of the UN Security Council to Exercise its Enforcement Powers under Chapter VII of the Charter," *Netherlands Yearbook of International Law*, Vol. 26 (1995), pp. 65–68.

67   *See generally* Jochen Abr. Frowein and Nico Krisch, "Article 41," in Bruno Simma ed., *The Charter of the United Nations: A Commentary* (2nd ed., Oxford University Press, 2002), pp. 745–746.

68   *See generally* Review and Assessment of the Implementation of the Humanitarian Programme Established Pursuant to Security Council Resolution 986(1995) (December 1996-November 1998), S/1999/481 (28 April 1999).

69   *See generally* Gian Luca Burci, "Interpreting the Humanitarian Exceptions through the Sanctions Committees," in Vera Gowlland-Debbas ed., *United Nations Sanctions and International Law* (2001), pp. 143 et seq.

70   *See generally* E. De Wet, *supra* note 28, pp. 226–247.

71   *See* Section II-1 of this chapter.

72   Vienna Convention on the Law of Treaties, *supra* note 63, Article 31(3)(b).

under international law.[73] In principle, however, international personality has no predetermined content in international law.[74] While the UN is "capable of possessing international rights and duties",[75] this capacity does not automatically dictate what rights and obligations the Organisation has.[76] The presumption that international organisations are born with no predestined entitlement and obligations is, of course, increasingly subject to qualification by the development of common rules on international organisations.[77] Yet the variance among international organisations has so far hampered the development of substantive rules, such as human rights law, into the corps of common institutional rules.

2   *By Soft Law*

Awaiting the time-consuming development by "hard" international law, non-binding standards have developed in order to regulate the listing decisions rendered by the sanctions regimes. The principles of "fair and clear" procedures, and more broadly, the principles of fairness and transparency, have been formulated through UN General Assembly and Security Council resolutions as the UN's institutional regulatory standards. In paragraph 109 of the World Summit Outcome in 2005, the UN General Assembly "call[ed] upon the Security Council…to ensure that *fair and clear procedures* exist for placing individuals and entities on sanctions lists and for removing them, as well as for granting humanitarian exemptions".[78] The principles of fairness and transparency have

---

73   A. Reinisch, *supra* note 28, pp. 858–859; Nigel D. White, *The Law of International Organisations* (2nd ed., Manchester University Press, 2005), p. 217. Similarly, Henry G. Schermers and Niels M. Blokker, *International Institutional Law Unity within Diversity* (4th revised ed., Martinus Nijhoff Publishers, 2003) p. 1002; Felice Morgenstern, *Legal Problems of International Organizations* (Cambridge: Grotius Publications, 1986), p. 32.
74   H. Schermers & N. Blokker, *ibid.*, p. 990, pp. 992–993; N. White, *ibid.*, pp. 40–41.
75   See *Reparation for Injuries Suffered in the Service of the United Nations*, Advisory Opinion, *I.C.J. Reports 1949*, p. 174, p. 179. The ICJ observed that "rights and duties [of the UN] are [not] the same as those of a State": *ibid.*
76   The personality refers to the capacity of a person, but his entitlement and duties require separate scrutiny: *see* Michael Byers, *Custom, Power and the Power of Rules: International Relations and Customary International Law* (Cambridge University Press, 1999), pp. 75–87.
77   Some examples include an *ultra vires* doctrine, the legal personality of international organisations, an implied power doctrine, interpretation of constituent instruments, and a series of rules on immunities and privileges: *see* D. Akande, *supra* note 5, p. 251.
78   2005 World Summit Outcome, A/RES/60/1 (24 October 2005), para. 109 (emphasis added). Similarly, Report of the Secretary-General, *Uniting against Terrorism: Recommendations for a Global Counter-Terrorism Strategy*, A/60/825 (27 April 2006), para. 42; The United Nations Global Counter-Terrorism Strategy, A/RES/60/288 (20 September 2006), para. 15.

also been incorporated into Security Council resolutions themselves. The first appearance was the preamble of Resolution 1730, concerning all targeted sanctions regimes, in which the Council "committed to ensuring that fair and clear procedures exist" for the listing and delisting of individuals and entities.[79] The principles were upgraded to the operative part of Resolution 1822 regarding the Al Qaeda and Taliban sanctions regime in particular.[80] In Resolution 1904 adopted in December 2009, the Security Council also "[took] note of challenges, both legal and otherwise" to the sanctions measures, and "express[ed] its intent to continue efforts to ensure that procedures are fair and clear".[81]

As suggested by the nuanced terms of "fair and clear" procedures, the principles do not necessarily signify the Security Council's obligation to "ensure" respect for human rights. Nevertheless, they still require the organ to incorporate procedural safeguards for the targeted individuals and entities with respect to its decisions to designate individuals. While the fairness and transparency can be understood in a range of different ways, the principles are broadly understood to realise not only the general improvement of the listing, but also the following four procedural safeguards: (i) *periodical review* by the Council, (ii) the respect for the individuals' *right to be informed* of the measures, (iii) the *right to be heard* directly by the decision-making body, and (iv) the *right to review* by an effective review mechanism.[82]

A series of the procedural improvements at the UN Security Council's sanctions committees can be understood as the incremental realisation of these procedural safeguards.[83] For instance, the sanctions-wide Focal Point established in December 2006 under Resolution 1730 can be understood as an

---

79   UN Doc. S/RES/1730 (19 December 2006), pre.para. 5 (original italics omitted).
80   UN Doc. S/RES/1822 (30 June 2008), para. 28. Similarly, UN Doc. S/RES/1904 (17 December 2009), para. 34; UN Doc. S/RES/1989 (17 June 2011), para. 42; UN Doc. S/RES/2083 (17 December 2012), para. 45.
81   UN Doc. S/RES/1904 (17 December 2009), pre.para. 9 (original emphasis omitted). Cf. UN Doc. S/RES/1822 (30 June 2008), pre.para. 12. Similarly, UN Doc. S/RES/1989 (17 June 2011), pre. para. 11; UN Doc. S/RES/2083 (17 December 2012), pre.para. 11.
82   Bardo Fassbender, *Targeted Sanctions and Due Process*, Study Commissioned by the UN Office of Legal Affairs (20 March 2006), at http://www.un.org/law/counsel/Fassbender_study.pdf (as of 31 October 2014); UN Doc. S/PV. 5474 (22 June 2006), p. 5 (statement by Mr. Michael, Legal Council of the UN, presenting the Secretary-General's view in the non-paper, presumably based on Fassbender's aforementioned paper); Report of the Special Rapporteur on the Promotion and Protection of Human Rights and Fundamental Freedoms while Countering Terrorism, UN Doc. A/61/267 (16 August 2006), paras. 38–41.
83   The main procedural improvements are chronologically listed in: M. Kanetake, *supra* note 32, Annex II.

incremental step for the element of the *right to be heard*.⁸⁴ The Ombudsperson established for the Al Qaeda sanctions regime is also one realisation of the *right to be heard* and the *right to review*. In December 2009, particularly with respect to the Al Qaeda sanctions regime alone, the Focal Point was replaced by the Office of the Ombudsperson established under Resolution 1904, who not only receives delisting requests from individuals and entities,⁸⁵ but also assists the Committee's consideration to such requests "in an independent and impartial manner".⁸⁶ Council Resolution 1989 in June 201 further awarded it the power to make recommendations on delisting.⁸⁷ Under the resolution, if the Ombudsperson recommends the Committee to consider "delisting", and if no decisions are rendered either by the Committee or the Council within the period of 60 days, the restrictive measures against the targeted individuals and entities would come to an end.⁸⁸ Council Resolution 1989 noted the Ombudsperson's "important role in improving fairness and transparency".⁸⁹

---

84 The Security Council unanimously adopted Resolution 1730 based on a French proposal, requesting the Secretary-General to establish a "focal point" to receive delisting requests as a mechanism to be applied to all Council sanctions involving designated individuals: UN Doc. S/RES/1730 (19 December 2006).

85 UN Doc. S/RES/1904 (17 December 2009), para. 21. On the establishment and function of the Ombudsperson under Resolution 1904, *see* Christopher Michaelsen, "The Security Council's Al Qaeda and Taliban Sanctions Regime: 'Essential Tool' or Increasing Liability for the UN's Counterterrorism Efforts?" *Studies in Conflict & Terrorism*, Vol. 33, No. 5 (2010), pp. 456–459.

86 UN Doc. S/RES/1904 (17 December 2009), para. 20. The delisting process under Resolution 1904 follows the three steps: information gathering by the Ombudsperson (two months), "dialogue" between the Ombudsperson and the petitioner (two months), and Committee discussion and decision (two months): *see ibid.*, Annex II. For the function of the Ombudsperson under Resolution 1904, *see Ibid.*; Laurence Boisson de Chazournes & Pieter Jan Kuijper, "Mr Kadi and Mrs Prost: Is the UN Ombudsperson Going to Find Herself between a Rock and a Hard Place?" in Henri de Waele and Eva Rieter eds., *Evolving Principles of International Law* (Martinus Nijhoff Publishers, 2012), pp. 81–90.

87 UN Doc. S/RES/1989 (17 June 2011), para. 21. *See also ibid.*, Annex II, para. 7(c).

88 *See* UN Doc. S/RES/1989 (17 June 2011), Annex II, para. 12. In cases where the Ombudsperson recommends *retaining the listing*, the restrictive measures on the petitioner remain in place "unless a Committee member submits a delisting request" which will be considered under its normal consensus procedures: *ibid.*, Annex II, para. 11.

89 UN Doc. S/RES/1989 (17 June 2011), pre.para. 13. The Monitoring Team of the Al Qaeda Sanctions Committee notes that this procedural development "came as close to meeting the calls for an independent and binding review mechanism as seemed possible": Thirteenth Report of the Analytical Support and Sanctions Implementation Monitoring Team Submitted Pursuant to Resolution 1989 (2011) concerning Al-Qaida and Associated Individuals and Entities, S/2012/968 (31 December 2012) para. 11.

The Council's incremental procedural developments, fostered by both governmental and non-governmental contestations, demonstrate that respect for the aforementioned four procedural safeguards has been, in principle, accepted and incrementally institutionalised within the targeted sanctions regimes. The concrete reforms in the listing procedures have led to the delisting of some of those targeted individuals and entities which brought court proceedings.[90] The principles of fairness and transparency are the UN's institutional standards and do not have any formal binding force upon the Security Council. Yet the principles are embedded in the discourse of the UN Security Council and its sanctions committees themselves, and have guided at least some of these incremental procedural reforms.

There is apparently a difference between hard and soft law with respect to the *identity of law-makers*. The interpretive development is ultimately a decision of member States.[91] On the other hand, the principles of fairness and transparency were formulated by the UN General Assembly, developed by the reports prepared by scholars and practitioners (e.g., those of the Watson Institute[92] and Fassbender[93]), and ultimately accepted and materialised by the UN Security Council and its sanctions committees.

V Why Catching Up?

The foregoing analysis finally brings us to the question of *why* the UN Security Council has accepted the principles of fairness and transparency and

---

90 See M. Kanetake, *supra* note 32, Annex I (The List of National, European and International Cases regarding UN Targeted Sanctions). The delisted individuals and targets include: Aaran Money Wide Service (26 August 2002), Global Services International (26 August 2002), Aden (26 August 2002), Abdulaziz Ali (26 August 2003), Yusuf (24 August 2006), Nasco (14 November 2007), Sayadi (20 July 2009), Vinck (20 July 2009), Nada (23 September 2009), Barakaat International Foundation (22 October 2009), Nada Management Organization (22 October 2009), Hassan (9 September 2010), Abdulrahim (22 December 2010), Elosta (22 December 2010), Al-Faqih (T-135/06) (22 June 2011), Sanabel Relief Agency (22 June 2011), Abdrabbah (22 June 2011), Ayadi (17 October 2011, after Ombudsperson review), Abdelrazik (30 November 2011, after Ombudsperson's review), Maftah Mohamed Elmabruk (22 December 2010), MIRA (2 July 2012, after Ombudsperson's review), Al-Faqih (2 July 2012, after Ombudsperson's review), and Kadi (Delisted on 5 October 2012 after Ombudsperson's review).

91 For instance, the interpretive development through practices must be done through the practices that establish the agreement of the "parties" regarding its interpretation: Vienna Convention on the Law of Treaties, *supra* note 63, Article 31(3)(b).

92 Watson Report, *supra* note 36.

93 B. Fassbender, *supra* note 82.

incrementally materialised them in the decision-making processes, apparently by way of responding to domestic and international human rights contestations.

1 For the Protection of Human Rights

A *liberalistic* answer to the question may well be that the UN Security Council accepted and materialised the principles in order to better protect the funda mental rights of those listed individuals. This human rights-based explanation should hold true in part. It was the domestic and international claims based upon human rights violations that fostered normative and procedural developments. For instance, the establishment of the Focal Point in 2006 followed the UN High-Level Panel's human rights criticisms in 2004 against the Al Qaeda sanctions regime,[94] *Kadi I* before the then CFI (now the EGC) in September 2005, and the World Summit Outcome document in October 2005.[95] The Focal Point has invited contestation by national judges on the grounds that it was "obvious that this procedure does not begin to achieve fairness for the person who is listed".[96] The establishment of the regime-specific Ombudsperson in December 2009 also followed a series of human rights contestations, including *Kadi I* before the ECJ in September 2008. The Ombudsperson's procedure met criticism from national judges as lacking any effective judicial remedy.[97]

---

94   A More Secure World: Our Shared Responsibility, *supra* note 51, para. 152.
95   2005 World Summit Outcome, *supra* note 78, para. 109.
96   *A, K, M, Q & G v. HM Treasury* [2008] EWHC 869 (Admin) (Justice Collins; High Court of Justice, UK) (Judgment of 24 April 2008), para. 18.
97   *HM Treasury v. Mohammed Jabar Ahmed and Others; HM Treasury v. Mohammed al-Ghabra; R (Hari El Sayed Sabaei Youssef) v. HM Treasury* [2010] UKSC 2 (UK Supreme Court) (Judgment of 27 January 2010) para. 78 (Lord Hope, with whom Lord Walker and Lady Hale agree). Lord Phillips observed that the Guidelines revised according to Resolution 1822 "fall far short" of providing the access to a court as well as the reasons for the listing to enable him to make an effective challenge: *ibid.*, para. 149 (Lord Phillips). Lord Mance also denounced the procedure of the 1267 committee, despite various modifications up to Resolution 1904, in that they do not provide judicial procedure for review, nor do they guarantee that individuals affected will know sufficiently about the case against them in order to be able to respond to it: *ibid.*, para. 239 (Lord Mance). *See also* Report of the Special Rapporteur on the Promotion and Protection of Human Rights and Fundamental Freedoms while Countering Terrorism, A/65/258 (6 August 2010), paras. 55–58 (the Special Rapporteur, Martin Scheinin, remains concerned that the revised delisting procedures do not meet the fundamental principles of the right to fair trial); Promotion and Protection of Human Rights and Fundamental Freedoms while Countering Terrorism, A/67/396 (26 September 2012), paras. 27–59 (the Special Rapporteur, Ben Emmerson, recommended that the Ombudsperson should be renamed the Office of the Independent Designations Adjudicator (IDA), and that States should be obligated to disclose information to the IDA

The human rights contestations have led to the conferral of recommendatory power on the Ombudsperson in June 2011.

At the same time, the liberalistic account provides only a part of the picture. First, the problem of procedural safeguards had existed already from the inception of targeted sanctions in 1994. It was, however, only after the Al Qaeda sanctions regime that the problem attracted wide international attention. The liberalist's view does not fully explain this point. Second, despite some normative and procedural developments, the principles of fairness and transparency and their concrete realisation still appear to be significantly departed from any strict observance of human rights law or domestic human rights standards. While the fairness and transparency principles have been used interchangeably with "due process",[98] the permanent members of the UN Security Council tend to avoid the use of human rights languages when they discuss the fairness and transparency in the sanctions regimes.[99]

2 *In Response to the Political Power of Judicial Contestations*

An alternative *realist*'s explanation may, in part, account for normative and procedural developments. A hallmark of realist thought is to capture law as a simple reflection of the prevailing balance of power and to serve the political purposes of powerful States.[100] From this perspective, it can be argued that the principles of fairness and transparency and their concrete realisation reflect the policy proactively pursued by the governments of some European States. They proactively push forward the procedural safeguard in the sanctions regimes through a range of diplomatic routes. Switzerland, Germany, and Sweden commissioned the project of the Watson Institute of Brown University

---

on conditions of confidentiality. The Rapporteur also suggested that the information obtained through torture should be excluded from consideration by the IDA.).

[98] See UN Doc. S/PV. 5474 (22 June 2006) p. 3 (Mr. Moeller/Ms. Løj of Denmark), p. 12 (Mr. Burian of Slovakia), p. 15 (Mr. Pereyra Plasencia of Peru), p. 20 (Mr. Mayoral of Argentina), p. 21 (Mr. Al-Nasser of Qatar); UN Doc. S/PV. 5474 (Resumption 1) (22 June 2006) p. 17 (Mrs. Núñez de Odremán of Venezuela), p. 19 (Mr. Adekanye of Nigeria); UN Doc. S/PV. 6347 (29 June 2010) (The promotion and strengthening of the rule of law in the maintenance of international peace and security); UN Doc. S/PV. 6347 (Resumption 1) (29 June 2010); UN Doc. S/PV. 6424 (15 November 2010) (Briefings by Chairmen of subsidiary bodies of the Security Council).

[99] See e.g., UN Doc. S/PV. 5474 (22 June 2006); UN Doc. S/PV. 5474 (Res. 1) (22 June 2006).

[100] Christian Reus-Smit, "The Politics of International Law," in Christian Reus-Smit ed., *The Politics of International Law* (Cambridge University Press, 2004), pp. 15–16.

on targeted sanctions' fair and clear procedures.[101] In April 2011, the like-minded European States proposed further improvement in the listing procedures.[102]

In addition to these governmental diplomatic initiatives, the role of judicial organs, especially that of EU courts, can be understood as part of political power. This is counter-intuitive, given that judicial bodies are generally supposed to restrain power, not create it. Nevertheless, no matter what EU courts and domestic courts decide, the legal effect of the decisions is formally confined in respective legal orders and does not reach to the UN Security Council's exercise of authority. Outside respective legal orders, the impact of decisions of domestic and EU courts should be understood as part of *political* influence.

This explains the fact that the problem of procedural safeguards attracted attention only after the Al Qaeda sanctions regime. What has helped the problem to emerge was the geographical proliferation of targets, which not only exacerbated the scale of human right problems but diversified political and judicial recourses available to the targeted individuals and entities. The use of national courts with which the individuals indirectly contested the UN Security Council's listing decisions has been an influential apparatus for attracting international political attention to the targeted individuals' claims. The international political significance of national courts greatly varies depending upon the geographical location. Suppose that *Kadi* decisions were rendered by a court of a small State, that the State is not a well-known advocate of the rule of law, and that the decisions were not readily available in English. As such, the normative and procedural developments at the sanctions committees might have been far more moderate.

Yet this power-based account is not satisfactory either. Apparently, the decisions of the Security Council often hinge on the positions of the US government, which is much less reluctant to provide procedural safeguards in

---

101 Watson Report, *supra* note 36. Switzerland, Germany, and Sweden also sponsored earlier initiatives to reform targeted sanctions, although the initiatives were primarily addressed the effectiveness of sanctions through robust domestic implementation and international monitoring: the Interlaken Process (1998–2001), the Bonn-Berlin Process (1999–2001), and the Stockholm Process (2001–2002), sponsored by Switzerland, Germany and Sweden, respectively. *See* further Thomas J. Biersteker, Sue E. Eckert, Aaron Halegua & Peter Romaniuk, "Consensus from the Bottom Up? Assessing the Influence of the Sanctions Reform Processes," in Peter Wallensteen and Carina Staibano eds., *International Sanctions: Between Words and Wars in the Global System* (London: Frank Cass, 2005), pp. 15 et seq.

102 "Improving Fair and Clear Procedures for a More Effective UN Sanctions System" (Document submitted to the Security Council by Switzerland and the Like-Minded States in April 2011) (a proposal submitted by Austria, Belgium, Costa Rica, Denmark, Finland, Germany, Liechtenstein, the Netherlands, Norway, Sweden, and Switzerland).

the sanctions regimes. With regard to the Al Qaeda sanctions regime, the vast majority of the names on the target list have been submitted by the US, either alone or in conjunction with other UN members,[103] and it has been a principal advisor of the Al Qaeda Sanctions Committee.[104] Since the UN does not have a general capacity to collect (as opposed to receive) international intelligence relating to them, national intelligence is the primary source.[105] The US, as a primary provider of the information, retains the political power in deciding how the sanctions regimes operate. Outside the sanctions' contexts, the US outweighs many other States with regard to many political and economic factors. This creates power disparities among UN member States. Given the predominant power of the US, it may be difficult to capture the normative and procedural developments as a good reflection of the balance of power.

3   To Secure the Effectiveness of Sanctions

A *rationalistic* or pragmatic account should remedy some of the shortcomings of liberal and realist explanations. Apparently, human rights contestations, especially those raised by domestic and EU courts, could hamper the effectiveness of sanction regimes.

Domestic organs have the ultimate authority to give effect to international decisions at the domestic level. No matter what decisions the UN Security Council makes, the international decisions would be binding only at the international level. This gives rise to the practical necessity for the UN to respond to legal impediments raised before domestic and EU courts. Also, the effective functioning of the sanctions regimes requires not only mere compliance through the adoption of appropriate domestic legislation, but also States' enhanced willingness to cooperate. In particular, the UN relies on member States' readiness to ensure that financial institutions within their jurisdictions

---

103   Eric Rosand, "The Security Council's Efforts to Monitor the Implementation of Al Qaeda/Taliban Sanctions," *American Journal of International Law*, Vol. 98, No. 4 (2004), p. 746.

104   Richard Barrett, the Coordinator of the Monitoring Team since 2004, states: "The United States, of course, is intensely engaged through this whole process [of the fight against terrorism]. We find great support from them in our work on the committee...": CNN, Diplomatic License: Current Events at the United Nations, 3 September 2004, available at http://transcripts.cnn.com/TRANSCRIPTS/0409/03/i_dl.00.html (as of 31 October 2014).

105   See Simon Chesterman, *Shared Secrets: Intelligence and Collective Security* (Longueville Media, published for Lowy Institute for International Policy, 2006), pp. 70–71.

are screening accounts and transactions in an effective and timely manner.[106] In order to maximise the effect of asset freeze measures, the UN Security Council needs to compromise its own procedures in line with the standards adopted at the domestic level.

This rationalistic explanation is sound, but still not complete. In particular, this pragmatic account does not explain the fact that the major normative and procedural developments had started *before* the critical decisions such as *Kadi I* in the ECJ were rendered.[107] The mere fact that that court proceedings were instigated in major political constituencies in the eyes of the UN Security Council facilitated the international reform. The driving factor for the normative and procedural reforms was therefore not entirely the decisions that eventually find in favour of the listed individuals and legally undermine the implementation of sanctions at the domestic level.

4 Constituted by Institutional Discourse

Finally, a *constructivist's* account may overcome some of the shortcomings of the above explanations. It holds that the UN Security Council's decisions are, after all, constituted by wider institutional discourse, including that of human rights. This constructivist perspective of international relations does not sanction the idea that law and society are the distinctive forms and they could be explained by the rationality of actors involved. It advances the account that normative and ideational structures construct actors' identities through the process of socialisation, as well as shape a public justificatory claim that the actors give for their behaviour. International law is a central component of the normative structures that are constitutive of the actors' internal identities and external logics of argument.[108]

This explanation appears to hold true in the case of targeted sanctions. The identity of the UN as a leading human rights advocate conditions their

---

106   Fourth Report of the Analytical Support and Sanctions Monitoring Team Appointed Pursuant to Security Council Resolutions 1526 (2004) and 1617 (2005) Concerning Al-Qaida and the Taliban and Associated Individuals and Entities, S/2006/154 (10 March 2006), para. 68.

107   The UN Security Council's meeting held two months *after Kadi I* (ECJ) is noteworthy. While some States expressed concern about *Kadi I* (ECJ), the attention was paid rather to the implementation of Resolution 1822, which introduced the procedural development (narrative summaries of reasons, notice to the targets, and comprehensive review) *before* the ECJ's decision. This meeting suggests that the ECJ's decision was not to change the overall direction of the procedural development which had started before. *See* UN Doc. S/PV.6015 (12 November 2008).

108   *See* C. Reus-Smit, *supra* note 100, pp. 21–23.

institutional discourse and behaviour, including those of the Security Council. Indeed, human rights discourse is deeply embedded in the practice of the UN.[109] The World Summit Outcome declared that human rights, along with the rule of law and democracy, belong to the universal and indivisible core values and principles "of the United Nations".[110] The UN Security Council is not immune from such human rights discourse. Through the deliberation and communications with member States outside the Council, other UN organs and experts, and the wider international community, the UN Security Council, whose identity and discourse are already conditioned by the institutional narrative on human rights, was required to justify its decisions with the language of human rights, which has led to the adoption of fairness and transparency principles and procedural improvements.

The practice of cross-referencing among judicial organs might have fostered the permeation of human rights contestations into the UN's discourse. For instance, with regard to the Al Qaeda sanctions regime, the Federal Supreme Court of Switzerland, in the case of *Nada* (2007), referred to the CFI's decision in *Kadi I* and reasoned the case in a similar line.[111] The UK Supreme Court in *Ahmed* (2010)[112] referred to the Canadian case of *Abdelrazik* (2009).[113] And *Kadi I*, *Abdelrazik*, and *Ahmed*, together with *Sayadi* (2008) before the Human Rights Committee of the International Covenant on Civil and Political Rights (ICCPR),[114] were referred to by the European Court of Human Rights (ECtHR)

---

109   See David Forsythe, "The United Nations and Human Rights," in Ramesh Thakur and Edward Newman eds., *New Millennium, New Perspectives: The United Nations, Security, and Governance* (United Nations University Press, 2000), pp. 220 et seq.

110   2005 World Summit Outcome, A/RES/60/1 (24 October 2005), para. 119.

111   The Swiss court conducted the *jus cogens* review and found that procedural deficiencies at the UN did not contradict *jus cogens*, as did the CFI in its 2005 decision. *Youssef Nada v State Secretariat for Economic Affairs and Federal Department of Economic Affairs*, Administrative appeal judgment, Case No 1A45/2007, DTF 133 II 450; ILDC 461 (CH 2007) (Switzerland, Federal Supreme Court, First Public Law Chamber) (14 November 2007). For details, see Johannes Reich, "Recent Developments: Due Process and Sanctions Targeted Against Individuals Pursuant to UN Resolution 1267 (1999)," *Yale Journal of International Law*, Vol. 33 (2008).

112   Ahmed (UK Supreme Court, 2010), *supra* note 97.

113   *Abousfian Abdelrazik v. The Minister of Foreign Affairs and the Attorney General of Canada*, 2009 FC 580 (Canada, Federal Court) (Judgment of 4 June 2009).

114   Nabil Sayadi and Patricia Vinck v. Belgium, CCPR/C/94/D/1472/2006 (views of the Human Rights Committee under Article 5, Paragraph 4, of the Optional Protocol to the ICCPR) (29 December 2008). The Human Rights Committee found that there was a violation of Articles 12 and 17 of the ICCPR by Belgium. In particular, the Committee found

in the case of *Nada* (2012).[115] The ECJ in *Kadi II* (2013) referred to the *Nada* cases of the ECtHR and the Federal Supreme Court of Switzerland in order to reiterate the insufficiency of the UN's procedure and the resulting importance of a judicial review at the EU level.[116]

In addition to the effect of decisions themselves, judges' specific reasoning and narratives also determine the extent to which domestic and EU court decisions generate political momentum at the international level. For instance, the CFI's *jus cogens* review in *Kadi I* added the material through which the European decision facilitated the international regulatory reform at that time—despite the ECJ's subsequent rejection of *jus cogens* review. The Canadian Federal Court in *Abdelrazik* (2009)[117] held that the Canadian government breached the applicant's right to enter Canada under Canadian constitutional jurisprudence. In *Abdelrazik*,[118] Justice Zinn of the Canadian Federal Court criticised the 1267 Committee regime against Al Qaeda as "a denial of basic legal remedies and as untenable under the principles of international human rights",[119] despite the fact that it was not strictly necessary to refer to the sanctions committee's procedure. In *A and Others* (2008) before the UK Court of Appeal, an English judge has chosen the powerful term "prisoners of the state" to characterise the State of those targeted, which was also reiterated by the Supreme Court, and also by the EGC in *Kadi II*.[120] The EGC also described targeted sanctions as "particularly draconian"[121] for the targeted individuals. These expressions and terms are reproduced by scholars and possibly by judges, and contribute to the gathering of political momentum to call for normative and procedural reforms on the international stage.

---

unjustified the way that Belgium initially transmitted complainants' names to the Sanction Committee: *see ibid.*, paras. 10.7–10.8.

115 *Nada v. Switzerland*, App. no. 10593/08, European Court of Human Rights Grand Chamber, Judgment, 12 September 2012.

116 Kadi II (ECJ, 2013), *supra* note 45, para. 133. The ECJ referred to *Nada*: Youssef Nada v State Secretariat for Economic Affairs and Federal Department of Economic Affairs, Administrative appeal judgment, *supra* note 111 paras. 8.1–8.3; Nada v. Switzerland, *supra* note 115, para. 211.

117 Abdelrazik (Canadian Federal Court, 2009), *supra* note 113.

118 *Ibid.*

119 *Ibid.*, para. 51.

120 *A and Others v. hm Treasury* [2008] EWCA Civ 1187 (UK Court of Appeal) (Judgment of 30 October 2008) para. 125 (Sedley LJ); Ahmed (UK Supreme Court, 2010), *supra* note 97, para. 4, para. 60; Kadi II (EGC, 2010), *supra* note 44, para. 149.

121 Kadi II (EGC, 2010), *supra* note 44, para. 149.

VI   Conclusion

If the "soft" branch of international law could be a good indicator for social transitions, the development of the principles of fairness and transparency and the incremental procedural improvements to regulate the decisions of the UN Security Council's sanctions committees seem to provide the following three contemporary features of international society.

First, the specific case discussed in this chapter is part of the broader trend to subject the institutional decisions of the UN and other international organisations to human rights norms. Human rights law has developed historically in the domestic legal order for the regulation of public authority exercised by States against individuals. Yet the exercise of authority by international organisations, including the UN, has great impact, not only on State organs, but also on individuals and entities within a State. The greater relevance of international organisations to domestic societies necessitates that the organisations justify their decisions in such a way as to address the concerns of individuals and non-governmental entities.[122] In addition, with regard to the UN, its institutional commitment to promote human rights has determined its own identity. As the case analysed in this chapter illustrates, this institutional identify circumscribes the way in which it responds to the human rights contestations—regardless of the fact that the UN Charter only imposes the abstract obligation to "promote" respect for human rights on the UN and its organs.

Second, the case of targeted sanctions highlights that national courts may no longer hesitate in reviewing the acts of national governments even if the acts in question concern the implementation of international obligations imposed by UN Security Council resolutions. Judicial contestations can be seen outside the context of targeted sanctions. While domestic courts proactively invoke international law and the decisions of international organisations, the active application of international law has inevitably augmented the occasions for domestic courts to encounter differences between two legal prescriptions. The promising trend of judicial amenability to international law has then increasingly coincided with domestic judicial contestations against international law, including the decisions of international organisations. Specific techniques and grounds under which domestic courts avoid and contest the decisions of international institutions vary depending on whether those decisions are rendered by political or judicial institutions, and whether

---

[122]   *See* Michael Zürn, "Global Governance and Legitimacy Problems," *Government and Opposition*, Vol. 39, No. 2 (2004), pp. 260 et seq.

States have monist or dualist traditions, the kind of treaties involved, and the wider political and judicial climate surrounding the judges.[123] The protection of fundamental rights has been one of the important grounds for contestation. Courts invoke the safeguarding of human rights as a basis for which they directly or indirectly review the decisions of international organisations, including those of the UN's targeted sanctions.

Finally, the social elements which UN law and its law-makers have been catching up with are not only those occasioned by member State authorities, but also those initiated by non-governmental actors. As illustrated by the example of targeted sanctions, individuals' claims before national courts have invited international attention and contestations against the decisions of international organisations. While the human rights claims by individuals and entities are often unable to attract sustained international attention, the claims before national courts, especially those of the geopolitically influential regions, have attracted international attention and support, which created the momentum for generating new regulatory standards at the international level.

Overall, the application of Professor Ida's analytical standpoint to the context of UN law helps us to analyse, not only the role of non-binding standards in remedying the gaps between the social demand for law and the rigidity of law-making process, but also simultaneously the features of international society in which international law and theories sustain their raison d'être. Professor Ida's analytical standpoint deserves continued academic attention from legal scholarships, as it serves not only to bridge a gap between social transitions and international law, but also to create a link between the social dynamics and international legal scholarship.

---

123   On the techniques and bases for national avoidance and contestations, see Machiko Kanetake, "The Interfaces between the National and International Rule of Law: A Framework Paper," in Machiko Kanetake and André Nollkaemper eds., *The Rule of Law at the National and International Levels: Contestations and Deference* (Oxford: Hart Publishing, 2015).

Bibliography of Professor Ryuichi Ida (With Abbreviations Used in This Book)

Books

1983	*Kaisetsu Joyakushu* [*Treaties and Conventions*] (Member of the Board of Editors, most recent edition in 2009, Sanseido).
1986	*Kokusai Kiko Joyaku Shiryoshu* [*Basic Documents of International Organizations*] (Member of the Board of Editors, Toshindo, 2nd edition in 2002).
2004	*Niju-u Isseiki no Kadai to Tembou* [*International Organizations in the 21st Century: Problems and Prospects*] (Co-editor, Toshido).
2010	*Rinri eno Toi to Daigaku no Shimei* [*Questions for Ethics and the Role of Universities*] (Co-editor, Kyoto University Press).
2011	*Adolescent et acte médical, regards croisés* (Co-directeur avec B. Feuillet-Liger, Bruylant).
2012	*Adolescent, Autonomy and Medical Treatment* (Co-editor with B. Feuillet-Liger and T. Callus, Bruylant).

Academic Articles

1974–75	Kokusai Keizai Kiko niokeru Jisshitsu-teki Byodo no Shucho: Kokuren Boeki Kaihatu Kaigi no Seiritsu (1) (2) [La revendication d'une réelle égalité entre les Etats au sein des organisations internationales économiques—Genèse de la CNUCED—(1) (2)], *Hogaku Ronso* [*Kyoto Law Review*], Vol. 96, No. 3; Vol. 97, No. 3: "La revendication d'une réelle égalité (1) (2)" (1974, 1975).
1979	Gijutsu Iten Code of Conduct to Kokusaiho no Hatten [Technology Transfer Code of Conduct and the Development of International Law], *Nihon no Shinro to Gijutsu Senryaku no Chousa Kenkyu* [*Research on Japan's Direction and Technology Strategy*] (Tsu-san Seisaku Kouhousha).
1979	Kokusai Nogyou Kaihatsu Kikin [International Agricultural Development Fund], *Kokusai Nourin Kyoryoku* [*International Agricultural and Forestry Cooperation*], Vol. 2, No. 3.
1979	Shin Kokusai Keizai Chitsujo no Kikoteki Imprimenteshon: Byodo Sankaken to Kokusai Nogyou Kaihatsu Kikin [La mise en œuvre institutionnelle du nouvel ordre économique international—Egalité de

participation et Fonds international pour le développement agricole—],
Okayama Daigaku Hogakkai Zasshi [*Okayama Law Journal*], Vol. 29, No. 1:
"La mise en œuvre institutionnelle" (1979).

1980 Kokusai Rengo Kogyo Kaihatsu Kiko Kensho [<Materials> The Constitution of the United Nations Industrial Development Organization], *Okayama Daigaku Hogakkai Zasshi* [*Okayama Law Journal*], Vol. 29, Nos. 3&4.

1981 <Shokai to Shiryo>Seigenteki Shokanko no Kokusaiteki Kisei—Takokuseki Kigyo Katsudo Kisei to Kodo Koryo no Kokusaihoteki Seikaku [Principes et règles pour le contrôle des pratiques commerciales restrictives—caractère juridique—], *Okayama Daigaku Hogakkai Zasshi* [*Okayama Law Journal*], Vol. 31, No. 2.

1982 Shin Kokusai Keizai Chitsujo no Hoteki Kozo—Kokka no Keizaiteki Kenri Gimu Kensho wo Sozai to Shite [The Legal Structure of the New International Economic Order: An Analysis of the Charter of Economic Rights and Duties of States], *Okayama Daigaku Souritsu 30 Shunen Kinen Ronbunshu "Hogaku to Seijigaku no Gendaiteki Tenkai"* [*Essays in Celebration of the 30th Anniversary of Okayama University: Modern Development of Legal and Political Studies*] (Yuhikaku): "The Legal Structure of the New International Economic Order," (1982).

1983 Kokusai Nogyo Kaihatsu Kikin—Kiko to Kino [Le Fonds international de développement agricol—d'après 4 ans d'expériences—], *Okayama Daigaku Hogakkai Zasshi* [*Okayama Law Journal*], Vol. 32, Nos. 3&4.

1985 Kaihatsu no Kokusaiho ni Okeru Hattentojokoku no Hoteki Chii—Kokka no Byodo to Hatten no Fubyodo [Statut juridique des pays en voie de développement en droit international du développement—Egalité des Etats et inégalité du développement—], *Hogaku Ronso* [*Kyoto Law Review*], Vol. 116, Nos. 1–6: "Statut juridique des pays en voie de développement" (1985).

1985 "Soft Law" towa Nani Ka—Kokusaiho-jo no Bunseki Gainen toshite no Yuyosei Hihan (1), (2) [Qu'est-ce que le "Soft Law"? (1)/(2)—Critique de son utilité en qu'instrument d'analyse—], *Hogaku Ronso* [*Kyoto Law Review*], Vol. 117, Nos. 5&6: "Qu'est-ce que le 'Soft Law'? (1) (2)" (1985).

1989 Saikin no Umi no Kyokai Kakutei Funso ni okeru Hireisei no Gensoku—Kokusaiho ni okeru Hireisei Gensokuno Kenkyu [Le concept de la proportionnalité dans les conflits récents sur la délimitation maritime—Le principe de la proportionnalité en droit international—], *Hogaku Ronso* [*Kyoto Law Review*], Vol. 124, Nos. 5&6.

1989 Kokusai Kiko niokeru Hyoketsu Seido no Tenkai—Kokusai Shakai Soshikika no Shihyo toshite—["The Evolution of Voting Systems in International Organisations as a Barometer of International Organisation"],

Kokusaiho no Shin Tenkai-Taijudo Sensei Kanreki Kinen Ronbunshu [*New Development of International Law*] (H. Hayashi, H. Yamate and S. Kozai eds., Toshindo): "The Evolution of Voting Systems" (1989).

1989 Keizaiteki Shakaiteki Kyoryoku to Kokusai Rengo—Kokuren no Kiki no Kaiketsu wo Motomete—[La coopération économique et sociale dans le système des Nations Unies: À la recherche d'une solution de la crise des Nations Unies], *Sekaiho Nempo* [*Yearbook of World Law*], Vol. 9: "La coopération économique et sociale dans le système des Nations Unies" (1989).

1989 "Kaihatsu no Kokusaiho" Riron—Furansu Kokusaihogaku no Ittan [The doctrine of droit international du développement: An Aspect of French Studies on International Law], *Nichifutsu Hogaku* [*La revue de la Société franco-japonaise des sciences juridiques*], Vol. 16: "The doctrine of droit international du developpement" (1989).

1990 Kokusaiho ni Okeru Jiei Gainen—Saikin no Kokka Jikko kara Mita Jiei Gainen no Tegakari [Légitime défense en droit international—Introduction à une tentative de réexamen du concept de légitime défense à travers la pratique récente—], *Hogaku Ronso* [*Kyoto Law Review*], Vol. 126, Nos. 4–6.

1991 Formation des normes internationales dans un monde en mutation - Critique de la notion de soft law -, *Le droit international au service de la paix, de la justice et du développement - Mélanges Michel Virally* (Pedone): "Formation des normes internationales dans un monde en mutation" (1991).

1991 Kokusai Rengo to Kokka Shuken—Kokusai Kiko no Jikkosei to Kokka Shuken ni Yoru Controle no Taiji [L'O.N.U. et la souveraineté: Dialectique de l'efficacite des organisations internationales et du contrôle exercé par les Etats], *Kokusaiho Gaiko Zassi* [*The Journal of International Law and Diplomacy*], Vol. 90, No. 4: "L'O.N.U. et la souveraineté" (1991).

1993 Nanboku Mondai to Kokusai Keizaiho [The North–South Problem and International Economic Law], *Shinpan Kokusai Keizaiho* [*International Economic Law, New Edition*] (A. Tanso, H. Yamate and Y. Ohara eds., Seirin Shoin).

1993 Kaihatsu no Kokusaiho ni Okeru Kokuyuka Funso no Kaiketsu—Chusai Saitei no Hensen kara Mita Jikkouteki Kaiketsu no Mosaku [Nationalisation pétrolière en droit international du développement—A la recherche de l'effectivité de solution arbitrale], *Hogaku Ronso* [*Kyoto Law Review*], Vol. 132, Nos. 4–6: "Nationalisation pétrolière en droit international du développement" (1993).

1996 International Lawmaking Process in Transition? A Comparative and Critical Analysis of Recent International Norm-Making Process, *Trilateral*

Perspectives on International Legal Issues: Relevance of Domestic Law and Policy (M.K. Young and Y. Iwasawa eds., Transnational Publishers): "International Lawmaking Process in Transition?" (1996).

1997 Kaihatsu Tojoukoku niokeru Kokuyu-uka Funsou no Jikkouteki Kaiketsu: Sono Houriron-teki Bunseki [Effective Settlement of Nationalization Disputes in the Developing Countries: Legal Theoretical Analysis], *Funsou Kaiketsu no Kokusaiho: Oda Shigeru Sensei Koki Shukuga [International Law of Dispute Settlement: Essays in Honour of Professor Shigeru Oda]* (T. Sugihara ed., Sanseido): "Effective Settlement of Nationalization Disputes" (1997).

1997 Le droit international du développement et le développement humain—A travers l'expérience japonaise—*Le droit international du développement social et culturel* (A. Pellet et J.-M. Sorel éds., L'Hermès).

1997 Japan in the International Community of the 21st Century, *Its Role in the U.N., Image and Reality: Philippine-Japan Relations towards the 21st Century* (La Cruz ed., University of Philippine Press).

1998 UNESCO "Hito Genomu oyobi Jinken ni Kansuru Sekai Sengen" [UNESCO: Universal Declaration on the Human Genome and Human Rights], *Idenshi Igaku [Gene & Medicine]*, Vol. 2, No. 1.

1998 Kokusai Boeki Taisei to Hattentojo-koku [The System of International Trade and Developing States], *Kokusai Mondai [International Affairs]*, Vol. 463: "The System of International Trade and Developing States" (1998).

1998 Sustainable Development in the APEC, *International Economic Law with a Human Face* (F. Weiss, E. Denters and P. de Waart eds., Kluwer Law International).

1998 Second Report of the Committee on Regional Economic Development Law, *International Law Association Report of the Conference*, Vol. 68.

1998 UNESCO "Hito Genomu oyobi Jinken ni Kansuru Sekai Sengen" ["Universal Declaration on the Human Genome and Human Rights" of UNESCO], *Kagaku to Seibutsu [Chemistry and Biology]*, Vol. 37, No. 1.

1999 Gendai Kokusaiho ni okeru Ho-Kihan Keisei—Saikin no Kokusaiho Keisei Purosesu ni Kansuru Ichi-kosatsu [Norm-Making Process in the Contemporary International Law: An Analysis of the Recent International Lawmaking Process], *Kyodai 100 Shunen Kinen Ronbunshu [Kyoto University Centenial Celebration]*, Vol. 2: "Norm Making Process in the Contemporary International Law" (1999).

1999 La mutation de la formation des normes internationales: richesse et limites du mythe de la paix par le droit, *René-Jean Dupuy: Une œuvre au service de l'humanité* (UNESCO): "La mutation de la formation des normes internationales" (1999).

1999	UNESCO "Hito Genomu oyobi Jinken ni Kansuru Sekai Sengen" no Kosatsu—Kokusai Seimei Rinri Iinkai An ni Kansuru Anketo Chosa Kekka no Kento [Déclaration universelle sur le génome humain et les droits de l'homme de l'UNESCO—A propos du résultat d'une enquête sur le Projet de déclaration établi par le C.I.B.], *Hogaku Ronso* [*Kyoto Law Review*], Vol. 144, Nos. 4&5.
1999	Seimei Kagakuto Junken: UNESCO "Hito Genomu to Jinken ni Kansuru Sekai Sengen" [Bio-science and Human Rights: UNESCO's Universal Declaration on the Human Genome and Human Rights], *Kokusai Jinken* [*Human Rights International*], Vol. 10.
2000	Tojo-koku no Kaihatsu Seisaku to Tsusho Mondai—WTO ni okeru Tojo-koku no Ho-teki Iso no Henka o Chushin ni [Development Policy of Developing Countries and International Trade System: Legal Status of Developing Countries in the WTO/Comments on Professor Hyuck-Soo Yoo's Paper] (Co-authored with Hyuck-Soo Yoo) *Nihon Kokusai Keizai Ho Gakkai Nempo* [*International Economic Law*], Vol. 9.
2000	Hito Soshiki Saibo no Kuron Riyo—Sono Ho-teki Rinri-teki Mondai [Cloning of Human Cells—Ethical and Legal Consideration—], *Idenshi Igaku* [*Gene & Medicine*], Vol. 4, No. 2.
2000	<Kaisetsu> Kuron Ningen Kinshi Ho "Hito no Songen ni Hansuru" Koui Saiko Choeki 5 Nen, Bakkin 500 Man-en [A Law Banning Human Cloning: Acts "Contrary to Human Dignity" Will Result in Five Years' Imprisonment and Fine of Five Million Yen], *SCIaS*, Vol. 5, No. 6.
2000	UNESCO "Hito Genomu Sengen" no Kokunai-teki Jisshi-Hito Kuron Kotai no Sansei Kinshi [Un suivi de la Déclaration universelle sur le génome humain et les droits l'homme de l'UNESCO—La prohibition du clonage humain reproductif au Japon—], *Hogaku Ronso* [*Kyoto Law Review*], Vol. 146, Nos. 5&6: "Un suivi de la Déclaration universelle sur le génome humain" (2000).
2000	Genomu Ikagaku ni Okeru Rinri Kihan no Sakutei to Rinri Shinsa Seido [Formation and Application of Ethical Principles in Genome Science], *Jikken Igaku* [*Experimental Medicine*], Vol. 18, No. 2.
2001	Kagaku Gijutsu to Jinken no Kokusai-teki Hogo—Seimei Kagaku no Hatten to Jinken Hogo [Science, Technology and International Protection of Human Rights: The Development of Life Science and the Protection of Human Rights], *Nihon to Kokusaiho no 100 Nen Dai 4 Kan Jinken* [*Japan and International Law: 100 Years, Vol. 4: Human Rights*] (Sanseido): "Science, Technology and International Protection of Human Rights" (2001).
2001	Hito Genomu Kenkyu wo Meguru Ho to Rinri: UNESCO "Hito Genome Sengen" wo Tegakari to Shite [Le droit et l'éthique dans le génomique—Autour de la Déclaration universelle sur le génome humain et les droits de l'homme de l'UNESCO], *Hogaku Ronso* [*Kyoto Law Review*], Vol. 148, Nos. 5&6.

2001 Hito ES Saibo no Kenkyu to Seimei Rinri [Human ES cells research and bioethics], *Jikken Kagaku* [*Experimental Medicine*], Vol. 19, No. 15.

2001 Kuron Gijutsu to Seimei Rinri [Cloning Technology and Bioethics], *Kagaku Gijutsu Journal* [*Science and Technology Journal*], Vol. 10, No. 3.

2001 Gan Kenkyu to Shakai to Seimei Rinri [Cancer Research, Society and Bioethics], *Gan no Rinsho* [*Japanese Journal of Cancer Clinics*], Vol. 47, No. 2.

2002 The Role of Proportionality in Maritime Delimitation Revisited: The Origin and Meaning of the Principle from the Early Decisions of the Court, *Liber Amicorum Judge Shigeru Oda* (N. Ando et al. eds., Kluwer Law International).

2002 Genomu, Kuron Kenkyu ga Jinrui ni Tsukitsuketa Toi—Seimei Rinri to Kagaku no Shinri Tankyu no Hazama de [Problems That Genome and Cloning Research Posed to Human Beings—Between Bioethics and Scientific Research], *Sekai* [*The World*], Vol. 699.

2002 21 Seiki no Jinbun Shakai-Kagaku no Shinko no Tame ni—Ho Gakusha no Seimei Rinri e no Torikumi no Keiken Kara [Toward Promoting 21st Century Humanities and Social Sciences—As Seen from a Law Scholar's Experience of Grappling with Life Theory], *Gakujutsu Geppo* [*Japanese Scientific Monthly*], Vol. 55, No. 11.

2002 Hito ES Saibono Kenkyu ni Okeru Rinri-teki Mondai [Ethical Questions of the Human Embryonic Stem Cells Research], *Rinsho Shinkeigaku* [*Clin. Neurol/Clinical Neurology*], Vol. 42, No. 11.

2002 Biotekunoroji Tokkyo to Seimei Rinri [Patent on Biotechnology and Bioethics], *Baiotekunoroji no Shinpo to Tokkyo* [*Development of Biotechnology and Patent*] (H. Nakayama ed., Yusho-do).

2002 Soshiki Teikyo no Infomudo Konsento ni Tsuite—Hito Soshiki Bank e no Soshiki Teikyo ni Kanren Shite—[Informed Consent on Providing Human Tissues—In Relation to Providing Tissues to Human Tissue Banks], *HAB Kenkyu Kiko Sousho* [*Series of HAB Research Institute*], No. 2.

2003 Sentan Iryo to Shakai to Seimei Rinri [Advanced Medicine, Society and Bioethics] (Co-authored with Tadao Kakizoe and Motoya Katsuki), *Nihon Hinyouki Kagaku Gakkai Zasshi* [*Japanese Journal of Urology*], Vol. 94, No. 2.

2003 "Asia ni Okeru Seimei Rinri no Taiwa to Fukyu" Purojekuto [Project on Dialogue and Promotion of Bioethics in Asia], *Idenshi Igaku* [*Gene & Medicine*], Vol. 7, No. 2.

2003 Posto-Hito-Genomu-Shikuensu Jidai no Rinri-teki Mondai [Ethical Issue in the Post-Human-Genome-Sequence Era], *Gakujutsu Geppo* [*Japanese Scientific Monthly*], Vol. 56, No. 8.

2003 Hito Genomu Kenkyu no Rinri Mondai—Seimei Kagaku no Hatten to Jinken Hogo—[Ethical Problems on Human Genome Research—Development of Life Science and Protection of Human Rights], *Kagaku* [*Science journal KAGAKU*], Vol. 73, No. 4.

2003	Bioethics and International Law, *Ordine internazionale e valori etici: VII Convegno, Verona, 26–27 giugno 2003* (Editoriale Scientifica, 2003): "Bioethics and International Law" (2003).
2004	Kokusai Jinken Hogaku no Shiten Kara—Seimei Kagaku no Hatten to Ningen no Songen Oyobi Jinken [From a View-Point of International Human Rights Law (Development of Life Science and Respect for Human Dignity and Human Rights)], *Hokudai Hogaku Ronshu* [*The Hokkaido Law Review*], Vol. 55, No. 2: "Development of Life Science and Respect for Human Dignity and Human Rights" (2004).
2004	Kokusai Kiko ni Yoru Kokusai Seimei Rinri Kihan Teiritsu to Sono Jikko-sei Kakuho—UNESCO Kokusai Seimei Rinri Iinkai no Baai [Making of International Norms on Bioethics and Ensuring Their Effectiveness by International Organizations: The Case of the UNESCO International Bioethics Committee], *21 Seiki no Kokusai Kiko: Kadai to Tembo* [*International Organizations in the 21st Century: Problems and Prospects*] (N. Ando, O. Nakamura and Ryuichi Ida eds., Toshindo): "Making of International Norms on Bioethics"(2004).
2004	Saisei Iryo no Shinten ni Tomonau Rinri-teki Mondai: Hito Kan Saibo Kenkyu wo Sozai ni [Ethical Issues in the Development of Regenerative Medicine: Research on Human Embryonic and Adult Stem Cells], *Rinsho Ketsueki* [*The Japanese Journal of Clinical Hematology*], Vol. 45, No. 6.
2004	Tokubetsu Kiko UNESCO "Hito Iden Joho ni Kansuru Kokusai Sengen" [UNESCO "International Declaration on Human Genetic Data"], *Gakujutsu Geppo* [*Japanese Scientific Monthly*], Vol. 57, No. 7.
2004	"Hito Hai no Toriatsukai ni Kansuru Kihonteki Kangaekata" ni Tsuite [Reflection on "Basic Idea on the Status of Embryo"], *Seimei Rinri* [*Journal of Japan Association for Bioethics*], Vol. 14, No. 1.
2004	"Saisei Iryo to Waga Kuni ni Seimei Rinri—Hito ES Saibo to Clone Hai, soshite Shibo Taiji—" oyobi "Sogo-o Toron" ["Regenerative Medicine and Bioethics in Japan—Human Embryonic Stem Cells, Human Somatic Cell Nuclear Transfer Embryo and Dead Unborn Child" and "Discussion"] *Ko-kai Symposium "Saisei Iryo to Seimei Rinri Project"* [21st century COE: Open symposium "Regenerative Medicine and Bioethics"].
2004	Post Sequence no Seimei Rinri—Ho Seimei Rinri no Tachiba Kara—Kojin Iden Joho to Seimei Rinri—[Bioethics in Post-sequence: From the Perspective of Law and Bioethics-Gene Analysis Information and Bioethics—], *Molecular Medicine*, Vol. 41.
2004	Juseiran Sakusei [Production of a Fertilized Egg], *Ashahi Shimbun Weekly AERA*.
2005	Current Focus Seimei Rinri "Asia ni Okeru Seimei Rinri no Taiwa to Fukyu" Project—Watashitachi ni Mijika na Seimei Rinri wo Motomete [Current

Focus: Bioethics "Dialogue about and Dissemination of Bioethics in Asia"—In Search of Bioethics Familiar to Asians], *Josan Zasshi* [*Japanese journal for midwives*], Vol. 59, No. 2.

2005 Asia no Kachikan ni Motozuku Seimei Rinri Kihan—"Asia ni Okeru Seimei Rinri no Taiwa to Fukyu" Project [Bioethics Based on Asian Values—Project for "Dialogue and Promotion of Bioethics in Asia"—], *Hogaku Ronso* [*Kyoto Law Review*], Vol. 156, Nos. 5&6.

2005 Iryo wo Kiritsu Suru Sofuto Ro no Igi [The Significance of Soft Law Regulating Medical Practice], *Seimei Rinri to Ho* [*Bioethics and Law*] (N. Higuchi and Y. Tsuchiya eds., Kobundo): "The Significance of Soft Law as Standards of Medical Practice" (2005).

2005 Kokusaiho to Seimei Rinri: Kokusai Seimei Rinri-Ho no Kouchiku ni Mukete [Le droit international et la bioéthique—Une esquisse du droit international de la bioéthique—], *Hogaku Ronso* [*Kyoto Law Review*], Vol. 156, Nos. 3&4: "Le droit international et la bioéthique" (2005).

2006 Kansaibo wo Mochiita Iryo no Rinri-teki Mondaiten [Ethical Issue in Regenerative Medicine Utilizing Human Stem Cells], *Gakujutsu Geppo* [*Japanese Scientific Monthly*], Vol. 59, No. 4.

2006 Waga Kuni ni Okeru Idenshi Kaiseki Kenkyu no Riri-teki Wakugumi [The Ethical Framework of Genetic Analysis in Japan], *Rinsho Iyaku* [*Journal of Clinical Therapeutics & Medicines*], Vol. 22, No. 10.

2006 Hito Kansaibo wo Mochiita Saisei Iryo no Rinri Mondai [Ethical Consideration on Regenerative Medicine Using Human Stem Cells], *Jikken Igaku* [*Experimental Medicine*], Vol. 24, No. 2.

2006 Kojin Joho Hogo Ho to Kongo no Iden Joho no Toriatsukai [Act on the Protection of Personal Information and the Treatment of Gene Information] *Rinsho Saibo Bunshi Iden* [*Cytomolecular Genetics*], Vol. 11.

2006 Kojin Joho Hogo Ho ga Genomu Kenkyu e Ataeta Eikyo [The Effect of the Act on the Protection of Personal Information on Genome Research], *Jikken Igaku* [*Experimental medicine*], Vol. 24, No. 1.

2007 Igaku Kenkyu no Arikata [Medical Research as It Ought to be], *Juristo*, Vol. 1339.

2008 Tokuron Saisei Iryo wo Meguru Rinriteki Shakiteki Hoteki Shomondai [Ethical, Legal and Social Issues of Regenerative Medicine], *Nippon-Rinsho*, Vol. 66, No. 5: "Ethical, Legal and Social Issues of Regenerative Medicine" (2008).

2008 Kokusai Seimei Rinri Kihan no Ho-teki Seikaku—UNESCO no 3 Sengen wo Sozai to Shite—[Nature juridique des normes internationales de la bioéthique—Cas des trois déclarations de l'UNESCO—], *Hogaku Ronso* [*Kyoto Law Review*], Vol. 162, Nos. 1–6: "Nature juridique des normes internationales de la bioéthique" (2008).

2008	La procréation médicalement assistée et l'anonymat au Japon: Dialectique de l'anonymat et du bien-être de l'enfant, Brigitte Feuillet-Liger (dir.), *Procréation médicalement assistée et anonymat* (Bruylant).
2009	Seimei Rinri to Jinken [Bioethics and Human Rights], *Kokusai Jinken [Human Rights International]*, Vol. 20.
2009	Saisei Iryo wo Meguru Rinri Mondai [Ethical issues of regenerative medicine], *Surgery Frontier*, Vol. 16, No. 3.
2009	"Post Genomu Shakai ni Okeru Seimei Rinri to Ho—Waga Kuni ni Okeru Seimei Rinri Kihon Ho no Teigen—" [Bioethics and Law in the Post-genomic Generation—Suggestions to Japan's Basic Law of Bioethics—], *Post Genome Shakai to Ijiho (Ijiho Koza Dai 1 Kan) [Post-genome Society and Medical Law]* (K. Kai ed., Shinzansha).
2009	Should We Improve Human Nature? An Interrogation from an Asian Perspective, *Human Enhancement* (J. Savulescu and N. Bostrom eds., Oxford University Press).
2009	La bioéthique: Un nouvel espace pour la gouvernance, la diversité et la partage dans les pays de Francophonie (Conférence d'ouverture), Rapport, 20–22 Octobre 2008, Québec Canada, Commission canadienne pour l'UNESCO.
2009	La bioéthique universelle dans le monde de la diversité culturelle: Dialectique de l'universalité de l'humanité et de la diversité de valeur humaine, *Valeurs universelles de la bioéthique et diversité culturelle—Colloque International*, 11–13 décembre 2008, Carthage, Tunisie.
2010	Dai 1 Sho: Seimei Rinri to Ho wo meguru Mondai Jokyo [Chapter 1: The Problematique of Bioethics and Law], *Rekucha Seimei Rinri to Ho [Lecture:Bioethics and Law]* (K. Kai, Horitsu Bunka Sha).
2010	What Ethics Framework for Global Governance of Biomedical Research?—From a Japanese and Asian Perspective, *The Role of Ethics in International Biomedical Research—Report of the 2nd Meeting of the European Commission's International Dialogue on Bioethics*, Madrid, 04–05 March (Publication Office of the European Commission).
2010	Stem Cell Policies and Regulations in Japan, *Singapore Academy of Law Journal*, Vol. 22.
2010	Anonymity and Assisted Reproduction in Japan: Dialectic of Anonymity and Well-being of the Child, *Who is My Genetic Parent? Donor Anonymity and Assisted Reproduction—A Cross-Cultural Perspective* (B. Feuillet-Liger, K. Orfali and T. Callus eds., Bruylant).
2011	Kojin Iden Joho wa Tokusyu ka?—Hito Genomu Zen-kaiseki Jidai ni okeru Iden Joho Hono Imi Suru Mono [Personal Genomic Data with Their Characteristics: How We Project and How We Make Best Use of?], *Igaku no Ayumi [Journal of Clinical and Experimental Medicine]*, Vol. 236, No. 6.

2011 Hito Hai Hito ES Saibo no Seimei Rinri, Dai XXIII Sho Seishoku no Seimei Rinri [Bioethics of Human Embryo and Human Embryonic Stem Cells, Chapter XXIII, Bioethics of Reproduction], *Ranshi Gaku [Oocytology]* (T. Mori ed., Kyoto University Press).

2012 Helsinki Sengen to Kokunai Ho Kihan [The Declaration of Helsinki and Domestic Laws and Regulations in Japan], *Rinsho Yakuri [Japanese Journal of Clinical Pharmacology]*, Vol. 43, No. 4.

2012 Iryo Rinri ni Kansuru Ronsetsu no Gendai-teki Igi [The Discourse on Medical Ethics in the Contemporary World], *Iryo to Ho no Kousaku-Iryo Funso no Kaiketsu [The Interplay of Medicine and Law-Medical Ethics and Resolution of Medial Dispute]* (T. Kuroyanagi ed., Shoji Homu).

2013 Takan-sei Kansaibo wo Mochiiru Saisei Iryo no Seimei Rinri [Bioethics in Regenerative Medicine with Induced Pluripotent Stem Cells], *Chizaiken Forum*, Vol. 93.

2013 La tradition japonaise, frein à une libéralisation du corps de la femme (avec Minori Kokado), *Corps de la femme et Biomédecine* (Amel Aouij-Mrad, Brigitte Feuillet dir., Bruylant).

2013 How Japanese Tradition Hampers Woman's Freedom over Her Body (Co-authored with Minori Kokado), *The Female Body: A Journey Through Law* (Thérèse Callus, Brigitte Feuillet-Liger and Kristina Orfali eds., Bruylant).

2013 The Family and End-of-Life Medical Treatment in Japan, *Families and End-of-Life Treatment Decisions—An International Perspective* (Thérèse Callus, Brigitte Feuillet-Liger and Kristina Orfali eds., Bruylant).

Miscellaneous

1992 <Jirei Kaisetsu> Daikan Kokuki Gekitsui Jiken [Case Study:The Korean Air Lines Flight Shoot-Down Incident], *Seminar Kokusaiho [International Law Seminar]*(Kanae Taijudo et al. eds., Toshindo).

1994 <Zadankai> Kokuren no Henyo to Nihon [Discussion: Changes of the United Nations and Japan], *Jurist*, Vol. 1058.

1997 <Zuiso> Taijudo Kanae Sensei no Omoide [Memories of Professor Kanae Taijudo], *Jurist*, Vol. 1105.

1999 <Tokushu "Idenshi Igaku"Sokan 2 Shu Kinen Zadankai> Idenshi Igaku to Seimei Rinri [<Feature: Discussions in Celebration of the Second Anniversary of "Gene & Medicine"> "Genetic Medicine and Bioethics"] (Co-authored with Tomoko Sakoda, Kaoru Suzumori and others), *Idenshi Igaku [Gene & Medicine]*, Vol. 3, No. 3.

2000	Hanrei Kaisetsu "Kokuren Kamei Shonin no Joken to Tetsuzuki" "Kokuren Daigaku Jiken" "Interhandel Jiken" [Case Notes: "Conditions and Procedures of Admission of a State to Membership in the United Nations", "Shigeko Ui v. United Nations University", "Affaire de l'Interhandel"], *Hanrei Kokusaiho [Case book of International Law]* (S. Tabata et al. eds., Toshindo).
2000	Zadankai Genome Kagaku no Shin-Tenkai—Hito Genomu wo Chushin ni [<Discussion> New Developments in Genomic Science-Emphasis on Human Genome], *Gakujutsu Geppo [Japanese Scientific Monthly]*, Vol. 53, No. 8.
2001	Hanrei Kaisetsu "Kabunushi no Kokusekikoku ni Yoru Gaikoteki-hogo—Barcelona Traction Kaisha Jiken" [Case note, "Diplomatic Protection by the State of Nationality of Shareholders—The Barcelona Traction Case"], *Kokusaiho Hanrei Hyakusen [100 Selected Cases of International Law]* (S. Yamamoto et al. eds., Yuhikaku).
2004	<Series> Hogakusha to Tomo ni Kangaeru Hito Yurai Kenkyu Shiryo ni Kansuru Informed Consent [Free Discussion with Jurist: Informed Consent for Researches Using Samples from Human Donors], *Saisei Iryo [Regenerative Medicine]*, Vol. 3, No. 1.
2006	Hanrei Kaisetsu "Kokuren Kamei Shonin no Joken to Tetsuzuki," "Kokuren Daigaku Jiken," "Interhandel Jiken" [Case note: "Conditions and Procedures of Admission of a State to Membership in the United Nations", "Shigeko Ui v. United Nations University", "Affaire de l'Interhandel"], *Hanrei Kokusaiho [Case book of International Law]* (2nd ed., Y. Matsui ed., Toshindo).
2006	<Shokai> Murase Shinya "Kokusaiho no Keizai-teki Kiso" [Shinya Murase, Economic Foundation of International Law (in Japanese)], *Kokusaiho Gaiko Zassi [Journal of International Law and Diplomacy]*, Vol. 105, No. 3.
2007	<Zadankai> Nihon ga Rido suru Kokuren Kaikaku—Aratana Jidai no Kokuren Gaiko no Arikata towa [Japan's Contribution to UN Reform—UN Diplomacy in the New Era], *Gaiko Forum*, Vol. 20, No. 1.
2011	Heiwa Iji Katsudo no Ho-teki Seishitsu to Tenkai—Kokuren Keihi Jiken—[The Legal Nature of Peacekeeping Operations and Its Developments—Advisory Opinion on Certain Expenses of the United Nations—], *Kokusaiho Hanrei Hyakusen [100 Selected Cases of International Law]* (2nd ed., A. Kotera et al. eds., Yuhikaku).

Index

acceptability   197, 201, 211
African Union (AU)   165–189
　- African Standby Force (ASF)   172, 173, 177
　- AU Mission in Burundi (AMIB)   177, 178
　- AU Mission in the Sudan (AMIS)   177, 178, 180
　- AU Mission in Somalia (AMISOM)   177, 178
　- AU/UN Hybrid Operation in Darfur (UNAMID)   178, 179
　- mechanism for conflict prevention, management and resolution   168
　- Peace and Security Council (PSC)   168–170, 172–175, 180, 181, 184, 185
Al Qaeda   262, 263, 266, 272, 273, 275–278, 280, 281
　- sanction   263, 266, 272, 273, 275–278, 280
　- Sanctions Committee   273, 278
amendment   27, 80, 100, 119, 123–125, 126, 129, 137–141, 170, 233, 234, 237, 243, 268
amnesty   96, 104, 105, 108–110
asset freeze   257, 262, 264, 279
aut dedere aut judicare   95

bilateral investment treaty (BIT) (traité bilatéral d'investissements (TBI))   9–14, 16, 121, 127, 132, 133, 155, 207, 208
bioethics   193–195, 224, 257–260
biological diversity (biodiversity)   194–202, 206–213
　- damage to   194–198, 200–202, 206–208, 211–213
biotechnology   197
Bretton Woods Institutions   54, 64
Biological Weapons Convention (BWC) regime   225, 226, 228, 232, 233, 236
　- review conference   222, 225–228, 232

catching up   191, 194, 225, 257, 258, 260, 274, 283
capacity-building   175, 187, 196, 213
Chemical Weapons Convention (CWC) regime   222, 226, 228, 230–233, 236
civilization   50
civilizing mission   40

community interest   91, 92, 94–96, 102, 110
comprehensive economic sanctions   261, 262
compensation   16, 17, 144, 150–153, 157–159, 198, 247
compensatory inequality   25, 28, 35
compliance   82, 87, 193, 194, 197, 218, 221, 223, 225, 227, 232, 239, 244, 254, 266, 269, 278
Conference of the Parties (COP)   196, 204, 210
　- Conference of the Parties serving as Meeting of the Parties (MOP)   196, 204
conflict   44, 46, 47, 52, 53, 61, 102–105, 116, 118, 128, 136, 142, 156, 166–168, 170–173, 175–182, 184, 187–189
consensus   35, 52, 73, 105, 110, 136, 210, 232, 235, 236, 273
contestation   257, 264, 267, 274–276, 278, 280, 282, 283
Court of First Instance (CFI)   95, 265, 275, 280, 281
Court of Justice of the European Union (ECJ)   265, 266, 275, 279, 281
crime against humanity   95, 96, 105, 169, 171
customary international law   89, 96, 105, 202, 220, 238, 240, 247, 248, 256, 269

damage   84, 93, 144, 145, 152, 155, 157–163, 178, 194–202, 205–213, 246, 247
　- environmental   194, 195, 200
　- traditional   198
　- to biodiversity (biodiversity damage)   194–198, 200–202, 206–208, 211–213
developed State (État développé)   3, 6, 7, 9, 17, 25, 26, 35, 39, 41, 44, 56, 65, 66, 69, 73, 75, 84, 86, 201
developing State (États en voie de développement)   3–8, 10, 17, 20, 21, 23, 37–39, 41–46, 49, 51–59, 61–75, 77, 78, 84–88, 115, 144, 201
differential and more favourable treatment (traitement différencié et plus favorable)   5, 6, 29

INDEX 297

discourse   59, 110, 194, 215, 274, 279, 280
discretion   95, 106, 144, 163, 200–204, 210, 212, 224, 230, 270
dispute settlement   33, 63, 64, 70–75, 77, 78, 82, 84, 88, 116, 117, 118, 123, 144
domestic law   95, 193–195, 197–202, 204–208, 210–213

economic development   24, 25, 37, 38, 44, 49, 62, 64, 65, 78, 221
economic sanction   261, 262
effectiveness   48, 72, 90, 102, 112, 181, 186, 188, 193–196, 203, 204, 206, 211–214, 221, 222, 225, 236, 239, 242, 243, 254
égalité réelle   3
enforcement   9, 10, 71, 94, 106, 151, 165, 176, 196, 240, 242, 243, 246, 250–253, 261
equality (of States)   24, 26, 27, 39, 41, 43, 45, 53, 57
equity   36, 48, 49, 57
État situé   3, 23–28, 30, 34–36, 43
European Court of Human Rights (ECtHR)   104, 280, 281
European Union (EU)   27, 117, 200, 207, 240, 241, 244, 245, 247, 249, 253, 264, 266, 277, 278, 281
  - Environmental Liability Directive   200
export-oriented industrialisation   66, 67

fair and clear procedure   261, 271, 272, 277
fair and equitable treatment (traitement juste et equitable)   8–10, 12–16, 18–22
fairness and transparency   257, 260, 271–274, 276, 280, 282
flag-State's exclusive jurisdiction   248
focal point   267, 272, 273, 275
formal equality   24, 26, 29, 259
framework treaty (convention)   196
free trade agreement (FTA)   115–117, 121, 122–124, 126–129, 132, 134–137, 140–142
functional approach   37–58, 61, 62
functional equality   26, 27, 43
functionalism   45–50, 54
functionalist   37, 45–49, 54
fundamental value   57, 193, 199

gap-filling   210
General Court of the European Union (EGC)   265, 275, 281

general international law   135
generalized scheme of preferences (GSP)   66–68, 70, 77, 78, 87, 88
genetically modified organism (GMO)   194, 195, 197, 198, 200–202, 204–206, 211–213
good faith (bonne foi)   49, 153, 193, 198, 199, 202, 204, 211, 212
grandfather clause   31, 32

Haiti   261, 262
hard law   215, 219, 220, 222–226, 229, 231–233, 235–237, 256, 258, 259, 267, 268
harmonisation   203
humanitarian intervention   168, 173, 185
human rights   38, 42, 47, 91, 102, 104, 105, 107–109, 170, 175, 214, 216, 220–222, 237, 247, 257, 260, 262–264, 266, 267, 269–272, 275, 276, 279–283
hybrid model   179

immunity   98
implementation   51, 116, 122–126, 168, 170, 172, 180, 182, 183, 193–196, 202–205, 207, 208, 211, 212, 223, 224, 226, 228, 229, 231–234, 236, 279, 282
industrialisation   65–67, 87
institutional mechanism   117, 221, 227
International Bank for Reconstruction and Development (IBRD)   25, 26, 54
international bioethics law (international law on bioethics)   193, 195, 257–259,
International Centre for Settlement of Investment Disputes (ICSID)   146–150, 157, 158, 160
international community   24, 25, 30, 36, 51, 57, 90, 92–94, 106, 109, 174, 179, 180, 189, 193, 198, 199, 216, 221, 222, 224, 227, 239, 280
International Court of Justice (ICJ)   39, 97–99, 145, 146, 149, 155–157, 163, 210, 220, 241, 246, 247, 249, 253, 268, 271
International Law Commission (ILC)   205, 239, 240, 251, 253
international law of development (droit international du développement)   3, 5, 21, 24–26, 28, 30, 35, 37–40, 44, 45, 48–50, 55–58, 61, 63, 257–259
International Monetary Fund (IMF)   25–27, 54

international organisation 25, 26, 31, 46, 54, 89, 100, 166, 168, 188, 222, 226, 228, 231, 236, 256, 257, 259, 260, 267, 270, 271, 282, 283
international peace and security 165, 166, 169, 172, 176, 177, 180, 182, 183, 186, 188
intuitive sociological method 38, 45, 52
investment 32, 64, 65, 70, 80, 121, 144–146, 149, 151–154, 159, 161–164, 207, 208, 211
investor 9, 14, 144–146, 149–152, 154, 155, 158, 159, 161–163
investor-State dispute settlement (ISDS) 144–146, 149, 151, 153–155, 157, 159, 162–164

jurisprudence 21, 50, 78, 88, 95, 96, 105, 107–109, 146–149, 154, 155, 157, 162, 163, 207, 212, 266, 281
jus cogens 92, 93, 95, 97, 102, 104, 216, 280, 281

Kadi 264–266, 275, 277, 279–281

law-making 191, 193–196, 199, 204, 211, 216, 217, 219, 220, 223, 224, 283
liability regime 193–195, 197, 198, 204–206, 211, 213
 - environmental 194, 197, 204–206
 - international 195, 198, 211, 213

military enforcement measure 165
monitoring 118, 196, 221, 222, 225, 232, 233, 270, 273, 277
 - mechanism 221
most-favoured-nation treatment 29
multilateral environmental agreement (MEA) 135, 136

necessity 40, 53, 54, 87, 104, 106, 158, 160, 232, 238–240, 248–254, 266, 278
New International Economic Order (NIEO) (Nouvel ordre économique international) 3–5, 7, 36, 44, 56–58, 61, 216
non-binding standard 255, 258–260, 271, 283
non-governmental organisation (NGO) 91, 197
non-intervention 60, 170, 171
non-State actor 206, 213, 221, 256

normative diplomacy 193, 194, 197
normativity 89, 193, 239, 254
Northwest Atlantic Fisheries Organization (NAFO) 241–247, 249, 252, 253

obligation
 - of maintenance 213
 - of means 196
 - of result 196, 200, 203, 212, 213
 - soft 196, 213
 - to prosecute 104–106, 108–110
  - non-performance of 106, 110
oil pollution liability regime 204
ombudsperson 273, 275, 276
one-country-one-vote system 25, 26
opinio juris 220
Organization for African Unity (OAU) 165–172
Organisation for the Prohibition of Chemical Weapons (OPCW) 222, 226, 228, 232, 233

payment of money 158
peacebuilding 168, 174
peacekeeping 168, 170, 172, 174–179, 181–184, 187, 189
 -robust 183, 184
peace operation 168, 172, 177, 178, 180, 182, 183
positivism 49, 235
positivist 40, 49, 60, 89, 219, 220
power 26, 27, 34, 35, 39–41, 47, 53–55, 58, 60, 71–74, 77, 84, 85, 88, 90–92, 94, 96, 98, 102, 109, 121, 122, 145, 146, 149, 150, 153–156, 163, 165, 166, 168–170, 181, 232–235, 256, 268, 271, 273, 276–278
pragmatic approach 37, 40, 186–189
preferential treatment 37, 41, 54, 55, 57, 80
principle
 - and rule(s) 196
 - fundamental 198, 199
 - general 134
 - jurisdictional 92
 - passive personality 94
proportionality 145, 152–154, 163
provisional measure 145–150, 152–155, 157–164

realist 40, 49, 50, 238, 276, 278
reciprocity 29, 41, 70, 87
regional organisation 167, 168, 172, 186, 187

INDEX 299

regional trade agreement (RTA)   115–122,
    126–130, 132, 134–137, 140–143
  - accession to   137
  - amendment of   140
  - termination of   137
  - governing body of   122–124, 126
reporting   68, 196
responsibility to protect   185, 186
restitution   150–158
right   30, 33, 34, 40, 65, 77, 106, 145, 146,
    148–154, 156, 160, 162, 163, 167, 169–171,
    184, 186, 199, 229, 244, 248, 250, 263,
    264, 266, 273, 275, 277, 281
  - to a fair hearing   264
  - to be heard   272, 273
  - to be informed   272

sanctions committee   261, 266, 273, 278
self-defence   183, 184, 250, 253
self-determination   258
social conflict perspective   53
social transition   255–260, 268, 282, 283
soft law   51, 52, 214–226, 228–237, 255–260,
    267, 271, 274
  - primary soft law   224, 236
  - secondary soft law   224–226, 228–237
    - adapting effect   233, 234
    - clarifying effect   231, 232
    - supplemental effect   232, 233
solidarity   24, 25, 36, 165, 167, 179
sovereignty   23, 24, 41, 53, 90, 91, 95–97,
    100–103, 110, 145, 153, 154, 216, 248
  - sovereign equality   25, 26, 30, 36, 60, 91,
    95, 97, 98, 103
  - resistance from sovereignty   90, 97, 102
Special and Different Treatment (S&D)   69, 87
specific performance   145, 148–153, 155, 157,
    158, 163
standard-setting   210
structural-functional approach   51
subsequent agreement   31, 210, 231, 234
subsequent practice   167, 210, 223, 269, 270
subsidiarity   102, 103, 108, 188
substantive equality   24, 25, 28, 35, 38, 39, 41,
    42, 49, 55–57, 61, 258, 259

targeted sanction   255, 257, 260–264, 267,
    270, 272, 274, 276, 277, 279, 281, 282
technology   42, 66, 216, 221

Third World   37, 38, 42, 53, 55, 57–61, 65
Third World Approaches to International Law
    (TWAIL)   58, 59, 60, 61
torture   92, 97, 104, 276
traditional international law   24, 25, 27, 28,
    38, 43, 44, 52, 54, 259
transition model   178, 179
travel ban   257, 262, 263
treaty   23, 92, 95–97, 99–101, 130, 140, 141, 185,
    195, 198, 199, 205, 207, 208, 210, 211, 214–219,
    222–226, 231, 232, 234–237, 243, 268, 269
  - organ   222, 226
  - regime   214
treaty on friendship, commerce and
    navigation (FCN Treaty)   122, 135, 136,
    140–142

United Nations (UN)   165–169, 171–185
  - Agenda for Peace   177
  - General Assembly   36, 60, 167, 174,
    216, 217, 220, 252, 258, 261, 267, 271, 274
  - Security Council (UNSC)   165, 168–173,
    175, 184, 185, 187, 226, 227, 257, 261,
    262–264, 267–280, 282
  - Resolution   185, 263, 271, 272, 279, 282
  - UN Mission in the Sudan (UNMIS)   178
  - UN Operation in Burundi (ONUB)   178
United Nations Commission on International
    Trade Law (UNCITRAL)   158, 160, 161, 162,
    210, 240
United Nations Conference on Trade and
    Development (UNCTAD) (Conférence des
    Nations Unies sur le commerce et le
    développement (CNUCED))   5, 65
universal jurisdiction   89, 91–111
use of force   165, 172, 173, 176, 183–185, 187,
    238, 243, 244, 247

voluntarism   216

Watson Institute   264, 267, 276
weighted voting system   24–28, 36
World Summit Outcome   174, 175, 271, 275
World Trade Organization (WTO)
    (Organisation modiale du commerce
    (OMC))   5, 6, 23–25, 27–36, 56, 63, 64,
    69–80, 82, 84, 86–88, 115–119, 128–132,
    134–136, 142
  - WTO-plus   33, 35

Printed in the United States
By Bookmasters